Kaplan Publishing are constantly finding new ways to make a difference to your studies and our exciting online resources really do offer something different to students looking for exam success.

This book comes with free MyKaplan online resources so that you can study anytime, anywhere

Having purchased this book, you have access to the following online study materials:

CONTENT	ACCA (including FFA,FAB,FMA)		FIA (excluding FFA,FAB,FMA)	
	Text	Kit	Text	Kit
iPaper version of the book	✓	✓	✓	✓
Interactive electronic version of the book	✓			
Progress tests with instant answers	✓			
Material updates	✓	✓	✓	✓
Latest official ACCA exam questions*		✓		
Extra question assistance using the signpost icon*		✓		
Timed questions with an online tutor debrief using the clock icon*		✓		
Interim assessment including questions and answers	✓			
Technical articles	✓	✓		

* Excludes F1, F2, F3, FFA, FAB, FMA

D1328973

How to access your online resources

Kaplan Financial students will already have a MyKaplan account and these extra resources will be available to you online. You do not need to register again, as this process was completed when you enrolled. If you are having problems accessing online materials, please ask your course administrator.

If you are already a registered MyKaplan user go to www.MyKaplan.co.uk and log in. Select the 'add a book' feature and enter the ISBN number of this book and the unique pass key at the bottom of this card. Then click 'finished' or 'add another book'. You may add as many books as you have purchased from this screen.

If you purchased through Kaplan Flexible Learning or via the Kaplan Publishing website you will automatically receive an e-mail invitation to MyKaplan. Please register your details using this email to gain access to your content. If you do not receive the e-mail or book content, please contact Kaplan Flexible Learning.

If you are a new MyKaplan user register at www.MyKaplan.co.uk and click on the link contained in the email we sent you to activate your account. Then select the 'add a book' feature, enter the ISBN number of this book and the unique pass key at the bottom of this card. Then click 'finished' or 'add another book'.

Your Code and Information

This code can only be used once for the registration of one book online. This registration and your online content will expire when the final sittings for the examinations covered by this book have taken place. Please allow one hour from the time you submit your book details for us to process your request.

Please scratch the film to access your MyKaplan code.

Please be aware that this code is case-sensitive and you will need to include the dashes within the passcode, but not when entering the ISBN. For further technical support, please visit www.MyKaplan.co.uk

ACCA

Paper F2

and

FIA

Diploma in Accounting and Business

Management Accounting (MA/FMA)

Complete Text

British library cataloguing-in-publication data

A catalogue record for this book is available from the British Library.

Published by:
Kaplan Publishing UK
Unit 2 The Business Centre
Molly Millars Lane
Wokingham
Berkshire
RG41 2QZ

ISBN 978-0-85732-816-8

Acknowledgements

We are grateful to the Association of Chartered Certified Accountants and the Chartered Institute of Management Accountants for permission to reproduce past examination questions. The answers have been prepared by Kaplan Publishing.

Contents

		Page
Chapter 1	The nature and purpose of management accounting	1
Chapter 2	Sources of data	27
Chapter 3	Presenting information	41
Chapter 4	Types of cost and cost behaviour	59
Chapter 5	Accounting for inventory	91
Chapter 6	Accounting for labour	135
Chapter 7	Accounting for overheads	161
Chapter 8	Marginal and absorption costing	193
Chapter 9	Job, batch and process costing	211
Chapter 10	Service and operation costing	261
Chapter 11	Alternative costing principles	273
Chapter 12	Forecasting techniques	291
Chapter 13	Budgeting	339
Chapter 14	Capital budgeting	391
Chapter 15	Standard costing	439
Chapter 16	Performance measurement techniques	489
Chapter 17	Performance measurement in specific situations	525
Chapter 18	Spreadsheets	555
Chapter 19	Questions	575
Chapter 20	Answers	615

Paper Introduction

How to Use the Materials

These Kaplan Publishing learning materials have been carefully designed to make your learning experience as easy as possible and to give you the best chances of success in your examinations.

The product range contains a number of features to help you in the study process. They include:

(1) Detailed study guide and syllabus objectives

(2) Description of the examination

(3) Study skills and revision guidance

(4) Complete text or essential text

(5) Question practice

The sections on the study guide, the syllabus objectives, the examination and study skills should all be read before you commence your studies. They are designed to familiarise you with the nature and content of the examination and give you tips on how to best to approach your learning.

The **complete text or essential text** comprises the main learning materials and gives guidance as to the importance of topics and where other related resources can be found. Each chapter includes:

- The **learning objectives** contained in each chapter, which have been carefully mapped to the examining body's own syllabus learning objectives or outcomes. You should use these to check you have a clear understanding of all the topics on which you might be assessed in the examination.

- The **chapter diagram** provides a visual reference for the content in the chapter, giving an overview of the topics and how they link together.

- The **content** for each topic area commences with a brief explanation or definition to put the topic into context before covering the topic in detail. You should follow your studying of the content with a review of the illustration/s. These are worked examples which will help you to understand better how to apply the content for the topic.

- **Test your understanding** sections provide an opportunity to assess your understanding of the key topics by applying what you have learned to short questions. Answers can be found at the back of each chapter.

- **Summary diagrams** complete each chapter to show the important links between topics and the overall content of the paper. These diagrams should be used to check that you have covered and understood the core topics before moving on.

- **Question practice** is provided at the back of each chapter. A **Question Bank** is also included at the back of the book. Appropriate question practice is fundamental – to increase your chances of passing the Exam, you must make sure that you have practised these questions before entering the Exam hall.

Icon Explanations

 Definition – Key definitions that you will need to learn from the core content.

 Key Point – Identifies topics that are key to success and are often examined.

 Expandable Text – Expandable text provides you with additional information about a topic area and may help you gain a better understanding of the core content. Essential text users can access this additional content on-line (read it where you need further guidance or skip over when you are happy with the topic)

 Illustration – Worked examples help you understand the core content better.

 Test Your Understanding – Exercises for you to complete to ensure that you have understood the topics just learned.

 **Tricky topic** – When reviewing these areas care should be taken and all illustrations and test your understanding exercises should be completed to ensure that the topic is understood.

For more details about the syllabus and the format of your exam, please see your Complete Text or go online.

On-line subscribers

Our on-line resources are designed to increase the flexibility of your learning materials and provide you with immediate feedback on how your studies are progressing. Ask your local customer services staff if you are not already a subscriber and wish to join.

If you are subscribed to our on-line resources you will find:

(1) On-line referenceware: reproduces your Complete or Essential Text on-line, giving you anytime, anywhere access.

(2) On-line testing: provides you with additional on-line objective testing so you can practice what you have learned further.

(3) On-line performance management: immediate access to your on-line testing results. Review your performance by key topics and chart your achievement through the course relative to your peer group.

Paper introduction

Paper background

The aim of ACCA Paper F2, **Management accounting**/FIA Diploma in Accounting and Business, **Management accounting**, is to develop knowledge and understanding of management accounting techniques to support management in planning, controlling and monitoring performance in a variety of business context.

Objectives of the syllabus

- Explain the nature, source and purpose of management information.
- Explain and apply cost accounting techniques.
- Prepare budgets for planning and control.
- Compare actual costs with standard costs and analyse any variances.
- Explain and apply performance measurements and monitor business performance.

Core areas of the syllabus

- The nature, source and purpose of management information
- Cost accounting techniques
- Budgeting
- Standard costing
- Performance measurement.

Syllabus objectives

We have reproduced the ACCA's syllabus below, showing where the objectives are explored within this book. Within the chapters, we have broken down the extensive information found in the syllabus into easily digestible and relevant sections, called Content Objectives. These correspond to the objectives at the beginning of each chapter.

KAPLAN PUBLISHING

Syllabus learning objective	Chapter reference

A   THE NATURE, SOURCE AND PURPOSE OF MANAGEMENT INFORMATION

(1) Accounting for management

(a) Describe the purpose and role of cost and management accounting within an organisation.[k]	1
(b) Compare and contrast financial accounting with cost and management accounting.[k]	1
(c) Outline the managerial processes of planning, decision making and control.[k]	1
(d) Explain the difference between strategic, tactical and operational planning.[k]	1
(e) Distinguish between data and information.[k]	1
(f) Identify and explain the attributes of good information.[k]	1
(g) Explain the limitations of management information in providing guidance for managerial decision-making [k]	1

(2) Sources of data

(a) Describe sources of information from within and outside the organisation (including government statistics, financial press, professional or trade associations, quotations and price list).[k]	2
(b) Explain the uses and limitations of published information/data (including information from the internet). [k]	2
(c) Describe the impact of general economic environment on costs/revenues. [k]	2
(d) Explain sampling techniques (random, systematic, stratified, multistage, cluster and quota). [k]	2
(e) Choose an appropriate sampling method in a specific situation. (Note: Derivation of random samples will not be examined) [s]	2

(3) Cost classification

(a) Explain and illustrate production and non-production costs. [k]	4
(b) Describe the different elements of non production costs – administrative, selling, distribution and finance [k]	4
(c) Describe the different elements of production cost – materials, labour and overheads.[k]	4

(d)   Explain the importance of the distinction between production and non-production costs when valuing output and inventories.[k]   4

(e)   Explain and illustrate with examples classifications used in the analysis of the product/service costs including by function, direct and indirect, fixed and variable, stepped fixed and semi variable costs. [s]   4

(f)   Explain and illustrate the use of codes in categorising transaction. [k]   4

(g)   Describe and illustrate, graphically, different types of cost behaviour [s]   4

(h)   Use high/low analysis to separate the fixed and variable elements of total costs including situations involving semi variable and stepped fixed costs and changes in the variable cost per unit.[s]   4

(i)   Explain the structure of linear functions and equations.[s]   4

(j)   Explain and illustrate the concept of cost objects, cost units[1], and cost centres.[s]   4

(k)   Distinguish between cost, profit, investment and revenue centres. [k]   1

(l)   Describe the differing needs for information of cost, profit, investment and revenue centre managers [k]   1

(4)   Presenting information

(a)   Prepare written reports representing management information in suitable formats according to purpose [s]   3

(b)   Present information using table, charts and graphs (bar charts, line graphs, pie charts and scatter graphs).[s]   3

(c)   Interpret information (including the above tables, charts and graphs) presented in management reports. [s]   3

KAPLAN PUBLISHING

B COST ACCOUNTING METHODS AND SYSTEMS

(1) Accounting for material, labour and overheads

(a) Accounting for materials

(i)	Describe the different procedures and documents necessary for the ordering, receiving and issuing of materials from inventory.[k]	5
(ii)	Describe the control procedures used to monitor physical and 'book' inventory and to minimise discrepancies and losses.[k]	5
(iii)	Interpret the entries and balances in the material inventory account.[s]	5
(iv)	Identify, explain and calculate the costs of ordering and holding inventory (including buffer inventory). [s]	5
(v)	Calculate and interpret optimal reorder quantities. [s]	5
(vi)	Calculate and interpret optimal reorder quantities when discounts apply. [s]	5
(vii)	Produce calculations to minimise inventory costs when inventory is gradually replenished.[s]	5
(viii)	Describe and apply appropriate methods for establishing reorder levels where demand in the lead time is constant. [s]	5
(ix)	Calculate the value of closing inventory and material issues using LIFO, FIFO and average methods. [s]	5

(b) Accounting for labour

(i)	Calculate direct and indirect costs of labour.[s]	6
(ii)	Explain the methods used to relate input labour costs to wor done.[k]	6
(iii)	Prepare the journal and ledger entries to record labour cost inputs and outputs.[s]	6
(iv)	Describe different remuneration methods: time-based systems, piecework systems and individual and group incentive schemes.[k]	6
(v)	Calculate the level, and analyse the costs and causes of labour turnover.[s]	6
(vi)	Explain and calculate labour efficiency, capacity and production volume ratios.[s]	6
(vii)	Interpret the entries in the labour account.[s]	6

(c) Accounting for overheads

    (i)   Explain the different treatment of direct and indirect expenses.[k]   7

    (ii) Describe the procedures involved in determining production overhead absorption rates.[k]   7

    (iii) Allocate and apportion production overheads to cost centres using an appropriate basis.[s]   7

    (iv) Reapportion service cost centre costs to production cost centres (using the reciprocal method where service cost centres work for each other).[s]   7

    (v)   Select, apply and discuss appropriate bases for absorption rates.[s]   7

    (vi) Prepare journal and ledger entries for manufacturing overheads incurred and absorbed.[s]   7

    (vii) Calculate and explain the under and over absorption of overheads.[s]   7

(2) **Absorption and marginal costing**

    (a) Explain the importance of, and apply, the concept of contribution.[s]   8

    (b) Demonstrate and discuss the effect of absorption and marginal costing on inventory valuation and profit determination.[s]   8

    (c) Calculate profit or loss under absorption and marginal costing.[s]   8

    (d) Reconcile the profits or losses calculated under absorption and marginal costing.[s]   8

    (e) Describe the advantages and disadvantages of absorption and marginal costing.[k]   8

(3) **Costing methods**

(a) Job and batch costing

    (i)   Describe the characteristics of job and batch costing.[k]   9

    (ii) Describe the situations where the use of job or batch costing would be appropriate.[k]   9

    (iii) Prepare cost records and accounts in job and batch costing situations.[k]   9

    (iv) Establish job and batch costs from given information.[s]   9

(b) Process costing

(i)	Describe the characteristics of process costing.[k]	9
(ii)	Describe the situations where the use of process costing would be appropriate.[s]	9
(iii)	Explain the concepts of normal and abnormal losses and abnormal gains.[k]	9
(iv)	Calculate the cost per unit of process outputs.[s]	9
(v)	Prepare process accounts involving normal and abnormal losses and abnormal gains.[s]	9
(vi)	Calculate and explain the concept of equivalent units.[s]	9
(vii)	Apportion process costs between work remaining in process and transfers out of a process using the weighted average and FIFO methods.[s]	9
(viii)	Prepare process accounts in situations where work remains incomplete.[s]	9
(ix)	Prepare process accounts where losses and gains are identified at different stages of the process.[s]	9
(x)	Distinguish between by-products and joint products.[k]	9
(xi)	Value by-products and joint products at the point of separation.[s]	9
(xii)	Prepare process accounts in situations where by-products and/or joint products occur.[s]	9

Note: Situations involving work in process and losses in the same process are excluded.

(c) Service/operation costing

(i)	Identify situations where the use of service/operation costing is appropriate.[k]	10
(ii)	Illustrate suitable unit cost measures that may be used in different service/operation situations.[s]	10
(iii)	Carry out service cost analysis in simple service industry situations.[s]	10

(4) Alternative costing principles

(a)	Explain activity based costing (ABC), target costing, life cycle costing and total quality management (TQM) as alternative cost management techniques. [k]	11
(b)	Differentiate ABC, target costing and life cycle costing from the traditional costing techniques (note: calculations are not required) [k]	11

C BUDGETING

(1) Nature and purpose of budgeting

(a) Explain why organisations use budgeting.[k]   12, 13

(b) Describe the planning and control cycle in an organisation [k]   13

(c) Explain the administrative procedures used in the budgeting process.[k]   13

(d) Describe the stages in the budgeting process (including sources of relevant data, planning and agreeing draft budgets and purpose of forecasting and how they link to budgeting).[k]   13

(2) Statistical techniques

(a) Explain the advantages and disadvantages of using high low method to estimate the fixed and variable element of costing [k]   4

(b) Construct scatter diagrams and lines of best fit [s]   3

(c) Analysis of cost data.

(i)   Explain the concept of correlation coefficient and coefficient of determination.[k]   12

(ii) Calculate and interpret correlation coefficient and coefficient of determination.[s]   12

(iii) Establish a linear function using regression analysis and interpret the results [s]   12

(d) Use liner regression coefficients to make forecasts of costs and revenues. [s]   12

(e) Adjust historical and forecast data for price movements. [s]   12

(f) Explain the advantages and disadvantages of linear regression analysis. [k]   12

(g) Describe the product life cycle and explain its importance in forecasting. [k]   11, 12

(h) Explain the principles of time series analysis (cyclical, trend, seasonal variation and random elements). [k]   12

(i) Calculate moving averages. [s]   12

(j) Calculation of trend, including the use of regression coefficients. [s]   12

(k) Use trend and seasonal variation (additive and multiplicative) to make budget forecasts [s]   12

(l) Explain the advantages and disadvantages of time series analysis [k] — 12

(m) Explain the purpose of index numbers [k] — 12

(n) Calculate simple index numbers for one or more variables [s] — 12

(o) Explain the role and features of a computer spreadsheet system [k] — 18

(p) Identify applications for computer spreadsheets and their use in cost and management accounting [s] — 18

(3) **Budget preparation**

(a) Explain the importance of principal budget factor in constructing the budget.[k] — 13

(b) Prepare sales budgets.[s] — 13

(c) Prepare functional budgets (production, raw materials usage and purchases, labour, variable and fixed overheads). [s] — 13

(d) Prepare cash budgets. [s] — 13

(e) Prepare master budgets (income statement and statement of financial position). [s] — 13

(f) Explain and illustrate 'what if' analysis and scenario planning. [s] — 13

(4) **Flexible budgets**

(a) Explain the importance of flexible budgets in control. [k] — 13

(b) Explain the disadvantage of fixed budgets in control. [k] — 13

(c) Identify situations where fixed or flexible budgetary control would be appropriate. [k] — 13

(d) Flex a budget to a given level of volume. [s] — 13

(5) **Capital budgeting and discounted cash flows**

(a) Discuss the importance of capital investment and planning and control. [k] — 14

(b) Define and distinguish between capital and revenue expenditure. [k] — 14

(c) Outline the issues to consider and the steps involved in the preparation of a capital expenditure budget. [k] — 14

(d) Explain and illustrate the difference between simple and compound interest, and between nominal and effective interest rates. [s] — 14

(e) Explain and illustrate compounding and discounting. [s] — 14

(f)   Explain the distinction between cash flow and profit and the   14
      relevance of cash flow to capital investment appraisal. [k]

(g)   Identify and evaluate relevant cash flows for individual   14
      investment decisions. [s]

(h)   Explain and illustrate the net present value (NPV) and   14
      internal rate of return (IRR) methods of discounted cash
      flow. [s]

(i)   Calculate present value using annuity and perpetuity   14
      formulae [s]

(j)   Calculate NPV, IRR and payback (discounted and non-   14
      discounted).[s]

(k)   Interpret the results of NPV, IRR and payback calculations   14
      of investment viability. [s]

(6) **Budgetary control and reporting**

(a)   Calculate simple variances between flexed budget, fixed   13
      budget and actual sales, costs and profits. [s]

(b)   Discuss the relative significance of variances. [k]   15

(c)   Explain potential action to eliminate variances. [k]   15

(d)   Define the concept of responsibility accounting and its   13
      significance in control. [k]

(e)   Explain the concept of controllable and uncontrollable costs.   13
      [k]

(f)   Prepare control reports suitable for presentation to   15
      management (to include recommendation of appropriate
      control action). [s]

(7) **Behavioural aspects of budgeting**

(a)   Explain the importance of motivation in performance   13
      management. [k]

(b)   Identify factors in a budgetary planning and control system   13
      that influence motivation. [k]

(c)   Explain the impact of targets upon motivation. [k]   13

(d)   Discuss managerial incentive schemes. [k]   13

(e)   Discuss the advantages and disadvantages of a   13
      participative approach to budgeting. [k]

(f)   Explain top down, bottom up approaches to budgeting. [k]   13

D   STANDARD COSTING

(1) Standard costing systems

(a) Explain the purpose and principles of standard costing. [k]	15
(b) Explain the difference between standard, marginal and absorption costing [k]	15
(c) Establish the standard cost per unit under absorption and marginal costing [k]	15

(2) Variance calculations and analysis

(a) Calculate sales price and volume variance. [s]	15
(b) Calculate materials total, price and usage variance. [s]	15
(c) Calculate labour total, rate and efficiency variance. [s]	15
(d) Calculate variable overhead total, expenditure and efficiency. [s]	15
(e) Calculate fixed overhead total, expenditure and, where appropriate, volume, capacity and efficiency. [s]	15
(f) Interpret the variances. [s]	15
(g) Explain factors to consider before investigating variances, explain possible causes of the variances and recommend control action. [s]	15
(h) Explain the interrelationships between the variances. [k]	15
(i) Calculate actual or standard figures where the variances are given.[k]	15

(3) Reconciliation of budgeted profit and actual profit

(a) Reconcile budgeted profit with actual profit under standard absorption costing.[s]	15
(b) Reconcile budgeted profit or contribution with actual profit or contribution under standard marginal costing.[s]	15

E   **PERFORMANCE MEASUREMENT**

(1) **Performance measurement overview**

(a) Discuss the purpose of mission statements and their role in performance measurement.[k]   1, 16

(b) Discuss the purpose of strategic and operational and tactical objectives and their role in performance measurement.[k]   1, 16

(c) Discuss the impact of economic and market condition on performance measurement.[k]   16

(d) Explain the impact of government regulation on performance measurement.[k]   16

(2) **Performance measurement – application**

(a) Discuss and calculate measures of financial performance (profitability, liquidity, activity and gearing) and non financial measures. [s]   16

(b) Perspectives of the balance scorecard.

(i) Discuss the advantages and limitations of the balance scorecard. [k]   16

(ii) Describe performance indicators for financial success, customer satisfaction, process efficiency and growth. [k]   16

(iii) Discuss critical success factors and key performance indicators and their link to objectives and mission statements. [k]   16

(iv) Establish critical success factors and key performance indicators in a specific situation. [s]   16

(c) Economy, efficiency and effectiveness

(i) Explain the concepts of economy, efficiency and effectiveness [k]   17

(ii) Describe performance indicators for economy, efficiency and effectiveness. [k]   17

(iii) Establish performance indicators for economy, efficient and effectiveness in a specific situation. [s]   17

(iv) Discuss the meaning of each of the efficiency, capacity and activity ratios. [k]   16

(v) Calculate the efficiency, capacity and activity ratios in a specific situation. [s]   16

(d) Unit costs

(i) Describe performance measures which would be suitable in contract and process costing environments. [k]   17

(e) Resources utilisation

    (i) Describe measures of performance utilisation in service and manufacturing environments. [k]   16

    (ii) Establish measures of resource utilisation in a specific situation. [s]   16

(f) Profitability

    (i) Calculate return on investment and residual income. [s]   17

    (ii) Explain the advantages and limitations of return on investment and residual income. [k]   17

(g) Quality of service

    (i) Distinguish performance measurement issues in service and manufacturing industries. [k]   16

    (ii) Describe performance measures appropriate for service industries. [k]   17

(3) Cost reductions and value enhancement

    (a) Compare cost control and cost reduction. [s]   11

    (b) Describe and evaluate cost reduction methods. [s]   11

    (c) Describe and evaluate value analysis. [s]   11

(4) Monitoring performance and reporting

    (a) Discuss the importance of non-financial performance measures. [k]   16

    (b) Discuss the relationship between short-term and long-term performance. [k]   16

    (c) Discuss the measurement of performance in service industry situations. [k]   17

    (d) Discuss the measurement of performance in non-profit seeking and public sector organisations [k]   17

    (e) Discuss measures that may be used to assess managerial performance and the practical problems involved [k]   17

    (f) Discuss the role of benchmarking in performance measurement [k]   16

    (g) Produce reports highlighting key areas for management attention and recommendations for improvement. [k]   3

The examination

Examination format

The syllabus is assessed by a two-hour paper or computer-based examination. Questions will assess all parts of the syllabus and will contain both computational and non-computational elements:

	Number of marks
Section A 35 two mark objective questions	70
Section B 3 ten mark multi-task questions	30
	100

Section B will examine Budgeting, Standard costing and Performance measurement

Total time allowed: 2 hours

Paper-based examination tips

Divide the time you spend on questions in proportion to the marks on offer. One suggestion for **this exam** is to allocate 1 minutes and 12 seconds to each mark available, so each 2-mark question should be completed in 2 minutes 24 seconds or approximately 2 and a half minutes.

Multiple-choice questions: Read the questions carefully and work through any calculations required. If you don't know the answer, eliminate those options you know are incorrect and see if the answer becomes more obvious. Guess your final answer rather than leave it blank if necessary.

Computer-based examination (CBE) – tips

Be sure you understand how to use the software before you start the exam. If in doubt, ask the assessment centre staff to explain it to you. Questions are **displayed on the screen** and answers are entered using keyboard and mouse. At the end of the exam, you are given a certificate showing the result you have achieved. Do not attempt a CBE until you have **completed all study material** relating to it. **Do not skip any of the material** in the syllabus.

Read each question very carefully.

Double-check your answer before committing yourself to it.

Answer every question – if you do not know an answer, you don't lose anything by guessing. Think carefully before you **guess.** With a multiple-choice question, eliminate first those answers that you know are wrong. Then choose the most appropriate answer from those that are left.

Remember that **only one answer to a multiple-choice question can be right**. After you have eliminated the ones that you know to be wrong, if you are still unsure, guess. But only do so after you have double-checked that you have only eliminated answers that are definitely wrong.

Don't panic if you realise you've answered a question incorrectly. Getting one question wrong will not mean the difference between passing and failing.

Study skills and revision guidance

This section aims to give guidance on how to study for your exams and to give ideas on how to improve your existing study techniques.

Preparing to study

Set your objectives

Before starting to study decide what you want to achieve – the type of pass you wish to obtain. This will decide the level of commitment and time you need to dedicate to your studies.

Devise a study plan

Determine which times of the week you will study.

Split these times into sessions of at least one hour for study of new material. Any shorter periods could be used for revision or practice.

Put the times you plan to study onto a study plan for the weeks from now until the exam and set yourself targets for each period of study – in your sessions make sure you cover the course, course assignments and revision.

If you are studying for more than one paper at a time, try to vary your subjects as this can help you to keep interested and see subjects as part of wider knowledge.

When working through your course, compare your progress with your plan and, if necessary, re-plan your work (perhaps including extra sessions) or, if you are ahead, do some extra revision/practice questions.

Effective studying

Active reading

You are not expected to learn the text by rote, rather, you must understand what you are reading and be able to use it to pass the exam and develop good practice. A good technique to use is SQ3Rs – Survey, Question, Read, Recall, Review:

(1) **Survey the chapter** – look at the headings and read the introduction, summary and objectives, so as to get an overview of what the chapter deals with.

(2) **Question** – whilst undertaking the survey, ask yourself the questions that you hope the chapter will answer for you.

(3) **Read** through the chapter thoroughly, answering the questions and making sure you can meet the objectives. Attempt the exercises and activities in the text, and work through all the examples.

(4) **Recall** – at the end of each section and at the end of the chapter, try to recall the main ideas of the section/chapter without referring to the text. This is best done after a short break of a couple of minutes after the reading stage.

(5) **Review** – check that your recall notes are correct.

You may also find it helpful to re-read the chapter to try to see the topic(s) it deals with as a whole.

Note-taking

Taking notes is a useful way of learning, but do not simply copy out the text. The notes must:

- be in your own words
- be concise
- cover the key points
- be well-organised
- be modified as you study further chapters in this text or in related ones.

Trying to summarise a chapter without referring to the text can be a useful way of determining which areas you know and which you don't.

KAPLAN PUBLISHING

Three ways of taking notes:

Summarise the key points of a chapter.

Make linear notes – a list of headings, divided up with subheadings listing the key points. If you use linear notes, you can use different colours to highlight key points and keep topic areas together. Use plenty of space to make your notes easy to use.

Try a diagrammatic form – the most common of which is a mind-map. To make a mind-map, put the main heading in the centre of the paper and put a circle around it. Then draw short lines radiating from this to the main sub-headings, which again have circles around them. Then continue the process from the sub-headings to sub-sub-headings, advantages, disadvantages, etc.

Highlighting and underlining

You may find it useful to underline or highlight key points in your study text – but do be selective. You may also wish to make notes in the margins.

Revision

The best approach to revision is to revise the course as you work through it. Also try to leave four to six weeks before the exam for final revision. Make sure you cover the whole syllabus and pay special attention to those areas where your knowledge is weak. Here are some recommendations:

Read through the text and your notes again and condense your notes into key phrases. It may help to put key revision points onto index cards to look at when you have a few minutes to spare.

Review any assignments you have completed and look at where you lost marks – put more work into those areas where you were weak.

Practise exam standard questions under timed conditions.

If you are stuck on a topic find somebody (a tutor) to explain it to you.

Read good newspapers and professional journals, especially ACCA's **Student Accountant** – this can give you an advantage in the exam.

Ensure you **know the structure of the exam** – how many questions and of what type you will be expected to answer. During your revision attempt all the different styles of questions you may be asked.

Further reading

You can find further reading and technical articles under the student section of ACCA's website.

FORMULAE AND TABLES

Regression analysis

$y = a + bx$

$$a = \frac{\Sigma y}{n} - \frac{b\,\Sigma x}{n}$$

$$b = \frac{n\,\Sigma xy - \Sigma x\,\Sigma y}{n\,\Sigma x^2 - (\Sigma x)^2}$$

$$r = \frac{n\,\Sigma xy - \Sigma x\,\Sigma y}{\sqrt{(n\,\Sigma x^2 - (\Sigma x)^2)(n\,\Sigma y^2 - (\Sigma y)^2)}}$$

Economic order quantity

$$= \sqrt{\frac{2C_o D}{C_h}}$$

Economic batch quantity

$$= \sqrt{\frac{2C_o D}{C_h(1 - \dfrac{D}{R})}}$$

Present value table

Present value of 1, i.e. $(1 + r)^{-n}$

Where   r = discount rate

n = number of periods until payment

Periods (n)	Discount rate (r)									
	1%	2%	3%	4%	5%	6%	7%	8%	9%	10%
1	0.990	0.980	0.971	0.962	0.952	0.943	0.935	0.926	0.917	0.909
2	0.980	0.961	0.943	0.925	0.907	0.890	0.873	0.857	0.842	0.826
3	0.971	0.942	0.915	0.889	0.864	0.840	0.816	0.794	0.772	0.751
4	0.961	0.924	0.888	0.855	0.823	0.792	0.763	0.735	0.708	0.683
5	0.951	0.906	0.863	0.822	0.784	0.747	0.713	0.681	0.650	0.621
6	0.942	0.888	0.837	0.790	0.746	0.705	0.666	0.630	0.596	0.564
7	0.933	0.871	0.813	0.760	0.711	0.665	0.623	0.583	0.547	0.513
8	0.923	0.853	0.789	0.731	0.677	0.627	0.582	0.540	0.502	0.467
9	0.914	0.837	0.766	0.703	0.645	0.592	0.544	0.500	0.460	0.424
10	0.905	0.820	0.744	0.676	0.614	0.558	0.508	0.463	0.422	0.386
11	0.896	0.804	0.722	0.650	0.585	0.527	0.475	0.429	0.388	0.350
12	0.887	0.788	0.701	0.625	0.557	0.497	0.444	0.397	0.356	0.319
13	0.879	0.773	0.681	0.601	0.530	0.469	0.415	0.368	0.326	0.290
14	0.870	0.758	0.661	0.577	0.505	0.442	0.388	0.340	0.299	0.263
15	0.861	0.743	0.642	0.555	0.481	0.417	0.362	0.315	0.275	0.239

Periods (n)	Discount rate (r)									
	11%	12%	13%	14%	15%	16%	17%	18%	19%	20%
1	0.901	0.893	0.885	0.877	0.870	0.862	0.855	0.847	0.840	0.833
2	0.812	0.797	0.783	0.769	0.756	0.743	0.731	0.718	0.706	0.694
3	0.731	0.712	0.693	0.675	0.658	0.641	0.624	0.609	0.593	0.579
4	0.659	0.636	0.613	0.592	0.572	0.552	0.534	0.516	0.499	0.482
5	0.593	0.567	0.543	0.519	0.497	0.476	0.456	0.437	0.419	0.402
6	0.535	0.507	0.480	0.456	0.432	0.410	0.390	0.370	0.352	0.335
7	0.482	0.452	0.425	0.400	0.376	0.354	0.333	0.314	0.296	0.279
8	0.434	0.404	0.376	0.351	0.327	0.305	0.285	0.266	0.249	0.233
9	0.391	0.361	0.333	0.308	0.284	0.263	0.243	0.225	0.209	0.194
10	0.352	0.322	0.295	0.270	0.247	0.227	0.208	0.191	0.176	0.162
11	0.317	0.287	0.261	0.237	0.215	0.195	0.178	0.162	0.148	0.135
12	0.286	0.257	0.231	0.208	0.187	0.168	0.152	0.137	0.124	0.112
13	0.258	0.229	0.204	0.182	0.163	0.145	0.130	0.116	0.104	0.093
14	0.232	0.205	0.181	0.160	0.141	0.125	0.111	0.099	0.088	0.078
15	0.209	0.183	0.160	0.140	0.123	0.108	0.095	0.084	0.074	0.065

KAPLAN PUBLISHING

Annuity table

Present value of an annuity of 1, i.e. $\dfrac{1-(1+r)^{-n}}{r}$

Where   r = discount rate

        n = number of periods

Periods (n)	Discount rate (r) 1%	2%	3%	4%	5%	6%	7%	8%	9%	10%
1	0.990	0.980	0.971	0.962	0.952	0.943	0.935	0.926	0.917	0.909
2	1.970	1.942	1.913	1.886	1.859	1.833	1.808	1.783	1.759	1.736
3	2.941	2.884	2.829	2.775	2.723	2.673	2.624	2.577	2.531	2.487
4	3.902	3.808	3.717	3.630	3.546	3.465	3.387	3.312	3.240	3.170
5	4.853	4.713	4.580	4.452	4.329	4.212	4.100	3.993	3.890	3.791
6	5.795	5.601	5.417	5.242	5.076	4.917	4.767	4.623	4.486	4.355
7	6.728	6.472	6.230	6.002	5.786	5.582	5.389	5.206	5.033	4.868
8	7.652	7.325	7.020	6.733	6.463	6.210	5.971	5.747	5.535	5.335
9	8.566	8.162	7.786	7.435	7.108	6.802	6.515	6.247	5.995	5.759
10	9.471	8.983	8.530	8.111	7.722	7.360	7.024	6.710	6.418	6.145
11	10.368	9.787	9.253	8.760	8.306	7.887	7.499	7.139	6.805	8.495
12	11.255	10.575	9.954	9.385	8.863	8.384	7.943	7.536	7.161	6.814
13	12.134	11.348	10.635	9.986	9.394	8.853	8.358	7.904	7.487	7.103
14	13.004	12.106	11.296	10.563	9.899	9.295	8.745	8.244	7.786	7.367
15	13.865	12.849	11.938	11.118	10.380	9.712	9.108	8.559	8.061	7.606

Periods (n)	Discount rate (r) 11%	12%	13%	14%	15%	16%	17%	18%	19%	20%
1	0.901	0.893	0.885	0.877	0.870	0.862	0.855	0.847	0.840	0.833
2	1.713	1.690	1.668	1.647	1.626	1.605	1.585	1.566	1.547	1.528
3	2.444	2.402	2.361	2.322	2.283	2.246	2.210	2.174	2.140	2.106
4	3.102	3.037	2.974	2.914	2.855	2.798	2.743	2.690	2.639	2.589
5	3.696	3.605	3.517	3.433	3.352	3.274	3.199	3.127	3.058	2.991
6	4.231	4.111	3.998	3.889	3.784	3.685	3.589	3.498	3.410	3.326
7	4.712	4.564	4.423	4.288	4.160	4.039	3.922	3.812	3.706	3.605
8	5.146	4.968	4.799	4.639	4.487	4.344	4.207	4.078	3.954	3.837
9	5.537	5.328	5.132	4.946	4.772	4.607	4.451	4.303	4.163	4.031
10	5.889	5.650	5.426	5.216	5.019	4.833	4.659	4.494	4.339	4.192
11	6.207	5.938	5.687	5.453	5.234	5.029	4.836	4.656	4.486	4.327
12	6.492	6.194	5.918	5.660	5.421	5.197	4.968	4.793	4.611	4.439
13	6.750	6.424	6.122	5.842	5.583	5.342	5.118	4.910	4.715	4.533
14	6.982	6.628	6.302	6.002	5.724	5.468	5.229	5.008	4.802	4.611
15	7.191	6.811	6.462	6.142	5.847	5.575	5.324	5.092	4.876	4.675

The nature and purpose of management accounting

Chapter learning objectives

Upon completion of this chapter you will be able to:

- distinguish between data and information

- identify and explain the attributes of good information

- outline the managerial processes of planning, decision making and control

- explain the difference between strategic, tactical and operational planning

- distinguish between cost, profit, investment and revenue centres

- describe the differing needs for information of cost, profit, investment and revenue centres managers

- describe the purpose and role of cost and management accounting within an organisation's management information system

- compare and contrast financial accounting with cost and management accounting

- explain the limitations of management information in providing guidance for managerial decision-making.

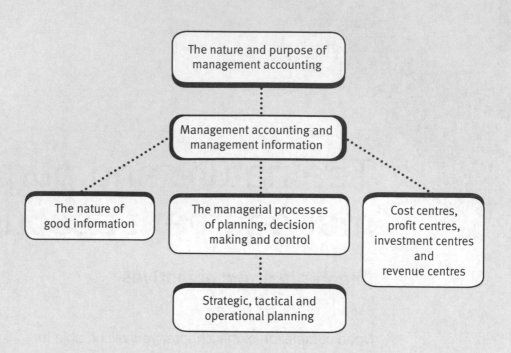

1 The nature of good information

Data and information

'Data' means facts. Data consists of numbers, letters, symbols, raw facts, events and transactions which have been recorded but not yet processed into a form suitable for use.

Information is data which has been processed in such a way that it is meaningful to the person who receives it (for making decisions).

- The terms data and information are often used interchangeably in everyday language. Make sure that you can distinguish between the two.

- As data is converted into information, some of the detail of the data is eliminated and replaced by summaries which are easier to understand.

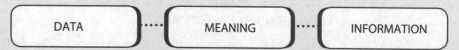

Test your understanding 1

What, if any, is the difference between data and information?

A   They are the same

B   Data can only be figures, whereas information can be facts or figures

C   Information results from sorting and analysing data

D   Data results from obtaining many individual pieces of information

Attributes of good information

Information is provided to management to assist them with planning, controlling operations and making decisions. Management decisions are likely to be better when they are provided with better quality information.

The attributes of good information can be identified by the **'ACCURATE'** acronym as shown below:

A Accurate

- The degree of accuracy depends on the reason why the information is needed.

- For example, reports may show figures to the nearest dollar, or nearest thousand dollars for a report on the performance of different divisions.

- Alternatively, when calculating the cost of a unit of output, managers may want the cost to be accurate to the nearest cent.

C Complete

- Managers should be given all the information they need, but information should not be excessive

- For example, a complete control report on variances should include all standard and actual costs necessary to understand the variance calculations.

C Cost-effective

- The value of information should exceed the cost of producing it.
- Management information is valuable, because it assists decision making.
- If a decision backed by information is different from what it would have been without the information, the value of information equates to the amount of money saved as a result.

U Understandable

- Use of technical language or jargon must be limited. Accountants must always be careful about the way in which they present financial information to non-financial managers.

R Relevant

- The information contained within a report should be relevant to its purpose.
- Redundant parts should be removed. For example, the sales team may need to know the total cost of producing a unit to calculate the selling price but will not need to know the breakdown into material, labour and overhead costs.

A Accessible

- Information should be accessible via the appropriate channels of communication (verbally, via a report, a memo, an email etc.)
- In the context of responsibility accounting, information about costs and revenues should be reported to the manager who is in a position to control them.

T Timely

- Information should be provided to a manager in time for decisions to be made based on that information.

E Easy to use!

The difference between information and data

Sometimes the issue of the quality of data is raised and often there is not a clear understanding of this issue. Quality data has several characteristics including being:

- error free;
- available at the right time;
- available at the right place;
- available to the appropriate individuals.

The arrival of the Internet has made it much easier for organisations and individuals to access data at the right time and the right place. However, at the same time the Internet has opened up questions about data being error free and about who can have access to it.

As well as the issue of data quality there is the question of how data, information and knowledge relate to one another. Russell Ackoff was one of the first people to speak of there being a hierarchy which he referred to as the Data Information Knowledge Wisdom (DIKW) Hierarchy. According to this model, data are simple facts or figures or maybe even a photograph or an illustration. In this form data is unstructured and uninterrupted. Information comes from processing or structuring data in a meaningful way. Another way of looking at this is that information is interpreted data. An Interesting story is told by Joan Magretta in her book *What Management is?* about Steve Jobs which clearly illustrates the difference between data and information.

Despite its small share of the total market for personal computers, Apple has long been a leader in sales to schools and universities. When CEO Steve Jobs learned that Apple's share of computer sales to schools was 12.5 per cent in 1999, he was dismayed, but unless you're an industry analyst who knows the numbers cold, you won't appreciate just how dismayed he was. That's because, in 1998, Apple was the segment leader with a market share of 14.6 per cent. And, while Apple slipped to the number two spot in 1999, Dell grew and took the lead with 15.1 per cent. Alone each number is meaningless. Together they spell trouble, if you're Steve Jobs, you see a trend that you'd better figure out how to reverse. This isn't number crunching, it's sense making. (Magretta, 2003, p. 123)

In this example the 12.5 per cent was data and when it was seen in conjunction with the 15.1 per cent it became information.

Knowledge is again different to data and information. Knowledge is much more personal and the presence or absence of knowledge can normally only be seen through the actions of individuals. When knowledge is written down it effectively becomes information.

Finally with respect to wisdom it is difficult to define this concept. Wisdom has something to do with understanding or insight. It is to do with achieving a good long-term outcome in relation to the circumstances you are in.

2 The managerial processes of decision making and control

The main functions that management are involved with are planning, decision making and control.

Planning

- Planning involves establishing the objectives of an organisation and formulating relevant strategies that can be used to achieve those objectives. In order to make plans, it helps to know what has happened in the past so that decisions about what is achievable in the future can be made. For example, if a manager is planning future sales volumes, he or she needs to know what sales volumes have been in the past.

- Planning can be either short-term (tactical planning) or long-term (strategic planning).

- Planning is looked at in more detail in the next section of this chapter.

Decision making

Decision making involves considering information that has been provided and making an informed decision.

- In most situations, decision making involves making a choice between two or more alternatives. Managers need reliable information to compare the different courses of action available and understand what the consequences might be of choosing each of them.

- The first part of the decision-making process is planning, the second part is control.

KAPLAN PUBLISHING

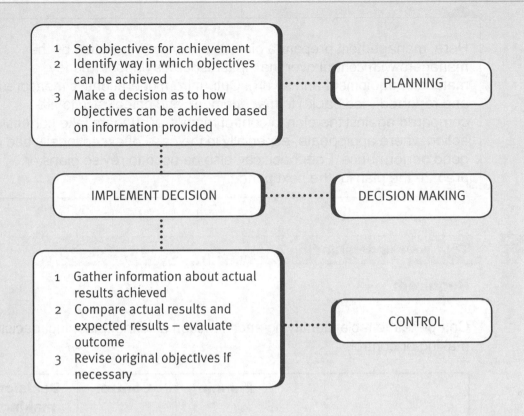

Control

Information relating to the actual results of an organisation is reported to managers.

- Managers use the information relating to actual results to take control measures and to re-assess and amend their original budgets or plans.

- Internally-sourced information, produced largely for control purposes, is called feedback.

- The 'feedback loop' is demonstrated in the following illustration.

Illustration 1 – The managerial processes of planning, decision

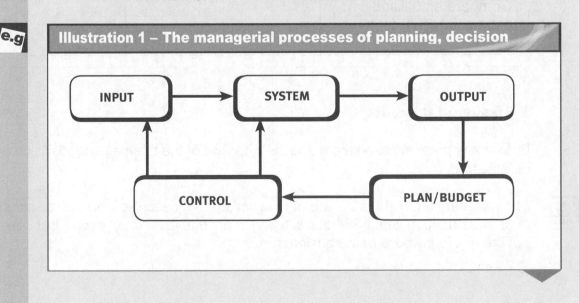

Here, management prepare a plan, which is put into action by the managers with control over the input resources (labour, money, materials, equipment and so on). Output from operations is measured and reported ('fed back') to management, and actual results are compared against the plan in control reports. Managers take corrective action where appropriate, especially in the case of exceptionally bad or good performance. Feedback can also be used to revise plans or prepare the plan for the next period.

Test your understanding 2

Required:

Complete the table identifying each function as either planning, decision making or control.

	Planning	Control	Decision making
Preparation of the annual budget for a cost centre			
Revise budgets for next period for a cost centre			
Implement decisions based on information provided			
Set organisation's objectives for next period			
Compare actual and expected results for a period			

3 Mission statements

Before any planning can take place the **mission** of the business needs to be established.

The mission statement is a statement in writing that describes the overall aims of an organisation, that is, what it is trying to accomplish. In other words it sets out the whole purpose of the business.

KAPLAN PUBLISHING

There are four key elements to a mission statement:

- **Purpose** – why does the business exist and who does it exist for?
- **Strategy** – what does the business provide and how is it provided?
- **Policies and culture** – how does the business expect its staff to act/behave?
- **Values** – What are the core principles of the business?

The mission should express what the business wants to achieve overall and the aims and objectives managers produce should all work towards achieving this.

Characteristics of mission statements

Mission statements will have some or all of the following characteristics:

- Usually a brief statement of no more than a page in length
- Very general statement of entity culture
- States the aims of the organisation
- States the business areas in which the organisation intends to operate
- Open-ended (not in quantifiable terms)
- Does not include commercial terms, such as profit
- Not time-assigned
- Forms a basis of communication to the people inside the organisation and to people outside the organisation
- Used to formulate goal statements, objectives and short term targets
- Guides the direction of the entity's strategy and as such is part of management information

Examples of mission statements

Honda

Maintaining a global viewpoint, we are dedicated to supplying products of the highest quality, yet at a reasonable price for worldwide customer satisfaction.

The Walt Disney Company

The mission of The Walt Disney Company is to be one of the world's leading producers and providers of entertainment and information. Using our portfolio of brands to differentiate our content, services and consumer products, we seek to develop the most creative, innovative and profitable entertainment experiences and related products in the world.

Virgin Atlantic

Safety, security and consistent delivery of the basics are the foundation of everything we do.

The success of our three year strategy requires us to build on these foundations by focusing on the business and leisure markets and driving efficiency and effectiveness.

Tesco PLC

Our vision is for Tesco to be most highly valued by the customers we serve, the communities in which we operate, our loyal and committed staff and our shareholders; to be a growth company; a modern and innovative company and winning locally, applying our skills globally.

4 Levels of planning

During the planning process the mission statement of a business is used to produce effective aims and objectives for employees and the company as a whole. Aims and objectives should be **SMART:**

- **Specific** – are the objectives well defined and understandable?

- **Measurable** – can achievement of the objectives be measured so that completion can be confirmed?

- **Attainable** – sometime referred to as achievable. Can the objectives set be achieved with the resources and skills available?

- **Relevant** - are the objectives relevant for the people involved and to the mission of the business?

- **Timed** – are deadlines being set for the objectives that are achievable? Are there are stage reviews planned to monitor progress towards the objective?

By following the SMART hierarchy a business should be able to produce plans that lead to **goal congruence** throughout the departments, centres and/or regional offices (the whole business).

There are three different levels of planning (known as 'planning horizons').These three levels differ according to their time span and the seniority of the manager responsible for the tasks involved.

Strategic planning

'Strategic planning' can also be known as 'long-term planning' or 'corporate planning'. It considers:

- the longer term (five years plus)
- the whole organisation

Senior managers formulate long-term objectives (goals) and plans (strategies) for an organisation as a whole. These objectives and plans should all be aiming to achieving the companies mission.

Tactical planning

Tactical planning takes the strategic plan and breaks it down into manageable chunks i.e. shorter term plans for individual areas of the business to enable the strategic plan to be achieved.

Senior and middle managers make short to medium term plans for the next year.

Operational planning

Operational planning involves making day-to-day decisions about what to do next and how to deal with problems as they arise.

All managers are involved in day to day decisions.

A simple hierarchy of management tasks can be presented as follows:

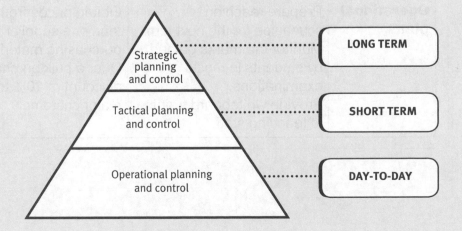

Strategic, tactical and operational planning

The table shown below illustrates the three different categories of planning.

	Private school	**Profit-making business**
Objective (Mission)	To provide a high quality of education so that, within five years, 95% of pupils achieve grades A or B in their final examinations.	To achieve a 20% return on capital every year. To increase earnings per share by 10% every year for the next five years.
Strategic plans	Reduce class sizes. Raise new funds to invest $1 million in new equipment and facilities. Attract the highest quality of teacher by paying good salaries.	Cut costs by 15% in domestic markets. Expand into markets in Asia. Increase domestic market share by 10% in the next five years.
Tactical plans	Set a target for this year for examination results. Increase the number of teachers by 10% by the end of the year. Plan the launch of a fund-raising campaign.	Carry out a cost reduction program next year. Establish business relationships with customers in Asia and carry out market research. Increase the size of the work force in order to improve total sales.
Operational plans	Prepare teaching schedules for the next term. Monitor the marks gained by students in mock examinations. Provide whiteboard training to teaching staff.	Obtain prices from more than one supplier before purchasing materials. Offer a bulk purchase discount of 10% to a major customer.

KAPLAN PUBLISHING

5 Cost centres, profit centres, investment centres and revenue centres

Responsibility accounting

Responsibility accounting is based on identifying individual parts of a business which are the responsibility of a single manager.

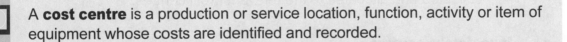

A **responsibility centre** is an individual part of a business whose manager has personal responsibility for its performance. The main responsibility centres are:

- cost centre
- revenue centre
- profit centre
- investment centre.

Cost centres

A **cost centre** is a production or service location, function, activity or item of equipment whose costs are identified and recorded.

- For a paint manufacturer cost centres might be: mixing department; packaging department; administration; or selling and marketing departments.

- For an accountancy firm, the cost centres might be: audit; taxation; accountancy; word processing; administration; canteen. Alternatively, they might be the various geographical locations, e.g. the London office, the Cardiff office, the Plymouth office.

- Cost centre managers need to have information about costs that are incurred and charged to their cost centres.

- The performance of a cost centre manager is judged on the extent to which cost targets have been achieved.

Revenue centres

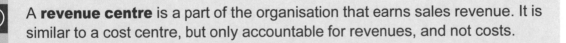

A **revenue centre** is a part of the organisation that earns sales revenue. It is similar to a cost centre, but only accountable for revenues, and not costs.

- Revenue centres are generally associated with selling activities, for example, a regional sales managers may have responsibility for the regional sales revenues generated.

- Each regional manager would probably have sales targets to reach and would be held responsible for reaching these targets.

- Sales revenues earned must be able to be traced back to individual (regional) revenue centres so that the performance of individual revenue centre managers can be assessed.

Profit centres

A **profit centre** is a part of the business for which both the costs incurred and the revenues earned are identified.

- Profit centres are often found in large organisations with a divisionalised structure, and each division is treated as a profit centre.

- Within each profit centre, there could be several costs centres and revenue centres.

- The performance of a profit centre manager is measured in terms of the profit made by the centre.

- The manager must therefore be responsible for both costs and revenues and in a position to plan and control both.

- Data and information relating to both costs and revenues must be collected and allocated to the relevant profit centres.

Investment centres

Managers of investment centres are responsible for investment decisions as well as decisions affecting costs and revenues.

- Investment centre managers are therefore accountable for the performance of capital employed as well as profits (costs and revenues).

- The performance of investment centres is measured in terms of the profit earned relative to the capital invested (employed). This is known as the return on capital employed (ROCE)

- ROCE = Profit/Capital employed. This calculation will be met in more detail in a later chapter.

Overview of responsibility centres

	Cost centre	Revenue centre	Profit centre	Investment centre
What is it?	Part of the business for which costs are identified and recorded	Part of the business for which revenues earned are identified and recorded	Part of the business for which costs incurred and revenue earned are identified and recorded	Part of the business for which profits and capital employed are measured
Where might it be found?	Any production or service location, function, activity, item of equipment	Sales divisions	Divisions of large organisations. May include several cost and revenue centres	Business units of large organisations
How is performance measured?	Have cost targets been achieved?	What revenue has been earned?	What profit has been made by the centre?	What is the return from investments?
What are the manager's information needs?	Costs incurred and charged to the cost centre	Sales revenue earned by the individual revenue centre	Information about costs and revenues allocated to the profit centre	Information on costs, revenues and capital employed by the investment centre
Example	Audit, tax, accountancy departments in an accountancy firm	Regional sales areas with the retail division of a manufacturing company	Wholesale and retail divisions in a paint company	UK and European divisions of a multinational company

6 Financial, cost and management accounting

Financial accounting

Financial accounting involves recording the financial transactions of an organisation and summarising them in periodic financial statements for external users who wish to analyse and interpret the financial position of the organisation.

- The main duties of the financial accountant include: maintaining the bookkeeping system of the nominal ledger, payables control account, receivables control account and so on and to prepare financial statements as required by law and accounting standards.

- Information produced by the financial accounting system is usually insufficient for the needs of management for decision making.

Cost accounting

Managers usually want to know about the costs and the profits of individual products and services. In order to obtain this information, details are needed for each cost, revenue, profit and investment centre. Such information is provided by cost accounting and management accounting systems.

Cost accounting is a system for recording data and producing information about costs for the products produced by an organisation and/or the services it provides. It is also used to establish costs for particular activities or responsibility centres.

- Cost accounting involves a careful evaluation of the resources used within the enterprise.

- The techniques employed in cost accounting are designed to provide financial information about the performance of the enterprise and possibly the direction that future operations should take.

- The terms 'cost accounting' and 'management accounting' are often used to mean the same thing.

Management accounting

Management accounting has cost accounting at its essential foundation.

KAPLAN PUBLISHING

Non-financial information

Information provided by cost accounting systems is financial in nature. Financial information is important for management because many objectives of an organisation are financial in nature, such as making profits and avoiding insolvency. Managers also need information of a non-financial nature.

- At a strategic level, management need to know about developments in their markets and in the economic situation. They also need to know about any new technology that emerges, and about the activities of competitors.

- At a tactical level, they might want to know about issues such as product or service quality, speed of handling customer complaints, customer satisfaction levels, employee skills levels and employee morale.

- At an operational level, they may want to know about the number of rejects per machine, the lead time for delivering materials and the number of labour and machine hours available.

The management accounting systems in many organisations are able to obtain non-financial as well as financial information for reporting to management. The importance of non-financial information within the reporting system should not be forgotten.

Differences between management accounting and financial accounting

The following illustration compares management accounting with financial accounting.

	Management accounting	Financial accounting
Information mainly produced for	Internal use e.g. managers and employees.	External use e.g. shareholders, payables, lenders, banks, government.
Purpose of information	To aid planning, controlling and decision making.	To record the financial performance in a period and the financial position at the end of that period.
Legal requirements	None.	Limited companies must produce financial accounts.
Formats	Management decide on the information they require and the most useful way of presenting it.	Format and content of financial accounts intending to give a true and fair view should follow accounting standards and company law.
Nature of information	Financial and non-financial.	Mostly financial.
Time period	Historical and forward-looking.	Mainly a historical record.

Illustration 2 – Management versus financial accounting

The role of management accounting within an organisation's management information system

The management information system of an organisation is likely to be able to prepare the following:

- annual statutory accounts

- budgets and forecasts

- product profitability reports

- cash flow reports

- capital investment appraisal reports

- standard cost and variance analysis reports

- returns to government departments, e.g. Sales Tax returns.

Management information is generally supplied to management in the form of reports. Reports may be routine reports prepared on a regular basis (e.g. monthly) or they may be prepared for a special purpose (e.g. ad hoc report).

Test your understanding 3

The following assertions relate to financial accounting:

(i) The main purpose of financial information is to provide a true and fair view of the financial position of an organisation at the end of an accounting period.

(ii) Financial information may be presented in any format deemed suitable by management.

Which of the following statements are true?

A   Assertions (i) and (ii) are both correct.

B   Only assertion (i) is correct.

C   Only assertion (ii) is correct.

Test your understanding 4

The Management Accountant has communicated a detailed budget to ensure that cost savings targets are achieved in the forthcoming period. This is an example of:

(a) Operational Planning

(b) Tactical Planning

(c) Strategic Planning

7 The limitations of management information

There are a number of respects in which management accounting information may fail to meet its objective of assisting management in the decision making process.

These can be summarised as follows:

- failure to meet the requirements of useful information

- the problem of relevant costs and revenues

- non-financial information

- external information.

Failure to comply with the qualities of useful information

If information supplied to managers is deficient in any of these respects then inappropriate management decisions may be made. Consider the following:

- **Accuracy** – overestimating costs may result in a decision not to produce a product which in fact is profitable; on the other hand, overestimating the price at which the output can be sold may result in the organisation producing output which cannot be sold profitably

- **Timeliness** – in connection with a decision to close a division or department if the information is presented to management after a decision had been made to lay off staff that could have been profitably employed in other divisions or activities, the company has incurred unnecessary redundancy costs, lost possible future revenues and demotivated the remaining employees when they learn of the redundancies.

- **Understandable** – excessive focus by management accountants on more complex techniques of which general management have little or no knowledge or understanding may mean that the accountant's advice will be ignored. There is significant attention being given to the role of the management accountant as an educator within the organisation – explaining the information and training general management to help them to understand the information better.

Relevant costs and revenues

Not all information produced by an accounting system is relevant to the decisions made by management. In particular, information produced mainly for financial reporting purposes and then taken as the basis for management decisions will often need significant modification to be useful to management. The principle here is that the figures presented to assist in management decision-making are those that will be affected by the decision, i.e. they should be:

- **Future** – costs and revenues that are going to be incurred some time in the future. Costs and revenues that have already been incurred are known as sunk costs and are not relevant to the decision to be made.

- **Incremental** – the **extra** cost or revenue that is created as a result of a decision taken

- **Cash flows** – actual cash being spent or received not monetary items that are produced via accounting convention e.g. book or carrying values, depreciation charges.

KAPLAN PUBLISHING

Non-financial information

Managers will not always be guided by the sort of financial and other (hard) information supplied by the management accounting system. They will also look at qualitative, behavioural, motivational, even environmental factors. These non-financial factors can be just as important in relation to a decision as financial information – but they are often more difficult to estimate and quantify.

Illustration 3 – Non-financial factors

A processing company needs to increase its output in order to take advantage of an increase in the total market for its product. The company has identified alternative ways of achieving this increase in output.

Alternative A

The cheapest (in financial terms) method of providing additional production capacity is to erect a new factory extension. However, there is a danger that the extension will be seen by the local council and by residents as an eyesore. Some landscaping and re-design work may be carried out at extra cost to company to make the extension more environmentally acceptable.

Alternative B

This entails keeping the factory at its current size but increasing the working hours per week for all production staff by 20%. The latter may be a cheaper solution in financial terms but may have an adverse impact on staff morale and result in a significant increase in staff turnover.

It is not easy for the company to build the non-financial costs into it's decision making process as they are often difficult to quantify.

External information

The environment refers to all of the external factors which affect a company and includes government actions, competitor actions, customer demands and other factors for example the weather.

Conventional accounting systems focus entirely on internal information such as production costs and volume of output produced. Companies and organisations do not, of course exist in a vacuum – they live in an environment in which they are influenced by a number of other organisations and forces arising from outside the organisation itself. This leads into an area of study often referred to as environmental analysis.

We do not need to go into this area in detail here, but, as with the non financial factors referred to above, you should be aware that the environment (this is simply the external circumstances in which the company operates) will have an influence on a company's actions which should be reflected in its decision making processes.

It follows from this that an organisation should have information on its environment available to it within its accounting information systems – the organisation needs external information as well as internal information.

8 Chapter summary

```
                    ┌─────────────────────────────┐
                    │  The nature and purpose of  │
                    │    management accounting    │
                    └─────────────────────────────┘
```

┌─────────────────────────────┐
│ Management accounting   │
│ and management   │
│ information   │
│ • Financial accounting   │
│ • Cost accounting   │
│ • Management accounting   │
└─────────────────────────────┘

┌─────────────────────────────┐
│ The nature of   │
│ good information   │
│ Accurate   │
│ Complete   │
│ Cost-effective   │
│ Understandable   │
│ Relevant   │
│ Accessible   │
│ Easy to use   │
└─────────────────────────────┘

┌─────────────────────────────┐
│ Cost centres   │
│ – costs identified   │
│   │
│ Profit centres   │
│ – cost and   │
│   revenues indentified   │
│   │
│ Investment centres   │
│ – profit centre   │
│   with responsibility   │
│   for investment   │
│   │
│ Revenue centres   │
│ – accountable for   │
│   revenues only   │
└─────────────────────────────┘

The managerial processes of planning, decision making and control

Plan – establish objectives of organisation and relevant strategies

Decision making – make informed decision using management information

Control – take control measures/feedback loop

Strategic, tactical and operational planning

Strategic – long term
Tactical – short term
Operational – day-to-day

Test your understanding answers

Test your understanding 1

Answer C

The two terms are frequently used synonymously but strictly speaking they mean different things. Data is obtained from a survey and is turned into information by sorting and analysis. Both data and information can comprise either facts or figures.

Test your understanding 2

	Planning	Control	Decision making
Preparation of the annual budget for a cost centre	√		√
Revise budgets for next period for a cost centre		√	√
Implement decisions based on information provided			√
Set organisation's objectives for next period	√		√
Compare actual and expected results for a period		√	√

Note that all planning and control functions are part of the decision making process and are therefore identified as being both. The only exception is 'implement decisions based on information provided' which is not part of planning and control, but the one decision making task that there is.

Test your understanding 3

Answer B

Test your understanding 4

Answer B

The management accountant is providing a new budget for the forthcoming period – i.e. a senior manager making a short term plan.

Sources of data

Chapter learning objectives

Upon completion of this chapter you will be able to:

- describe sources of information from within and outside the organisation (including government statistics, financial press, professional or trade associations, quotations and price list)

- explain the uses and limitations of published information/data (including information from the internet)

- describe the impact of general economic environment on costs/revenue

- explain sampling techniques (random, systematic, stratified, multistage, cluster and quota)

- choose an appropriate sampling method in a specific situation

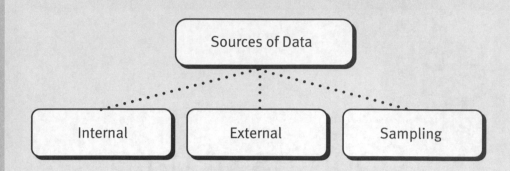

1 Internal sources of information

Internal information may come from various sources.

Accounting system

The accounting system will collect data from source documents such as invoices, timesheets and journal entries. The data will be sorted and analysed by the coding system by type of expense, department, manager and job. Reports of direct and indirect costs compared to budgets may be produced at regular intervals to help managers plan and control costs. Ad hoc reports may be produced to help managers make specific decisions.

Consider the examples listed below:

- Sales analysed by product will help management to assess the patterns of demand for each product.

- This same information will help plan production and inventory levels.

- In turn, production information will enable the organisation to plan its requirements for raw materials, labour and machine hours.

- Information on material, labour and other costs will allow the organisation to set estimated costs for its products. This will be the basis for a budgetary control and standard costing system, as we shall see in a later chapter.

- In the context of long-term, strategic decision making, the sales analysis given above may help management to assess future product strategies – expand output of those for which demand is increasing, reduce output of those for which demand is falling.

- An aged receivables report would provide the basis for debt collection decisions taken by a credit control manager.

- Figures for wastage rates or product reject rates may allow management to reach decisions on the product quality aspect of the organisation's operations.

Payroll system

The payroll system may provide information concerning detailed labour costs. Hours paid may be analysed into productive work and non-productive time such as training, sick leave, holiday and idle time. Labour turnover by department or manager may be analysed and may help management to assess the employment and motivation policies

Strategic planning system

The strategic planning system may provide information relating to the organisation's objectives and targets. Assumptions relating to the external environment may be detailed. Details of the organisation's capital investment programme and product launch programme may also be recorded here. Some of this information will be commercially sensitive and only accessed by senior managers in the organisation.

Benefits and limitations of internal sources

Benefits	Limitations
• Readily available data	• Data may need to be further analysed to be of use to management accountants
• Data can easily be sorted and analysed	
• Reports can easily be produced when required	
• Data relates to the organisation concerned	

2 External sources of information

Businesses are finding it increasingly difficult to succeed if they ignore the external environment which will influence their activities. The process known as environmental scanning or environmental monitoring is becoming an increasingly important part of the role of the management accountant. These terms are used to describe the process whereby data is collected from outside, as well as from inside the organisation and used in the decision-making process.

The main sources of external information which we shall consider here are:

• government sources

• business contacts – customers and suppliers

• trade associations and trade journals

• the financial and business press and other media.

Government sources

There is a wealth of published statistical data covering many aspects of the nation's economy: population, manpower, trade, agriculture, price levels, capital issues and similar matters. Most, but not all of this is produced by national governments.

The primary purpose of this data is to provide information for economic planning at the national level. The data serves the secondary purpose of providing industry with useful background information for deciding on future policies such as raising new finance or recruiting specialised labour. The data is only published in general terms (e.g. for a particular industry or geographical area).

The following list shows some (there are many others) of the main sources of this type of information in the UK. Other countries will usually have similar information available. Copies are generally available in reference libraries and on government websites.

Title	Frequency of publication	Main topics covered
Employment Gazette	Monthly	Earnings, basic wage rates, unemployment, indices of wholesale and retail prices.
British Business	Weekly	Wholesale and retail prices, production for specific sectors of industry, capital expenditure
National Income and Expenditure Blue Book	Annually	Personal income and expenditure, gross national product.
Financial Statistics	Monthly	Money supply, interest rates, hire purchase liabilities, building societies
Price Index numbers for Current Cost Accounting	Annually, but updated by monthly supplement	Retail price index, also industry specific and asset specific price indices.

All the above publications relate to the UK. Publications concerned with statistics relating to the European Union include European Economy Annual Statistical Yearbook, Eurostat (monthly) and OECD Main Economic Indicators (monthly). Information on the World Economy is available from the United Nations (Demographic Yearbook and Statistical Yearbook), the International Labour Organisation (Yearbook of Labour Statistics) and UNESCO (Statistical Yearbook).

Business contacts

Government produced information will be broadly based and general, dealing with the economy as a whole or particular sectors or industries. An organisation may be looking for information more focused on its own position. Its day-to-day business contacts, customers and suppliers, can be a useful source of this information – and often it is available free.

Customers can provide information on such matters as:

- the product specification which they require

- their quality requirements

- requirements for delivery periods

- preference for packaging and distribution methods

- feedback on the above and on general aspects of customer service.

Suppliers may be able to provide information on:

- quantity discounts and volume rebates which may help the organisation to decide on order size

- availability of products and services

- alternative products or services which may be available or may become available

- technical specifications of their product.

Trade associations and trade journals

Most major industries have their own trade association. The role of these organisations includes:

- representing their member firms in legal and other disputes

- providing quality assurance schemes for customers of member organisations

- laying down codes of practice to be followed by their member organisations

- publishing trade journals and other information useful for the management and development of their businesses.

There follows a very brief list of just a small selection of trade associations operating in the UK – it is taken from an alphabetical listing of associations and shows the first few starting with the letter A. There are hundreds more!

- Agricultural Industries Confederation

- Airport Operators Association

- Association for Payment Clearing Services APCS
- Association for Road Traffic Safety & Management
- Association of Art and Antique Dealers
- Association of British Fire Trades Ltd.

Many of these organisations publish their own industry or trade journals which will contain useful news and other information for organisations operating in that industry. Trade journals are also published by many publishing organisations. In the UK one of the best known of these journals is The Grocer aimed at the food and drink retail sector. Again, many others exist.

The financial press, business press and other media

In the UK, The Financial Times, the Guardian, The Times and the Daily Telegraph together with some regional newspapers provide statistics and financial reviews as well as business and economic news and commentary. These include:

- the FTSE 100 Index – the stock market index of the leading 100 leading companies based on tradeable share value
- the FT Actuaries All-share Index – an index of all share prices quoted on the stock exchange.

Such information is now also widely available via electronic media. Digital television services available on satellite or cable systems carry specialist business and financial channels and programmes (such as Bloomberg TV) which give both national and world-wide coverage. There is also the internet as a widely available source of up-to-date financial information.

Benefits and limitations of external sources

Internal information is produced by the company itself so the users are aware of any limitations in its quality or reliability. External information is not under the control of the organisation – the users may not be aware of any limitations in its quality.

Benefits	Limitations
• Wide expanse of external sources of information	• Data may not be accurate
• Easily accessible especially using the internet	• Finding relevant information can be time consuming
• More general information available	
• Can source specific information needs	

KAPLAN PUBLISHING

3 General economic environment

The general economic environment will have an impact on the costs and revenues of a business.

If the **economy is strong** then attitudes are more confident about the future. There will be more disposable income so more money will be available to spend.

A business will be able to increase prices, if desired, to follow this upward trend. This means that revenues of a business will increase. Suppliers to the business may also increase their prices so costs could increase.

The increased disposable income will also cause consumers to purchase or demand more products. As these products become scarce, the price charged by suppliers will rise.

If the **economy is weak** then attitudes will be less confident about the future. This does not mean that costs and revenues will both drop.

There will be less disposable income available so revenues will decline. It may not be possible for suppliers to drop their prices so costs may continue to be high.

4 Sampling techniques

The purpose of sampling is to gain as much information as possible about the population by observing only a small proportion of that population i.e. by observing a sample.

The term population is used to mean all the items under consideration in a particular enquiry.

A sample is a group of items drawn from that population. The population may consist of items such as metal bars, invoices, packets of tea, etc; it need not be people.

For example:

*   in order to ascertain which television programmes are most popular, a sample of the total viewing public is interviewed and, based on their replies, the programmes can be listed in order of popularity with all viewers.

*   during the quality control procedures in a manufacturing business, a sample of the product is taken for testing.

There are three main reasons why sampling is necessary:

(1) The whole population may not be known.

(2) Even if the population is known the process of testing every item can be extremely costly in time and money, for example, gaining information about the popularity of TV programs by interviewing every viewer.

(3) The items being tested may be completely destroyed in the process, for example in order to check the lifetime of an electric light bulb it is necessary to leave the bulb burning until it breaks and is of no further use.

The characteristics of a population can be ascertained by investigating only a sample of that population provided that the following two rules are observed:

(1) The sample must be of a certain size. In general terms the larger the sample the more reliable the results will be.

(2) The sample must be chosen in such a way that it is representative of the population.

There are several methods of obtaining a sample and these are considered in turn.

Random Sampling

A simple random sample is defined as a sample taken in such a way that every member of the population has an equal chance of being selected. The normal way of achieving this is by numbering each item in the population.

If 10% of a population of 200 is the required sample size then 20 numbers from a table of random numbers can be taken and the corresponding items are extracted from the population to form the sample e.g. in selecting a sample of invoices for an audit. Since the invoices are already numbered, this method can be applied with the minimum of difficulty.

This method has obvious limitations when either the population is extremely large or, in fact, not known. The following methods are more applicable in these cases.

Systematic sampling

If the population is known to contain 50,000 items and a sample of size 500 is required, then 1 in every 100 items is selected. The first item is determined by choosing randomly a number between 1 and 100 e.g. 67, then the second item will be the 167th, the third will be the 267th... up to the 49,967th item.

Strictly speaking, systematic sampling (also called quasi-random) is not truly random as only the first item is selected randomly. However, it gives a very close approximation to random sampling and it is very widely used.

There is danger of bias if the population has a repetitive structure. For example, if a street has five types of house arranged in the order, A B C D E A B C D E... etc, an interviewer visiting every fifth home would only visit one type of house.

Stratified sampling

If the population under consideration contains several well defined groups (called strata or layers), e.g. men and women, smokers and non-smokers, different sizes of metal bars, etc, then a random sample is taken from each group. This is done in such a way that the number in each sample is proportional to the size of that group in the population and is known as sampling with probability proportional to size (pps).

For example, in selecting a sample of people in order to discover their leisure habits, age could be an important factor. So if 20% of the population are over 60 years of age 65% between 18 and 60 and 15% are under 18, then a sample of 200 people should contain 40 who are over 60 years old, 130 people between 18 and 60 and 30 under 18 years of age, i.e. the subsample should have sizes in the ratio 20 : 65 : 15.

This method ensures that a representative cross-section of the strata in the population is obtained, which may not be the case with a simple random sample of the whole population.

This method is often used by auditors to choose a sample to confirm receivables' balances. In this case a greater proportion of larger balances will be selected.

Multi-stage sampling

This method is often applied if the population is particularly large. The process involved here would be as follows:

Step 1 The country is divided into areas (counties) and a random sample of areas is taken.

Step 2 Each area chosen in Step 1 is then subdivided into towns and cities or boroughs and a random sample of these is taken.

Step 3 Each town or city chosen in Step 2 is further divided into roads and a random sample of roads is then taken.

Step 4 From each road chosen in Step 3 a random sample of houses is taken and the occupiers interviewed.

This method is used, for example, in selecting a sample for a national opinion poll of the type carried out prior to a general election.

Cluster sampling

This method is similar to the previous one in that the country is split into areas and a random sample taken. Further sub-divisions can be made until the required number of small areas have been determined. Then every house in each area will be visited instead of just a random sample of houses. In many ways this is a simpler and less costly procedure as no time is wasted finding particular houses and the amount of travelling by interviewers is much reduced.

Quota sampling

With quota sampling the interviewer will be given a list comprising the different types of people to be questioned and the number or quota of each type e.g. 20 males, aged 20 to 30 years, manual workers; 15 females, 25 to 35, not working; 10 males, 55 to 60, professional men, etc. The interviewer can use any method to obtain such people until the various quotas are filled. This is very similar to stratified sampling, but no attempt is made to select respondents by a proper random method, consequently the sample may be very biased.

Sampling methods compared

The objective of a sample is to collect data upon which an opinion can be formed, and a conclusion drawn in respect of the population of which the sample is representative.

Ideally the sample would be chosen at random, and would be large enough so as to be representative of the population. Unfortunately both of these aspects introduce costs which are often unacceptably high.

Alternatives to the truly random sampling method have been outlined above. They are all concerned with minimising costs whilst maintaining the representative nature of the sample compared to the population.

In order to use these alternatives it is often necessary to have some knowledge of the population. Systematic sampling should not be used if the population follows a repetitive pattern. Quota sampling must be used with caution. The data collector may introduce bias because they choose how to fill the quota.

KAPLAN PUBLISHING

Test your understanding 1

The essence of systematic sampling is that:

A   each element of the population has an equal chance of being chosen

B   members of various strata are selected by the interviewers up to predetermined limits

C   every nth member of the population is selected

D   every element of one definable subsection of the population is selected

Test your understanding 2

A sample is taken by dividing the population into different age bands and then sampling randomly from the bands, in proportion to their size. What is such a sample called?

A   Simple random

B   Stratified random

C   Quota

D   Cluster

Test your understanding 3

In a survey on the opinions of employees in a large company headquarters, one of the following is a cluster sample. Which is it?

A   Staff are randomly selected from each department in proportion to departmental size

B   Staff are selected from the list of employees, taking every nth name

C   A sample, which is as representative as possible of the composition of the staff in terms of gender, age and department, is taken by stopping appropriate staff in the corridors and canteen

D   One department is selected and all the staff in that department are surveyed

Test your understanding 4

Associate with each of the following sampling methods (A)–(F) the most appropriate example from the list, (P)–(U), given below.

A   Simple random sample

B   Stratified random sample

C   Cluster sample

D   Systematic sample

E   Quota sample

F   Multistage sample

Examples

P   One city is chosen at random from all cities in the United Kingdom, then the electoral register is used to select a 1-per-1,000 sample.

Q   Names picked from a hat.

R   Every 10th person is chosen randomly from each ward in a hospital.

S   One secondary school in a town is selected at random, then every pupil in that school is surveyed.

T   One person in ten is chosen from an alphabetical list of employees.

U   People are stopped in the street according to instructions such as 'stop equal numbers of men and women'.

5 Chapter summary

```
                    ┌─────────────────────┐
                    │   Sources of Data   │
                    └─────────────────────┘
```

┌──────────────────────┐ ┌──────────────────────┐ ┌──────────────────────┐
│ Internal   │ │ External   │ │ Sampling   │
│ • Accounting system │ │ • Government   │ │ • Random   │
│ • Payroll   │ │ • Journals   │ │ • Systematic   │
│ • Planning   │ │ • Newspapers   │ │ • Cluster   │
│   │ │   │ │ • Quota   │
│   │ │   │ │ • Stratified   │
│   │ │   │ │ • Multi-staged   │
└──────────────────────┘ └──────────────────────┘ └──────────────────────┘

Test your understanding answers

Test your understanding 1

Answer C

In systematic sampling, population members are listed and members selected at regular intervals along the list.

Test your understanding 2

Answer B

In simple random sampling, there is no division of the population into groups. In cluster sampling, only one group is selected and all its members are surveyed. Quota sampling and stratified random sampling are both as described in the question but quota sampling is not random.

Test your understanding 3

Answer D

A is a stratified random sample, B is systematic and C is a quota sample

Test your understanding 4

The associations are as follows:

A   Most appropriate example is (Q)

B   Most appropriate example is (R)

C   Most appropriate example is (S)

D   Most appropriate example is (T)

E   Most appropriate example is (U)

F   Most appropriate example is (P)

KAPLAN PUBLISHING

3

Presenting information

Chapter learning objectives

Upon completion of this chapter you will be able to:

- prepare written reports representing management information in suitable formats according to purpose

- present information using tables, charts and graphs (bar charts, line graphs, pie charts and scatter graphs)

- construct scatter diagrams and lines of best fit

- interpret information (including the above tables, charts and graphs) presented in management reports.

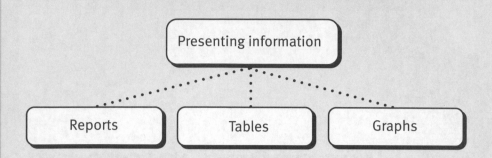

1 Introduction

The major theme underlying management accounting is information. The previous chapter dealt with the processes involved in collecting that information – this can be seen as the input into the management accounting process. We now turn our attention to the output from the management accounting department – the presentation of information to management.

One of the desirable qualities of information is that it should be understandable to the user. Management accountants have been criticised in the past for presenting information in a form which is unclear to the non-expert. Very often, graphical methods of presentation are clearer to the user than written or numerical presentation.

2 Writing reports

The information given below on writing reports can be applied, in not only a business environment, but also in an examination environment.

The four-stage approach to report writing

When producing written reports, the management accountant needs to carry out four steps.

Prepare

- determine the type of document required: detailed report, short memo, discussion notes, etc.

- establish the user of the information: the type of language used and the level of knowledge assumed will be largely determined by the end user.

- find out what the report will be used for – the report will often be aimed at providing information to help management make a decision.

Plan

- select the relevant data: summarise, analyse, illustrate (if appropriate) to turn the raw data into useful information. This will often involve the use of management accounting techniques.

- produce a logical order for the material.

Write

- determine the writing style that is appropriate.

- take care over spelling, use of language and arithmetic – your meaning must be clear and logical.

Review

- re-read what you have written.

- check that it meets the requirements of the document.

- ensure that it is complete and clear.

The structure of a report

A typical report structure will be as follows:

- **Title** – At the top of your report show who the report is to, who it is from, the date and a heading.

- **Introduction** – showing what information was requested, the work done and where results and conclusions can be found.

- **Analysis** – presenting the information required in a series of sub-sections.

- **Conclusion** – including, where appropriate, recommendations. Never introduce new material into a conclusion.

- **Appendices** – containing detailed calculations, tables of underlying data, etc. If you use appendices refer to them in your report.

Numbered headings and cross referencing between sections make reports easier to follow (or navigate).

Use of English

English is technically a complicated language – if you try to write lengthy complex sentences or paragraphs, it may go wrong.

The single most important point is to make sure that the reader can understand what you are saying.

Some specific guidelines are:

- avoid excessively long sentences

- avoid over-long words

- do not use jargon, clichés, metaphors – the aim is to communicate in a professional manner

- if acronyms (e.g. ACCA) are used – they should be explained the first time they are introduced into the report

- take care with punctuation and grammar to make sure your ideas are communicated clearly.

3 Tables

Tabulation is the process of presenting data in the form of a table – an arrangement of rows and columns.

The purpose of tabulation is to summarise the information and present it in a more understandable way.

Rules of tabulation

The following rules or principles of tabulation should be considered when preparing tables:

(a) Title: the table must have a clear and self-explanatory title.

(b) Source: the source of the material used in drawing up the table should be stated (usually by way of a footnote).

(c) Units: the units of measurement that have been used must be stated e.g. 000s means that the units are in thousands.

(d) Headings: all column and row headings should be clear and concise.

(e) Totals: these should be shown where appropriate, and also any subtotals that may be applicable to the calculations.

(f) Percentages and ratios: these should be shown, if meaningful, with an indication of how they were calculated.

KAPLAN PUBLISHING

Columns and rows

A table is set up in the form of a number of columns headed up across the page and then a number of rows of information moving down the page. A typical table would be set up as follows:

	Column 1	Column 2	Column 3
Row 1			
Row 2			
Row 3			

A key element of setting up a good table is to decide upon the optimal arrangement of columns and rows.

Three general rules apply here:

(1) Try to ensure that the table fits on one page

(2) The columns should be arranged so that related information is shown alongside each other.

(3) The information shown in the rows should be arranged so that there is a logical progression through the information and any meaningful totals or subtotals can be clearly made.

4 Graphs and charts

In some cases clarity of presentation can be improved if data is presented pictorially – in the form of charts or graphs. We shall refer to these two techniques together as diagrams.

A diagram should be as clear and unambiguous as possible. In order to help to achieve this aim a number of rules should be followed:

- give each diagram a name or a title
- state the source of any data that has been used
- state the units of measurement that have been used
- give a scale so that the diagram can be properly interpreted
- ensure that the presentation is neat
- use a key to explain the contents
- if axes are used, they should be properly labelled.

These guidelines are similar to those suggested above for the construction of tables.

The types of diagrams which are covered by your examination syllabus are:

- bar charts
- line graphs
- scatter graphs
- pie charts.

Bar charts

A bar chart is a widely used method of illustrating quantitative data. There are a number of different types of bar chart and the ones to be considered in this chapter are:

- simple bar charts
- component (or stacked) bar charts
- percentage component bar charts
- compound (or multiple) bar charts.

Simple bar charts

A simple bar chart is where only one variable only is being illustrated. The bars on a simple bar chart should be of equal widths as the height or length of the bar represents the 'value' of the variable.

Illustration 1

The production of grain in the UK for the years 20X1 to 20X3 was as follows:

Year	Production (m tonnes)
20X1	150
20X2	375
20X3	600

Illustrate this data using a simple bar chart.

A bar chart showing the production of grain in the UK from 20X1 to 20X3

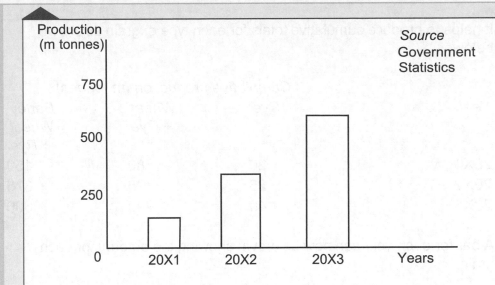

Interpretation

A simple bar chart shows not only the actual amount of the data which can be read off from the vertical axis but also the relationship between the data.

In the example the actual amount of wheat production each year can be determined by reading off the amounts on the vertical axis. It is also possible to see at a glance that grain production was increasing over the three-year period.

Component bar chart

A component bar chart is used when each total figure in the data is made up of a number of different components and it is important that these component elements are shown as well as the total figure.

Illustration 2

Continuing with the previous grain production example suppose that annual production can now be split into that of rye, wheat and barley as follows:

	Production (m tonnes)		
Year	Rye	Wheat	Barley
20X1	20	60	70
20X2	25	150	200
20X3	40	250	310

Draw a component bar chart to illustrate this data.

It helps to produce cumulative totals for each type of grain as shown below:

Year	Cumulative production (m tonnes)		
	Rye	Wheat + Rye	Barley + Wheat + Rye
20X1	20	80	150
20X2	25	175	375
20X3	40	290	600

A bar for each year can now be drawn showing the amount for each grain.

Grain production in the UK, 20X1 to 20X3

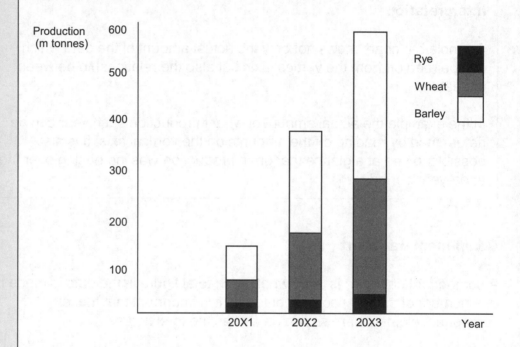

Interpretation

The component bar chart still shows that the volume of grain as a whole has been increasing by significant amounts but it also shows the breakdown of this information into types of grain.

Percentage component bar chart

A percentage component bar chart is one where the actual values of each component are not shown but the percentage of the total for each component is. The bars in this type of chart are all the same height (representing 100%) and are split according to the proportions of each component element – rye, wheat and barley in our example above.

Illustration

To create a percentage component bar chart you need to calculate the percentage of the total that each variable takes up.

	Production (m tonnes)		
Year	Rye	Wheat	Barley
20X1	20	60	70
20X2	25	150	200
20X3	40	250	310

Convert the above figures into percentages:

	Production %			
Year	Total	Rye	Wheat	Barley
20X1	150	13	40	47
20X2	375	7	40	53
20X3	600	7	42	52

Show these on a percentage component bar chart.

A bar chart showing the percentage of grain produced from 20X1 to 20X3

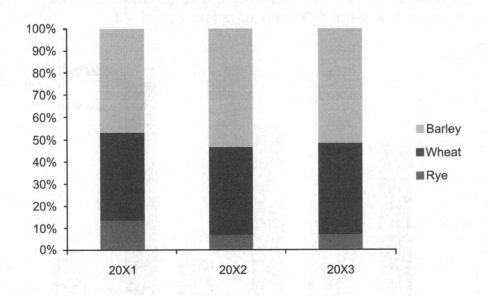

Interpretation

From the percentage graph it is clear to see that even though the total amount of grain produced is increasing – the proportion of the different types of grain is remaining fairly constant.

Compound (multiple) bar charts

Compound bar charts are sometimes termed multiple bar charts. A compound bar chart is one where there is more than one bar for each sub-division of the chart. For example a business makes 3 products and wants to show each products sales over the last 4 years. A compound bar chart could be used with 3 bars (one for each product) in each year.

Illustration 3

An accountancy tuition provider uses a delivery company to deliver its book and manuals to customers and retailers. Using the following information construct a compound bar chart to show how the following variables have changed over the last 3 years.

(a) the sales value of the manuals and text books sold

(b) the van expenses

(c) the drivers wages

	Year 1	Year 2	Year 3
Sales $	200,000	222,200	272,630
Van expenses $	14,000	15,000	18,000
Drivers' wages $	52,000	56,600	68,150

A compound bar chart showing the sales value, the van expenses and the drivers wages for years 1 – 3

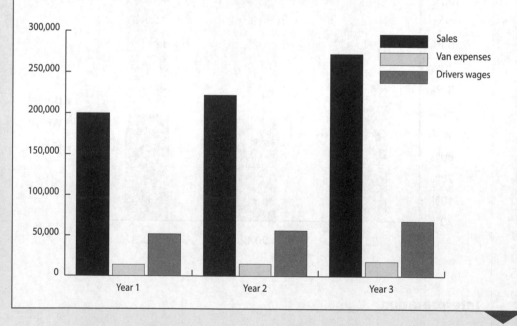

Interpretation

This compound bar graph has been used to show how the value of 3 different items has changed over time. It is clear from the graph that sales have grown and in comparison van and driver expenses have stayed almost static.

Line graphs

In many instances it will be found that data can be more clearly and understandably presented in the form of a line graph, especially if we are consider the change in an item over time.

Things to consider when producing a line graph:

- **Independent and dependent variables** – the dependent variable must always be plotted on the vertical (y) axis and the independent variable on the horizontal (x) axis. For example - sales over the last 12 months. the sales volume would be plotted on the y-axis and the time periods (months) on the x-axis. The sales are dependent on the month rather than the sale determining the month. The month of the year is independent of the sales volume.

- **Scales of the axes** – there is no necessity for the same scale to be used on each axis. Even if the units on the x and y axis are the same a different scale is quite permissible.

- **Starting point of the axes** – in most cases the scales on both axes should start at zero, however if starting at zero is not practical then it is possible to show a break in the scale with a zig zag line.

- **Multiple line graphs** – plotting more than one set of variables on the same graph. This is quite acceptable as long as the graph still remains clear and informative. If more than one line is to appear on a graph then they must also be drawn to the same scale and the different lines should be clearly indicated by use dashed or dotted lines or coloured lines.

Illustration 4

You are an accountant working for a group of companies. In one sector of the business there are two divisions, A and B. Some concern has been expressed in recent years regarding the growth in administrative costs in the two divisions.

Details of administrative costs for the past five years are:

	20X1 £m	20X2 £m	20X3 £m	20X4 £m	20X5 £m
Division A					
Actual	2.7	3.0	3.4	3.6	4.0
Adjusted cost	3.04	3.25	3.62	3.69	4.00
Division B					
Actual	1.7	2.1	2.5	3.0	3.6
Adjusted cost	1.92	2.27	2.66	3.07	3.60

Draw a line graph to show the administrative costs for both divisions at both original and adjusted prices for the period from 20X1 to 20X5.

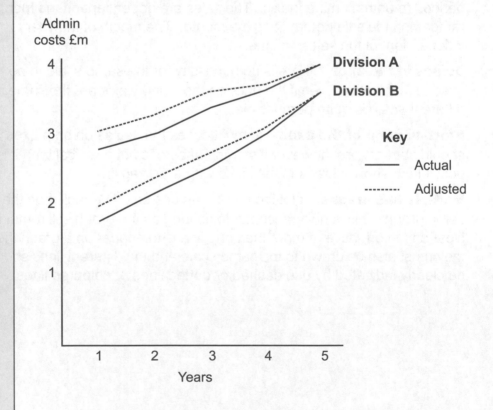

Interpretation

From the graph, it can be seen that the rise in Division B costs is steeper than in A, in both the actual and adjusted costs.

Scatter Diagram

Information about two variables that are considered to be related in some way can be represented by using a graph known as a 'scatter diagram' or scattergraph, where each axis of the scatter diagram represents one variable.

For example, the sales revenue for a product could be plotted against time (months) to show how the sales revenue has varied over the year; or production costs could be plotted against units produced to show how costs change as production changes:

- The x-axis (horizontal) represents the **independent** variable i.e. time or units produced
- The y-axis (vertical) represents the **dependent** variable i.e. sales revenue or production costs

Sales revenue is dependent on the month and production costs are dependent on volume produced not vice versa.

To produce a scatter diagram a number of **pairs of data** are required e.g. sales revenue for January, sales revenue for February, sales revenue for March etc. These pairs of data are plotted on the graph to produce a scattering of points.

The way in which these points are scattered or dispersed indicates if any relationship is likely to exist between the variables. When the points on a scatter diagram lie in a narrow band, there is a strong relationship between the variables. When the points are widely dispersed there is less likely to be a relationship between the variables.

Line of best fit or trend line

Scatter diagrams are often used to show how two variables relate to each other i.e. is there a **trend**. A 'line of best fit' can be plotted through the points on a scatter diagram to demonstrate the trend. To plot a line of best fit it is necessary to try to estimate visually a line through the points that is the same distance away from each point. Some computer packages that can be used to produce graph, for example Excel, have a facility included to plot a line of best fit through data points.

Scatter diagrams with lines of best fit can be useful as a forecasting technique and has the advantage of relative simplicity – this is looked at in more detail in a Chapter 12.

Illustration 5

Consider the following data which relates to the total costs incurred at various output levels in a factory:

Output (units)	Total cost ($)
26	6,566
30	6,510
33	6,800
44	6,985
48	7,380
50	7,310

If the data shown above is plotted on a scattergraph and a line of best fit is drawn on it would look like this:

A scatter graph showing the relationship between output and cost

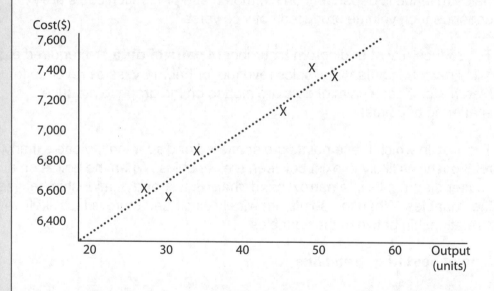

Interpretation

It is clear to see from the line on the graph that there is a positive relationship between output in units and costs ($). As output increases the costs also increase.

Pie Charts

A pie chart is a circle broken down into sections, each section is representing a component of the data.

Pie charts are used to illustrate different components of data as part of a whole, similar to percentage component bar charts.

Constructing a pie chart

(1) Calculate the total value of the numerical data that is to be represented

(2) Calculate the number of degrees per item of data:

   360°/Total value of data = Number of degrees per item of data

(3) Calculate the size of section required to represent for each element of data

   Number of degrees per unit × number of items in each set of data

(4) Draw a circle and split it into sections accordingly

Illustration 6

Suppose a family's income in 20X0 is $1,000 per month, and their expenditure splits down as follows:

	Amount
	$
Mortgage and insurance	300
Electricity and gas	50
Food and drink	200
Clothes	40
Car and petrol	150
Telephone	10
Savings	70
Fares	60
Miscellaneous	120
	1,000

(1) Calculate the total value of the numerical data that is to be represented

   $1,000

(2) Calculate the number of degrees per item of data:

360°/Total value of data = Number of degrees per item of data

360°/$1,000 = 0.36° per $

(3) Calculate the size of section required to represent for each element of data

Number of degrees per unit × number of items in each set of data

Mortgage and insurance = 0.36 × 300 = 108°

Electricity and gas = 0.36 × 50 = 18°

Food and drink = 0.36 × 200 = 72°

etc

(4) Draw a circle and split it into sections accordingly

A pie chart showing how the family's income is spent

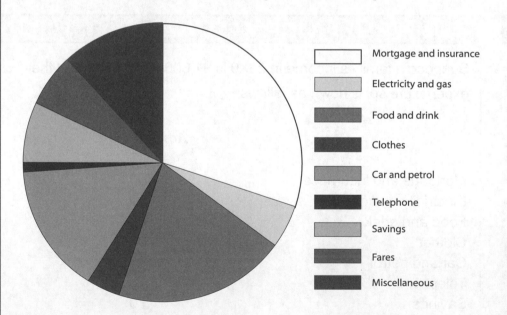

Interpretation

Without actually measuring the angles or having the raw data input on the pie chart it is not possible to read the actual figures. However it is very easy to see what the largest proportion of the families income is spent on. Over a quarter of the income is spent on the mortgage and insurance, with food and drink being the next biggest section.

Interpretation of tables, charts and graphs

Although the information presented in diagrammatic form should be presented in a way which is easy to understand, part of the role of the management accountant may nevertheless involve interpreting the information, perhaps in the form of a brief report to management.

It will generally be the case that the better prepared the diagram is, the less interpretation that will be required to assist management to understand the information.

Your objective in carrying out this sort of interpretation exercise is to bring out the meaning in the information and, perhaps, to help management reach conclusions based on the information presented. As a result of your interpretation, you may also be able to make suitable recommendations to management.

5 Chapter summary

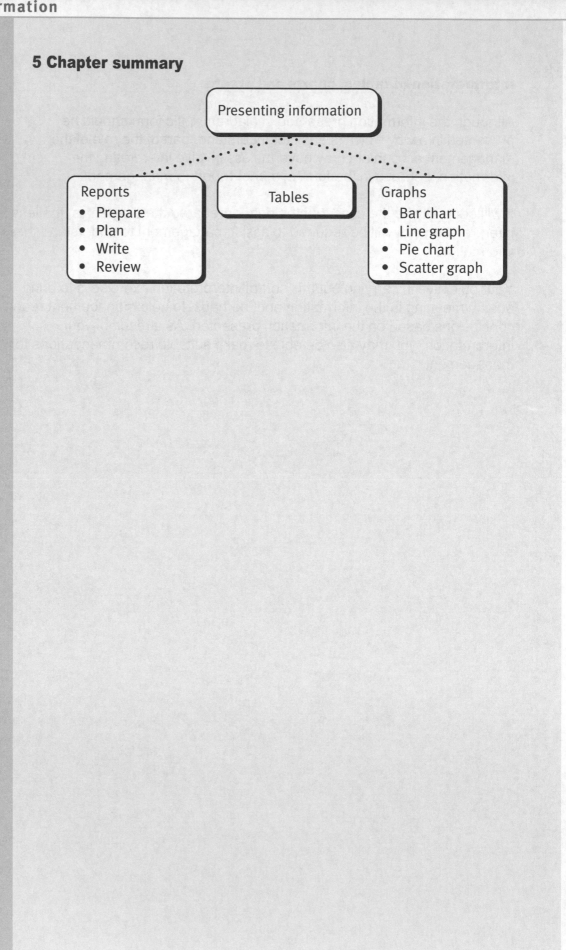

Types of cost and cost behaviour

Chapter learning objectives

Upon completion of this chapter you will be able to:

- explain and illustrate production and non-production costs

- describe the different elements of non-production cost – administrative, selling, distribution and finance

- describe the different elements of production cost – materials, labour and overheads

- explain the importance of the distinction between production and non-production costs when valuing output and inventories

- explain and illustrate with examples classifications used in the analysis of the product/service costs including by function, direct and indirect, fixed and variable, stepped fixed and semi variable costs

- describe and illustrate, graphically, different types of cost behaviour

- use high/low analysis to separate the fixed and variable elements of total costs including situations involving semi variable and stepped fixed costs and changes in the variable cost per unit

- explain the advantages and disadvantages of using high low method to estimate the fixed and variable element of costing

- explain the structure of linear functions and equations

- explain and illustrate the concepts of cost objects, cost units and cost centres

- explain and illustrate the use of codes in categorising transaction.

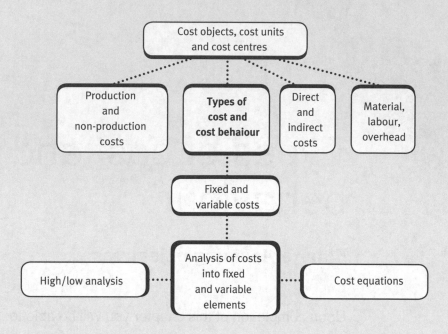

1 Analysing costs

Management will require a variety of different cost summaries, including:

- costs for a particular product – cost unit or cost object

- costs for use in the preparation of external financial reports

- costs for a particular department – cost centre

- costs that may be used for decision making

- costs that are useful for planning and control.

To be able to produce these summaries the type of cost and the cost behaviour will need to be analysed.

Cost objects

A cost object is any activity for which a separate measurement of cost is undertaken.

Examples of cost objects:

- cost of a product

- cost of a service

- cost of running a department

- cost of running a regional office.

Cost units

A cost unit is a unit of product or service in relation to which costs are ascertained.

Examples of cost units:

- a room (in a hotel)
- a litre of paint (paint manufacturers)
- in-patient (in a hospital).

Cost centres

A cost centre is a production or service location, function, activity or item of equipment for which costs can be ascertained.

Examples of cost centres:

- a department
- a machine
- a project
- a ward (in a hospital).

2 Classifying costs

Costs can be classified in a number of different ways.

- **Element** – costs are classified as materials, labour or expenses.
- **Function** – costs are classified as being production or non-production costs.
- **Nature** – costs are classified as being direct or indirect.
- **Behaviour** – costs are classified as being fixed, variable, semi-variable or stepped fixed.

3 Classification by element

The cost elements that you need to know about are materials, labour and expenses. To classify by element you need to decide if a cost is a material cost, a labour cost or cost relating to something else – an expense.

- **Materials** – all costs of materials purchased for production or non-production activities. For example, raw materials, components, cleaning materials, maintenance materials and stationery.

- **Labour** – all staff costs relating to employees on the payroll of the organisation.

- **Expenses** – all other costs which are not materials or labour. This includes all bought-in services, for example, rent, telephone, sub-contractors and costs such as the depreciation of equipment.

4 Classification by function

Production costs

Production costs are the costs which are incurred when raw materials are converted into finished goods and part-finished goods (work in progress).

Production costs, such as direct materials, direct labour, direct expenses and production overheads, are used to **value inventory**.

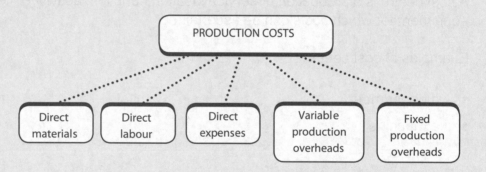

Examples of production costs

- Direct materials – the direct materials that go into making a product. For example, cloth in the manufacture of shirts.

- Direct labour – the cost of labour directly engaged in making a product. For example, the wages of the machinists making the shirts.

- Direct expenses – the cost of expenses directly involved in making a product. For example, the royalties paid to a designer.

- Variable production overheads – overheads that vary in direct proportion to the quantity of product manufactured. For example, cost of fuel used to run machinery.

- Fixed production overheads – overheads that are fixed whatever the quantity of product manufactured. For example, rent of the factory.

Non-production costs

Non-production costs are costs that are not directly associated with the production of the businesses output.

Non-production costs, such as administrative costs, selling costs and finance costs, are charged to the income statement as expenses for the period in which they are incurred. Non-production costs are **not** used to value inventory.

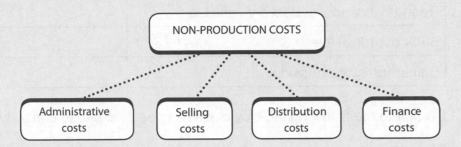

Examples of non-production costs

- Administrative costs – the costs involved in running the general administration departments of an organisation, for example, the accounts department.

- Selling costs – costs associated with taking orders from customers who wish to buy an organisation's products (sales department costs) and also marketing costs.

- Distribution costs – the costs involved in distributing an organisation's finished products, such as the cost of running the warehouse or delivery costs.

- Finance costs – the costs that are incurred in order to finance an organisation, for example, loan interest.

Test your understanding 1

Cost	Classification
Overalls for machine workers	
Cost of printer cartridges in general office	
Salary of factory supervisor	
Salary of payroll supervisor	
Rent of warehouse for storing goods ready for sale	
Loan interest	
Salary of factory security guard	

Early settlement discounts for customers who pay early	
Salary of the Chairman's PA	
Road tax licence for delivery vehicles	
Bank overdraft fee	
Salesmen's commissions	

Complete the following table by classifying each expense correctly.

Classifications

(1) = Production

(2) = Selling

(3) = Distribution

(4) = Administrative

(5) = Finance

Test your understanding 2

ILCB has the following information relating to one of its products:

- Direct material cost per unit $1

- Direct labour cost per unit $3

- Variable production cost per unit $3

- Selling costs $10 per unit

- Fixed production overhead $30,000 per month

- Budgeted production 15,000 units per month

- Budgeted sales 12,000 units per month

Required

What is the total cost of the budgeted monthly production?

5 Classification by nature

Direct costs

Direct costs are costs which can be directly identified with a specific cost unit or cost centre. There are three main types of direct cost:

- direct materials – for example, cloth for making shirts
- direct labour – for example, the wages of the workers stitching the cloth to make the shirts
- direct expenses – for example, the royalties paid to a designer.

The total of direct costs is known as the **prime cost**.

Indirect costs

Indirect costs are costs which cannot be directly identified with a specific cost unit or cost centre. Examples of indirect costs include the following:

- indirect materials – these include materials that cannot be traced to an individual item for example cleaning fluids for cleaning the machinery
- indirect labour – for example, the cost of a supervisor who supervises the shirt makers
- indirect expenses – for example, the cost of renting the factory where the shirts are manufactured.

The total of indirect costs is known as **overheads**.

Test your understanding 3

Identify whether the following costs are materials, labour or expenses and whether they are direct or indirect.

Cost	Materials, labour or expense	Direct or indirect?
The hire of tools or equipment		
Rent of a factory		
Packing materials, e.g. cartons and boxes		
Supervisors' salaries		
Oil for lubricating machines		

Wages of factory workers involved in production		
Depreciation of equipment		

Test your understanding 4

(a) Which of the following would be classed as indirect labour?

    A   Assembly workers

    B   A stores assistant in a factory storeroom

    C   Plasterers in a building company

    D   An audit clerk in an accountancy firm

(b) Direct costs are:

    A   costs which can be identified with a cost centre but not a single cost unit

    B   costs which can be identified with a single cost unit or cost centre

    C   costs which can be attributed to an accounting period

    D   none of the above.

6 Classification by behaviour

Costs may be classified according to the way that they behave in relation to changes in levels of activity. Cost behaviour classifies costs as one of the following:

* variable cost

* fixed cost

* stepped fixed cost

* semi-variable cost.

Variable costs

Variable costs are costs that vary in direction proportion with the level of activity. As activity levels increase then total variable costs will also increase.

- Variable costs can be shown graphically as follows:

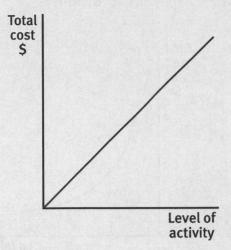

- Note that as total costs increase with activity levels, the cost per unit of variable costs remains constant.

- Examples of variable costs include direct costs such as raw materials and direct labour.

Numerical example of variable costs

- A factory is producing widgets. It takes $4m^2$ to make one widget and it costs $2 per square metre. If the factory makes 50 widgets it costs $400, if the factory makes 100 widgets it costs $800. The cost incurred increases in line with the volume being produced – graph 1 demonstrates this.

- The material for each widget costs $4 \times \$2 = \$8$ and it does not change if more or less widgets are made. The variable cost per unit remains constant – graph 2 demonstrates this.

Fixed costs

A fixed cost is a cost which is incurred for an accounting period, and which, within certain activity levels remains constant.

Fixed costs can be shown graphically as follows:

GRAPH 1   **GRAPH 2**

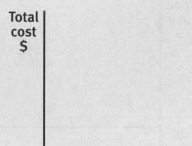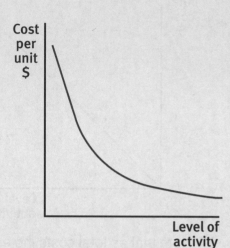

- Note that the total cost remains constant over a given level of activity but that the cost per unit falls as the level of activity increases.

- Examples of fixed costs:
    - rent
    - business rates
    - executive salaries.

Numerical example of fixed costs

- If factory rent is $5,000 per month, this cost will be incurred whether 2 widgets are made, or 200 widgets are made – graph 1 demonstrates this.

- If 2 widgets are made the fixed cost per unit is $5,000 ÷ 2 , i.e. $2,500 per widget.

- If 200 widgets are made the fixed cost per unit is $5,000 ÷ 200, i.e. $25 per widget.

- Therefore, the fixed cost per unit falls at a reducing rate but never reaches zero – graph 2 demonstrates this.

Stepped fixed costs

This is a type of fixed cost that is only fixed within certain levels of activity. Once the upper limit of an activity level is reached then a new higher level of fixed cost becomes relevant.

- Stepped fixed costs can be shown graphically as follows:

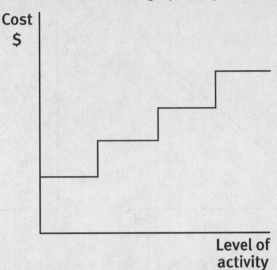

- Examples of stepped fixed costs:
  - warehousing costs (as more space is required, more warehouses must be purchased or rented)
  - supervisors' wages (as the number of employees increases, more supervisors are required).

Numerical example of stepped costs

- For production of up to 50 widgets, only one supervisor is required but if production is between 50 and 100 widgets, two supervisors are required.

- The cost of one supervisor is $18,000 per annum and the cost of two supervisors is therefore $36,000.

- The fixed costs therefore increase in steps as shown in the stepped fixed cost graph above.

Semi-variable costs

Semi-variable costs contain both fixed and variable cost elements and are therefore partly affected by changes in the level of activity.

- Semi-variable costs can be shown graphically as follows:

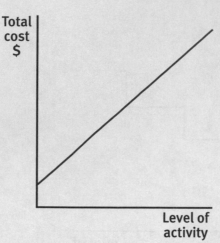

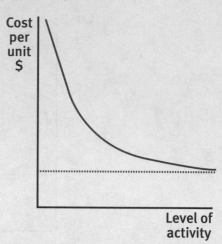

- Examples of semi-variable costs:

   – electricity bills (fixed standing charge plus variable cost per unit of electricity consumed)

   – telephone bills (fixed line rental plus variable cost per call)

Test your understanding 5

Classify the following items of expenditure according to their behaviour i.e. as fixed, variable, semi-variable or stepped fixed costs.

(1) Monthly Rent
(2) Council tax charge
(3) Petrol
(4) Electricity bill
(5) Telephone bill
(6) Annual salary
(7) Depreciation of 1, 2 or 3 machines
(8) Raw materials

Test your understanding 6

Study the following graphs, where the vertical axis represents 'Total Costs' or 'Cost per unit'. Then answer the questions shown below.

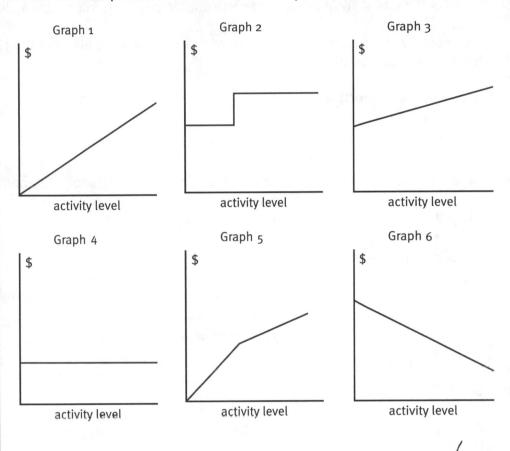

Total fixed cost is shown in graph

Total variable cost is shown in graph

Total semi-variable cost is shown in graph

Fixed cost per unit is shown in graph

Variable cost per unit is shown in graph

A stepped fixed cost is shown in graph

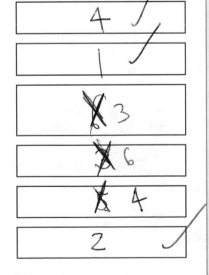

7 The high/low method used for separating a semi-variable cost

The total cost of a semi-variable cost can be shown as:

Total costs = Total Fixed costs + (Variable cost per unit × Activity level)

To separate the fixed cost element from the variable cost element the High-low method can be used.

The High/low method

Step 1

Select the highest and lowest **activity levels**, and their associated costs.

Step 2

Calculate the variable cost (VC) per unit:

$$\text{VC per unit} = \frac{\text{Cost at high level of activity} - \text{cost at low level of activity}}{\text{High level of activity} - \text{low level of activity}}$$

Step 3

Calculate the fixed cost by substitution, using either the high or low activity level.

Fixed cost = Total cost at activity level – (Variable cost × Activity level)

Step 4

Use the total fixed cost and the variable cost per unit values from steps 2 and 3 to calculate the estimated cost at different activity levels.

Total costs = Total Fixed costs + (Variable cost per unit × Activity level)

Assumptions underlying the high/low method

Assumptions of the high/low method are as follows:

- the only thing causing any change in cost is the change in activity
- the cost under consideration is potentially semi-variable (i.e. it has both fixed and variable elements)
- the linear model of cost behaviour is valid i.e. $y = a + bx$ (we will study this in more detail later on in this chapter)

Illustration 1 – The high-low method

Output (Units)	Total cost ($)
200	7,000
300	8,000
400	9,000

Required:

(a) Find the variable cost per unit.

(b) Find the total fixed cost.

(c) Estimate the total cost if output is 350 units.

(d) Estimate the total cost if output is 600 units.

Solution

(a) Variable cost per unit = ($9,000 – $7,000)/(400 – 200) = $2,000/200 = $10 per unit

(b) Total fixed cost by substituting at high activity level:

Total cost	=	$9,000
Total variable cost	= 400 × $10	$4,000
Therefore Fixed cost	=	$5,000

(c) If output is 350 units:

Variable cost	= 350 × $10 =	$3,500
Fixed cost	=	$5,000
		_____
Total cost	=	$8,500

(d) If output is 600 units:

Variable cost	= 600 × $10 =	$6,000
Fixed cost	=	$5,000
		_____
Total cost	=	$11,000

Test your understanding 7

The total costs incurred at various output levels in a factory have been measured as follows:

Output (units)	Total cost ($)
26	6,566
30	6,510
33	6,800
44	6,985
48	7,380
50	7,310

Required:

Using the high/low method, analyse the total cost into fixed and variable components.

KAPLAN PUBLISHING

High/low method with stepped fixed costs

Sometimes fixed costs are only fixed within certain levels of activity and increase in steps as activity increases (i.e. they are stepped fixed costs).

- The high/low method can still be used to estimate fixed and variable costs. Simply choose 2 activity levels where the fixed costs remain unchanged.

- Adjustments may need to be made for the fixed costs based on the activity level under consideration.

Illustration 2 – The high/low method with stepped fixed costs

An organisation has the following total costs at three activity levels:

Activity level (units)	4,000	6,000	7,500
Total cost	$40,800	$50,000	$54,800

Variable cost per unit is constant within this activity range and there is a step up of 10% in the total fixed costs when the activity level exceeds 5,500 units.

What is the total cost at an activity level of 5,000 units?

A $44,000

B $44,800

C $45,400

D $46,800

Solution

A

Calculate the variable cost per unit by comparing two output levels where fixed costs will be the same:

Variable cost per unit = [(54,800 − 50,000) ÷ (7,500 − 6,000)] = $3.20

Total fixed cost above 5,500 units = [54,800 − (7,500 × 3.20)] = $30,800

Total fixed cost below 5,500 units = 30,800/110 × 100 = $28,000

Total cost for 5,000 units = [(5,000 × 3.20) + 28,000] = $44,000

High/low method with changes in the variable cost per unit

Sometimes there may be changes in the variable cost per unit, and the high/low method can still be used to determine the fixed and variable elements of semi-variable costs. As with the stepped fixed costs – choose activity levels where the variable costs per unit remain unchanged.

Illustration 3 – The high/low method with changes in the variable

The following information relates to the manufacture of Product LL in 20X8:

Output (Units)	Total cost ($)
200	7,000
300	8,000
400	8,600

For output volumes above 350 units the variable cost per unit falls by 10%. (Note: this fall applies to all units – not just the excess above 350).

Required:

Estimate the cost of producing 450 units of Product LL in 20X9.

Solution

$$\text{Variable cost per unit } (<350) = \frac{\$8,000 - \$7,000}{300 - 200} = \frac{\$1,000}{100} = \$10 \text{ per unit}$$

Total cost at 300 units	=	$8,000
Total variable cost	= 300 × $10	$3,000
Therefore Fixed cost	=	$5,000

If output is 450 units in 20X9:

Variable cost	= 450 × $9 (W1)	$4,050
Fixed cost	=	$5,000
		————
Total cost	=	$9,050

(W1) Variable cost per unit in 20X9 (when output > 350 units) = $10 × 0.9 = $9 per unit

Test your understanding 8

The total costs incurred in 20X3 at various output levels in a factory have been measured as follows:

Output (units)	Total cost ($)
26	6,566
30	6,510
33	6,800
44	6,985
48	7,380
50	7,310

When output is 80 units or more, another factory unit must be rented and fixed costs therefore increase by 100%.

Variable cost per unit is forecast to rise by 10% in 20X4.

Required:

Calculate the estimated total costs of producing 100 units in 20X4.

Advantages and limitations of the high/low method

The main advantage of the high/low method is that it is easy to understand and easy to use.

The limitations of the high/low method are as follows:

- it relies on historical cost data and assumes this data can reliably predict future costs

- it assumes that activity levels are the only factor affecting costs

- it uses only two values (highest and lowest) to predict future costs and these results may be distorted because of random variations which may have occurred.

- bulk discounts may be available for purchasing resources in large quantities.

8 Cost equations

Cost equations are derived from historical cost data. Once a cost equation has been established, for example distinguishing the fixed and variable costs using the high/low method, it can be used to estimate future costs. Cost equations are assumed to have a linear function and therefore the equation of a straight line can be applied:

$y = a + bx$

Where:

- 'a' is the intercept, i.e. the point at which the line $y = a + bx$ cuts the y axis (the value of y when x = 0).

- 'b' is the gradient/slope of the line $y = a + bx$ (the change in y when x increases by one unit).

- 'x' = independent variable.

- 'y' = dependent variable (its value depends on the value of 'x').

This formula can be related to the results of the high/low calculation as follows:

- 'a' is the fixed cost per period (the intercept)

- 'b' is the variable cost per unit (the gradient)

- 'x' is the activity level (the independent variable)

- 'y' is the total cost = fixed cost + variable cost (dependent on the activity level)

Suppose a cost has a cost equation of y = $5,000 + 10x, this can be shown graphically as follows:

Graph of cost equation y = 5,000 + 10x

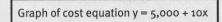

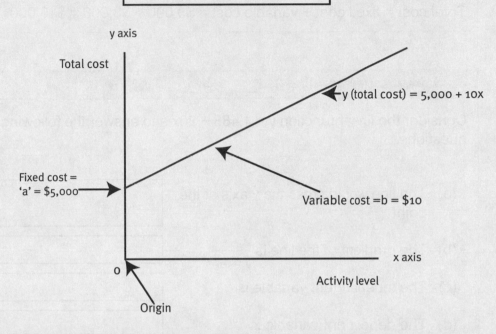

Graph of cost equation y = 5,000 + 10x

y axis

Total cost

y (total cost) = 5,000 + 10x

Fixed cost =
'a' = $5,000

Variable cost =b = $10

x axis

0

Activity level

Origin

e.g

Illustration 4 – Cost equations

If y = 8,000 + 40x

(a) Fixed cost = $

(b) Variable cost per unit = $

(c) Total cost for 200 units = $

Solution

(a) Fixed cost = $ | 8,000

(b) Variable cost per unit = $ | 40

(c) Total cost for 200 units = $ | 16,000

Working

Fixed cost = $8,000

Variable cost = 200 × $40 = $8,000

Total cost = fixed cost + variable cost = $8,000 + $8,000 = $16,000

Test your understanding 9

Consider the linear function y = 1,488 + 20x and answer the following questions.

(a) The line would cross the y axis at the point

(b) The gradient of the line is

(c) The independent variable is

(d) The dependent variable is

Test your understanding 10

If the total cost of a product is given as:

Y = 4,800 + 8x

(a) The fixed cost is $ 4800

(b) The variable cost per unit is $ 8

(b) The total cost of producing 100 units is $ 5600

9 Cost cards

The following costs are brought together and recorded on a cost card:

- direct materials
- direct labour
- direct expenses
- prime cost (total direct costs)
- variable production overheads
- fixed production overheads
- non-production overheads.

COST CARD – statement of the total cost of one unit of a product

	$
Direct materials	X
Direct labour	X
Direct expenses	X
	—
PRIME COST	XX
Variable production overheads	X
	—
TOTAL VARIABLE (MARGINAL) PRODUCTION COST	XX
Fixed production overheads	X
	—
TOTAL PRODUCTION (ABSORPTION) COST	XX
Non-production overheads:	
– Administration	X
– Selling	X
– Distribution	X
	—
TOTAL COST	XX
Profit	X
	—
Sales price	XXX

Illustration 5 – Cost card

A cost card for a hand-made wooden train set is shown below.

- The cutting and assembly department and the painting department are cost centres.

- One hand-made wooden train set is a cost unit (but may also be classed as a cost object).

		$
Direct materials		
Wood	5m^2 @ $2.50 per m^2	12.50
Paint	0.1 litre at $10 per litre	1.00
Direct labour		
Cutting and assembly department	0.5 hours at $6.00 per hour	3.00
Painting department	1.0 hours @ $7.00 per hour	7.00
Direct expenses	Licence fee @ $2 per train set	2.00
		_____
PRIME COST		25.50
Variable production overheads		
Power for electric saws	0.25 hours @ $2.00 per hour	0.50
		_____
TOTAL VARIABLE (MARGINAL) PRODUCTION COST		26.00
Fixed production overheads	1.5 labour hours @ $10.00 per labour hour	15.00
		_____
TOTAL PRODUCTION (ABSORPTION) COST		41.00
Non-production overheads:		
Administration, selling and distribution	20% of total production cost	8.20
		_____
TOTAL COST		49.20
Profit	30% of total cost	14.76
		_____
		63.96

KAPLAN PUBLISHING

10 Cost coding

Cost accountants need to determine the costs that relate to each cost centre. To make this simpler each cost is classified according to its cost centre and type. A cost code is then allocated to the cost to represent this classification.

A code is a system of letters/numbers designed to give a brief accurate reference, which helps entry to the records, collation and analysis.

The main purpose of cost codes is to:

- Assist precise information

- Facilitate data processing

- Facilitate logical arrangement of records

- Simplify comparisons of similar costs

- Incorporate checking for accuracy

There are no set methods for designing a cost code, the organisation will decide on the most appropriate coding system for their business.

Illustration

Suppose that the cost coding system for the JJ Ltd the shirt manufacturer is as follows:

Production cost centre

(1) Cutting department

(2) Sewing department

(3) Pressing department

(4) Packaging department

Non Production cost centres

(5) Stores department

(6) Maintenance department

(7) Administration department

(8) Selling & Marketing department

Cost code

(15) Production labour

(16) Production materials

(17) Production expenses

(18) Non-production labour

(19) Non-production materials

(20) Non-production expenses

The following invoices would be coded as:

Salesman's travel expenses	820
Wages of pressing department operatives	315
1000 metres white cotton thread	216
Cleaning of the stores department	518
Salary of the administration supervisor	718

11 Chapter summary

Cost object, cost unit and cost centre

Cost object – activity for which costs can be separately measured

Cost unit – unit of product or service in relation to which costs are ascertained

Cost centre – production or service location, function, activity or item of equipment for which costs can be ascertained

---

Production and non-production costs

Production costs = prime cost (total direct costs) plus overheads

Non-production costs = admin, selling, distribution and finance

Types of cost behaviour

Direct and indirect costs

Direct costs – directly involved in production

Indirect costs – not directly involved in production

Material, labour, overhead

Fixed and variable costs

Fixed – do not vary with level of activity

Variable – vary with level of activity

Analysis of semi-variable costs into fixed and variable elements

Cost equations
(linear function) $y = a + bx$

High/low analysis
Variable cost per unit = $\dfrac{\text{Cost at high level of activity} - \text{Cost at low level of activity}}{\text{High level of activity} - \text{Low level of activity}}$

Fixed cost = Total cost at activity level – Total variable cost

Test your understanding answers

Test your understanding 1

Cost	Classification
Overalls for machine workers	1
Cost of printer cartridges in general office	4
Salary of factory supervisor	1
Salary of payroll supervisor	4
Rent of warehouse for storing goods ready for sale	3
Loan interest	5
Salary of factory security guard	1
Early settlement discounts for customers who pay early	2
Salary of the Chairman's PA	4
Road tax licence for delivery vehicles	3
Bank overdraft fee	5
Salesmen's commissions	2

Test your understanding 2

The production cost includes:

	Per unit $	Total $
Direct material cost	1	15,000
Direct labour cost	3	45,000
Variable production cost	3	45,000
Fixed production cost	2	30,000
		135,000

The selling costs are not included as these are non-production costs.

Test your understanding 3

Cost	Materials, labour or expense	Direct or indirect?
The hire of tools or equipment	Expense	Direct
Rent of a factory	Expense	Indirect
Packing materials, e.g. cartons and boxes	Material	Direct
Supervisors' salaries	Labour	Indirect
Oil for lubricating machines	Material	Indirect
Wages of factory workers involved in production	Labour	Direct
Depreciation of equipment	Expense	Indirect

Test your understanding 4

(a) B Store assistants are not directly involved in producing the output (goods or services) of an organisation.

(b) B This is a basic definition question. Direct costs are costs which can be identified with a single cost unit, or cost centre.

Test your understanding 5

The items of expenditure would be analysed as follows.

(1) Fixed

(2) Fixed

(3) Variable

(4) Semi-variable

(5) Semi-variable

(6) Fixed

(7) Stepped Fixed

(8) Variable

Note: the depreciation charge for the factory machines (7) is a stepped fixed cost – when activity increases to such a level that a second and third machine is required, the fixed cost will step up.

Test your understanding 6

Total fixed cost is shown in graph	4
Total variable cost is shown in graph	1
Total semi-variable cost is shown in graph	3
Fixed cost per unit is shown in graph	6
Variable cost per unit is shown in graph	4
A stepped fixed cost is shown in graph	2

Test your understanding 7

$$\text{Variable cost per unit} = \frac{\$7{,}310 - \$6{,}566}{50 - 26} = \frac{\$744}{24} = \$31 \text{ per unit}$$

Substituting at high activity level:

Total cost	=	$7,310
Total variable cost	= 50 × $31	$1,550
Therefore Fixed cost	=	$5,760

Test your understanding 8

$$\text{Variable cost per unit (20X3)} = \frac{\$7{,}310 - \$6{,}566}{50 - 26} = \frac{\$744}{24} = \$31 \text{ per unit}$$

Substituting at high activity level:

Total cost	=	$7,310
Total variable cost	= 50 × $31	$1,550
Therefore Fixed cost (in 20X3)	=	$5,760

Estimated total costs of producing 100 units in 20X4:

Variable cost	= 100 × $31 × 1.1	$3,410
Fixed cost	= $5,760 × 2	$11,520
Total cost	=	$14,930

Test your understanding 9

(a) The line would cross the y axis at the point | 1,488

(b) The gradient of the line is | 20

(c) The independent variable is | x

(d) The dependent variable is | y

Test your understanding 10

(a) The fixed cost is $ | 4,800

(b) The variable cost per unit is $ | 8

(b) The total cost of producing 100 units is $ | 5,600

Working

Fixed cost = $4,800

Variable cost = 100 × $8 = $800

Total cost = fixed cost + variable cost = $4,800 + $800 = $5,600

Accounting for inventory

Chapter learning objectives

Upon completion of this chapter you will be able to:

- describe the different procedures and documents necessary for the ordering, receiving and issuing of materials from inventory

- identify, explain and calculate the costs of ordering and holding inventory (including buffer inventory)

- describe and apply appropriate methods for establishing reorder levels where demand in the lead time is constant

- calculate and interpret the optimal order quantities

- calculate and interpret the optimal order quantities when quantity discounts are available

- produce calculations to minimise inventory costs when inventory is gradually replenished

- calculate the value of closing inventory and material issues using LIFO, FIFO and average methods

- describe the control procedures used to monitor physical and 'book' inventory and to minimise discrepancies and losses

- interpret the entries and balances in the material inventory account.

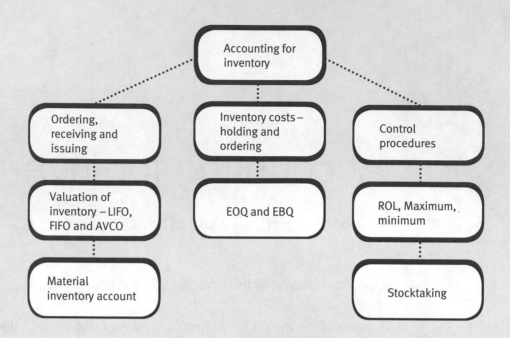

1 Ordering, receiving and issuing inventory

In a manufacturing business inventory (materials) may be the largest item of cost so it is essential that the material purchased is the most suitable for the intended purpose.

When inventory is purchased it must be ordered, received by the stores department, recorded, issued to the manufacturing department that requires it and eventually paid for. This process needs a great deal of paperwork and strict internal controls.

Internal control consists of full documentation and appropriate authorisation of all transactions, movements of materials and of all requisitions, orders, receipts and payments.

If control is to be maintained over purchasing, it is necessary to ensure that:

• only necessary items are purchased

• orders are placed with the most appropriate supplier after considering price and delivery details

• the goods that are actually received are the goods that were ordered and in the correct quantity/quality

• the price paid for the goods is correct (i.e. what was agreed when the order was placed).

To ensure that all of this takes place requires a reliable system of checking and control.

The procedures for ordering, purchasing and receiving materials are as follows:

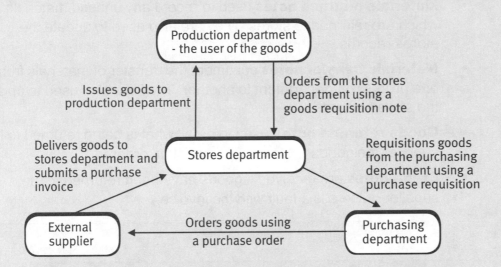

Notes for the diagram

- **Goods or Materials requisition notes** are issued by production departments. Their purpose is to authorise the storekeeper to release the goods which have been requisitioned and to update the stores records.

- A **purchase requisition** is completed by the stores department (including authorisation by the relevant manager) and sent to the **purchasing department.**

- On receipt of a properly authorised requisition, the purchasing department will select a supplier and create an order on a **purchase order form**.

- The purchase order form is sent to the supplier and copies are also sent to the accounts department and the stores department.

- On receipt of the goods, the stores department will check the goods against the relevant purchase order, and check the **delivery note** which accompanies the goods. Full details of the goods are then entered onto a **goods received note (GRN).**

- A copy of the GRN is attached to the relevant purchase order and they are both sent to the purchasing department where they are matched to the relevant supplier's purchase invoice. Once approved, the **purchase invoice** can be paid.

Other documentation a business may encounter include:

- **Materials returned notes** used to record any unused materials which are returned to stores. They are also used to update the stores records.

- **Materials transfer notes** document the transfer of materials from one production department to another. They are also used to update the stores records.

- **Goods returned notes** used to detail what is being returned to the supplier the goods are damaged or not as ordered.

- **Credit notes** are received if goods have been returned to the supplier or there is a fault with the invoice.

Specimen forms

PURCHASE REQUISITION

Date ....20............   Serial No: ....

Purpose*: inventory/special
capital equipment/(budget reference)
*Delete as appropriate

Quantity and units	Description	Material code	Job or dept. code	Delivery required		Purchase order		
				Date	Place	No.	Date	Supplier

Origination department ....   Authorisation ....

PURCHASE ORDER

To: ....   Serial No: ....
....   Date: ....
....   Purchase Req. No: ....

Please supply, in accordance with the attached conditions

Quantity	Description	Code	Delivery date	Price	Per

Your quotation ....
To be delivered, carriage paid, to .... Terms
Please quote our Purchase Order number on all correspondence.

For ABC Ltd

....

GOODS RECEIVED NOTE

To: ....   Serial No: ....
....   Date issued: ....
Carrier: ....   Purchase Order No: ....
Date of delivery: ....

Description	Code	Quantity	Packages	Gross Weight

INSPECTION REPORT			Received by: ....
Quantity passed	Quantity rejected	Remarks	Required by: ....
			Accepted: ....

Inspector .... Date ....   Date: ....

MATERIAL REQUISITION

Charge job/
Cost Centre No: ....

Serial No: ....
Date: ....

Code No.	Description	Quantity or weight	Cost office only				
			Rate	Unit	$	$	Stores ledger

Authorised by:	Storekeeper:	Prices entered by:
Received by:	Bin card entered:	Calculations checked:

Test your understanding 1

A goods received note (GRN) provides (tick all that apply):

✓	Information used to update inventory records.
—	Information to check that the correct price has been recorded on the supplier's invoice.
✓	Information to check that the correct quantity of goods has been recorded on the supplier's invoice.
—	Information to record any unused materials which are returned to stores.

Test your understanding 2

The following documents are used within a cost accounting system:

✓ (i) invoice from supplier

✓ (ii) purchase order

(iii) purchase requisition

(iv) stores requisition

Which TWO of the documents are matched with the goods received note in the buying process?

A   (i) and (ii) ✓

B   (i) and (iv)

C   (ii) and (iii)

D   (iii) and (iv)

Test your understanding 3

The following documents are used in accounting for raw materials:

(i)   Goods received note

(ii) Materials returned note

(iii) Materials requisition note

(iv) Delivery note

Which of the documents may be used to update stores ledger cards for inventory?

A   (i) and (ii) ✓

B   (i) and (iv)

C   (ii) only

D   (ii) and (iii)

2 Inventory holding and ordering costs

Most businesses, whatever their size, will be concerned with the problem of which items to have in inventory and how much of each item should be kept.

Functions of inventory

The principal reasons why a business needs to hold inventory are as follows:

- It acts as a buffer in times when there is an unusually high rate of consumption.

- It enables the business to take advantage of quantity discounts by buying in bulk.

- The business can take advantage of seasonal and other price fluctuations (e.g. buying coal in the summer when it is cheaper).

- Any delay in production caused by lack of parts is kept to a minimum, so production processes will flow smoothly and efficiently.

- It may be necessary to hold inventory for a technical reason: for example, some food items need to 'matured'.

Costs of having inventory

Irrespective of the nature of the business, a certain amount of inventory will need to be held.

However, holding inventory costs money and the principal 'trade-off' in an inventory holding situation is between the costs of acquiring and storing inventories on the one hand and the level of service that the company wishes to provide on the other.

The total cost of having inventory consists of the following:

- Purchase price
- Holding costs:
  - the opportunity cost of capital tied up
  - insurance
  - deterioration
  - obsolescence
  - damage and pilferage
  - warehouse upkeep
  - stores labour and administration costs.

Holding costs can be distinguished between fixed holding costs and variable holding costs:

  - Fixed holding costs include the cost of storage space and the cost of insurance. Note that the cost of storage space may be a stepped fixed cost if increased warehousing is needed when higher volumes of inventory are held.

  - Variable holding costs include interest on capital tied up in inventory. The more inventory that is held, the more capital that is tied up.

  - Holding costs can be calculated as follows:

Total annual holding cost = holding cost per unit of inventory × average inventory (Ch × Q/2).

Where average inventory held is equal to half of the order quantity (Q/2).

KAPLAN PUBLISHING

- Ordering costs:
  - clerical and administrative costs – the total administrative costs of placing orders will increase in proportion to the number of orders placed. They therefore exhibit the behaviour of variable costs.
  - transport costs.
  - ordering costs can be calculated as follows:

Total annual ordering cost = cost of placing an order × number of orders (Co × D/Q).

Where the number of orders in a year = Expected annual demand/order quantity (D/Q).

- Stock-out costs (items of required inventory are not available):
  - loss of sales, therefore lost contribution
  - long-term damage to the business through loss of goodwill
  - production stoppages caused by a shortage of raw materials
  - extra costs caused by the need for emergency orders.

- Inventory recording systems costs:
  - maintaining the stores record card

There is also a formula that allows us to calculate the Total Annual Costs (TAC) i.e. the total of purchasing costs (purchase cost per unit P×D), ordering costs (Co × D/Q) and holding costs (Ch × Q/2):

Total Annual Cost = PD + (Co × D/Q) + (Ch × Q/2)

Disadvantages of low and high inventory levels

Disadvantages of low inventory levels

To keep the holding costs low it may be possible to reduce the volume of inventory that is kept but this can cause some problems:

- Customer demand cannot always be satisfied; this may lead to loss of business if customers become dissatisfied.

- In order to fulfil commitments to important customers, costly emergency procedures (e.g. special production runs) may become necessary in an attempt to maintain customer goodwill.

- It will be necessary to place replenishment orders more frequently than if higher inventories were held, in order to maintain a reasonable service. This will result in higher ordering costs being incurred.

Disadvantages of high inventory levels

To reduce the problems mentioned above management may consider holding high levels of inventory but again this can have issues:

- Storage or holding costs are very high; such costs will usually include rates, rent, labour, heating, deterioration, etc.

- The cost of the capital tied up in inventories, i.e. the cash spent to buy the inventory is not available to pay other bills.

- If the stored product becomes obsolete, a large inventory holding of that item could, at worst, represent a large capital investment in an unsaleable product whose cash value is only that of scrap.

- If a great deal of capital is invested in inventories, there will be proportionately less money available for other requirements such as improvement of existing production facilities, or the introduction of new products.

- When a high inventory level of a raw material is held, a sudden drop in the market price of that material represents a cash loss to the business for having bought at the higher price. It follows that it would seem sensible to hold higher inventories during an inflationary period and lower inventories during a period of deflation.

Illustration 1 – The cost of holding inventory

A company uses components at the rate of 6,000 units per year, which are bought in at a cost of $1.20 each from the supplier. The company orders 1,000 units each time it places an order and the average inventory held is 500 units. It costs $20 each time to place an order, regardless of the quantity ordered.

The total holding cost is 20% per annum of the average inventory held.

The annual holding cost will be $ $500 \times 1.2 \times 0.2$ | 120 |

The annual ordering cost will be $ $\dfrac{6000}{1000} \times 20$ | 120 |

$CH \times Q/2$
$CB \times P/Q$

Solution

The annual holding cost will be $ | 120 |

The annual ordering cost will be $ | 120 |

KAPLAN PUBLISHING

Workings

Annual holding cost
= average inventory held x cost per unit × 20%
= 500 units × $1.20 × 20%
= $120

Annual ordering cost $= \dfrac{\text{Annual usage}}{\text{Order size}} \times \$20$

$= \dfrac{6,000}{1,000} \times \$20$

$= \$120$

Test your understanding 4

A company has recorded the following details for Component 427 which is sold in boxes of 10 components.

Ordering cost	$32 per order placed
Purchase price	$20 per box of 10 components
Holding cost	10% of purchase price
Monthly demand	1,500 components

Component 427 is currently ordered in batches of 240 boxes at a time. The average inventory held is 120 boxes.

Required:

Calculate the annual holding cost and the annual ordering cost for Component 427.

ORDERING

$\dfrac{1500}{10} \times 12 = 1800$ $\div 240 \times 32 = 240$

HOLDING

$120 \times 20 \times 0.1 = 240$

3 Reorder levels

Reorder level

The reorder level is the quantity of inventory in hand when a replenishment order should be placed. It is calculated with reference to the time it will take to receive the order (the lead time) and the possible requirements during that time.

If the demand in the lead time is constant, the reorder level is calculated as follows:

Reorder level = Maximum Usage x Maximum Lead time

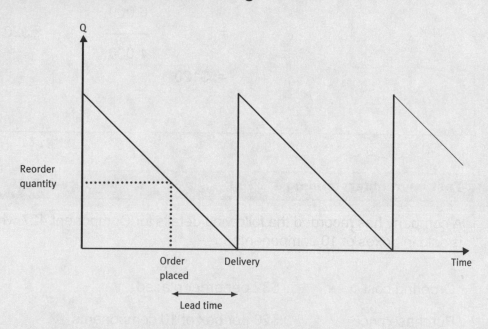

Illustration 2 – Reorder levels

A company uses Component M at the rate of 1,500 per week. The time between placing an order and receiving the components is five weeks. The reorder quantity is 12,000 units.

Required:

Calculate the reorder level.

Solution

Reorder level = Usage × Lead time

= 1,500 units × 5 weeks = 7,500 units

Test your understanding 5

A national chain of tyre fitters stocks a popular tyre for which the following information is available:

Usage – 175 tyres per day

Lead time – 16 days

Reorder quantity – 3,000 tyres

Based on the data above, at what level of inventory should a replenishment order be issued in order to ensure that there are no stock-outs?

A   2,240

B   2,800

C   3,000

D   5,740

(handwritten annotations: 175 × 16 = 2,800. ↑ USAGE, ↑ LEAD TIME, ↑ RE-ORDER LEVEL.)

4 The economic order quantity (EOQ)

The EOQ is the reorder quantity which minimises the total costs associated with holding and ordering inventory (i.e. holding costs + ordering costs) are at a minimum.

We can estimate the EOQ graphically by plotting holding costs, ordering costs and total costs at different levels of activity.

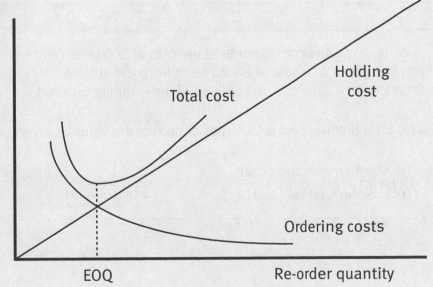

EOQ formula

The formula for the EOQ (or Q) is as follows:

$$Q = EOQ = \sqrt{\frac{2C_o D}{C_h}}$$

Where:

D = Demand per **annum**

C_o = Cost of placing **one** order

C_h = Cost of holding **one** unit for **one** year

Q = Reorder quantity (EOQ)

Note that the formula for the EOQ is provided in your exam. You must make sure that you know what the different symbols represent so that you can use the formula correctly.

EOQ assumptions

There are a number of important assumptions and formulae related to the EOQ that you should note:

- Demand and lead time are constant and known
- Purchase price is constant
- No buffer inventory is held

Illustration 3 – The economic order quantity (EOQ)

A company uses components at the rate of 500 units per month, which are bought in at a cost of $1.20 each from the supplier. It costs $20 each time to place an order, regardless of the quantity ordered.

The total holding cost is 20% per annum of the value of inventory held.

The company should order _____ components

The total annual cost will be $ _____

Solution

The company should order [1,000] components

The total annual cost will be $ [7,440]

Workings

Economic order quantity = $\sqrt{\dfrac{2 \times 20 \times 500 \times 12}{0.2 \times 1.2}}$ = 1,000 components

$\sqrt{(2 \times 20 \times 500 \times 12 / (0.2 \times 1.2))} = 1000$

 ?

$TAC = (\$1.20 \times 500 \times 12) + (\$20 \times \dfrac{500 \times 12}{1,000}) + (\$1.20 \times 0.2 \times \dfrac{1,000}{2}) = \$7,440$

Test your understanding 6

A company is planning to purchase 90,800 units of a particular item in the year ahead. The item is purchased in boxes each containing 10 units of the item, at a price of $200 per box. A safety inventory of 250 boxes is kept.

The cost of holding an item in inventory for a year (including insurance, interest and space costs) is 15% of the purchase price. The cost of placing and receiving orders is to be estimated from cost data collected relating to similar orders, where costs of $5,910 were incurred on 30 orders. It should be assumed that ordering costs change in proportion to the number of orders placed. 2% should be added to the above ordering costs to allow for inflation. Assume that usage of the item will be even over the year.

.24

The order quantity which minimises total costs is [ ] boxes

This will mean ordering the item every [ ] weeks

5 The EOQ with discounts

Quantity discounts

It is often possible to negotiate a quantity discount on the purchase price if bulk orders are placed.

* If a quantity discount is accepted this will have the following effects:
    - The annual purchase price will decrease.
    - The annual holding cost will increase.
    - The annual ordering cost will decrease

* To establish whether the discount should be accepted or not, the following calculations should be carried out.
    - Calculate TAC with the discount.
    - Compare this with the annual costs without the discount (at the EOQ point).

EOQ when quantity discounts are available

The steps involved in calculating the EOQ when quantity discounts are available are as follows:

(1) Calculate the EOQ, ignoring discounts.

(2) If the EOQ is smaller than the minimum purchase quantity to obtain a bulk discount, calculate the total for the EOQ of the annual inventory holding costs, inventory ordering costs and inventory purchase costs.

(3) Recalculate the annual inventory holding costs, inventory ordering costs and inventory purchase costs for a purchase order size that is only just large enough to qualify for the bulk discount.

(4) Compare the total costs when the order quantity is the EOQ with the total costs when the order quantity is just large enough to obtain the discount. Select the minimum cost alternative.

(5) If there is a further discount available for an even larger order size, repeat the same calculations for the higher discount level.

Illustration 4 – The EOQ with discounts

A company uses components at the rate of 500 units per month, which are bought in at a cost of $1.20 each from the supplier. It costs $20 each time to place an order, regardless of the quantity ordered.

The supplier offers a 5% discount on the purchase price for order quantities of 2,000 items or more. The current EOQ is 1,000 units.

The total holding cost is 20% per annum of the value of inventory held.

Required:

Should the discount be accepted?

Solution

Order quantity =	**1,000**		**2,000**
	$		$
Order cost (6,000/1,000 × $20)	120	(6,000/2,000 × $20) =	60
Holding cost (20% × $1.20 × 1,000/2)	120	($0.24 × 0.95 × 2,000/2) =	228
Purchase cost (6,000 × $1.20)	7,200	(6,000 × $1.20 × 0.95) =	6,840
Total annual costs	7,440		7,128

The discount should be accepted because it saves the company $312 ($7,440 – $7,128).

Test your understanding 7

Watton Ltd is a retailer of beer barrels. The company has an annual demand of 36,750 barrels. The barrels cost $12 each. Fresh supplies can be obtained immediately, but ordering costs and the cost of carriage inwards are $200 per order. The annual cost of holding one barrel in inventory is estimated to be $1.20. The economic order quantity has been calculated to be 3,500 barrels.

The suppliers introduce a quantity discount of 2% on orders of at least 5,000 barrels and 2.5% on orders of at least 7,500 barrels.

Required:

Determine whether the least-cost order quantity is still the EOQ of 3,500 barrels.

6 Gradual replenishment of inventory

Gradual replenishment of inventory

The situations we have looked at so far have involved inventory levels being replenished immediately when organisations buy inventory from suppliers. Similar problems are faced by organisations who replenish inventory levels gradually by manufacturing their own products internally.

- The decisions faced by organisations that manufacture and store their own products involve deciding whether to produce large batches at long intervals OR produce small batches at short intervals.

- An amended EOQ model is used to help organisations to decide which course of action to take.

- The amended EOQ model is known as the EBQ (economic batch quantity) model.

- As the items are being produced, there is a machine setup cost. This replaces the ordering cost of the EOQ.

- In the EOQ, inventory is replenished instantaneously whereas here, it is replenished over a period of time.

- Depending on the demand rate, part of the batch will be sold or used while the remainder is still being produced.

- For the same size of batch (Q), the average inventory held in the EOQ model (Q/2) is greater than the average in this situation (see diagram on the next page).

- The EBQ model can be shown graphically as follows.

Inventory

(units)

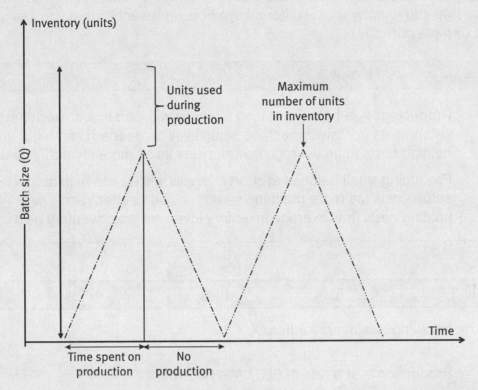

- The maximum inventory level will never be as great as the batch size, because some of the batch will be used up while the remainder is being produced.

The EBQ

The EBQ model is primarily concerned with determining the number of items that should be produced in a batch (compared to the size of an order with the EOQ).

The formula for the EBQ is as follows:

$$\text{Economic batch quantity} = \sqrt{\frac{2C_o D}{C_h \left(1-\frac{D}{R}\right)}}$$

Where:

Q = Batch size

D = Demand per **annum**

C_h = Cost of holding **one** unit for **one** year

C_o = Cost of setting up **one** batch ready to be produced

R = **Annual** replenishment rate

Note that the formula for the EBQ is provided in your exam. You must make sure that you know what the different symbols represent so that you can use the formula correctly.

Large or small batches?

- Producing large batches at long intervals will lead to low machine setup costs (as fewer machine setups will be needed) and high holding costs (high average inventory levels as more inventory held).

- Producing small batches at short intervals will lead to high machine setup costs (as more machine setups will be needed) and low holding costs (low average inventory levels as less inventory held).

Illustration 5 – Gradual replenishment of inventory

The following is relevant for Item X:

- Production is at a rate of 500 units per week.

- Demand is 10,000 units per annum; evenly spread over 50 working weeks.

- Setup cost is $2,700 per batch.

- Storage cost is $2.50 per unit for a year.

Required:

Calculate the economic batch quantity (EBQ) for Item X.

Solution

Annual production rate, R = 500 × 50 = 25,000 units
Annual demand rate = 10,000 units
Cost per setup, C_o = $2,700
Cost of holding one item in inventory per year, C_h = $2.50

$$EBQ = \sqrt{\frac{2\,C_o\,D}{C_h\,(1-(D/R))}} = \sqrt{\frac{2 \times 2{,}700 \times 10{,}000}{2.5\,(1-10{,}000/25{,}000)}} = 6{,}000 \text{ units}$$

Test your understanding 8

AB Ltd makes a component for one of the engines that it builds. It uses, on average, 2,000 of these components, steadily throughout the year. The component costs $16 per unit to make and it costs an additional $320 to setup the production process each time a batch of components is made. The holding cost per unit is 10% of the unit production cost. The company makes these components at a rate of 200 per week, and the factory is open for 50 weeks per annum.

Required:

Calculate the EBQ.

Maximum and minimum inventory

Many inventory systems will also incorporate maximum and minimum inventory 'warning' levels, above or below which (respectively) inventory should not be allowed to rise/fall.

In practice, the maximum inventory level is fixed by taking into account:

- rate of consumption of the material
- time needed to obtain new supplies
- financial considerations due to high inventories tying up capital
- storage space with regard to the provision of space and maintenance costs
- extent to which price fluctuates
- risks of changing specifications
- possibility of loss by evaporation, deterioration, etc
- seasonal considerations as to both price and availability
- economic order quantities.

The minimum inventory level is fixed by taking into account:

- rate of consumption
- time needed to obtain delivery of supplies
- the costs and other consequences of stock-outs.

A simplified method of determining these control levels is by reference to the re-order level, re-order quantity and estimates of possible lead times and usage rates, as follows:

> **Minimum level** = Re-order level – (Average usage × Average lead time)
>
> **Maximum level** = Re-order level + Re-order quantity – (Minimum usage × Minimum lead time)
>
> If at any time inventories fall below the minimum level, this is a warning that usage or lead time are above average. Thus the storekeeper will need to keep an eye on inventory levels and be prepared to place an emergency order if inventories get too low.
>
> If inventories rise above the maximum level then usage or lead time have actually been lower than the expected minimum. If it is usage, this may indicate a general decline in the demand for the inventory and the order quantity (and possibly the re-order level) should be reviewed to avoid holding excess inventory with associated holding costs.

7 Control procedures to minimise discrepancies and losses

The level of investment in inventory and the labour costs of handling and recording/controlling them is considerable in many organisations. It is for this reason that organisations must have control procedures in place in order to minimise discrepancies and losses.

Stocktaking

The process of stocktaking involves checking the physical quantity of inventory held on a certain date and then checking this balance against the balances on the stores ledger (record) cards or bin cards. Stocktaking can be carried out on a **periodic basis** or a **continuous basis**.

- **Periodic stocktaking** involves checking the balance of every item of inventory on the same date, usually at the end of an accounting period.

- **Continuous stocktaking** involves counting and valuing selected items of inventory on a rotating basis. Specialist teams count and check certain items of inventory on each day. Each item is checked at least once a year with valuable items being checked more frequently.

- Any differences (or discrepancies) which arise between 'book' inventory and physical inventory must be investigated.

- In theory any differences, as recorded in the stores ledger or the bin card, must have arisen through faulty recording.

- Once the discrepancy has been identified, the stores ledger card is adjusted in order that it reflects the true physical inventory count.

- Any items which are identified as being **slow-moving** or **obsolete** should be brought to the attention of management as soon as possible.

- Management will then decide whether these items should be disposed of and written off to the income statement.

- Slow-moving items are those inventory items which take a long time to be used up.

- Obsolete items are those items of inventory which have become out of date and are no longer required.

Examples of other issues and controls

Issue	Control procedure
Ordering goods at inflated prices	• Use of standard costs for purchases
	• Quotation for special items
Fictitous purchases	• Separation of ordering and purchasing
	• Physical controls over materials receipts, usage and inventory
Shortages on receipts	• Checking in all goods inwards at gate
	• Delivery signatures
Losses from inventory	• Regular stocktaking
	• Physical security procedures
Writing off obsolete or damaged inventory which is good	• Control of responsible official over all write-offs
Losses after issue to production	• Records of all issues
	• Standard usage allowance

Inventory losses and waste

- Inventory losses may be quantified by comparing the physical quantity of an item held with the balance quantity recorded on the bin card and/or stores ledger card.

- There are two categories of loss: those which occur because of theft, pilferage, damage or similar means and those which occur because of the breaking of bulk receipts into smaller quantities.

- It is the second of these which are more commonly referred to as waste.

- Inventory losses must be written off against profits as soon as they occur. If the value to be written off is significant then an investigation should be made of the cause.

- When waste occurs as a result of breaking up bulk receipts, it is reasonable to expect that the extent of such wastage could be estimated in advance based upon past records. Either of two accounting treatments could then be used:
  - Issues continue to be made and priced without any adjustment and the difference at the end of the period is written off.

  - Alternatively, the issue price is increased to compensate for the expected waste.

- Suppose that a 100 metre length of copper is bought for $99. The estimated loss caused by cutting into shorter lengths as required is 1%.

- The issue price could be based on the expected issues of 99 metres, i.e. $1 per metre rather than pricing the copper at:

$$\text{Issue price} = \frac{\$99}{100} = \$0.99/\text{metre}$$

8 Valuing inventory

Perpetual inventory

Perpetual inventory is the recording as they occur of receipts, issues and the resulting balances of individual items of inventory in either quantity or quantity and value.

- Inventory records are updated using stores ledger cards and bin cards.

- Bin cards also show a record of receipts, issues and balances of the quantity of an item of inventory handled by stores.

- As with the stores ledger card, bin cards will show materials received (from purchases and returns) and issued (from requisitions).
- A typical stores ledger card is shown below.

STORES LEDGER CARD

Description: .... Unit: .... Location: .... Code: ....
Maximum: .... Minimum: .... Reorder level: .... Reorder quantity: ....

Receipts			Issues			On order		
Date/ref	Quantity	$	Date/ref	Quantity	$	Date/ref	Quantity	$

Inventory valuation is important for:

- Financial reporting
  - for inclusion in the Financial statements of a business

- Costing
  - to calculate how much to charge for a product based on the amount of inventory consumed.

To charge units of inventory at appropriate amount to cost of production or cost of sales, the business will consistently use an appropriate basis:

- **FIFO (First In First Out)** basis.
- **LIFO (Last In First Out)** basis.
- **AVCO or WACO (Weighted Average Cost)** basis.

All will be illustrated using following information.

Illustration 6 – Inventory valuation

M Ltd had the following material transactions during the first week in March.

		Quantity (units)	Unit cost $
Opening balance	1st March	10	2.00
Receipts	2nd March	70	2.20
Issues	3rd March	40	
Receipts	4th March	50	2.30
Issues	5th March	70	

FIFO

- Assumes that materials are issued out of inventory in the order in which they were delivered into inventory.

- Appropriate for many businesses (e.g. retailer selling fresh food using sell-by date rotation techniques).

Illustration 7 – FIFO inventory valuation

Date	Receipts			Issues			Balance		
	Units	Unit cost $	Total cost $	Units	Unit cost $	Total cost $	Units	Unit cost $	Total cost $
Op/Bal							10	2.00	20.00
2nd Mar	70	2.20	154.00				10	2.00	20.00
							70	2.20	154.00
									———
									174.00
3rd Mar				10	2.00	20.00	40	2.20	88.00
				30	2.20	66.00			
						———			
						86.00			
4th Mar	50	2.30	115.00				40	2.20	88.00
							50	2.30	115.00
									———
									203.00
5th Mar				40	2.20	88.00	20	2.30	46.00
				30	2.30	69.00			
						———			
						157.00			

- Closing inventory valuation = 20 units @ $2.30 = $46

- Closing inventory valuation = Opening inventory + receipts – issues

  = $20 + ($154 + $115) – ($86 + $157) = $46

Features of FIFO

Advantages:	Disadvantages:
• Logical – reflects the most likely physical flow. • Easily understood. • Inventory values at up-to-date prices. • Acceptable to HM Revenue and Customs and IAS2.	• Issues may be at out-of-date prices. • In times of rising prices (as in this example), reported profits are high ('high' closing inventory valuations). • Cost comparisons between jobs are difficult.

LIFO

- Assumes that materials are issued out of inventory in the reverse order to which they were delivered. An uncommon method which is only appropriate for a few businesses
  - e.g. a coal merchant who stores coal inventories in a large 'bin'.

Illustration 8 – LIFO inventory valuation

Date	Receipts			Issues			Balance		
	Units	Unit cost ($)	Total cost ($)	Units	Unit cost ($)	Total cost ($)	Units	Unit cost ($)	Total cost ($)
Op/Bal							10	2.00	20.00
2nd Mar	70	2.20	154.00				10 70	2.00 2.20	20.00 154.00 174.00
3rd Mar				40	2.20	88.00	10 30	2.00 2.20	20.00 66.00 86.00
4th Mar	50	2.30	115.00				10 30 50	2.00 2.20 2.30	20.00 66.00 115.00 201.00
5th Mar				50 20	2.30 2.20	115.00 44.00 159.00	10 10	2.00 2.20	20.00 22.00 42.00

- Closing Inventory valuation = 10 units @ $2.00 + 10 units @ $2.20 = $42

- Closing inventory valuation = Opening inventory + receipts – issues

  $20 + ($154 + $115) – ($88 + $159) = $42

Features of LIFO

Advantages:	Disadvantages:
• Issue prices are up-to-date. • In times of rising prices, reported profits are reduced (as in this example where closing inventory is valued at 'lower' cost).	• Not usually acceptable to the HM Revenue & Customs and accounting standards. • Inventory values may become very out-of-date. • Cost comparisons between jobs are difficult.

Cumulative Weighted Average

- All issues and inventory are valued at average price.

- The average price is recalculated after each receipt.

- Cumulative weighted average price = $\dfrac{\text{Running total of costs}}{\text{Running total of units}}$

- Could be appropriate for businesses such as an oil merchant, where deliveries are fully mixed in with existing inventory.

KAPLAN PUBLISHING

Illustration 9 – Cumulative weighted average inventory valuation

Cumulative Weighted Average

Date	Receipts			Issues			Balance		
	Units	Unit cost ($)	Total cost ($)	Units	Unit cost ($)	Total cost ($)	Units	Unit cost ($)	Total cost ($)
Op/Bal							10	2.00	20.00
2nd Mar	70	2.20	154.00				80	2.175	174.00
3rd Mar				40	2.175	87.00	40		87.00
4th Mar	50	2.30	115.00				90	2.244	202.00
5th Mar				70	2.244	157.08	20		44.92

- Cumulative weighted average price after 2nd March delivery

  = ($20 + $154) / (10 + 70) = $174 / 80 = $2.175 per unit

- Closing Inventory valuation = $44.92
- Closing inventory valuation = Opening inventory + receipts – issues

  = $20 + ($154 + $115) – ($87 + $157.08) = $44.92

Features of Cumulative Weighted Average

Advantages:	Disadvantages:
• Acceptable to Accounting Standards and HM Revenue & Customs. • Logical because units all have the same value.	• Issue prices and inventory values may not be an actual purchase price (as in above example). • Inventory values and issue prices may both lag behind current values (e.g. issue on 5 March is at $2.244/unit whereas most recent purchase price = $2.30/unit).

The following information relates to TYUs 9 to 12.

A business had opening inventory of 300 units valued at $4.50 per unit on 1 May. The following receipts and issues were recorded in May:

2 May	Issue	200 units
7 May	Receipt	500 units @ $4.80 per unit
13 May	Issue	400 units
20 May	Receipt	500 units @ $5.00 per unit
28 May	Issue	450 units

Test your understanding 9

What is the value of issues during the month using the FIFO method?

A $4,750

B $5,000 ✓

C $5,030

D $5,080

Test your understanding 10

What is the value of issues during the month using the LIFO method?

A $4,750

B $5,000

C $5,030

D $5,070 ✓

Test your understanding 11

What is the value of closing inventory?

OI + Rec – Issues

	FIFO method	LIFO method
A	$1,180	$1,250
(B)	$1,250 ✓	$1,180 ✓
C	$1,250	$730
D	$1,180	$730

Test your understanding 12

What is the value of closing inventory using the weighted average cost method?

A $1,180

B $1,232

C $1,250

D $1,282

9 Accounting for inventory – the material inventory account

Material inventory account

Materials held in store are an asset and are recorded as inventory in the statement of financial position of a company.

Accounting transactions relating to materials are recorded in the material inventory account.

Material inventory account

Debit entries reflect an **increase** in inventory	Credit entries reflect a **decrease** in inventory
• purchases • returns to stores	• issues to production • returns to suppliers

Illustration 10 – Accounting for inventory

Material inventory account

	$000		$000
Opening balance (1)	33	Work-in-progress (4)	137
Payables (2)	146	Materials returned to suppliers (5)	2
		Production overhead account (6)	4
Materials returned to stores (3)	4		
		Income statement (7)	3
		Closing balance (8)	37
	183		183

(1) The opening balance of materials held in inventory at the beginning of a period is shown as a debit in the material inventory account.

(2) Materials purchased on credit are debited to the material inventory account.

(3) Materials returned to stores cause inventory to increase and so are debited to the material inventory account.

(4) **Direct** materials used in production are transferred to the **work-in-progress** account by crediting the material inventory account.

(5) Materials returned to suppliers cause inventory levels to fall and are therefore 'credited out' of the material inventory account.

(6) **Indirect** materials are not a direct cost of manufacture and are treated as **overheads**. They are therefore transferred to the production overhead account by way of a credit to the material inventory account.

(7) Any material write-offs are 'credited out' of the material inventory account and transferred to the income statement where they are written off.

(8) The balancing figure on the material inventory account is the closing balance of material inventory at the end of a period. It is also the opening balance at the beginning of the next period.

Test your understanding 13

Transaction	Debit which account?	Credit which account?
Issue materials to production.	WIP	Invent ✓
Purchase new materials on credit.	Invent	Payables ✓
Materials returned to store from production.	Invent	WIP ✓
Materials written off.	Income State	Invent ✓
Indirect materials transferred to production overheads.	Overhead	Invent ✓

10 Chapter summary

Accounting for inventory

Ordering:
- Purchase requisition
- Purchase order form

Receiving:
- Delivery note
- Goods received note

Issuing:
- Material requisition note
- Material returned note
- Materials transfer note

Valuation of inventory:
- LIFO
- FIFO
- AVCO

Material inventory account:
- Dr when material enters stores
- Cr when material leaves stores

Inventory costs

Holding costs:
- Interest on capital
- Storage
- Insurance
- Stock outs

Ordering:
- Administrative
- Clerical
- Delivery

EOQ and EBQ

$$EOQ = \sqrt{\frac{2 \times C_o \times D}{C_h}}$$

$$EBQ = \sqrt{\frac{2C_oD}{C_n(1-D/R)}}$$

Control procedures
- Re-order level
- Maximum and minimum inventory levels

Stocktaking:
- Periodic
- Continuous

Test your understanding answers

Test your understanding 1

√	Information used to update inventory records.
	Information to check that the correct price has been recorded on the supplier's invoice.
√	Information to check that the correct quantity of goods has been recorded on the supplier's invoice.
	Information to record any unused materials which are returned to stores.

Test your understanding 2

Answer A

Test your understanding 3

A – the goods received note would be used rather than the delivery note in case the delivery note is wrong.

Test your understanding 4

Annual holding cost = average inventory held x cost per box x 10%

= 120 × $20 × 10% = $240

Annual usage (in boxes) $= \dfrac{1,500}{10} \times 12$ months = 1,800 boxes

Annual ordering cost $= \dfrac{\text{Annual usage}}{\text{Order size}} \times \$32$

$= \dfrac{1,800}{240} \times \$32$

= $240

Test your understanding 5

B   Reorder level = Usage × Lead time

= 175 × 16

= 2,800 units

Test your understanding 6

The order quantity which minimises total costs is

| 349 boxes |

This will mean ordering the item every

| 2 weeks |

Workings

To avoid confusion this question is best tackled by working in boxes not units.

C_o =   5,910/30   ×1.02= $200.94

C_h =   0.15   ×$200= $30 per box

D =   90,800/10   = 9,080 boxes

EOQ = $\sqrt{(2 \times 200.94 \times 9,080/30)}$ = 349 boxes

Number of orders per year   9,080/349   = 26

26 orders per annum is equivalent to placing an order every 2 weeks (52 weeks / 26 orders).

Order quantity = EOQ of 3,500 barrels

	$
Purchase costs (36,750 × $12)	441,000
Annual stockholding costs ($1.20 × 3,500/2)	2,100
Annual ordering costs ($200 × 36,750/3,500)	2,100
	———
Total costs	445,200
	———

Order quantity = 5,000 barrels

	$
Purchase costs (36,750 × $12 × 98%)	432,180
Annual stockholding costs ($1.20 × 5,000/2)	3,000
Annual ordering costs ($200 × 36,750/5,000)	1,470
	———
Total costs	436,650
	———

Order quantity = 7,500 barrels

	$
Purchase costs (36,750 × $12 × 97.5%)	429,975
Annual stockholding costs ($1.20 × 7,500/2)	4,500
Annual ordering costs ($200 × 36,750/7,500)	980
	———
Total costs	435,455
	———

Total costs are minimised with an order size of 7,500 barrels.

D		= 2,000 units
R	= 200 × 50	= 10,000 units
C_o		= $320
C_h	= 10% of $16	= $1.60

$$EBQ = \sqrt{\frac{2C_oD}{C_h(1 - D/R)}} = \sqrt{\frac{2 \times 320 \times 2,000}{1.60\,(1 - 2,000/10,000)}} = 1,000 \text{ units}$$

Test your understanding 9

B

				$
	Opening Inventory	300 units × $4.50		
3 May	Issue	200 units × $4.50	=	900
7 May	Receipts	500 units × $4.80		
13 May	Issue	100 units × $4.50	=	450
		300 units × $4.80	=	1,440
20 May	Receipt	500 units × $5.00		
28 May	Issue	200 units × $4.80	=	960
		250 units × $5.00	=	1,250
				5,000

Test your understanding 10

D

				$
	Opening inventory	300 units × $4.50		
3 May	Issue	200 units × $4.50	=	900
7 May	Receipt	500 units × $4.80		
13 May	Issue	400 units × $4.80	=	1,920
20 May	Receipt	500 units × $5.00		
28 May	Issue	450 units × $5.00	=	2,250
				5,070

Test your understanding 11

Answer B

			$
FIFO	250 units × $5.00	=	1,250
LIFO	100 units × $4.50	=	450
	100 units × $4.80	=	480
	50 units × $5.00	=	250
			1,180

Test your understanding 12

Answer B

			$
Opening inventory	300	$4.50	1,350
Issue	(200)	$4.50	(900)
Receipt	500	$4.80	2,400
	600	$4.75	2,850
Issue	(400)	$4.75	(1,900)
Receipt	500	$5.00	2,500
	700	$4.929	3,450
Issue	(450)	$4.929	(2,218)
Closing inventory	250		1,232

Test your understanding 13

Transaction	Debit which account?	Credit which account?
Issue materials to production.	Work-in-progress.	Material inventory account.
Purchase new materials on credit.	Material inventory account.	Payables.
Materials returned to store from production.	Material inventory account.	Work-in-progress account.
Materials written off.	Income statement.	Material inventory account.
Indirect materials transferred to production overheads.	Production overhead account.	Material inventory account.

6

Accounting for labour

Chapter learning objectives

Upon completion of this chapter you will be able to:

- calculate direct and indirect costs of labour

- explain the methods used to relate input labour costs to work done

- prepare the journal and ledger entries to record labour costs inputs and outputs

- interpret entries in the labour account

- describe different remuneration methods: time-based systems; piecework systems and individual and group incentive schemes

- calculate the level, and analyse the costs and causes of labour turnover

- explain and calculate labour efficiency, capacity and production volume ratios.

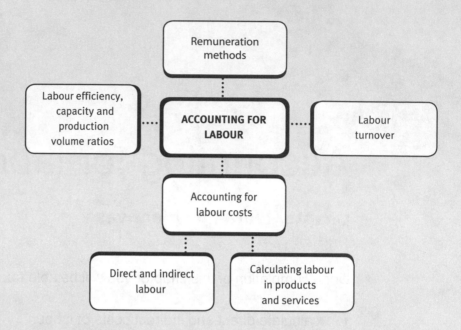

1 Direct and indirect labour

Direct and indirect labour costs

Labour is often one of the major costs to a business. One of the most important distinctions of labour is between **direct** and **indirect** costs.

- Direct labour costs make up part of the prime cost of a product and include the basic pay of direct workers.

- Direct workers are those employees who are directly involved in making an organisation's products.

- Indirect labour costs make up part of the overheads (indirect costs) and include the basic pay of indirect workers.

- Indirect workers are those employees who are **not** directly involved in making products, (for example, maintenance staff, factory supervisors and canteen staff).

- Indirect labour costs also include the following.
  - Bonus payments.
  - Benefit contributions.
  - Idle time (when workers are paid but are not making any products, for example when a machine breaks down).
  - Sick pay.
  - Time spent by direct workers doing 'indirect jobs' for example, cleaning or repairing machines.

Test your understanding 1

Which one of the following should be classified as direct labour?

A   Supervisors' salaries in a factory

B   Maintenance workers looking after equipment in a hospital

(C)   Bricklayers in a house building company

D   Wages of cleaning and housekeeping personnel

Overtime and overtime premiums

If employees are entitled to extra pay when hours in excess of contracted hours are worked then they will be paid for **overtime**. When employees work overtime, they receive an **overtime payment** which includes a **basic pay** element and an **overtime premium**.

- For example, if Fred is paid $8 per hour and overtime is paid at time and a half, when Fred works overtime, he will receive an overtime payment of $12 per hour ($8 basic + $4 premium (50% × $8)).

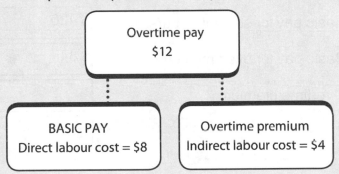

It is important that the overtime payment is analysed correctly into direct and indirect labour costs.

- Basic pay (whether it relates to overtime or normal working hours) is always classified as a direct labour cost for direct labour workers.

- Overtime premiums are usually classified as an indirect labour cost but if the extra hours are at the **specific request of a customer** because they want a job to be finished as soon as possible they can be classified as direct labour.

- Employees who work night shifts, or other anti-social hours may be entitled to a shift allowance or shift premium. Shift premiums are similar to overtime premiums where the extra amount paid above the basic rate is treated as an indirect labour cost.

Illustration 1 – Direct and indirect labour

Vienna is a direct labour employee who works a standard 35 hours per week and is paid a basic rate of $12 per hour. Overtime is paid at time and a third. In week 8 she worked 42 hours and received a $50 bonus. Complete the following table.

	Direct labour cost	Indirect labour cost
Basic pay for standard hours	$ 420	$
Basic pay for overtime hours	$ 84	$
Overtime premium	$	$ 28
Bonus	$	$ 50

Solution

	Direct labour cost	Indirect labour cost
(1) Basic pay for standard hours	$ 420	
(2) Basic pay for overtime hours	$ 84	
(3) Overtime premium		**$28**
(4) Bonus		$50

Workings:

(1) Basic pay for standard hours = 35 hours × $12 per hour = $420

Basic pay for standard hours is a **direct labour cost** because the work involved is directly attributable to production.

(2) Basic pay for overtime hours = 7 hours × $12 = $84
This is also a **direct labour cost** because the **basic rate for overtime** is part of the direct labour cost. It is the **overtime premium** which is usually part of the indirect labour cost.

(3) Overtime premium = 1/3 of $12 = $
Total overtime premium = 7 hours × $4 = $28

Unless overtime is worked at the specific request of a customer, overtime premium is part of the **indirect labour costs** of an organisation.

Test your understanding 2

A company operates a factory which employed 40 direct workers throughout the four-week period just ended. Direct employees were paid at a basic rate of $4.00 per hour for a 38-hour week. Total hours of the direct workers in the four-week period were 6,528. Overtime, which is paid at a premium of 35%, is worked in order to meet general production requirements. Employee deductions total 30% of gross wages. 188 hours of direct workers' time were registered as idle.

Calculate the following for the four-week period just ended.

Gross wages (earnings)	$ 26739.20
Deductions	$ 8021.76
Net wages	$ 18717.44
Direct labour cost	$ 25360
Indirect labour cost	$ 1379.20

2 Calculating labour in products and services

Determining time spent

Methods for recording the length of time an employee spends working can include:

- time sheets
- time cards
- job sheets.

Time records

It is essential that organisations employ relevant methods in both manufacturing and service industries to relate the labour costs incurred to the work done. One of the ways in which this can be done is to make records of the time spent by employees doing jobs.

- Time recording is required both for payment purposes and also for determining the costs to be charged to specific jobs.

- In many manufacturing industries both direct and indirect workers will be supplied with an attendance record on which to record their time of arrival and departure from the factory. Such records are known as time cards (gate or clockcards) and are used to calculate wages and rates of pay.

- Plastic 'swipe' cards directly linked to a central computer can also be used.

Activity time records

Another method of relating work done to costs incurred is by the use of activity time records. Activity time records may be either period related or time related.

- Period-related timesheets are commonly used in service industries, for example in accountancy firms where time spent working for different clients is analysed, often to the nearest 15 minutes.

- Period-related timesheets are records that may cover days, weeks or sometimes longer periods.

- Task-related activity time records are known as job sheets, operations charts or piecework tickets. They are generally more accurate and reliable than time-related activity time records, and are essential when incentive schemes are in use.

An example of a daily timesheet is illustrated on the next page.

Time Sheet					
Employee name:				No:	
Start date:				Finish date:	
Department:				Operation:	

Day	Start	Finish	Time	Production	Supervisor's signature
1					
2					
3					
4					
5					
Total Time allowed Time saved					

	Hours	Rate $	Paid $
Time wages Bonus Total wages			

Payroll department

The payroll department is involved in carrying out functions that relate input labour costs to the work done.

- Preparation of the payroll involves calculating gross wages from time and activity records.

- The payroll department also calculates net wages after deductions from payroll.

- The payroll department also carries out an analysis of direct wages, indirect wages, and cash required for payment.

3 Accounting for labour costs

Labour costs are recorded in an organisation's income statement. Accounting transactions relating to labour are recorded in the labour account.

- The labour account is debited with the labour costs incurred by an organisation. The total labour costs are then analysed into direct and indirect labour costs.

- **Direct labour costs** are credited from the labour account and debited in the work-in-progress (WIP) account. Remember, direct labour costs are directly involved in production and are therefore transferred to WIP before being transferred to finished goods and then cost of sales.

- **Indirect labour costs** are also credited 'out of' the labour account but debited to the production overheads account. It is important that total labour costs are analysed into their direct and indirect elements.

Illustration 2 – Accounting for labour costs

Labour account

	$000		$000
Bank (1)	80	WIP (2)	60
		Production overheads (3)	
		Indirect labour	14
		Overtime premium	2
		Shift premium	2
		Sick pay	1
		Idle time	1
	——		——
	80		80
	——		——

(1) Labour costs incurred are paid out of the bank before they are analysed further in the labour account.

(2) The majority of the labour costs incurred by a manufacturing organisation are in respect of direct labour costs. Direct labour costs are directly involved in production and are transferred out of the labour account via a credit entry to the WIP account.

(3) Indirect labour costs include indirect labour (costs of indirect labour workers), overtime premium (unless overtime is worked at the specific request of a customer), shift premium, sick pay and idle time. All of these indirect labour costs are collected in the production overheads account. They are transferred there via a credit entry out of the labour account and then debited in the production overheads account.

KAPLAN PUBLISHING

Test your understanding 3

The following information is taken from the payroll records of a company.

	Direct workers $	Indirect workers $	Total $
Basic pay for basic hours	43,000	17,000	60,000
Overtime – basic pay	10,000	4,500	14,500
Overtime – premium	5,000	2,250	7,250
Training	2,500	1,250	3,750
Sick pay	750	250	1,000
Idle time	1,200	–	1,200

Required:

Using the information given, complete the labour account shown below:

Labour account

BANK	$ 87,700	WIP Indirect labour Overtime prem Training Sick pay Idle time	$ 53,500 21,500 7250 3750 1000 1200
	87,700		87,700

4 Remuneration methods

There are two basic approaches to remuneration – time-related or output-related.

Time-related systems

The most common remuneration method is to base pay or wages on the number of hours an employee works.

- Employees are paid a basic rate per hour, day, week or month.

- Basic time-based systems do not provide any incentive for employees to improve productivity and close supervision is often necessary.

- Overtime is paid if any extra hours are worked.

- The basic formula for a time-based system is as follows.

**Total wages = (hours worked x basic rate of pay per hour) +
(overtime hours worked x overtime premium per hour)**

- A guaranteed minimum wage is often required due to minimum wage requirements.

Output related systems

A **piecework** system pays a fixed amount per unit produced. The basic formula for a piecework system is as follows.

Total wages = (units produced x rate of pay per unit)

- A guaranteed minimum wage is often required due to minimum wage requirements.

- Piecework is often combined with a time-based system to provide an added incentive to employees.

Types of piecework system

There are two main piecework systems that you need to know about:

- **Straight piecework systems** – these systems are almost extinct today as employees are more likely to be paid a guaranteed minimum wage within a straight piecework system.

- **Differential piecework systems** – these systems are the most widely used piecework systems and involve different piece rates for different levels of production.

Illustration 3 – Piecework schemes

A company operates a piecework system of remuneration, but also guarantees its employees 75% of a time-based rate of pay which is based on $19 per hour for an eight hour working day. Each unit should take 3 minutes to produce (standard time). Employees are paid based on the number of hours their output should have taken them (standard hours). Piecework is paid at the rate of $18 per standard hour.

KAPLAN PUBLISHING

If an employee produces 200 units in eight hours on a particular day, what is the employee gross pay for that day?

A $114

B $152

C $180

D $190

Handwritten annotations:
1. £19 × 8 = 152
2. 200 × 3 = 600 ÷ 60 = 10 hours
   UNITS MINS MINS
   £18 × 10 = £180 ✓✓
   GROSS PAY > GUARANTEED AMOUNT.

Solution

C

200 units × standard time of 3 minutes per unit = 600 minutes, or 10 hours.

Employee gross pay = 10 hours × $18 = $180

Guaranteed ($19 × 8 hours) × 75% = $152 × 75% = $114

As gross pay exceeds the guaranteed amount, the answer is $180.

Test your understanding 4

The following graph shows the wages earned by an employee during a single day.

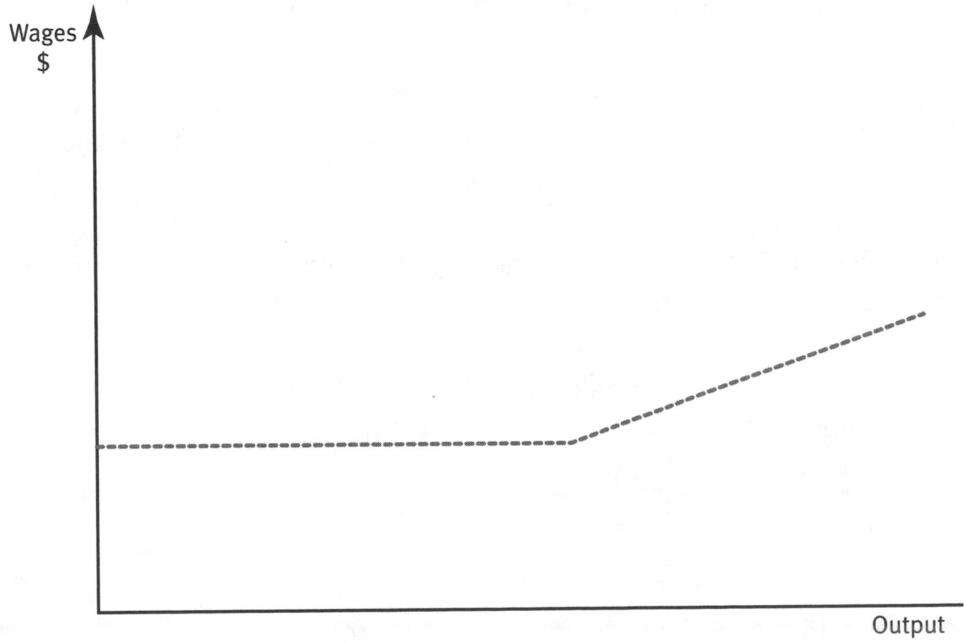

Which one of the following remuneration systems does the graph represent?

A   Differential piecework

B   A flat rate per hour with a premium for overtime working

C   Straight piecework

(D)   Piecework with a guaranteed minimum daily wage

5 Incentive schemes

Incentive schemes can be aimed at individuals and/or groups.

- Many different systems exist in practice for calculating bonus schemes. General rules are as follows:

  - They should be closely related to the effort expended by employees.

  - They should be agreed by employers/employees before being implemented.

  - They should be easy to understand and simple to operate.

  - They must be beneficial to all of those employees taking part in the scheme.

- Most bonus schemes pay a basic time rate, plus a portion of the time saved as compared to some agreed allowed time. These bonus schemes are known as **premium bonus plans**. Examples of such schemes are Halsey and Rowan.

- **Halsey** – the employee receives 50% of the time saved.

$$\text{Bonus} = \frac{\text{Time allowed} - \text{Time taken}}{2} \times \text{Time rate}$$

- **Rowan** – the proportion paid to the employee is based on the ratio of time taken to time allowed.

$$\text{Bonus} = \frac{\text{Time taken}}{\text{Time allowed}} \times \text{Time rate} \times \text{Time saved}$$

- **Measured day work** – the concept of this approach is to pay a high time rate, but this rate is based on an analysis of past performance. Initially, work measurement is used to calculate the allowed time per unit. This allowed time is compared to the time actually taken in the past by the employee, and if this is better than the allowed time an incentive is agreed, e.g. suppose the allowed time is 1 hour per unit and that the average time taken by an employee over the last three months is 50 minutes. If the normal rate is $12/hour, then an agreed incentive rate of $14/hour could be used.

- **Share of production** – share of production plans are based on acceptance by both management and labour representatives of a constant share of value added for payroll. Thus, any gains in value added – whether by improved production performance or cost savings – are shared by employees in this ratio.

Illustration 4 – Incentive schemes

The following data relate to Job A.

Employee's basic rate = $4.80 per hour
Allowed time for Job A = 1 hour
Time taken for Job A = 36 minutes

The employee is paid the basic rate for the allowed time for the job and then the bonus based on any time saved.

Halsey scheme – Total payment for Job A = $ [   ]

Rowan scheme – Total payment for Job B = $ [   ]

Solution

Halsey scheme – Total payment for Job A = $ [5.76]

Rowan scheme – Total payment for Job B = $ [5.95]

Workings:

Halsey

$$\text{Bonus} = \frac{60 - 36}{2} \times \frac{\$4.80}{60} \qquad 0.96$$

(Allowed 60, taken 36, 2 = AVERAGE, $4.80 = RATE, 60 = TIME)

		$
Bonus	=	0.96
Basic rate	=	4.80
		———
Total payment for Job A		5.76

Rowan	$
Bonus $= \dfrac{36}{60} \times \dfrac{\$4.80}{60} \times 24$	1.15
Basic rate $=$	4.80
___
Total payment for Job A	5.95

Test your understanding 5

Ten employees work as a group. When production of the group exceeds the standard – 200 pieces per hour – each employee in the group is paid a bonus for the excess production in addition to wages at hourly rates.

The bonus is computed thus: the percentage of production in excess of the standard quantity is found, and one half of the percentage is regarded as the employees' share. Each employee in the group is paid as a bonus this percentage of a wage rate of $5.20 per hour. There is no relationship between the individual worker's hourly rate and the bonus rate.

The following is one week's record:

	Hours worked	Production
Monday	90	24,500
Tuesday	88	20,600
Wednesday	90	24,200
Thursday	84	20,100
Friday	88	20,400
Saturday	40	10,200
	___	___
	480	120,000
	___	___

(handwritten annotations in right margin: 18000, 176 00, 18000)

(handwritten working below the table):

Standard = 480 × 200 = 96,000
Actual = 120,000
Excess = 24,000

Bonus rate = $\dfrac{24,000}{96,000} \times 0.5 \times \cancel{5.20} = 0.65$

Total bonus = 0.65 × ~~24,000~~ 480 = 312

During this week, Jones worked 42 hours and was paid $3 per hour basic.

Complete the following.

(1) The bonus rate for the week was $

(2) The total bonus for the group for the week was $

(3) The total pay for Jones for the week was $

In an examination you will be given clear instructions on any bonus scheme in operation. You should follow the instructions given carefully in order to calculate the bonus payable from the data supplied.

6 Labour turnover

Labour turnover is a measure of the proportion of people leaving relative to the average number of people employed.

- Management might wish to monitor labour turnover, so that control measures might be considered if the rate of turnover seems too high.

- Labour turnover is calculated for any given period of time using the following formula:

$$\frac{\text{Number of leavers who require replacement}}{\text{Average number of employees}} \times 100$$

Illustration 5 – Labour turnover

At 1 January a company employed 3,641 employees and at 31 December employee numbers were 3,735. During the year 624 employees chose to leave the company. What was the labour turnover rate for the year?

Solution

Labour turnover rate =

$$\frac{\text{Number of leavers who require replacement}}{\text{Average number of employees}} \times 100$$

Average number of employees in the year = (3,641 + 3,735) ÷ 2 = 3,688.

Labour turnover rate = $\frac{624}{3,688} \times 100\% = 16.9\%$.

Test your understanding 6

A company had 4,000 staff at the beginning of 20X8. During the year, there was a major restructuring of the company and 1,500 staff were made redundant and 400 staff left the company to work for one of the company's main competitors. 400 new staff joined the company in the year to replace those who went to work for the competitor.

Required:

$\frac{400}{3250} \times 100 = 12.3\%$ $4000 + 400 - 400 - 1500 = 2500$

$(4000 + 2500)/2 = 3250$

Calculate the labour turnover rate for 20X8.

Causes and costs of labour turnover

Causes

It is important to try to identify why people leave an organisation and to distinguish between avoidable and unavoidable causes of labour turnover.

- Causes of labour turnover – avoidable:
  - poor remuneration
  - poor working conditions
  - lack of training opportunities
  - lack of promotion prospects
  - bullying in the workplace.

- Causes of labour turnover – unavoidable:
  - retirement
  - illness/death
  - family reasons (e.g. pregnancy)
  - relocation.
- Efficient managers will investigate high levels of labour turnover and aim to keep that turnover rate at a minimum.

Costs

Every time an employee leaves, an organisation will incur costs that are associated with replacing the employee. These costs are known as replacement costs.

- Replacement costs include the following:
  - advertising costs
  - cost of selection (time spent interviewing etc.)
  - training new employees
  - reduced efficiency until the new employee reaches the required skill.
- A high labour turnover rate tends to lower the performance of employees who remain in the organisation. Such employees may become restless and resentful of the extra burden of training new members and of additional temporary duties imposed upon them.
- In order to keep the labour turnover rate to a minimum, organisations should aim to prevent employees from leaving. Such preventive measures come with their own costs, known as preventive costs.
- Preventive costs include the costs associated with escaping the avoidable causes of labour turnover:
  - pay competitive wages and salaries if remuneration is poor
  - improve poor working conditions
  - offer good training opportunities
  - make sure promotion prospects arise as necessary.
  - stamp out bullying in the workplace
  - investigate high labour turnover rates objectively.

7 Labour efficiency, capacity and production volume ratios

Labour efficiency ratio

Labour is a significant cost in many organisations and it is important to continually measure the efficiency of labour against pre-set targets.

- The labour efficiency ratio measures the performance of the workforce by comparing the actual time taken to do a job with the expected or standard time.

- The standard time is how long it should take to complete the actual output.

- The labour efficiency ratio is calculated using the following formula:

$$\frac{\text{Standard Hours for actual output}}{\text{Actual hours worked to produce output}} \times 100$$

Idle time ratio

Sometimes the workforce is 'idle' through no fault of its own, and cannot get on with productive work. This happens if machines break down, or needs to be reset for a new production run. An idle time ratio can be calculated as follows:

$$\frac{\text{Idle hours}}{\text{Total hours}} \times 100$$

Labour capacity ratio

The labour capacity ratio measures the number of hours spent actively working as a percentage of the total hours available for work (full capacity or budgeted hours). The labour capacity ratio is calculated using the following formula:

$$\frac{\text{Actual hours worked to produce output}}{\text{Total budgeted hours}} \times 100$$

KAPLAN PUBLISHING

Labour production volume ratio ('activity' ratio)

- The labour production volume ratio compares the number of hours expected to be worked to produce actual output with the total hours available for work (full capacity or budgeted hours).

- The labour production volume ratio is calculated using the following formula:

$$\frac{\textbf{Standard hours for actual output}}{\textbf{Total budgeted hours}} \quad \textbf{x} \quad \textbf{100}$$

Labour efficiency, capacity and production volume ratios

Labour efficiency, capacity and production volume ratios

Standard hours

A **standard hour** can be used to state the number of production units which should be achieved within a period of one hour.

Standard time allowed per unit	30 minutes
Actual output in period	840 units
Actual hours worked	410
Budgeted hours	400

An employee would be expected to make 2 units in one hour. Therefore the standard hours to produce the actual output = 840 units × 0.5 hours per unit = 420 standard hours

Labour efficiency ratio:

$$\frac{\text{Standard hours for actual output}}{\text{Actual hours worked to produce output}} \times 100\%$$

$$= 420/410 \qquad \times 100\% = 102\%$$

Labour capacity ratio:

$$\frac{\text{Actual hours worked to produce actual output}}{\text{Total budgeted hours}} \times 100\%$$

$$= 410/400 \qquad \times 100\% = 102.5\%$$

Production volume ratio:

$$\frac{\text{Standard hours for actual output}}{\text{Total budgeted hours}} \times 100\%$$

$$= 420/400 \qquad \times 100\% = 105\%$$

Test your understanding 7

A company budgets to make 40,000 units of Product DOY in 4,000 hours (each unit is budgeted to take 0.1 hours each) in a year.

Actual output during the year was 38,000 units which took 4,180 hours to make.

Required:

Calculate the labour efficiency, capacity and production volume ratios.

Labour Efficiency = $\dfrac{\text{Actual Standard}}{\text{Budget Actual}}$ $\dfrac{3800}{4080} \times 1000 = 900.9\%$

Capacity Efficiency = $\dfrac{\text{Standard Actual}}{\text{Budget Budget}}$ $\dfrac{4180}{4000} \times 100 = 104.5\%$

Production Volume = $\dfrac{\text{Actual Standard}}{\text{Standard Budget}}$ $\dfrac{3800}{4000} \times 100 = 95\%$

Budget = 40,000 units — 4,000 hours
Actual = 38,000 units — 4,180 hours
3,800 hours
Standard =

8 Chapter summary

Remuneration methods
- Time-based systems
- Piecework systems
- Individual incentive schemes
- Group incentive schemes

ACCOUNTING FOR LABOUR

Labour efficiency capacity and production volume ratios

Labour is significant cost in many organisations – important to use these ratios to continually 'measure' how it is doing by reference to effciency, capacity and production volume ratios

Accounting for labour costs

Debit labour account with labour costs incurred

Credit labour account with direct labour – transfer to WIP

Credit labour account with indirect labour – transfer to production overheads account

Labour turnover

Measure of proportion of employees leaving relative to the average number of people employed

Many causes and costs of labour turnover – both avoidable and unavoidable

Direct and indirect labour

Direct labour – makes up part of prime cost and includes basic pay of direct workers

Indirect labour – makes u p part of overheads and Includes basic pay of indirect workers

Overtime premiums are treated as overheads unless worked at specific request of customer when treated as direct cost

Calculating labour in products and services

Times records
- Time cards
- Clock cards

Activity records
- Period-related

Test your understanding answers

Test your understanding 1

C

Test your understanding 2

Gross wages (earnings)	$26,739.20
Deductions	$8,021.76
Net wages	$18,717.44
Direct labour cost	$25,360
Indirect labour cost	$1,379.20

Workings:

Basic time	= 40 workers × 38 hrs/week × 4 weeks	= 6,080 hrs
Overtime	= Total time – Basic time = 6,528 – 6,080	= 448 hrs
Total wages	= Basic pay + Overtime premium	
	= 6,528 hours at $4.00 per hour	= $26,112.00
	+ 448 hours at $1.40 per hour	= $627.20
		_____
Gross wages		$26,739.20
		_____
Deductions	= $26,739.20 × 30%	= $8,021.76
		_____
Net pay	= $26,739.20 × 70%	= $18,717.44
		_____

Productive time = Total time – Idle time

           = 6,528 – 188   = 6,340 hours

Direct labour   = 6,340 hours at $4.00 per hour   = $25,360

Indirect labour   = Overtime premium + Idle time costs

                = $627.20 + $752 (188 hours × $4.00/hr)   = $1,379.20

Gross wages $26,739.20

Test your understanding 3

Labour account

	$		$
Bank	87,700	WIP (43,000 + 10,000)	53,000
		Production overheads	
		Indirect labour (17,000 + 4,500)	21,500
		Overtime premium	7,250
		Training	3,750
		Sick pay	1,000
		Idle time	1,200
	87,700		87,700

Test your understanding 4

D   The graph represents a piecework system (as shown by the gentle upward-sloping line) with a guaranteed minimum daily wage (as shown by the horizontal line).

Test your understanding 5

(1) The bonus rate for the week was $ | 0.65 |

(2) The total bonus for the week was $ | 312 |

(3) The total pay for Jones for the week was $ | 153.30 |

Workings

Standard production for the week = 480 hours × 200 = 96,000 pieces
Actual production for the week = 120,000 pieces
Excess production = 120,000 – 96,000 = 24,000

(1) Bonus rate = 24,000 ÷ 96,000 × 0.5 × $5.20
= $0.65 per hour

(2) Total bonus = 480 hours × $0.65
= $312

(3) Pay for Jones = 42 × (3.00 + 0.65)
= $153.30

Test your understanding 6

Number of staff at beginning of year = 4,000

Number of staff at end of year = 4,000 – 1,500 – 400 + 400 = 2,500

Labour turnover rate =

$$\frac{\text{Number of leavers who require replacement}}{\text{Average number of employees}} \times 100$$

Average number of employees in the year = $\dfrac{4,000 + 2,500}{2}$ = 3,250

Labour turnover rate = $\dfrac{400}{3,250} \times 100\%$ = 12.3%.

Test your understanding 7

Standard hours for actual output = 38,000 × 0.1 hours = 3,800 standard hours.

Labour efficiency ratio:

$$\frac{\text{Standard hours for actual output}}{\text{Actual hours worked to produce output}} \times 100\%$$

$$= (3,800/4,180) \qquad \times 100\% = 91\%$$

Labour capacity ratio:

$$\frac{\text{Actual hours worked to produce output}}{\text{Total budgeted hours}} \times 100\%$$

$$= (4,180/4,000) \qquad \times 100\% = 104.5\%$$

Production volume ratio:

$$\frac{\text{Standard hours for actual output}}{\text{Total budgeted hours}} \times 100\%$$

$$= \frac{3,800}{4,000} \times 100\% = 95\%$$

Accounting for overheads

Chapter learning objectives

Upon completion of this chapter you will be able to:

- explain the different treatment of direct and indirect expenses

- describe the procedures involved in determining production overhead absorption rates

- allocate and apportion production overheads to cost centres using an appropriate basis

- reapportion service cost centre costs to production cost centres (using the reciprocal method where service cost centres work for each other)

- select, apply and discuss appropriate bases for absorption rates

- prepare journal and ledger entries for manufacturing overheads incurred and absorbed

- calculate and explain the under- and over-absorption of overheads

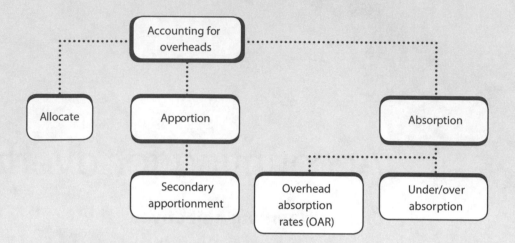

1 Direct and indirect expenses

Direct expenses are expenses that can be directly identified with a specific cost unit or cost centre. There are few examples of direct expenses but royalties paid to a designer or fees paid to a subcontractor for a specific job could be classed as direct expenses.

- Direct expenses are part of the prime cost of a product.

Indirect expenses cannot be directly identified with a specific cost unit or cost centre.

- For example, the cost of renting a factory where shirts are manufactured is classified as an indirect cost because it would be impossible to relate such costs to shirts only, if other clothes, such as dresses and suits were also made in the same factory.

- Indirect expenses are also known as **overheads**.

2 Production overhead absorption

Fixed production overheads

Production overheads are the total of indirect production costs:

Fixed production overheads = indirect materials + indirect labour + indirect expenses

- Fixed production overheads of a factory will include the following costs:
  - heating the factory
  - lighting the factory
  - renting the factory.

- The total cost of a product also needs to include a share of the fixed production overheads.

- This is because organisations must cover the cost of their fixed production overheads and they do this by absorbing a fixed amount into each product that they make.

Absorption costing

Production overheads are recovered by absorbing them into the cost of a product and this process is therefore called absorption costing.

- The main aim of absorption costing is to recover overheads in a way that fairly reflects the amount of time and effort that has gone into making a product or service.

- Absorption costing involves the following stages:
    - allocation and apportionment of overheads to the different cost centres
    - reapportionment of service (non-production) cost centre overheads to the production cost centres
    - absorption of overheads into the products.

3 Allocation and apportionment

Allocation and apportionment of overheads

The first stage of the absorption costing process involves the allocation and apportionment of overheads.

- Allocation involves charging overheads directly to specific departments (production and service).

- If overheads relate to more than one specific department, then they must be shared between these departments using a method known as apportionment.

- Overheads must be apportioned between different production and service departments on a fair basis.

Bases of apportionment

There are no hard and fast rules for which basis of apportionment to use except that whichever method is used to apportion overheads, it must be fair. Possible bases of apportionment include the following:

- floor area – for rent and rates overheads

- carrying amount of non-current assets – for depreciation and insurance of machinery

- number of employees – for canteen costs.

Illustration 1 – Allocation and apportionment

LS Ltd has two production departments (Assembly and Finishing) and two service departments (Maintenance and Canteen).

The following are budgeted costs for the next period:

Indirect materials   – $20,000
Rent   – $15,000
Electricity   – $10,000
Machine depreciation   – $5,000
Indirect labour   – $16,520

The following information is available:

	Assembly	Finishing	Maintenance	Canteen	Total
Area (sq metres)	1,000	2,000	500	500	4,000
kW hours consumed	2,750	4,500	1,975	775	10,000
Machine value ($)	45,000	35,000	11,000	9,000	100,000
Staff	18	30	12	2	62
Direct labour hours	3,175	3,800	–	–	6,975
Indirect w\l materials budget ($)	7,000	8,000	3,000	2,000	20,000
Indirect labour budget ($)	1,600	2,220	11,200	1,500	16,520

KAPLAN PUBLISHING

Required:

Complete the extract from the overhead analysis sheet shown below.

Overhead analysis sheet

Overhead	Basis of apportionment	Assembly $	Finishing $	Maintenance $	Canteen $	Total $
Indirect materials	Allocated Floor area WI	7000	8,000	3000	2000	20,000
Rent	Floor area	3750	7500	1875	1875	
Electricity	Floor area	2750	4500	1975	775	
Machine depreciation	Carrying amount	2250	1750	550	450	
Indirect labour	N° of employees	1600	2220	11,200	1500	

Solution

Overhead analysis sheet

Overhead	Basis of apportionment	Assembly $	Finishing $	Maintenance $	Canteen $	Total $
Indirect materials	Allocated (W1)	7,000	8,000	3,000	2,000	20,000
Rent	Area (W2)	3,750	7,500	1,875	1,875	15,000
Electricity	kW Hours (W3)	2,750	4,500	1,975	775	10,000
Machine depreciation	Machine value (W4)	2,250	1,750	550	450	5,000
Indirect labour	Allocated (W5)	1,600	2,220	11,200	1,500	16,520

Workings:

(W1)

Indirect materials are allocated directly to the relevant departments.

(W2)

Rent is apportioned to all departments based on the area occupied.

Total rent cost	= $15,000
Total area occupied	= 4,000 sq metres
Apportioned to Assembly department	= 1,000/4,000 × $15,000 = $3,750

(W3)

Electricity is apportioned to all departments on the basis of kW hours.

Total electricity costs	= $10,000
Total kW hours consumed	= 10,000 kW hours
Apportioned to Finishing department	= 4,500/10,000 × $10,000 = $4,500

(W4)

Machine depreciation is apportioned to all departments on the basis of machine value.

Total machine depreciation costs	= $5,000
Total machine value	= $100,000
Apportioned to Maintenance department	= 11,000/100,000 × $5,000 = $550

(W5)

Indirect labour costs are allocated directly to all departments based on the indirect labour budget for each department.

4 Reapportionment of service cost centre costs to production cost centres

Reapportionment

Service cost centres (departments) are not directly involved in making products and therefore the fixed production overheads of service cost centres must be shared out between the production cost centres (departments) using a suitable basis.

- Examples of service cost centres are as follows:
    - stores
    - canteen
    - maintenance department
    - payroll department.

Basic reapportionment

- The basic method of reapportionment is used when one service department works or provides a service for other service departments as well as the production departments

- Using the example in the previous illustration – the canteen feeds all the staff that work for the company in maintenance, finishing and assembly but the maintenance staff do not provide support for the canteen equipment.

Illustration 2 – Reapportionment of service cost centre costs

The total overheads allocated and apportioned to the production and service departments of LS Ltd are as follows:

Assembly = $17,350
Finishing = $23,970
Maintenance = $18,600
Canteen = $6,600

A suitable basis for sharing out the maintenance costs is the time spent servicing equipment. The amount of time spent by the maintenance department servicing equipment in the Assembly and Finishing departments has been analysed as follows:

Assembly 60%
Finishing 40%

The Canteen department's overheads are to be reapportioned on the basis of the number of employees in the other three departments.

	Assembly	Finishing	Maintenance	Canteen
Number of employees	18	30	12	2

(handwritten: 60 above Canteen)

Required:

Complete the overhead analysis sheet overleaf.

(handwritten in left margin: A = 60% F = 40%)

	Basis of apportionment	Assembly $	Finishing $	Maintenance $	Canteen $	Total $
Total from above		17,350	23,970	18,600	6,600	66,520
Reapportion canteen	Nº of employees	1980	3300	1320	(6,600)	
Sub-total		19330	27270	19920	—	66520
Reapportion maintenance	% of maint	11,952	7968	—	—	
Total		31,282	35238	—	—	66520

Solution

	Basis of apportionment	Assembly $	Finishing $	Maintenance $	Canteen $	Total $
Total from above		17,350	23,970	18,600	6,600	66,520
Reapportion canteen	Employees (W1)	1,980	3,300	1,320	(6,600)	–
Sub-total		19,330	27,270	19,920	0	66,520
Reapportion maintenance	% time (W2)	11,952	7,968	(19,920)	–	–
Total		31,282	35,238	0	0	66,520

KAPLAN PUBLISHING

Workings:

(W1)

Canteen overheads are reapportioned on the basis of number of employees that work in the departments it services.

Total employees = 18 + 30 + 12 = 60

Reapportioned to Assembly department = 18/60 × $6,600 = $1,980

(W2)

Assembly = 60% × $19,920 = $11,952

Maintenance = 40% × $19,920 = $7,968

Test your understanding 1

A manufacturing company runs two production cost centres C1 and C2, and two service cost centres S1 and S2. The total allocated and apportioned overheads for each is as follows:

C1	C2	S1	S2
$12,000	$17,000	$9,500	$8,000

It has been estimated that each service cost centre does work for other cost centres in the following proportions:

	C1	C2	S1	S2
Percentage of service cost centre S1 to:	60%	40%	–	–
Percentage of service cost centre S2 to:	35%	35%	30%	–

1440 | 0.3 × 8 000 × 0.6

After the reapportionment of service cost centre costs has been carried out, what is the total overhead for production cost centre C1?

A $17,700

B $19,140

C $21,940 //

D $23,240

you have to re-apportion S2 first

Reciprocal reapportionment

Reciprocal reapportionment (or the repeated distribution method) is used where service cost centres (departments) do work for each other.

- It involves carrying out many reapportionments until all of the service departments' overheads have been reapportioned to the production departments.

Illustration 3 – Reapportionment of service cost centre costs

The total overheads allocated and apportioned to the production and service departments of LS Ltd are as follows.

Assembly = $17,350
Finishing = $23,970
Maintenance = $18,600
Canteen = $6,600

A suitable basis for sharing out the maintenance costs is the time spent servicing equipment. The amount of time spent by the maintenance department servicing equipment in the other three departments has been analysed as follows.

Assembly   50%
Finishing   40%
Canteen   10%

The Canteen department's overheads are to be reapportioned on the basis of the number of employees in the other three departments.

	Assembly	Finishing	Maintenance	Canteen
Number of employees	18	30	12	2

Complete the overhead analysis sheet below and reapportion the service departments' overheads to the production departments.

	Assembly $	Finishing $	Maintenance $	Canteen $	Total $
Total from above	17,350	23,970	18,600	6,600	66,520
Reapportion canteen	1980	3300	1320	(6,600)	6,600
Reapportion maintenance	9960	7968	(19,920)	1992	19,920

Reapportion canteen	598	996	398	(1992)	1992
Reapportion maintenance	199	159	(398)	40	398
Reapportion canteen	12	20	8	(40)	40
Reapportion maintenance	4	3	(8)	1	8
Reapportion canteen	+	1	–	–	–
Total	30,103	36,417	–	–	66,520

Solution – Reciprocal reapportionment

	Assembly $	Finishing $	Maintenance $	Canteen $	Total $
Total from above	17,350	23,970	18,600	6,600	66,520
Reapportion canteen	1,980	3,300	1,320	(6,600)	–
Reapportion maintenance	9,960	7,968	(19,920)	1,992	–
Reapportion canteen	598	996	398	(1,992)	–
Reapportion maintenance	199	159	(398)	40	–
Reapportion canteen	12	20	8	(40)	–
Reapportion maintenance	4	3	(8)	1	–
Reapportion canteen	0	1	–	(1)	–
Total	30,103	36,417	0	0	66,520

Solution – Using Equations

There is another option for calculating the total overhead in each production department. Some people will find it a quicker option but others prefer to reapportion as in the previous solution. Whichever you choose you should arrive at the same answer.

Often you will find that the data for reapportioning is given in percentages. The amount of time spent by the maintenance department servicing equipment in the other three departments has been analysed as percentages.

Assembly   50%
Finishing   40%
Canteen   10%

In this illustration we need to convert the relevant number of employees into percentages.

	Assembly	*Finishing*	*Maintenance*
Number of employees	18	30	12
Number of employees as a %	18/60 × 100 = 30%	30/60 × 100 = 50%	12/60 × 100 = 20%

Now we can produce two calculations that show the relationship between Maintenance and Canteen - the two service departments.

Maintenance = $18,600 (overhead already apportioned) + 20% of the Canteen overhead

Canteen = $6,600 (overhead already apportioned) + 10% of the Maintenance overhead

These can be shorten to:

M = 18,600 + 20%C

C = 6,600 + 10%M

Currently each formula has 2 unknowns in them – M and C. We can substitute one of the formulae into the other to calculate the unknowns:

M = 18,600 + 20%(6,600 + 10%M)

M is the only unknown

Change the % to decimals

M = 18,600 + 0.2(6,600 + 0.1M)

Remove the brackets

M = 18,600 + (0.2 × 6,600) + (0.2 × 0.1M)

M = 18,600 + 1,320 + 0.02M

Put the 'unknowns' together

$M - 0.02M = 18,600 + 1,320$

$0.98M = 19,920$

Therefore **M = 19,920/0.98 = \$20,327**

We now know M so can substitute into the formula for C

$C = 6,600 + 10\%M$

$C = 6,600 + 0.1 \times 20,327$

C = \$8,633

Final step is to then relate these amounts to the production centres:

Assembly $= 17,350 + 0.5M + 0.3C$

Assembly $= 17,350 + (0.5 \times 20,327) + (0.3 \times 8,633)$

Assembly = \$30,103

Finishing $= 23,970 + 0.4M + 0.5C$

Finishing $= 23,970 + (0.4 \times 20,327) + (0.5 \times 8,633)$

Finishing = \$36,417

Test your understanding 2

A company has three production departments, Alpha, Beta and Gamma, and two service departments, Maintenance (M) and Payroll (P). The following table shows how costs have been allocated and the relative usage of each service department by other departments.

Department	Production			Service	
	Alpha	Beta	Gamma	M	P
Costs	$3,000	$4,000	$2,000	$2,500	$2,700
Proportion M (%)	20	30	25	–	25
Proportion P (%)	25	25	30	20	–

Required:

Complete the overhead analysis sheet below and reapportion the service department overheads to the production departments using the reciprocal method.

Overhead	Alpha $	Beta $	Gamma $	M $	P $
Total overheads	3,000	4,000	2,000	2,500	2700
Reapportion M	500	750	625	(2,500)	625
	3500	4750	2625	–	3325
Reapportion P	831	831	998	665	(3325)
	4331	5581	3623	665	–
Reapportion M	133	200	166	(665)	166
	4464	5781	3789	–	166
Reapportion P	42	42	50	32	(166)
	4506	5823	3839	32	–
Reapportion M	6	10	8	(32)	8
	4512	5833	3847	–	(8)
Reapportion P	2	2	2	2	
Total	4515	5835	3849	✓	

KAPLAN PUBLISHING

5 Absorption of overheads

Bases of absorption

Once the overheads are allocated, apportioned and re-apportioned into the production departments the overheads need to be related to or absorbed into the units of product.

- Overheads can also be absorbed into cost units using the following absorption bases:
  - units produced
  - machine-hour rate (when production is machine intensive)
  - labour-hour rate (when production is labour intensive)
  - percentage of prime cost
  - percentage of direct wages.
- Production overheads are usually calculated at the beginning of an accounting period in order to determine how much cost to assign a unit before calculating a selling price
- The overhead absorption rate (OAR) is calculated as follows:

$$\text{OAR} = \frac{\textbf{Budgeted production overhead}}{\textbf{Budgeted total of absorption basis}}$$

- The absorption basis is most commonly units of a product, labour hours, or machine hours.

Departmental OARs

It is usual for a product to pass through more than one department during the production process. Each department will normally have a separate departmental OAR.

- For example, a machining department will probably use a machine-hour OAR.
- Similarly, a labour-intensive department will probably use a labour-hour OAR.
- An alternative to a departmental OAR is what is termed a blanket OAR.
- With blanket OARs, only one absorption rate is calculated for the entire factory regardless of the departments involved in production.
- Blanket OARs are also known as single factory-wide OARs.

Illustration 4 – OAR per unit

RS Ltd is a manufacturing company producing Product P, which has the following cost card.

		$
Direct labour	2 hrs @ $5 per hour	10
Direct materials	1 kg @ $5 per kg	5
Direct expenses		1
Prime cost		**16**

RS Ltd produces and sells 1,000 units in a month. RS absorbed overheads based on the number of units produced.

Based on past experience, RS Ltd estimates its monthly overheads will be as follows.

	$
Heating	3,000
Power	2,000
Maintenance	500
Total	5,500

The overhead cost allocated to each unit of Product P is $ ☐

The cost per unit of Product P is $ ☐

Monthly OH

$$\frac{£5500}{1000 \text{ units}} = £5.50$$

$$\frac{£16.00 +}{5.50}$$
$$\overline{21.50}$$

Solution

The overhead cost allocated to each unit of Product P is	$5.50
The cost per unit of Product P is	$21.50

Workings

The overhead per unit is $5,500/1,000 = $5.50 per unit.

The cost per unit is:

	$
Prime cost	16.00
Overheads	5.50
	————
Total	**21.50**
	————

Illustration 5 – OAR per hour

Ballard Ltd makes three products A, B and C. Each passes through two departments: Machining and Assembly.

Budgeted production in each department by each product

	Units		Machining	Assembly	
Product A	1,000	x	1 hr =1000	1 hr = 1000	
Product B	2,000	y	2 hrs =4000	1/2 hr = 1000	
Product C	500	x	None = 0	4 hrs = 2000	
			5000	4000	

Overheads are budgeted as follows:

Machining	Assembly
$100,000	$150,000

Complete the following.

Machining department OAR per hour = $ [   ]

Assembly department OAR per hour = $ [   ]

Blanket OAR per hour = $ [   ]

Overhead absorbed by Product B using a
separate departmental overhead rate [   ]

Solution

Machining department OAR per hour = | $20
Assembly department OAR per hour = | $37.50
Blanket OAR per hour = | $27.78
Overhead absorbed by Product B using a separate departmental overhead rate | $58.75

Workings

Product	Units	Mach-ining	Total Machining hours	Asse-mbly	Total Assembly hours	Blanket OAR
A	1,000	1 hr	1,000	1 hr	1,000	
B	2,000	2 hrs	4,000	1/2 hr	1,000	
C	500	None	0	4 hrs	2,000	
		Total hours	5,000		4,000	9,000
		Over-heads	$100,000		$150,000	$250,000
		OAR per hour	$20		$37.50	$27.78

Apply to Product:	Machining	Assembly	Total
B	2 hours @ $20 per hour = $40	½ hour @$37.50 per hour = $18.75	$40 + $18.75 = $58.75

Test your understanding 3

The Major Gnome Manufacturing Company has two departments – Moulding and Painting – and uses a single production OAR based on direct labour hours. The budget and actual data for Period 6 are given below:

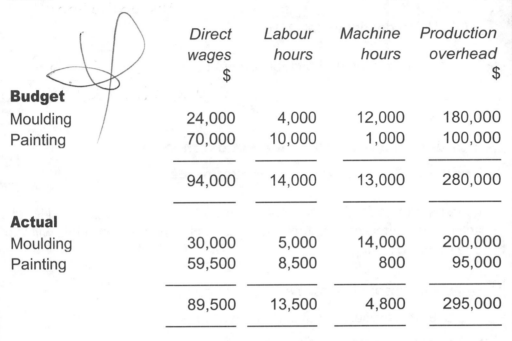

	Direct wages $	Labour hours	Machine hours	Production overhead $
Budget				
Moulding	24,000	4,000	12,000	180,000
Painting	70,000	10,000	1,000	100,000
	94,000	14,000	13,000	280,000
Actual				
Moulding	30,000	5,000	14,000	200,000
Painting	59,500	8,500	800	95,000
	89,500	13,500	4,800	295,000

During Period 6, a batch of Pixie Gnomes was made, with the following costs and times:

	Direct wages $	Labour hours	Machine hours
Moulding	726	120	460
Painting	2,490	415	38
	3,216	535	498

The direct material cost of the batch was $890.

Complete the following.

(a) Using a single blanket OAR based on labour hours:

The cost of the batch of Pixie Gnomes is $ 20

$$\frac{280,000}{14,000} \rightarrow$$

IT MAKES PERFECT SENSE TO APPROPRIATE THE MOULDING OAR TO MACHINE HOURS AND PAINTING OAR TO LABOUR HOURS.

(b) It has been suggested that appropriate departmental OARs may be more realistic. The OAR in:

180,000/12,000

(i) the moulding department is $ 15

(ii) the painting department is $ 10

100,000/10,000

(c) Using departmental OARs:

The cost of the batch of Pixie Gnomesis $ 11050

(10 x 415) + (15 x 460)

6 Under- and over-absorption of overheads

Under- and over-absorption of overheads

If the estimates for the budgeted overheads and/or the budgeted level of activity are different from the actual results for the year then this will lead to one of the following:

- under-absorption (recovery) of overheads
- over-absorption (recovery) of overheads.

Calculating an under- or over-absorption

There is a three step procedure:

Step 1 – calculate the OAR (based on budget)

$$OAR = \frac{\textbf{Budgeted overheads}}{\textbf{Budgeted level of activity}}$$

Step 2 – calculate the overhead absorbed by actual activity

Overheads absorbed = predetermined OAR × actual level of activity

Step 3 – Compare absorbed to actual

If at the end of this period, the overheads absorbed are greater than the actual overheads, then there has been an over-absorption of overheads.

If, on the other hand, the overheads absorbed are less than the actual overheads, then there has been an under-absorption of overheads.

Illustration 6 – Under- and over-absorption of overheads

The following data relate to Lola Ltd for Period 8.

	Budget	Actual
Overheads	$80,000	$90,000
Labour hours worked	20,000	22,000

Overheads were under/over-absorbed by (delete as appropriate) $ 2000

Solution

Overheads were under-absorbed by $2,000

Workings

$$OAR = \frac{\$80,000}{20,000} = \$4 \text{ per labour hour worked}$$

Overhead absorbed = 22,000 × $4 = $88,000

Actual overhead = $90,000

Under-absorbed overhead = $2,000

Test your understanding 4

The following data relate to Lola Ltd for Period 9.

	Budget	Actual
Overheads	$148,750	$146,200
Machine hours	8,500	7,928
Overheads were under-absorbed by:	$ 7460	

$$\frac{148,750}{8500} \times 7928 = 138740$$

Budget < Actual
138740 − 146200 = (7460)

Working backwards

Sometimes you may be given information relating to the actual under- or over-absorption in a period and be expected to calculate the budgeted overheads or the actual number of hours worked.

Approach to working backwards

- As long as you remember the basic formula involved in calculating under/over-absorption, you shouldn't have any problems.

- The main thing to remember is that if actual overheads are greater than absorbed overheads then we have under-absorption and any under-absorbed overheads need to be deducted from actual overheads incurred in order to calculate the actual overheads absorbed.

- Similarly, if over-absorption occurs, the over-absorbed overhead needs to be added to actual overhead in order to calculate the actual overheads absorbed.

Illustration 7 – Under- and over-absorption of overheads

A business absorbs its fixed production overhead on the basis of direct labour hours. The budgeted direct labour hours for week 24 were 4,200. During that week 4,050 direct labour hours were worked and the production overhead incurred was $16,700. The overhead was under-absorbed by $1,310.

The budgeted fixed overhead for the week (to the nearest $10) was $ [   ]

Solution

The budgeted fixed overhead for the week (to the nearest $10) was $ | 15,960 |

Working

Actual overhead	$16,700
Under-absorbed	$(1,310)
Overhead absorbed	$15,390

$$OAR = \frac{15{,}390}{4{,}050} = \$3.80 \text{ per hour}$$

Budgeted fixed overhead = 4,200 × $3.80 = $15,960

Test your understanding 5

A business absorbs its fixed overheads on the basis of machine hours worked. The following figures are available for the month of June:

Budgeted fixed overhead	$45,000
Budgeted machine hours	30,000
Actual fixed overhead	$49,000

If there was an over-absorption of overhead of $3,500, how many machine hours were worked in the month?

A   30,334

B   32,667

C   35,000

D   49,000

7 Journal and ledger entries for manufacturing overheads

Production overheads account

- Indirect production costs are debited into the production overheads account.

- Absorbed production overheads are credited out of the production overheads account and debited into the WIP account.

- Any difference between the actual and absorbed overheads is known as the under- or over-absorbed overhead and is transferred to the income statement at the end of an accounting period.

- Non-production overheads are debited to one of the following:
  - administration overheads account
  - selling overheads account
  - distribution overheads account
  - finance overheads account.

Illustration 8 – Journal and ledger entries for manufacturing

Production overheads

	$000		$000
Labour (1)	20	WIP (2)	108
Expenses (1)	92	Under-absorption (Bal. figure) (3)	9
Material (1)	5		
	117		117

Over/under-absorption of overheads

	$000		$000
Production overheads (3)	9	Income statement (4)	9
	9		9

(1) The production overheads account acts as a collecting place for all the indirect costs of a production process. All the costs are debited to this account.

(2) Production overheads are absorbed into production on the basis of actual activity. The absorbed overheads are 'credited out' of the production overheads account and transferred to the WIP account where they are added to the cost of production, and hence the cost of sales.

(3) The difference between the overheads absorbed and the overheads actually incurred is known as the under- or over-absorbed overhead. This is a balancing figure and is transferred to the Over/under-absorption of overheads account. A debit balancing amount in the production overheads accounts is an over-absorption and a credit balancing amount is an under-absorption.

(4) At the end of an accounting period, the balance on the over/under-absorption account is transferred to the income statement where it is written off (under-absorbed overhead) or increases profit (over-absorbed overhead).

Test your understanding 6

Transaction	Debit which account?	Credit which account?
Indirect materials issued from stores		
Indirect wages analysed in the labour account		
Indirect expenses purchased (cash)		
Production overheads absorbed into the cost of production		
Direct materials issued from stores		

8 Chapter summary

Recap of direct and indirect expenses
- **Direct expenses are part of the prime cost of a product**
- **Indirect expenses are known as overheads**

Journal and ledger entries for manufacturing overheads	**Accounting for overheads**	Relating non-production overheads to cost units

Allocation and apportionment
- Allocation charges overheads directly to specific departments
- If overheads relate to more than one specific department they must be apportioned (shared) between departments
- Apportioned fixed production overheads include: rent, rates, heating and electricity costs

Reapportionment of service cost centre costs to production cost centres
Reapportionment involves sharing out the fixed production overheads of service cost centres betweerp roduction cost centres

Basic method – one service department does work for another, but not vice versa	**Production overhead absorption**	Reciprocal method – both service departments do work for each other

Appropriate bases for absorption
- Machine-hour rate
- Labour-hour rate
- Percentage of prime cost
- Percentage of direct wages

Under- and over-absorption of overheads
If either or both of the estimates for budgeted overheads or budgeted level of activity are different from actual results then this will lead to under-or-over-absorption (recovery) of overheads

KAPLAN PUBLISHING

Test your understanding answers

Test your understanding 1

Answer C

Allocated and apportioned overheads $12,000

Add: reapportionment of S1: 60% × $9,500 = $5,700

Add: reapportionment of S2 overhead apportioned to S1: $8000 × 30% × 60% = $1,440

Add: reapportionment of S2: 35% × $8,000 = $2,800

Total = $21,940

Test your understanding 2

Overhead	Alpha $	Beta $	Gamma $	M $	P $
Total overheads	3,000	4,000	2,000	2,500	2,700
Reapportion M	500 (20%)	750 (30%)	625 (25%)	(2,500)	625 (25%)
					3,325
Reapportion P	831 (25%)	831 (25%)	998 (30%)	665 (20%)	(3,325)
Reapportion M	133 (20%)	200 (30%)	166 (25%)	(665)	166 (25%)
Reapportion P	41 (25%)	42 (25%)	50 (30%)	33 (20%)	(166)
Reapportion M	7 (20%)	10 (30%)	8 (25%)	(33)	8 (25%)
Reapportion P	3 (25%)	2 (25%)	3 (30%)		(8)
Total	4,515	5,835	3,850		

Alternative answer (using equations)

M = 2,500 + 20% P
and
P = 2,700 + 25% M

Substitute the equation for P into the equation for M to have one unknown:

M = 2,500 + 20% (2,700 + 25% M)

Turn the percentages to decimals and multiply out the brackets:

M = 2,500 + (0.2 × 2,700) + (0.2 × 0.25M)
M = 2,500 + 540 + 0.05M

Put the unknowns together:

M – 0.05M = 2,500 + 540
0.95M = 3,040

Calculate was M equals:

M = 3,040 / 0.95
M = 3,200

Go to original equations to calculate P:

P = 2,700 + 25% M
P = 2,700 + 0.25 × 3,200
P = 3,500

Using the percentages in the original data for Alpha, Beta and Gamma we can calculate how much overhead each department receives:

Alpha = 3,000 + (20% × 3,200) + (25% × 3,500)
Alpha = $4,515

Beta = 4,000 + (30% × 3,200) + (25% × 3,500)
Beta = $5,835

Gamma = 2,000 + (25% × 3,200) + (30% × 3,500)
Gamma = $3,850

Test your understanding 3

(a) Using a single blanket OAR based on labour hours, the cost of the batch of Pixie Gnomes is:

$14,806

It has been suggested that appropriate departmental OARs may be more realistic.

(b) The OAR in:

   (i) the moulding department is $15

   (ii) the painting department is $10

(c) Using departmental absorption rates, the cost of the batch of Pixie Gnomes is

$15,156

Workings

Blanket OAR = $\dfrac{\$280,000}{14,000}$ = $20 per labour hour

(a) Cost of batch of Pixie Gnomes

	$
Direct materials	890
Direct labour	3,216
Overheads (535 hours @ $20 per hour)	10,700
TOTAL COST	14,806

(b)

	(i) Moulding	(ii) Painting
Budgeted overheads	$180,000	$100,000
Budgeted hours	12,000 machine hours	10,000 labour hours
OAR	$15 per machine hour	$10 per labour hour

(c) Cost of a batch of Pixie Gnomes using separate departmental OARs

	$
Direct materials	890
Direct labour	3,216
Moulding overheads (460 × $15)	6,900
Painting overheads (415 × $10)	4,150
TOTAL COST	15,156

Test your understanding 4

Overheads were under-absorbed by: $7,460

$$OAR = \frac{\$148,750}{8,500} = \$17.50 \text{ per machine hour}$$

Overhead absorbed	= 7,928 × $17.50 = $138,740
Actual overhead	= $146,200
Under-absorbed overhead	= $7,460

Test your understanding 5

Answer C

35,000 machine hours were worked in the month.

Workings

$$\text{OAR} = \frac{\$45,000}{30,000} = \$1.50 \text{ per hour}$$

Actual overhead	$49,000
Over-absorbed overhead	$3,500
Absorbed overhead	$52,500

$$\text{Machine hours worked} = \frac{\text{Overheads absorbed}}{\text{Overhead absorption rate}}$$

$$= \frac{\$52,000}{\$1.50}$$

$$= 35,000 \text{ hours}$$

Test your understanding 6

Transaction	Debit which account?	Credit which account?
Indirect materials issued from stores	Production overheads account	Material inventory account
Indirect wages analysed in the labour account	Production overheads account	Labour account
Indirect expenses purchased (cash)	Production overheads account	Bank
Production overheads absorbed into the cost of production	WIP account	Production overheads account
Direct materials issued from stores	WIP account	Material inventory account

Marginal and absorption costing

Chapter learning objectives

Upon completion of this chapter you will be able to:

- explain the importance of, and apply, the concept of contribution

- demonstrate and discuss the effect of absorption and marginal costing on inventory valuation and profit determination

- calculate profit or loss under absorption and marginal costing

- reconcile the profits or losses calculated under absorption and marginal costing

- describe the advantages and disadvantages of absorption and marginal costing

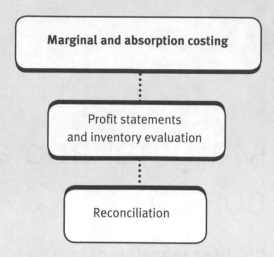

1 Introduction

Marginal and absorption costing are two different ways of valuing the cost of goods sold and finished goods in inventory. With absorption costing fixed overhead are treated as a product cost and an amount is assigned to each unit. In marginal costing fixed overheads are treated as period costs and are charged in full against the profit for the period.

2 Marginal costing

The **marginal** cost of a unit of inventory is the total of the **variable** costs required to produce the unit (the marginal cost). This includes direct materials, direct labour, direct expenses and variable overheads.

No fixed overheads are included in the inventory valuation; they are treated as a period cost and deducted in full lower down the income statement.

 The marginal production cost is the cost of one unit of product or service which would be avoided if that unit were not produced, or which would increase if one extra unit were produced.

Marginal costing is also the principal costing technique used in decision making. The key reason for this is that the marginal costing approach allows management's attention to be focused on the changes which result from the decision under consideration.

The contribution concept

The contribution concept lies at the heart of marginal costing. Contribution can be calculated as follows:

Contribution = Sales price – Variable costs

Illustration 1 – The concept of contribution

The following information relates to a company that makes a single product, a specialist lamp, which is used in the diamond-cutting business.

The cost card for the lamp is as follows.	$	$
Sales price		600
Direct materials	200	
Direct labour	150	
Direct expenses	Nil	
	―――	
Prime cost	350	
Variable production overheads	50	
Fixed production overheads	100	
	―――	
Total cost	500	

Fixed costs have been estimated to be $120,000 based on a production level of 1,200 lamps.

Let us look at the costs and revenues involved when different volumes of lamps are sold.

		Sales of 1,200 lamps		Sales of 1,500 lamps
		$		$
Sales revenue		720,000		900,000
Direct materials	240,000		300,000	
Direct labour	180,000		225,000	
Direct expenses	Nil		Nil	
	―――		―――	
Prime cost	420,000		525,000	
Variable production overheads	60,000		75,000	
Marginal cost of production		**480,000**		**600,000**
CONTRIBUTION		**240,000**		**300,000**
Fixed production overheads		120,000		120,000
Total profit		120,000		180,000
Contribution per unit		**200**		**200**
Profit per unit		100		120

- We can see that the profit per lamp has increased from **$100** when 1,200 lamps are sold to **$120** when 1,500 lamps are sold.

- This is because all of the variable costs (direct materials, direct labour, direct expenses and variable overheads) have increased but the fixed costs have remained constant at $120,000.

Based on what we have seen above, the idea of profit is not a particularly useful one as it depends on how many units are sold. For this reason, the contribution concept is frequently employed by management accountants.

- Contribution gives an idea of how much 'money' there is available to 'contribute' towards paying for the fixed costs of the organisation.
- At varying levels of output and sales, contribution per unit is constant.
- At varying levels of output and sales, profit per unit varies.
- **Total contribution = Contribution per unit × Sales volume.**
- **Profit = Total contribution – Fixed overheads**.

Test your understanding 1

Buhner Ltd makes only one product, the cost card of which is:

	$
Direct materials	3
Direct labour	6
Variable production overhead	2
Fixed production overhead	4
Variable selling cost	5

The selling price of one unit is $21.

Budgeted fixed overheads are based on budgeted production of 5,000 units. Opening inventory was 1,000 units and closing inventory was 4,000 units.

Sales during the period were 3,000 units and actual fixed production overheads incurred were $25,000.

(a) Calculate the total contribution earned during the period.

(b) Calculate the total profit or loss for the period.

3 Absorption costing

Absorption costing values each unit of inventory at the cost incurred to **produce** the unit. This includes an amount added to the cost of each unit to represent the fixed **production** overheads incurred by that product. The amount added to each unit is based on estimates made at the start of the period.

To calculate a fixed production cost per unit the budgeted fixed production costs are divided by the budgeted activity. The calculation of the fixed cost per unit was looked at in more detail in the previous chapter – Accounting for overheads.

Absorption costing is a method of building up a full product cost which adds direct costs and a proportion of production overhead costs by means of one or a number of overhead absorption rates.

4 The effect of absorption and marginal costing on inventory valuation and profit determination

Absorption and marginal costing

Marginal costing values inventory at the total variable production cost of a unit of product.

Absorption costing values inventory at the full production cost of a unit of product.

- Inventory values will therefore be different at the beginning and end of a period under marginal and absorption costing.

- If inventory values are different, then this will have an effect on profits reported in the income statement in a period.

- Profits determined using marginal costing principles will therefore be different to those using absorption costing principles.

Absorption costing income statement

In order to be able to prepare income statements under absorption costing, you need to be able to complete the following proforma.

Absorption costing income statement

	$	$
Sales		X
Less Cost of sales:		
Opening inventory	X	
Variable cost of production	X	
Fixed overhead absorbed	X	
less closing inventory	(X)	
		(X)
		X
(under)/over-absorption		(X) / X
Gross profit		X
Less Non-production costs		(X)
Profit/loss		X

- **Valuation of inventory** – opening and closing inventory are valued at full production cost under absorption costing.

- **Under/over-absorbed overhead** – an adjustment for under or over absorption of overheads is necessary in absorption costing income statements.

Marginal costing income statement

In order to be able to prepare income statements under marginal costing, you need to be able to complete the following proforma.

Marginal costing income statement

	$	$
Sales		X
Less Cost of sales:		
Opening inventory	X	
Variable cost of production	X	
Less Closing inventory	(X)	
		(X)
		X
Less Other variable costs		(X)
Contribution		X
Less fixed costs		(X)
Profit/loss		X

- **Valuation of inventory** – opening and closing inventory are valued at marginal (variable) cost under marginal costing.

- The **fixed costs** actually incurred are deducted from contribution earned in order to determine the profit for the period.

Illustration 2 – Impact of inventory on profit

A company commenced business on 1 March making one product only, the cost card of which is as follows:

	$
Direct labour	5
Direct material	8
Variable production overhead	2
Fixed production overhead	5
	—
Standard production cost	20
	—

The fixed production overhead figure has been calculated on the basis of a budgeted normal output of 36,000 units per annum. The fixed production overhead incurred in March was $15,000 each month.

Selling, distribution and administration expenses are: *PRODUCTION COSTS* *NON*

Fixed	$10,000 per month
Variable	15% of the sales value

The selling price per unit is $50 and the number of units produced and sold were:

	March (units)
Production	2,000
Sales	1,500

Prepare the absorption costing and marginal costing income statements for March.

Absorption costing income statement – March

	$	$
Sales		
Less Cost of sales:		
Opening inventory		
Variable cost of production		
Fixed overhead absorbed		
Closing inventory		
(under)/over-absorption		
Gross profit		
		___
Less non-production costs		
Profit/loss		
		___

Value of closing inventory at the end of March (using absorption costing) $ _____

Marginal costing income statement – March

	$	$
Sales		
Less Cost of sales:		
Opening inventory		
Variable cost of production		
Less Closing inventory		___
Less Other variable costs		
Contribution		___
Less Fixed costs (actually incurred)		
Less non-production costs		
		___
Profit/loss		

Value of closing inventory at the end of March (using marginal costing) $ _____

Solution

Absorption costing income statement – March

	$	$
Sales		75,000
Less Cost of sales: (valued at full production cost)		
Opening inventory	–	
Variable cost of production (2,000 × $15)	30,000	
Fixed overhead absorbed (2,000 × $5)	10,000	
Less Closing inventory (500 × $20)	(10,000)	
		(30,000)
		45,000
(Under) / over-absorption (W1)		(5,000)
Gross profit		40,000
Less Non-Production Costs (W2)		(21,250)
Profit / loss		18,750

Value of closing inventory at the end of March (using absorption costing)	$10,000

Workings

(W1)

March	$
Overheads absorbed (2,000 × $5)	10,000
Overheads incurred	15,000
Under-absorption on overheads	5,000

(W2)

Non-production costs
Fixed = 10,000
Variable = 15% × $75,000 = $11,250
Total = $(10,000 + 11,250) = $21,250

Marginal costing income statement – March

	$	$
Sales		75,000
Less Cost of sales: (marginal production costs only)		
Opening inventory	–	
Variable cost of production (2,000 × $15)	30,000	
less Closing inventory (500 × $15)	(7,500)	
		(22,500)
		52,500
Less other variable costs (15% × $75,000)		(11,250)
Contribution		41,250
Less Fixed costs (actually incurred) $(15,000 + 10,000)		(25,000)
Profit / loss		16,250

Value of closing inventory at the end of March (using marginal costing)	$7,500

Test your understanding 2

Duo Ltd makes and sells one product, the Alpha. The following information is available for period 3:

	Alpha
Production (units)	2,500
Sales (units)	2,300
Opening inventory (units)	0

Financial data:	Alpha
	$
Unit selling price	90
Unit cost:	
direct materials	15
direct labour	18
variable production overheads	12
fixed production overheads	30
variable selling overheads	1

Fixed production overheads for the period were $52,500 and fixed administration overheads were $13,500.

Required:

(a) Prepare an income statement for period 3 based on marginal costing principles.

(b) Prepare an income statement for period 3 based on absorption costing principles.

Reconciling profits reported under the different methods

When inventory levels increase or decrease during a period then profits differ under absorption and marginal costing.

- If inventory levels increase, absorption costing gives the higher profit.

  This is because fixed overheads held in closing inventory are carried forward (thereby reducing cost of sales) to the next accounting period instead of being written off in the current accounting period (as a period cost, as in marginal costing).

- If inventory levels decrease, marginal costing gives the higher profit.

  This is because fixed overhead brought forward in opening inventory is released, thereby increasing cost of sales and reducing profits.

- If inventory levels are constant, both methods give the same profit.

Illustration 3 – Reconciling profits

A company commenced business on 1 March making one product only, the cost card of which is as follows.

	$
Direct labour	5
Direct material	8
Variable production overhead	2
Fixed production overhead	5
Full production cost	20

- Marginal cost of production = $(5 + 8 + 2) = $15

- Full cost of production = $20 (as above)

- Difference in cost of production = $5 which is the fixed production overhead element of the full production cost.

- This means that each unit of opening and closing inventory will be valued at $5 more under absorption costing.

The number of units produced and sold was as follows.

	March (units)
Production	2,000
Sales	1,500

Closing inventory at the end of March is the difference between the number of units produced and the number of units sold, i.e. 500 units (2,000 – 1,500).

- Profit for March under absorption costing = $18,750 (as calculated in **Illustration 2**).

- Profit for March under marginal costing = $16,250 (as calculated in **Illustration 2**).

- Difference in profits = $18,750 – $16,250 = $2,500.

- This difference can be analysed as being due to the fixed overhead held in inventory, i.e. 500 units of inventory 'holding' $5 fixed overhead per unit.

- 500 × $5 = $2,500 which is the difference between the profit in the profit statements under the different costing methods for March.

In an exam question you may be told the profit under either marginal or absorption costing and be asked to calculate the alternative profit for the information provided.

There is a short cut to reconciling the profits:

Absorption costing profit		18,750
(Opening inventory – closing inventory) × OAR	(0–500) × 5	–2,500
		————
Marginal costing profit		16,250

Test your understanding 3

(a) In a period where opening inventory was 5,000 units and closing inventory was 3,000 units, a company had a profit of $92,000 using absorption costing. If the fixed overhead absorption rate was $9 per unit, calculate the profit using marginal costing.

(b) When opening inventory was 8,500 litres and closing inventory was 6,750 litres, a company had a profit of $62,100 using marginal costing. The fixed overhead absorption rate was $3 per litre. Calculate the profit using absorption costing.

5 The advantages and disadvantages of absorption and marginal costing

Advantages of marginal costing	Advantages of absorption costing
• Contribution per unit is constant unlike profit per unit which varies with changes in sales volumes. • There is no under or over absorption of overheads (and hence no adjustment is required in the income statement). • Fixed costs are a period cost and are charged in full to the period under consideration. • Marginal costing is useful in the decision-making process. • It is simple to operate.	• Absorption costing includes an element of fixed overheads in inventory values (in accordance with IAS 2). • Analysing under/over absorption of overheads is a useful exercise in controlling costs of an organisation. • In small organisations, absorbing overheads into the costs of products is the best way of estimating job costs and profits on jobs.

- The main disadvantages of marginal costing are that closing inventory is not valued in accordance with IAS 2 principles and that fixed production overheads are not 'shared' out between units of production, but written off in full instead.

- The main disadvantages of absorption costing are that it is more complex to operate than marginal costing and it does not provide any useful information for decision making (like marginal costing does).

6 Chapter summary

The effect of absorption and marginal costing on inventory value and profit determination

Inventory up:
AC----→MC profits

Inventory down:
AC←----MC profits

MARGINAL AND ABSORBTION COSTING

The concept of contribution

Contribution = Sales Price – Variable costs

Widely used in decision-making process

The advantages and disadvantages of absorption and marginal costing

Each costing method has a number of advantages and disadvantages

Test your understanding answers

Test your understanding 1

(a) Total variable costs = $(3 + 6 + 2 + 5) = $16

Contribution per unit (selling price less total variable costs) = $21 – $16 = $5

Total contribution earned = 3,000 × $5 = $15,000

(b) Total profit/(loss) = Total contribution – Fixed production overheads incurred

= $(15,000 – 25,000)

= $(10,000)

Test your understanding 2

(a) Marginal costing

	$000	$000
Sales		207
Opening inventory	–	
Variable production cost (2,500 × 45)	112.5	
Closing inventory (200 × 45)	(9)	
		(103.5)
		103.5
Variable selling costs		(2.3)
Contribution		101.2
Fixed production costs		(52.5)
Fixed administration costs		(13.5)
Profit		35.2

(b) Absorption costing

	$000	$000
Sales		207
Opening inventory	–	
Full production costs		
(2,500 × 75)	187.5	
Closing inventory	(15)	
(200 × 75)	———	
		(172.5)
		———
		34.5
Over-absorbed overhead (working)		22.5
		———
Gross profit		57
Less: non-production overheads		
variable selling overheads		(2.3)
fixed administration overheads		(13.5)
		———
Profit		41.2
		———

Working

	$
Overhead absorbed = (2,500 × $30)	75,000
Overheads incurred =	52,000
	———
Over-absorbed overhead	22,500

Test your understanding 3

(a)

Absorption costing profit =	$92,000
Difference in profit = change in inventory x fixed cost per unit = 2,000 × $9 =	$18,000
Marginal costing profit =	$110,000

Since inventory levels have fallen in the period, marginal costing shows the higher profit figure, therefore marginal costing profit will be $18,000 higher than the absorption costing profit, i.e. $110,000.

(b)

Marginal costing profit	$62,100
Difference in profit = change in inventory × fixed cost per unit = (8,500 – 6,750) × $3	$(5,250)
	———
Absorption costing profit	$56,850
	———

Inventory levels have fallen in the period and therefore marginal costing profits will be higher than absorption costing profits. Absorption costing profit is therefore $5,250 less than the marginal costing profit.

Job, batch and process costing

Chapter learning objectives

Upon completion of this chapter you will be able to:

- describe the characteristics of job costing, batch costing, process costing and describe situations in which each would be appropriate

- prepare cost records and accounts in job and batch costing situations

- establish job and batch costs from given information

- for process costing explain the concepts of normal and abnormal losses and abnormal gains

- calculate the cost per unit of process outputs

- prepare process accounts involving normal and abnormal losses and abnormal gains

- calculate and explain the concept of equivalent units

- apportion process costs between work remaining in process and transfers out of a process using the weighted average and FIFO method (Note: situations involving work-in-progress (WIP) and losses in the same process are excluded)

- prepare process accounts in situations where work remains incomplete

- prepare process accounts where losses and gains are identified at different stages of the process

- distinguish between by-products and joint products

- value by-products and joint products at the point of separation

- prepare process accounts in situations where by-products and/or joint products occur.

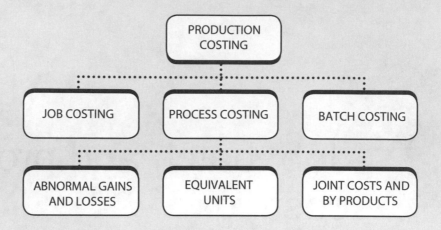

1 Different types of production

Costing systems

- **Specific order costing** is the costing system used when the work done by an organisation consists of **separately identifiable jobs** or **batches**.

- **Continuous operation costing** is the costing method used when goods or services are produced as a direct result of a **sequence of continuous operations or processes**, for example process and service costing.

Job costing

Job costing is a form of specific order costing and it is used when a customer orders a specific job to be done. Each job is priced separately and each job is unique.

- The main aim of job costing is to identify the costs associated with completing the order and to record them carefully.

- Individual jobs are given a unique job number and the costs involved in completing the job are recorded on a job cost sheet or job card.

- The selling prices of jobs are calculated by adding a certain amount of profit to the cost of the job.

- Job costing could be used by landscape gardeners where the job would be to landscape a garden; or decorators where the job would be to decorate a room.

Illustration 1 – Job costing

Individual job costs are recorded on a job card similar to the one shown below.

JOB CARD

Customer	Green & Co. Ltd		Job No: 342
Description	Transfer machine	Promised delivery date	3.11.X1
Date commenced	25.9.X1	Actual delivery date	13.11.X1
Price quoted	$2,400		
Despatch note no:	7147		

	Materials estimate $1,250		Labour estimate $100		Overhead estimate $176		Other charges estimate $25	
Date Ref					Hourly rate $11			
	Cost $	Total $	Hrs	Total $	Cost $	Total $	Cost $	Total $
20X1 b/f		1,200	17	110		187		13
6 Nov Material Requisition 1714	182	1,382						
7 Nov Consultant's test fee							10	23
8 Nov Material Requisition 1937	19	1,401						
9 Nov Material Returns Note	(26)	1,375						
10 Nov Labour analysis			5	138	55	242		

Summary

	$
Materials	1,375
Labour	138
Overhead	242
Other charges	23
	1,778
Invoice price	
(invoice number 7147 dated 12.12.X1)	2,400
Profit	622

The flow of documents in a job costing system is shown as follows:

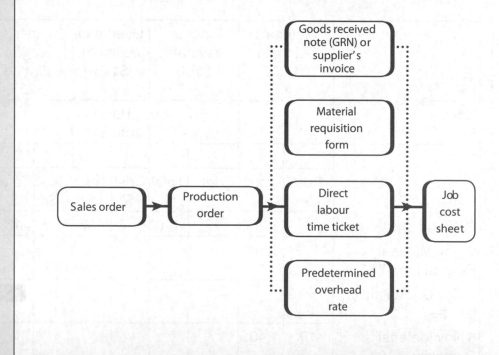

Batch costing

Batch costing is also a form of specific order costing. It is very similar to job costing.

- Within each batch are a number of identical units but each batch will be different.

- Each batch is a separately identifiable cost unit which is given a batch number in the same way that each job is given a job number.

- Costs can then be collected for each batch number. For example materials requisitions will be coded to a batch number to ensure that the cost of materials used is charged to the correct batch.

- When the batch is completed the unit cost of individual items in the batch is found by dividing the total batch cost by the number of items in the batch.

$$\text{Cost per unit in batch} = \frac{\textbf{Total production cost of batch}}{\textbf{Number of units in batch}}$$

- Batch costing is very common in the engineering component industry, footwear and clothing manufacturing industries where identical items are produced; for example a batch could contain 100 pairs of size 6 trainers for a retailer outlet.

- The selling prices of batches are calculated in the same ways as the selling prices of jobs, i.e. by adding a profit to the cost of the batch.

Test your understanding 1

Which of the following are characteristics of job costing?

(i)   Homogenous products.

(ii) Customer-driven production.

(iii) Production can be completed within a single accounting period.

A   (i) only

B   (i) and (ii) only

C   (ii) and (iii) only

D   (i) and (iii) only

Illustration 2 – Costing for job and batch costing

Jetprint Ltd specialises in printing advertising leaflets and is in the process of preparing its price list. The most popular requirement is for a folded leaflet made from a single sheet of A4 paper. From past records and budgeted figures, the following data has been estimated for a typical batch of 10,000 leaflets:

Artwork	$65
Machine set up	4 hours @ $22 per hour
Paper	$12.50 per 1,000 sheets
Ink and consumables	$40
Printer's wages 4 hours at	$8 per hour

Note: Printer's wages vary with volume.

General fixed overheads are $15,000 per period during which a total of 600 labour hours are expected to be worked.

Required:

(a) Calculate the job cost for 10,000 leaflets.

(b) Calculate the job cost for 20,000 leaflets.

Solution

	(a) *Producing 10,000 leaflets*	(b) *Producing 20,000 leaflets*
	$	$
Artwork	65	65
Machine set up (4 hours @ $22)	88	88
Paper (variable)	125	250
Ink and consumables (variable)	40	80
Printer's wages ($8 per hour)	32	64
	———	———
Production cost	350	547
General fixed overheads (W1)	100	200
	———	———
Absorption cost	450	747
	———	———

Workings

Artwork and machine set up are only required once at the start of the production run and are not batch size dependant therefore they are fixed costs.

(W1) Overhead absorption rate = $15,000 ÷ 600 = $25 per hour

For 10,000 leaflets, general fixed overheads = 4 hours × $25 = $100

For 20,000 leaflets, general fixed overheads = 8 hours × $25 = $200

Test your understanding 2

A business has a job costing system and prices jobs using total absorption costing. The cost estimates for Job 264 are as follows:

Direct materials 50 kg @ $4 per kg

Direct labour 30 hours @ $9 per hour

Variable production overhead $6 per direct labour hour

Fixed production overheads are budgeted as $80,000 and are absorbed on the basis of direct labour hours. The total budgeted direct labour hours for the period are 20,000.

Other overheads are recovered at the rate of $40 per job.

Calculate the total job cost for Job 264.

2 Process costing

Introduction

Process costing is a costing method used when mass production of many identical products takes place, for example, the production of bars of chocolate, cans of soup or tins of paint. It is an example of continuous operation costing.

- One of the distinguishing features of process costing is that all the products in a process are identical and indistinguishable from each other.

- For this reason, an average cost per unit is calculated for each process.

$$\text{Average cost per unit} = \frac{\text{Net costs of inputs}}{\text{Expected output}}$$

- Expected output is what we expect to get out of the process.

- Another main feature of process costing is that the output of one process forms the material input of the next process.

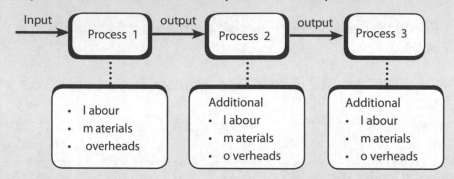

- Also, where there is closing work-in-progress (WIP) at the end of one period, this forms the opening WIP at the beginning of the next period.

The details of process costs and units are recorded in a process account which shows (in very general terms) the materials, labour and overheads input to the process and the materials output at the end of the process.

Illustration 3 – A process account

Process 2 Account

	Units	$		Units	$
Input transferred from Process 1	1,000	24,000	Output transferred to Process 3	1,000	
Additional raw materials		5,000			
Direct labour		4,000			
Departmental overheads		3,000			
	1,000			1,000	

Calculate the average cost per unit in Process 2 and complete the Process 2 Account shown above.

Solution

$$\text{Average cost per unit} = \frac{\text{Net costs of input}}{\text{Expected output}}$$

Net costs of input = $24,000 + $5,000 + $4,000 + $3,000 = $36,000

Expected output = 1,000 units

$$\text{Average cost per unit in Process 2} = \frac{\$36,000}{1,000} = \$36 \text{ per unit}$$

Process 2 Account

	Units	$		Units	$
Transfer from Process 1	1,000	24,000	Transfer to Process 3	1,000	36,000
Additional raw materials		5,000			
Direct labour		4,000			
Departmental overheads		3,000			
	1,000	36,000		1,000	36,000

Note that the units completed in Process 1 form the material input into Process 2 and that the units completed in Process 2 form the material input into Process 3.

3 Process costing with losses and gains

Normal losses

Sometimes in a process, the total of the input units may differ from the total of the output units.

- Losses may occur due to the evaporation or wastage of materials and this may be an expected part of the process.

- Losses may sometimes be sold and generate a revenue which is generally referred to as scrap proceeds or scrap value.

- **Normal loss** is the loss that is **expected** in a process and it is often expressed as a percentage of the materials input to the process.

Illustration 4 – Normal losses

The following data relates to Process 1.

Materials input   – 1,000 units costing $10,000
Labour costs   – $8,000
Departmental overheads – $6,000

Normal loss is 4% of input.

Actual output = 960 units

Required:

Calculate the average cost per unit in Process 1 and produce the process account.

Solution

Process 1 Account

	Units	$		Units	$
Raw materials	1,000	10,000	Normal loss	40	0
Direct labour		8,000			
Departmental overheads		6,000	Transfer to Finished goods (W2)	960	24,000
	1,000	24,000		**1,000**	24,000

(W1)

$$\text{Average cost per unit} = \frac{\text{Net cost of inputs}}{\text{Expected output}}$$

Where:

Net cost of inputs = $24,000
Units input = 1,000 units
Normal loss = 4% of 1,000 units = 40 units
Therefore expected output is 1,000 units – 40 units = 960 units

$$\text{Average cost per unit} = \frac{\$24,000}{960} = \$25 \text{ per unit}$$

(W2)

Units transferred to finished goods are valued at the average cost per unit, $25.

Value of goods transferred = 960 × $25 = $24,000

Normal loss and scrap value

If normal loss is sold as scrap the revenue is used to reduce the input costs of the process.

(1) If normal loss is sold as scrap then the formula for calculating the average cost of the units output does not really change – simply the costs of inputs are reduced by the revenue received from the scrap that is sold i.e. giving the **net** cost.

$$\textbf{Average cost per unit} = \frac{\textbf{Net cost of inputs}}{\textbf{Expected output}}$$

$$\textbf{Average cost per unit} = \frac{\textbf{Total cost of inputs – Scrap value of normal loss}}{\textbf{Expected output}}$$

(2) If normal loss has a scrap value, it is valued in the process account at this value.

(3) If normal loss does not have a scrap value, it is valued in the process account as $Nil.

Illustration 5 – Normal losses and scrap value

The following data relates to Process 1.

Materials input	– 1,000 units costing $10,000
Labour costs	– $8,000
Departmental overheads	– $6,000

Normal loss is 4% of input and is sold as scrap for $12 per unit.

Actual output = 960 units

Required:

Calculate the average cost per unit in Process 1 and produce the process account and the scrap account.

Solution

Average cost per unit in Process 1 (W2) = $24.50

Process 1 Account

	Units	$		Units	$
Raw materials	1,000	10,000	Normal loss (W1)	40	480
Direct labour		8,000			
Departmental overheads		6,000	Transfer to Finished goods (W3)	960	23,520
	1,000	24,000		1,000	24,000

Scrap Account

	$		$
Process 1	480	Cash	480
	480		480

Workings

(W1) Normal loss = 4% × 1,000 = 40 units

Scrap value of normal loss = 40 × $12 = $480

This amount is credited to the process account and debited to the scrap account and used to reduce the cost of inputs to the process.

(W2)

$$\text{Average cost per unit} = \frac{\text{Net costs of input}}{\text{Expected output}}$$

$$\text{Average cost per unit} = \frac{\$24,000 - \$480 \text{ (W1)}}{1,000 - 40 \text{ (W1)}}$$

$$= \frac{\$23,520}{960} = \$24.50 \text{ per unit}$$

(W3)

Units transferred to finished goods are valued at the average cost per unit, $24.50.

Value of goods transferred = 960 × $24.50 = $23,520

Abnormal losses and gains

Normal loss is the expected loss in a process. If the loss in a process is different to what we are expecting then we have an abnormal loss or an abnormal gain in the process.

 Abnormal loss is more loss than expected

 Abnormal gain is less loss than expected

Abnormal losses and gains and the process account

- The costs associated with producing abnormal losses or gains are not absorbed into the cost of good output.

- Abnormal loss and gain units are valued at the same cost as units of good output in the process account.

Abnormal losses and gains and the scrap account

Losses and gains are transferred from the process account to the abnormal loss/gain account.

If there is no scrap value the losses or gains are transferred to the Income statement at the value given in the process account.

If there is a scrap value then:

- the abnormal loss is transferred from the abnormal loss/gain account to the scrap account at the scrap value. The cost of the loss transferred to the Income statement is reduced by the scrap value of these loss units and the cash received for scrap sales is increased by the same amount.

- the abnormal gain is transferred from the abnormal loss/gain account to the scrap account at the scrap value. The saving associated with the gain is transferred to the Income statement but it also reduces the cash received for the scrap sale.

Illustration 6 – Abnormal losses with no scrap value

The following data relates to Process 1.

Materials input	– 1,000 units costing $10,000
Labour costs	– $8,000

Departmental overheads – $6,000

Normal loss is 4% of input which cannot be sold.

Actual output = 944 units

Required:

Calculate the average cost per unit in Process 1 and produce the process account and the abnormal gains and losses account.

Solution

Process 1 Account

	Units	$		Units	$
Raw materials	1,000	10,000	Normal loss (W1)	40	0
Direct labour		8,000	Abnormal loss (W3)	16	400
Departmental overheads		6,000	Transfer to Finished goods (W4)	944	23,600
	1,000	24,000		1,000	24,000

Average cost per unit in Process 1 (W2) = $25.00

Abnormal gains and losses account

	$		$
Process 1	400	Income statement	400
	400		400

Workings:

(W1) Normal loss = 4% × 1,000 = 40 units

(W2)

$$\text{Average cost per unit} = \frac{\text{Net costs of input}}{\text{Expected output}}$$

$$\text{Average cost per unit} = \frac{\$24,000}{1,000 - 40}$$

$$= \frac{\$24,000}{960} = \$25.00 \text{ per unit}$$

(W3) Actual output   = 944 units

Abnormal loss = expected output – actual output = 960 – 944 = 16 units

Abnormal loss is valued at the same cost as good output, i.e. $25.00 per unit.

Abnormal loss value = 16 × $25.00 = $400

(W4) Value of units transferred to finished goods = 944 × $25.00 = $23,600

Illustration 7 – Abnormal losses with scrap value

The following data relates to Process 1.

Materials input   – 1,000 units costing $10,000

Labour costs   – $8,000

Departmental overheads – $6,000

Normal loss is 4% of input and is sold as scrap for $12 per unit.

Actual output = 944 units

Required:

Calculate the average cost per unit in Process 1 and produce the process account, abnormal gains and losses account and the scrap account .

Process 1 Account

	Units	$		Units	$
Raw materials	1,000	10,000	Normal loss (W1)	40	480
Direct labour		8,000	Abnormal loss (W3)	16	392
Departmental overheads		6,000	Transfer to Finished goods (W4)	944	23,128
	1,000	24,000		1,000	24,000

Average cost per unit in Process 1 (W2) = $24.50

Abnormal gains and losses account

	$		$
Process 1	392	Scrap (W5)	192
		Income statement	200
	392		392

Scrap account

	$		$
Process 1 (normal loss)	480	Cash (56 × $12)	672
Abnormal gain and loss	192		
	672		672

Workings:

(W1) Normal loss = 4% × 1,000 = 40 units

Scrap value of normal loss = 40 × $12 = $480

(W2)

$$\text{Average cost per unit} = \frac{\text{Net costs of input}}{\text{Expected output}}$$

$$\text{Average cost per unit} = \frac{\$24,000 - \$480 \ (\text{W1})}{1,000 - 40 \ (\text{W1})}$$

$$= \frac{\$23,520}{960} = \$24.50 \text{ per unit}$$

(W3) Actual output = 944 units

Abnormal loss= expected output – actual output = 960 – 944 = 16 units

Abnormal loss is valued at the same cost as good output, i.e. $24.50 per unit

Abnormal loss value = 16 × $24.50 = $392

(W4) Value of units transferred to finished goods = 944 × $24.50 = $23,128

(W5) Value of abnormal loss transferred to the scrap account = 16 × $12 = $192

Illustration 8 – Abnormal gains with no scrap value

The following data relates to Process 1.

Materials input   – 1,000 units costing $10,000

Labour costs   – $8,000

Departmental overheads – $6,000

Normal loss is 4% of input which cannot be sold.

Actual output = 980 units

Required:

Calculate the average cost per unit in Process 1 and produce the process account and the abnormal gains and losses account.

Solution

Process 1 Account

	Units	$		Units	$
Raw materials	1,000	10,000	Normal loss (W1)	40	0
Direct labour		8,000	Transfer to Finished goods (W4)	980	24,500
Departmental overheads		6,000			
Abnormal gain (W3)	20	500			
	1,020	24,500		1,020	24,500

Average cost per unit in Process 1 (W2) = $25.00

Abnormal gains and losses account

	$		$
Income statement	500	Process 1	500
	──		──
	500		500
	──		──

Workings:

(W1) Normal loss = 4% × 1,000 = 40 units

(W2)

$$\text{Average cost per unit} = \frac{\text{Net costs of input}}{\text{Expected output}}$$

$$\text{Average cost per unit} = \frac{\$24,000}{1,000 - 40}$$

$$= \frac{\$24,000}{960} = \$25.00 \text{ per unit}$$

(W3) Actual output = 980 units

Abnormal gain = expected output – actual output = 960 – 980 = 20 units

Abnormal gain is valued at the same cost as good output, i.e. $25.00 per unit.

Abnormal loss value = 20 × $25.00 = $500

(W4) Value of units transferred to finished goods = 980 × $25.00 = $24,500

Illustration 9 – Abnormal gains with scrap value

The following data relates to Process 1.

Materials input   – 1,000 units costing $10,000

Labour costs   – $8,000

Departmental overheads – $6,000

Normal loss is 4% of input which can be sold for $12 per unit.

Actual output = 980 units

Required:

Calculate the average cost per unit in Process 1 and produce the process account, abnormal gains and losses account and the scrap account.

Solution

Process 1 Account

	Units	$		Units	$
Raw materials	1,000	10,000	Normal loss (W1)	40	480
Direct labour		8,000	Transfer to Finished goods (W4)	980	24,010
Departmental overheads		6,000			
Abnormal gain (W3)	20	490			
	1,020	24,490		1,020	24,490

Average cost per unit in Process 1 (W2) = $24.50

Abnormal gains and losses account

	$		$
Scrap (W5)	240	Process 1	490
Income statement	250		
	——		——
	490		490
	——		——

Scrap account

	$		$
Process 1 (normal loss)	480	Abnormal gain and loss	240
		Cash	240
	——		——
	480		480
	——		——

Workings:

(W1) Normal loss = 4% × 1,000 = 40 units

Scrap value of normal loss = 40 × $12 = $480

(W2)

$$\text{Average cost per unit} = \frac{\text{Net costs of input}}{\text{Expected output}}$$

$$\text{Average cost per unit} = \frac{\$24,000 - \$480 \ (\text{W1})}{1,000 - 40 \ (\text{W1})}$$

$$= \frac{\$23,520}{960} = \$24.50 \text{ per unit}$$

(W3) Actual output = 980 units

Abnormal gain = expected output – actual output = 960 – 980 = 20 units

Abnormal gain is valued at the same cost as good output, i.e. $24.50 per unit

Abnormal gain value = 20 × $24.50 = $490

(W4) Value of units transferred to finished goods = 980 × $24.50 = $24,010

(W5) Value of abnormal gain transferred to the scrap account = 20 × $12 = $240

Suggested approach for answering normal loss, abnormal loss/gain questions

(1) Calculate any normal loss units

(2) Draw the process account and enter the units or produce a flow of units (input units = output units). The balancing figure for the units is either an abnormal loss or gain.

(3) Value the inputs.

(4) Value the normal loss (if any).

(5) Calculate the average cost per unit:

$$\frac{\textbf{Net costs of input}}{\textbf{Expected output}}$$

(6) Value the good output and abnormal loss or gain at this average cost per unit.

(7) Transfer the normal loss to the scrap account (if any).

(8) Transfer the abnormal loss or gain to the abnormal loss/gain account.

(9) Transfer the abnormal loss or gain to the scrap account at the scrap value (if any).

(10) Balance the abnormal loss/gain account and the scrap account.

Test your understanding 3

W&B Ltd produce a breakfast cereal that involves several processes. At each stage in the process, ingredients are added, until the final stage of production when the cereal is boxed up ready to be sold.

In Process 2, W&B Ltd have initiated a quality control inspection. This inspection takes place BEFORE any new ingredients are added in to Process 2. The inspection is expected to yield a normal loss of 5% of the input from Process 1. These losses are sold as animal fodder for $1 per kg.

The following information is for Process 2 for the period just ended:

	Units	$
Transfer from Process 1	500 kg	750
Material added in Process 2	300 kg	300
Labour	200 hrs	800
Overheads	–	500
Actual output	755 kg	–

Prepare the process account, abnormal loss and gain account, and scrap account for Process 2 for the period just ended.

4 Work-in-progress (WIP) and equivalent units (EUs)

Work in progress (WIP)

At the end of an accounting period there may be some units that have entered a production process but the process has not been completed. These units are called closing work in progress (or CWIP) units.

- The output at the end of a period will consist of the following:
  - fully-processed units
  - part-processed units (CWIP).

- CWIP units become the Opening WIP (OWIP) units in the next accounting period.

- It would not be fair to allocate a full unit cost to part-processed units and so we need to use the concept of equivalent units (EUs) which spreads out the process costs of a period fairly between the fully-processed and part-processed units.

Concept of EUs

Process costs are allocated to units of production on the basis of EUs.

- The idea behind this concept is that a part-processed unit can be expressed as a proportion of a fully-completed unit.

- For example, if 100 units are exactly half-way through the production process, they are effectively equal to 50 fully-completed units. Therefore the 100 part-processed units can be regarded as being equivalent to 50 fully-completed units or 50 EUs.

Illustration 10 – CWIP and EUs

For process 1 in ABC Co the following is relevant for the latest period:

Period costs $4,440
Input   800 units
Output   600 fully -worked units and 200 units only 70% complete

There were no process losses.

Required:

Produce the process account

Solution

Statement of EUs

	Output	%	EUs
Fully-worked units	600	100%	600
CWIP	200	70%	140
Total	800		**740**
Costs			**$4,440**
Cost per EU			**$6**

Cost per EU = $4,440/740 units = $6 per unit

The Process 1 account can be completed as follows:

Process 1 Account

	Units	$		Units	$
Input	800	4,440	Transferred to next process (600 × $6)	600	3,600
			CWIP(140 EUs × $6)	200	840
	800	4,440		800	4,440

Different degrees of completion

For most processes the **material** is input at the **start** of the process, so it is only the addition of **labour** and **overheads** that will be **incomplete** at the end of the period.

- This means that the material cost should be spread over all units, but conversion costs should be spread over the EUs.

- This can be achieved using an expanded Statement of EUs which separates out the material, labour and overhead costs.

- Note that the term conversion costs is often used to describe the addition of labour and overheads together in a process.

Illustration 11 – CWIP and EUs

For Process 1 in LJK Ltd the following is relevant for the latest period:

Material costs	500 units @ $8 per unit
Labour	$2,112
Overheads	150% of labour cost

Output: 400 fully-worked units, transferred to Process 2. 100 units only 40% complete with respect to conversion, but 100% complete with respect to materials.

There were no process losses.

Required:

Produce the process account

Solution

The value of fully-worked units and CWIP are calculated as follows:

Statement of EUs

	Output	Materials		Conversion	
		%	EUs	%	EUs
Fully-worked units	400	100	400	100	400
CWIP	100	100	100	40	40
Total	500		500		440
Costs		Material	$4,000	Labour	$2,112
				Overheads	$3,168
					$5,280
Cost per EU			$8		$12

The value of fully-worked units is (W1) $8,000

The value of CWIP is (W2) $1,280

Workings

(W1) Fully-worked units are valued at $20 per unit ($8 + $12).

    400 × $20 = $8,000

(W2) CWIP is valued as follows:

    Materials 100 units × $8   = $800

    Conversion 40 units × $12   = $480

    Total CWIP value = $800 + $480 = $1,280

The Process 1 account can be completed as follows:

Process 1 Account

	Units	$		Units	$
Input	500	4,000	Transferred to next process	400	8,000
Labour		2,112	**CWIP**	100	1,280
Overheads		3,168			
	500	9,280		500	9,280

Test your understanding 4

A firm operates a process costing system. Details of Process 2 for Period 1 are as follows.

During the period 8,250 units were received from the previous process at a value of $453,750, labour and overheads were $350,060 and material introduced was $24,750.

At the end of the period the closing WIP was 1,600 units which were 100% complete in respect of materials, and 60% complete in respect of labour and overheads. The balance of units was transferred to Finished goods.

There was no opening WIP or process losses. Calculate the cost per EU, the value of finished goods and closing WIP.

Statement of EUs

	Output	Materials		Conversion	
		%	EUs	%	EUs
Fully-worked					
Closing WIP					
Total units					
Costs					
Total cost					
Cost per EU					

The value of finished goods is $ [ ]

The value of WIP is $ [ ]

5 Opening work in progress (OWIP)

If OWIP is present then:

- Work remaining in the process (CWIP) and transfers out of a process (fully-completed units) can be valued on different bases: weighted average method and the FIFO method.

- These methods are similar to the valuation methods studied when we looked at materials in an earlier chapter.

Weighted average costing of production

- In the weighted average method no distinction is made between units in process at the start of a period and those added during the period.

- Opening inventory costs are added to current costs to provide an overall average cost per unit.

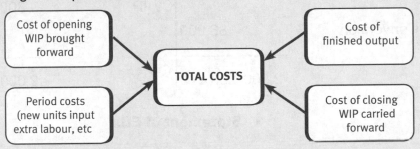

Illustration 12 – Weighted average costing of production

BR Ltd makes a product requiring several successive processes. Details of the first process for August are as follows:

Opening WIP:	400 units
Degree of completion:	
Materials (valued at $19,880)	100 %
Conversion (valued at $3,799)	25 %
Units transferred to Process 2	1,700 units
Closing WIP	300 units
Degree of completion:	
Materials	100 %
Conversion	50 %
Costs incurred in the period:	
Material	$100,000
Conversion	$86,000

There were no process losses.

Required:

Prepare the process account for August using the weighted average method.

Solution

Process 1 Account

	Units	$		Units	$
OWIP	400	23,679	Transferred to		
			Process 2	1,700	184,416
Materials	1,600	100,000			
			CWIP	300	25,263
Conversion		86,000			
	——	——		——	——
	2,000	209,679		2,000	209,679

Statement of EUs

	Output	Materials		Conversion	
		%	EUs	%	EUs
Transferred to Process 2	1,700	100%	1,700	100%	1,700
CWIP	300	100%	300	50%	150
Total units	2,000		2,000		1,850
Costs:					
OWIP			19,880		3,799
Period			100,000		86,000
Total cost			119,880		89,799
Cost per EU			$59.94		$48.54

Valuation of transfers to Process 2:

Materials   = (1,700 × $59.94)   = $101,898
Conversion = (1,700 × $48.54)   = $82,518
Total   = $184,416

Valuation of CWIP:

Materials   = (300 × $59.94)   = $17,982
Conversion = (150 × $48.54)   = $7,281
Total   = $25,263

Test your understanding 5

A business makes one product that passes through a single process. The business uses weighted average costing. The details of the process for the last period are as follows:

Materials	$98,000
Labour	$60,000
Production overheads	$39,000
Units added to the process	1,000

There were 200 units of opening WIP which are valued as follows:

Materials	$22,000
Labour	$6,960
Production overheads	$3,000

There were 300 units of closing WIP fully complete as to materials but only 60% complete for labour and 50% complete for overheads.

There were no process losses.

Calculate the following:

(a) The value of the completed output for the period.

(b) The value of the closing WIP.

FIFO costing of production

With the FIFO method it is assumed that the OWIP units need to be completed first before any more units can be started. Therefore:

- completed output is made up of OWIP that has been finished in the period and units that have been made from beginning to end in the period.

- if OWIP units are 75% complete with respect to materials and 40% complete with respect to labour, only 25% **more work** will need to be carried out with respect to materials and 60% with respect to labour.

- the OWIP b/f costs are not considered to be a period cost so are not included in the EU table. They are used in the final valuation of the completed units.

- This means that the process costs in the period must be allocated between:
  - OWIP units
  - units started and completed in the period (fully-worked units)
  - CWIP units.

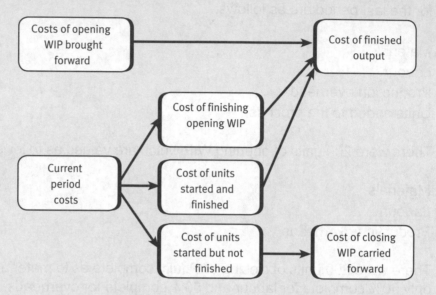

Illustration 13 – FIFO costing of production

BR Ltd makes a product requiring several successive processes. Details of the first process for August are as follows:

Opening WIP:	400 units
Degree of completion:	
Materials (valued at $19,880)	100%
Conversion (valued at $3,775)	25%
Units transferred to Process 2	1,700 units
Closing WIP	300 units
Degree of completion:	
Materials	100%
Conversion	50%

Costs incurred in the period:

Material	$100,000
Conversion	$85,995

There were no process losses.

Required:

Prepare the process account for August using the FIFO method.

Solution

Process 1 Account

	Units	$		Units	$
OWIP	400	23,655	Transferred to Process 2	1,700	183,529
Materials	1,600	100,000	CWIP	300	26,121
Conversion		85,995			
	2,000	209,650		2,000	209,650

Statement of EUs

	Output	Materials		Conversion	
		%	EUs	%	EUs
OWIP completed	400	0	0	75	300
Fully-worked in process	1,300	100	1,300	100	1,300
CWIP	300	100	300	50	150
Total	2,000		1,600		1,750
Costs			$100,000		$85,995
Cost per EU			$62.50		$49.14

Valuation of transfers to Process 2:

OWIP value from last period = $19,880 + $3,775 = **$23,655**

OWIP completed this period:

Conversion only = 300 × $49.14 = **$14,742**

Fully-worked current period

Materials	= 1,300 × $62.50	= $81,250
Conversion	= 1,300 × $49.14	= $63,882
Total		= **$145,132**

> **Total valuation of transfers to Process 2 = $183,529**
>
> **Valuation of CWIP:**
>
> Materials = (300 × $62.50)   = $18,750
> Conversion = (150 × $49.14)   = $7,371
> Total   = **$26,121**

Additional notes for solution to Illustration

Materials

Units completed in period	1,700
OWIP	(400)
Units completed from start to finished in the period	1,300

OWIP

The OWIP is 100% complete with respect to materials and therefore no further work or costs are involved in completing the opening WIP units.

The OWIP is 25% complete with respect to conversion costs and therefore 75% of the conversion work/costs are still outstanding.

Costs to complete OWIP and fully-worked units

Each unit started and finished in the period costs $(62.50 + 49.14) = $111.64

1,300 units were fully-worked in the process = 1,300 × $111.64 = $145,132

Costs to complete 400 units of OWIP = 300 units (conversion EUs) × $49.14 = $14,742

Costs to complete units transferred to Process 2

Cost of completing 1,700 units (1,300 fully-worked plus 400 OWIP) = $145,132 + $ 14,742 = $159,874

Total cost of units transferred to Process 2 = cost of completing 1,700 units plus costs already incurred in OWIP, i.e. $(19,880 + 3,775) = $23,655

Therefore, cost of 1,700 units transferred to Process 2 = $159,874 + $23,655 = $183,529

Test your understanding 6

AXL Ltd operates a process costing system. Details of Process 1 are as follows.

All materials used are added at the beginning of the process. Labour costs and production overhead costs are incurred evenly as the product goes through the process. Production overheads are absorbed at a rate of 100% of labour costs.

The following details are relevant to production in the period:

	Units	Materials	Labour and production overheads
Opening inventory	200	100% complete	75% complete
Closing inventory	100	100% complete	50% complete

Opening inventory

Costs associated with these opening units are $1,800 for materials. In addition $4,000 had been accumulated for labour and overhead costs.

Period costs

Costs incurred during the period were:

Materials $19,000

Labour costs $19,000

During the period, 2,000 units were passed to Process 2. There were no losses.

The company uses a FIFO method for valuing process costs.

Calculate the total value of the units transferred to Process 2.

6 Losses made part way through production

It is possible that losses (or gains) to be identified part way through a process. In such a case, EUs must be used to assess the extent to which costs were incurred at the time at which the loss/gain was identified.

Illustration 14 – Losses made part way through production

BLT manufactures chemicals and has a normal loss of 15% of material input. Information for February is as follows:

Material input 200 kg costing $4.93 per kg

Labour and overheads $4,100

Transfers to finished goods 160 kg

Losses are identified when the process is 40% complete

No opening or closing WIP.

Required:

Prepare the process account for February.

Solution

Normal loss is 15% of input, i.e. 15% × 200 kg = 30 kg

Actual loss is 40 kg. Thus abnormal loss is 10 kg.

Calculate the EUs for completed output plus the abnormal loss units. Normal loss is absorbed into good output so does not appear in the statement of EUs

Statement of EUs		EUs	
	Total	Materials	Conversion
Finished units	160	160	160
Abnormal loss	10	10	4
Total EUs	170	170	164
Process costs		986	4100
Cost per EU		$5.80	$25

Valuation of completed output

Total cost of completed unit =160EU × $(5.80 + 25) = $4,928

Valuation of abnormal loss

Abnormal loss = (10EU × $5.80) + (4EU × $25) = $158

Process account

	Kg	$		Kg	$
Materials	200	986	Normal loss	30	–
Labour and overheads		4,100	Finished goods	160	4,928
			Abnormal loss	10	158
	200	5,086		200	5,086

Normal loss account

	Kg	$		Kg	$
Process account	30	–			

Abnormal loss account

	Kg	$		Kg	$
Process account	10	158	Income statement		158
	10	158			158

7 Joint and by-products

Introduction

The nature of process costing is such that processes often produce more than one product. These additional products may be described as either joint products or by-products. Essentially joint products are main products whereas by-products are incidental to the main products.

Joint products

Joint products are two or more products separated in the course of processing, each having a sufficiently **high saleable value** to merit recognition as a main product.

- Joint products include products produced as a result of the oil-refining process, for example, petrol and paraffin.

- Petrol and paraffin have similar sales values and are therefore equally important (joint) products.

By-products

By-products are outputs of **some value** produced incidentally in manufacturing something else (main products).

- By-products, such as sawdust and bark, are secondary products from the timber industry (where timber is the main or principal product from the process).

- Sawdust and bark have a relatively low sales value compared to the timber which is produced and are therefore classified as by-products.

8 Treatment of joint costs

Accounting treatment of joint products

The distinction between joint and by-products is important because the accounting treatment of joint products and by-products differs.

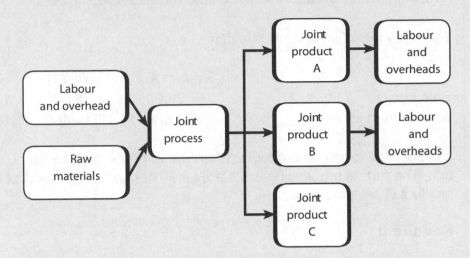

- Joint process costs occur before the split-off point. They are sometimes called pre-separation costs or common costs.

- The joint costs need to be apportioned between the joint products at the split-off point to obtain the cost of each of the products in order to value closing inventory and cost of sales.

- The basis of apportionment of joint costs to products is usually one of the following:
    - sales value of production (also known as market value)
    - production units
    - net realisable value.

Accounting treatment of by-products

As by-products have an insignificant value the accounting treatment is different.

- The costs incurred in the process are shared between the joint products alone. The by-products do not pick up a share of the costs, like normal loss.

- The sales value of the by-product at the split-off point is treated as a reduction in costs instead of an income, again just the same as normal loss.

- If the by-product has no known value at the split-off point but does have a value after further processing, the net income of the by-product is used to reduce the costs of the process

Net income (or net realisable value) =Final sales value – Further processing costs

Illustration 15 – Treatment of joint costs

Process M produces two joint products (A and B) and one by-product (C). Joint costs are apportioned on the basis of sales units.

The following information is relevant.

	Product A	Product B	Total
Sales units	2,000	8,000	10,000
Apportioned joint cost	$3,600	$14,400	$18,000

It is possible to sell by-product C after further processing for $0.50 per unit. The further processing costs are $0.20 per unit. 2,000 units of by-product C are produced.

Required:

How are the joint costs of $18,000 apportioned when by-product C is produced?

Solution

With the production of by-product C, joint costs are reduced by the net income from the process.

Income from by-product = $(0.5 – 0.2) × 2,000 = $600

Joint costs are now $18,000 – $600 = $17,400

Total output units = 2,000 + 8,000 = 10,000

$$\text{Joint costs allocated to Product A} = \frac{2,000}{10,000} \times \$17,400 = \$3,480$$

$$\text{Joint costs allocated to Product B} = \frac{8,000}{10,000} \times \$17,400 = \$13,920$$

Test your understanding 7

A company operates a manufacturing process which produces joint products A and B, and by-product C.

Manufacturing costs for a period total $272,926, incurred in the manufacture of:

Product A 16,000 kg (selling price $6.10 per kg)

Product B 53,200 kg (selling price $7.50 per kg)

Product C 2,770 kg (selling price $1.20 per kg)

Product B requires further processing after separation from the other two products. This costs a total of $201,930.

Product C also requires further processing to make it saleable, and this costs $0.40 per kg.

Calculate the total profit earned by Products A and B in the period, using the net realisable values (net income) to apportion joint costs.

9 Process accounts for joint and by-products

You may be required to deal with joint and by-products when preparing process accounts. Joint products should be treated as 'normal' output from a process. The treatment of by-products in process accounts is similar to the treatment of normal loss.

- The by-product income is credited to the process account and debited to a by-product account.

- To calculate the number of units in a period, by-product units (like normal loss) reduce the number of units output.

- When by-products are produced, the cost per unit is calculated as follows:

Process costs (materials & conversion costs) – Scrap value of normal loss – Sales value of by-product

───────────────────────────────────────

Expected number of units output (Input units – Normal Loss Units – By-Product units)

OR

Net costs of inputs

─────────────────

Expected output

10 Chapter summary

Joint and by-products
- Joint products are two or more products separated in processing, each having sufficiently high saleable value
- By-products are outputs of some value produced at the same time as joint products

Job costing

Form of specific order costing used when customer orders a specific job to be done. Each job is priced separately and is unique.

Different types of production

Batch costing

Form of specific order costing which is very similar to job costing. Each batch is a separately identifiable cost unit which is given a batch number.

Simple process costings

Costing method used when mass production of many identical products takes place, e.g. manufacture of bars of chocolate or cans of soup. All products manufactured are indistinguishable from each other and so an average cost per unit is calculated for each process.

Process costing with gains and losses
- Normal loss = expected loss. Value is $0 unless it has a scrap value.
- Abnormal loss is extra unexpected loss.
- Abnormal gain occurs when actual loss is less than expected.
- Abnormal loss and gain are valued at same value as good output.

Process costing with opening WIP

Weighted average method does not distinguish between opening WIP units and units added in process. FIFO method distinguishes between opening WIP, units started and finished in process ('fully- worked' units) and closing WIP.

Process costing with WIP and EUs

Not fair to allocate full unit cost to a part-processed unit. Idea behind the concept of EUs is that a part-processed unit can be expressed as a proportion of a fully-completed unit.

Process costs are allocated to units in a process on the basis of EUs.

Test your understanding answers

Test your understanding 1

Answer C

Job costing is customer-driven with customers ordering a specific job to be done. It is also possible for production to be completed within a single accounting period.

Test your understanding 2

	$
Direct materials 50 kg × $4	200
Direct labour 30 hours × $9	270
Variable production overhead 30 × $6	180
Fixed overheads $80,000/20,000 × 30	120
Other overheads	40
	___
Total cost	810

Test your understanding 3

Process 2 Account

	Kg	$		Units	$
Transfer from Process 1	500	750	Normal loss	25	25
Additional raw materials	300	300	Finished goods	755	2,265
Direct labour		800	Abnormal loss	20	60
Departmental overheads		500			
	___	___		___	___
	800	2,350		800	2,350

Normal loss = 5% of transfer from Process 1 = 500 kg × 0.05 = 25 kg

Scrap value of normal loss = 25 kg × $1 = $25

Cost per unit = ($2,350 − $25) / (800 kg − 25 kg) = $3

Abnormal gains and losses account

	$		$
Process 2	60	Scrap (20 × $1)	20
		Income statement	40
	___		___
	60		60
	___		___

Scrap account

	$		$
Process 2 (normal loss)	25	Cash (45 × $1)	45
Abnormal gain and loss	20		
	___		___
	45		45
	___		___

Test your understanding 4

	Output	Materials %	Materials EUs	Conversion %	Conversion EUs
Fully-worked	6,650	100	6,650	100	6,650
CWIP	1,600	100	1,600	60	960
Total units			8,250		7,610
Costs:			$453,750		$350,060
			$24,750		
Total cost			$478,500		$350,060
Cost per EU			$58		$46

The value of finished goods is (W1)   **$691,600**

The value of CWIP is (W2)   **$136,960**

Workings

(W1)   Value of finished goods
       Materials: 6,650 × $58   = $385,700
       Conversion: 6,650 × $46   = $305,900
       Total   = $691,600

(W2)   Value of CWIP
       Materials: 1,600 × $58   = $92,800
       Conversion: 960 × $46   = $44,160
       Total   = $136,960

Test your understanding 5

Statement of EUs

	Materials		Labour		Overheads	
	%	EU	%	EU	%	EU
Output	100	900	100	900	100	900
CWIP	100	300	60	180	50	150
Total EUs		1,200		1,080		1,050

		Materials	Labour	Overheads
		$	$	$
Costs – **period**		98,000	60,000	39,000
OWIP		22,000	6,960	3,000
Total costs		120,000	66,960	42,000
Cost per unit		$100	$62	$40

(Total costs/total EUs)

(a) Value of completed output = 900 × $(100 + 62 + 40) = $181,800

(b)

		$
Materials	300 × $100	30,000
Labour	180 × $62	11,160
Overheads	150 × $40	6,000
Value of CWIP		47,160

Test your understanding 6

Statement of EUs

	Output	Materials %	Materials EUs	Conversion %	Conversion EUs
OWIP completed	200	0	0	25	50
Fully-worked in process	1,800	100	1,800	100	1,800
CWIP	100	100	100	50	50
Total	2,100		1,900		1,900
Costs			$19,000		$19,000 + $19,000*= $38,000
Cost per EU			$10		$20

* Overheads are absorbed at 100% of labour cost.

Value of units passed to Process 2:

OWIP value from last period   = $1,800 + $4,000 = $5,800

OWIP completed this period:

Conversion only   = 50 × $20   = $1,000
Fully-worked current period
Materials   = 1,800 × $10   = $18,000
Conversion   = 1,800 × $20   = $36,000

Total = $54,000

Total value of units transferred to Process 2   = $60,800

Test your understanding 7

Net revenue from product C = $(1.2 − 0.4) = $0.80

Costs to apportion = Joint process costs − net revenue from product C

$$= \$272,926 - (2,770 \times \$0.80)$$

$$= \$270,710$$

	A	B	Total
	$	$	$
Revenue	97,600	399,000	496,600
Further processing costs	–	(201,930)	(201,930)
Net realisable values	97,600	197,070	294,670
Joint costs (W1)	(89,664)	(181,046)	(270,710)
Total profits	**7,936**	**16,024**	**23,960**

Total net realisable values = $97,600 + $197,070 = $294,670

(W1)

Joint costs apportioned to Product A = $\dfrac{97,600}{294,670} \times \$270,710 = \$89,664$

Joint costs apportioned to Product B = $\dfrac{197,070}{294,670} \times \$270,710 = \$181,046$

Service and operation costing

Chapter learning objectives

Upon completion of this chapter you will be able to:

- identify situations where the use of service/operation costing is appropriate

- illustrate suitable unit cost measures that may be used in different service/operation situations

- carry out service cost analysis in simple service industry situations.

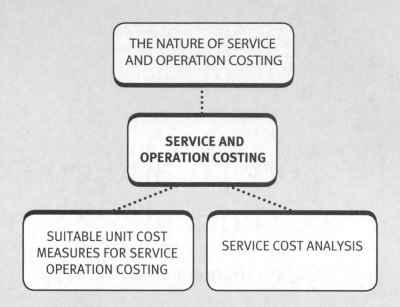

1 The nature of service and operation costing

Service costing

Service costing is used when an organisation or department provides a service, such as an accountancy firm preparing the accounts for a company.

There are four main differences between the 'output' of service industries and the products of manufacturing industries.

- **Intangibility** – output is in the form of 'performance' rather than tangible ('touchable') goods.

- **Heterogeneity** – the nature and standard of the service will be variable due to the high human input.

- **Simultaneous production and consumption** – the service that you require cannot be inspected in advance of receiving it.

- **Perishability** – the services that you require cannot be stored.

Illustration 1 – The nature of service and operation costing

Examples of service industries include the following:

- hotel
- college
- hairdressers
- restaurant.

We can ask the following questions about, e.g. the hotel industry.

(1) Is output in the form of performance? Yes – the hotel provides a bed and possibly breakfast. You will judge the service of the hotel on how comfortable the bed was and how tasty the breakfast was. You cannot really 'touch' the performance of the hotel

(2) Is the standard of the service variable? Yes – your stay at the hotel may vary each time you stay there. You may not have such a comfortable bed and your breakfast may not be very tasty each time you visit. The standard of service is therefore variable because lots of different staff work at the hotel – the standard of the service you receive may depend on which staff are on duty.

(3) Can you inspect the services in advance of receiving them? In general, you cannot sleep in a hotel bed or eat breakfast at the hotel until you have booked in and made a contract to buy the services of the hotel.

(4) Can the hotel services be stored? No - you cannot take your bed away with you, nor can you keep your breakfast – it must be eaten during the morning of your stay.

2 Suitable unit cost measures for service/operation costing

Unit cost measures for service costing

One of the main difficulties in service costing is the establishment of a suitable cost unit.

- Service organisations may use several different cost units to measure the different kinds of service that they are providing.

- Examples for a hotel might include:
    - Meals served for the restaurant
    - Rooms occupied for the cleaning staff
    - Hours worked for the reception staff.

- A **composite cost unit** is more appropriate if a service is a function of two variables.

- Examples of composite cost units are as follows:
    - How much is carried over what distance (tonne-miles) for haulage companies
    - How many patients are treated for how many days (patient-days) for hospitals
    - How many passengers travel how many miles (passenger-miles) for public transport companies.

Test your understanding 1

Which of the following are characteristics of service costing?

(i)   High levels of direct labour costs as a proportion of total cost.

(ii) Use of composite cost units.

(iii) Use of equivalent units.

A   (i) only

B   (i) and (ii) only √√

C   (ii) only

D   (ii) and (iii) only

Cost per service unit

The total cost of providing a service will include labour, materials, expenses and overheads (the same as the costs associated with the products produced in manufacturing industry).

	$
Direct materials	X
Direct labour	X
Direct expenses	X
Overheads absorbed	X
	───
TOTAL COST	XX

- In service costing, it is not uncommon for labour to be the only direct cost involved in providing a service and for overheads to make up most of the remaining total costs.

- In service costing costs can be classified as being fixed, variable or semi-variable. If costs are semi-variable, it is necessary to separate them into their fixed and variable constituents using the high/low method.

- The cost per service unit is calculated by establishing the total costs involved in providing the service and dividing this by the number of service units used in providing the service.

- The calculation of a cost per service unit is as follows.

$$\text{Cost per service unit} = \frac{\textbf{Total costs for providing the service}}{\textbf{Number of service units used to provide the service}}$$

Illustration 2 – Suitable unit cost measures for service/operation

The canteen of a company records the following income and expenditure for a month.

	$	$
Income		59,010
Food	17,000	
Drink	6,000	
Bottled water	750	
Fuel costs (gas for cooking)	800	
Maintenance of machinery	850	
Repairs	250	
Wages	15,500	
Depreciation	1,000	

During the month the canteen served 56,200 meals. The canteen's cost unit is one meal.

Required:

Calculate the average cost per meal served and the average income per meal served.

Solution

Total canteen expenditure in month = $42,150
Total meals served in the month = 56,200

$$\text{Average cost per meal served} = \frac{\$42,150}{56,200} = \$0.75 \text{ per meal}$$

0.3 margin

$$\text{Average income per meal} = \frac{\$59,010}{56,200} = \$1.05 \text{ per meal}$$

3 Service cost analysis

If organisations in the same service industry use the same service cost units then comparisons between the companies can be made easily.

Illustration 3 – Service cost analysis

The following figures were taken from the annual accounts of two electricity supply boards working on uniform costing methods.

Meter reading, billing and collection costs:

	Board A $000	Board B $000
Salaries and wages of:		
Meter readers	150	240
Billing and collection staff	300	480
Transport and travelling	30	40
Collection agency charges	–	20
Bad debts	10	10
General charges	100	200
Miscellaneous	10	10
	600	1,000

	Board A	Board B
Units sold (millions)	2,880	9,600
Number of consumers (thousands)	800	1,600
Sales of electricity (millions)	$18	$50
Size of area (square miles)	4,000	4,000

Comparative costs for Boards A and B may be collected as follows and are useful in showing how well (or otherwise) individual services are performing.

Electricity Boards A and B

Comparative costs – year ending 31.12X5

	Board A $000	% of total	Board B $000	% of total
Salaries and wages:				
Meter reading	150	25.0	240	24.0
Billing and collection	300	50.0	480	48.0
Transport/travelling	30	5.0	40	4.0
Collection agency	–	–	20	2.0
Bad debts	10	1.7	10	1.0
General charges	100	16.6	200	20.0
Miscellaneous	10	1.7	10	1.0
	600	100.0	1,000	100.0

The information contained in the following table is much more useful for comparison purposes than the meter reading and billing costs information given above.

	$	$
Cost per:		
Million units sold	208	104
Thousand consumers	750	625
$m of sales	33,333	20,000
Square mile area	150	250

Test your understanding 2

Happy Returns Ltd operates a haulage business with three vehicles. The following estimated cost and performance data is available:

Petrol	$0.50 per kilometre on average
Repairs	$0.30 per kilometre
Depreciation	$1.00 per kilometre, plus $50 per week per vehicle
Drivers' wages	$300.00 per week per vehicle
Supervision and general expenses	$550 per week
Loading costs	$6.00 per tonne

During week number 26 it is expected that all three vehicles will be used, 280 tonnes will be loaded and a total of 3,950 kilometres travelled (including return journeys when empty) as shown in the following table:

Working

Journey	Tonnes carried (one way)	Kilometres (one way)
1	34	180
2	28	265
3	40	390
4	32	115
5	26	220
6	40	480
7	29	90
8	26	100
9	25	135
	280	1,975

Calculate the average cost per tonne-kilometre in week 26.

4 Chapter summary

The nature of service and operation costing

- Intangibility
- Heterogeneity
- Simultaneous production and consumption
- Perishability

Examples of service industries

- Hotels
- Airlines
- Public transport
- College/university
- Accountancy/audit firms
- Utility companies
- Distribution/haulage companies

Service and operation costing

Used when an organisation or department provides a service·

Suitable unit cost measures for service and operation coasting

Composite cost unit used if service is function of two variables, for example:

- Patient-day
- Passenger-mile
- Guest-day
- Tonne-mile (or km)

Service cost analysis

If organisations in the same industry use the same service cost units then comparisons between companies can be made easily

Test your understanding answers

Test your understanding 1

B

Direct labour costs may be a high proportion on the total cost of providing a service and composite cost units are characteristic features of service costing. (i) and (ii) are therefore applicable and the correct answer is B.

Test your understanding 2

Total costs in Week 26

		$
	$/km	
Petrol	0.50	
Repairs	0.30	
Depreciation	1.00	
	─────	
	1.80 × 3,950	7,110
	─────	
	$/week	
Depreciation ($50 × 3)	150	
Wages ($300 × 3)	900	
Supervision and general expenses	550	
	─────	
		1,600
Loading costs ($6 × 280)		1,680
		─────
		10,390
		─────
Tonne-km in week 26 (see working)		66,325

(Costs averaged over the outward journeys, not the return, as these are necessary, but carry no tonnes.)

Average cost per tonne-km $= \dfrac{\text{Total cost}}{\text{Total tonne-km}}$

$= \dfrac{\$10,390}{66,325}$

$= \$0.157$ per tonne-km

Working

Journey	Tonnes carried (one way)	Kilometres (one way)	Tonne- kilometres
1	34	180	6,120
2	28	265	7,420
3	40	390	15,600
4	32	115	3,680
5	26	220	5,720
6	40	480	19,200
7	29	90	2,610
8	26	100	2,600
9	25	135	3,375
	280	1,975	66,325

Alternative costing principles

Chapter learning objectives

Upon completion of this chapter you will be able to:

- explain activity based costing (ABC), target costing, life cycle costing and total quality management (TQM) as alternative cost management techniques

- differentiate ABC, target costing and life cycle costing from the traditional costing techniques

- compare cost control and cost reduction

- describe and evaluate cost reduction methods

- describe and evaluate value analysis

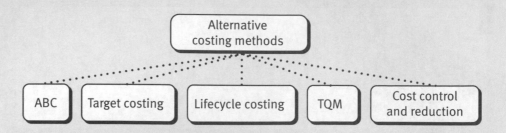

1 Modern production environments

Modern manufacturing is different from traditional manufacturing techniques:

- much more machinery and computerised manufacturing systems are used

- smaller batch sizes are manufactured at the request of customers

- less use of 'direct' labour due to the higher use of computers and machinery

This has had an impact on production costs:

- more indirect costs (overheads)
- less direct labour costs

This means that the traditional methods of costing using Absorption costing and Marginal costing are less useful.

- **Absorption costing** charges overheads to products in an arbitary way – usually based on volume of production in units or hours

- **Marginal costing** value products based on the variable cost to produce them and fixed cost are a period charge. In modern environments the variable costs might be small in comparison to the fixed costs and the fixed cost may not be truly fixed if considering all aspects of the production process.

2 Activity based costing (ABC)

Activity based costing (ABC) is an alternative approach to product costing. It is a form of absorption costing, but, rather than absorbing overheads on a production volume basis it firstly allocates them to **cost pools** before absorbing them into units using **cost drivers**.

- A **cost pool** is an **activity** that consumes resources and for which overhead costs are identified and allocated. For each cost pool there should be a cost driver.

- A **cost driver** is a **unit** of activity that consumes resources. An alternative definition of a cost driver is the factor influencing the level of cost.

Illustration 1 – Absorption costing versus ABC

Imagine the machining department in a traditional absorption costing system. The overhead absorption rate would be based on machine hours because many of the overheads in the machine department would relate to the machines, for example power, maintenance, machine depreciation etc. Using only machine hours as the basis would seem fair, however not only does the machine department have machine related costs, but also in an absorption costing system it would have had a share of rent and rates, heating, lighting apportioned to it. These costs would also be absorbed based on machine hours and this is inappropriate as the machine hours are not directly responsible for the rent or rates.

ABC overcomes this problem by not using departments as gathering points for costs, but instead it uses activities to group the costs (cost pools) which are caused (driven) by an activity. There would be an activity that related to each of the following: power usage, machine depreciation and machine maintenance. Machining would not pick up a share of personnel costs or rent and rates as these would be charged to another activity. For example:

- the cost of setting up machinery for a production run might be driven by the number of set-ups (jobs or batches produced)

- the cost of running machines might be driven by the number of machine hours for which the machines are running

- the cost of order processing might be related to the number of orders dispatched or to the weight of items dispatched

- the cost of purchasing might be related to the number of purchase orders made.

ABCs flexibility reduces the need for arbitrary apportionments.

Advantages and disadvantages of ABC

ABC has a number of advantages:

- It provides a more accurate cost per unit. As a result, pricing, sales strategy, performance management and decision making should be improved.

- It provides much better insight into what causes overhead costs.

- ABC recognises that overhead costs are not all related to production and sales volume.

- In many businesses, overhead costs are a significant proportion of total costs, and management needs to understand the drivers of overhead costs in order to manage the business properly. Overhead costs can be controlled by managing cost drivers.

- It can be applied to calculate realistic costs in a complex business environment.

- ABC can be applied to all overhead costs, not just production overheads.

- ABC can be used just as easily in service costing as in product costing.

Disadvantages of ABC:

- ABC will be of limited benefit if the overhead costs are primarily volume related or if the overhead is a small proportion of the overall cost.

- It is impossible to allocate all overhead costs to specific activities.

- The choice of both activities and cost drivers might be inappropriate.

- ABC can be more complex to explain to the stakeholders of the costing exercise.

- The benefits obtained from ABC might not justify the costs.

3 Target costing

A target cost is a product cost estimate derived by subtracting a desired profit margin from a competitive market price. This may be less than the planned initial product cost, but will be expected to be achieved by the time the product reaches the mature production stage.

The conventional approach to product costing is an internal approach. The organisation builds up the cost of the product incurred in its production and will often determine its selling price by adding on an amount to the cost of production. This approach ignores the external environment within which the organisation operates – the market demand conditions and the prices set by competitors may not be fully reflected in the organisation's pricing policy.

Target costing is designed primarily to avoid this problem.

The starting point for target costing is an estimate of a selling price for a new product that will enable a firm to capture a required share of the market. The next step is to reduce this figure by the firm's required level of profit. This will take into account the return required on any new investment and on working capital requirements. This will produce a target cost figure for the organisation. All departments responsible for getting the product to market will estimate costs and must jointly find ways to achieve the target. Value analysis and/or value engineering can be used to reduce costs (discussed later in this chapter).

In essence, conventional costing and pricing methods can be described as bottom up in their approach, they start with internal costs and build up to a selling price.

Target costing is a top down approach – it starts with a target price and derives a cost from that price.

4 Life cycle costing

Life cycle costing tracks and accumulates the actual costs and revenues attributable to each product from inception to abandonment.

This is a technique which compares the revenues from a product with all the costs incurred over the entire product life cycle.

The product life cycle

The product life cycle suggests that all products pass through a number of stages from development to decline and is the basis for life cycle costing.

A diagram depicting the standard life cycle model for a product is shown below:

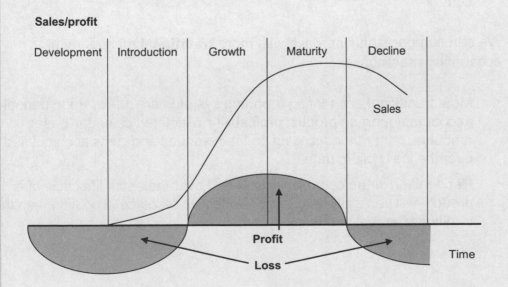

The interpretation of this model, is as follows:

- At the **development** stage the product is not yet being sold. Sales are nil and development costs are creating a loss.

- At the **introduction** the product is launched on to the market. Sales volume is likely to be at a low level during this stage whilst the product establishes itself in the market place. In addition, potential customers may not be fully aware of the existence of the product or may be reluctant to try a new product, preferring to remain loyal to the products already established in the market place.

- During the **growth** stage it is hoped that sales volume will increase rapidly (note the sharply upward sloping curve in the diagram above) as consumers become more familiar with the product and it begins to take over from existing products in the market.

- At some point the growth in sales will slow and probably stop. The product has now reached the **maturity** stage in its life cycle. Sales are still at a high level. At this stage form of modification may be required to prevent the product from going into the final stage.

- During the **decline** stage, sales will fall, perhaps slowly at first, but the pace of decline is likely to increase. The product may have become outdated or unfashionable, or new products may have entered the market and attracted customers away.

The advantages of life cycle costing are:

- the forecast profitability of a given product over its **entire life** is determined before production begins

- accumulated costs at any stage can be compared with life cycle budgeted costs, product by product, for the purposes of planning and control.

We can compare this approach with more **traditional** management accounting practices.

- Most traditional accounting reporting systems are based upon periodic accounts, reporting product profitability in isolated calendar-based amounts, rather than focusing on the revenues and costs accumulated over the life cycle to date.

- Recognition of the commitment needed over the entire life cycle of a product will generally lead to more effective resource allocation than the traditional annual budgeting system.

- Research and development, design, production set-up, marketing and customer service costs are traditionally reported on an aggregated basis for all products and recorded as a period expense. Life cycle costing traces these costs to individual products over their entire life cycles, to aid comparison with product revenues generated in later periods.

- Relationships between early decisions on product design and production methods and ultimate costs can therefore be identified and used for subsequent planning.

With decreasing product lives, it is important to recognise and monitor the relatively high pre-production and early stage costs product by product.

There are a number of factors that need to be managed in order to maximise a product's return over its lifecycle:

Design costs out of the product:

Around 70% of a product's costs are often incurred at the design and development stages of its life. Decisions made then commit the organisation to incurring the costs at a later date, because the design of the product determines the number of components, the production method, etc. It is absolutely vital therefore that design teams do not work in isolation but as part of a cross-functional team in order to minimise costs over the whole life cycle. Value engineering helps here.

Minimise the time to market:

In a world where competitors watch each other keenly to see what new products will be launched, it is vital to get any new product into the market place as quickly as possible. The competitors will monitor each other closely so that they can launch rival products as soon as possible in order to maintain profitability. It is vital, therefore, for the first organisation to launch its product as quickly as possible after the concept has been developed, so that it has as long as possible to establish the product in the market and to make a profit before competition increases. Often it is not so much costs that reduce profits as time wasted.

Maximise the length of the life cycle itself:

Generally, the longer the life cycle, the greater the profit that will be generated, assuming that production ceases once the product goes into decline and becomes unprofitable. One way to maximise the life cycle is to get the product to market as quickly as possible because this should maximise the time in which the product generates a profit.

Another way of extending a product's life is to find other uses, or markets, for the product. Other product uses may not be obvious when the product is still in its planning stage and need to be planned and managed later on. On the other hand, it may be possible to plan for a staggered entry into different markets at the planning stage.

Many organisations stagger the launch of their products in different world markets in order to reduce costs, increase revenue and prolong the overall life of the product. A current example is the way in which new films are released in the USA months before the UK launch. This is done to build up the enthusiasm for the film and to increase revenues overall. Other companies may not have the funds to launch worldwide at the same moment and may be forced to stagger it.

The implications of life-cycle costing

Pricing

- Pricing decisions can be based on total life-cycle costs rather than simply the costs for the current period.

Decision making

- In deciding to produce a product, a timetable of life-cycle costs helps show what costs need to be allocated to a product so that an organisation can recover its costs. If all costs cannot be recovered, it would not be wise to produce the product or service.

- Life-cycle costing allows an analysis of links between business functions, e.g. a decision taken now to reduce research and development costs may lead to a fall in sales in the future.

Performance management

- Improved control – many companies find that 90% of the product's life-cycle costs are determined by decisions made in the development and launch stages. Focusing on costs after the product has entered production results in only a small proportion of life-cycle costs being manageable. Life-cycle costing thus reinforces the importance of tight control over locked-in costs, such as research and development in the development stage.

- Improved reporting – costs such as research and development and marketing are traditionally reported on an aggregated basis for all products and recorded as a period expense. Life-cycle costing traces these costs to individual products over their entire life cycles, to aid comparison with product revenues generated in later periods

5 Total quality management (TQM)

Total quality management (TQM) is a philosophy of quality management and cost management that has a number of important features.

- **Total** – means that everyone in the value chain is involved in the process, including employees, customer and suppliers
- **Quality** – products and services must meet the customers' requirements
- **Management** – quality is actively managed rather than controlled so that problems are prevented from occurring.

There are three basic principles of TQM:

(1) Get it right, first time

TQM considers that the costs of prevention are less than the costs of correction. One of the main aims of TQM is to achieve zero rejects and 100% quality

(2) Continuous improvement

The second basic principles of TQM is dissatisfaction with the status-quo. Realistically a zero-defect goal may not be obtainable. It does however provide a target to ensure that a company should never be satisfied with its present level of rejects. The management and staff should believe that it is always possible to improve next time.

(3) Customer focus

Quality is examined from a customer perspective and the system is aimed at meeting customer needs and expectations.

Quality related costs

Failing to satisfy customers' needs and expectations, or failing to do so first time, costs the average company between 15 and 30 per cent of sales revenue.

A quality-related cost is the 'cost of ensuring and assuring quality' as well as the loss incurred when quality is not achieved. Quality costs are classified as prevention costs, appraisal cost, internal failure cost and external failure cost.

(1) **Prevention cost**

Prevention costs represent the cost of any action taken to prevent or reduce defects and failures. Examples include:

- customer surveys
- research of customer needs
- field trials
- quality education and training programmes
- supplier reviews
- investment in improved production equipment
- quality engineering.

(2) **Appraisal costs**

Appraisal costs are the costs incurred, such as inspection and testing, in initially ascertaining the conformance of the product to quality requirements. Examples might be:

- the capital cost of measurement equipment
- inspection and testing
- product quality audits
- process control monitoring
- test equipment expense.

(3) **Internal failure cost**

Internal failure costs are the costs arising from inadequate quality where the problem is discovered before the transfer of ownership from supplier to purchaser. Examples include:

- rework or rectification costs
- net cost of scrap
- disposal of defective products
- downtime or idle time due to quality problems.

(4) **External failure cost**

The cost arising from inadequate quality discovered after the transfer of ownership from supplier to purchaser. Examples include:

- complaint investigation and processing
- warranty claims
- cost of lost sales
- product recalls.

Conformance costs and non-conformance costs

Appraisal and prevention costs may also be referred to as conformance costs, whilst internal and external failure costs may be referred to as non-conformance costs.

6 Cost control and cost reduction

Cost control

Cost control essentially involves the setting of targets for cost centre managers and then monitoring performance against those targets.

Two management accounting authors, Crowningshield and Gorman, have identified six requirements of such a system.

(1) Effective delegation of authority and assignment of responsibility for costs. This requires proper delegation of authority with clear cut accountability, with terms of reference and limits of responsibility clearly defined and agreed by all parties concerned.

(2) An agreed plan that sets up objectives and goals to be achieved. In the context of cost savings, this cannot be reiterated often enough. Without such clearly defined and agreed goals, management is working in the dark, having no benchmark by which to measure whether or not it is achieving its desired activity levels.

(3) Motivation to encourage individuals to reach the goals established and agreed. Cost reduction, like anything else within an organisation, is an exercise requiring the agreement of the involved parties for its ultimate success. Agreement implies participation, and these days, this may well mean interdisciplinary participation, with each function of the business making an effective contribution. The goals or target costs must be realistic and reasonably attainable. Ideally, they must optimise that fine balance between maximising managerial potential without making management despondent, and the easily reached target that causes complacency.

(4) Timely reporting. This is an essential prerequisite of control and certainly of any cost reduction exercise. However, the resultant reports must provide detailed and instructive information on the implications of the alternative options. The alternative suggestions must be clearly presented with the cost savings and profit gains highlighted.

(5) The recommendations and action must follow.

(6) More importantly there must be an effective system of follow-up to ensure that the corrective measures are being effectively implemented.

Cost reduction

Cost reduction is the reduction in unit cost of goods or services without impairing suitability for the use intended i.e. without reducing value to the customer.

Cost reduction has rather negative connotations. It is perceived as being about cutting back, about saving money, even about penny pinching. Profit improvement is about accepting the possibility that costs may go up but because they add further value to the product, and make the product more attractive to the customer, profit goes up even further.

Note the important point here – any reduction in cost should not be seen as a reduction in value in the eyes of the consumer.

Cost reduction techniques

A number of techniques are widely used as a means of attempting to achieve cost reduction, particularly in manufacturing organisations.

Value analysis

Value analysis is a systematic examination of factors affecting the cost of a product or service, in order to devise means of achieving the specified purpose most economically at the required standard of quality and reliability.

Value analysis is basically a form of cost reduction i.e. a method of improving profitability by reducing costs without necessarily increasing prices; it is particularly useful to manufacturers or suppliers who are unable to fix their own price because of, for example, a competitive market. However it can be used in all circumstances to try to improve profitability.

Value analysis resulted from a realisation by manufacturers that they were incorporating features into their product which the user of the product did not require and was not prepared to pay for. For example, for a car manufacturer are customers really willing to pay for upholstery or trim which is relatively expensive for the manufacturer to buy? If customers would pay the same price for a car produced with slightly cheaper trim, the company could modify the specification.

Value analysis takes a critical look at each feature of a product, questioning its need and its use, and eliminating any unjustifiable features.

One of the problems with value analysis is placing a meaning on the word 'value'.

It is useful to distinguish two types of value:

- **Utility value** is the value an item has because of the uses to which it can be put.
- **Esteem value** is the value put on an item because of its beauty, craftsmanship, etc.

An individual who wants a basic, functional car to get from A to B will be considering utility value of the car and will not be too concerned with its colour, image or top speed. Other individuals may be looking more at the esteem value of a car than its utility value. They will be concerned about the image of the car, its design, its specification and so on.

The value analysis method

Value analysis can be carried out in five key steps:

Step 1 Establish the precise requirements of the customer. By a process of enquiry it should be possible to discover precisely why customers want an item, whether the item has any esteem value, etc. Only in this way can the manufacturer be certain that each function incorporated into the product contributes some value to it.

Step 2 Establish and evaluate alternative ways of achieving the requirements of the customers. There may be methods of producing the item which have not been considered e.g. replacing metal panels with plastic. Each alternative method must be costed out in units of:

(i)   Materials – amount required, acceptable level of wastage (can it be improved?), alternative, cheaper materials.

(ii) Labour – can the cost be reduced by eliminating operations or changing production methods?

(iii) Other factors – can new, cheaper processes be found? Would a cheaper finish be acceptable?

Step 3 Authorise any proposals put forward as a result of step 2. The assessment in step 2 may be carried out by middle management and, if so, it will require ratification by top management before implementation.

Step 4 Implementation of proposals.

Step 5 Evaluate feedback from new proposals to establish the benefits from the change.

Several benefits will result from value analysis;

- many customers will be impressed by the interest shown in their requirements and this will lead to increased sales.

- a firm which adopts this approach is likely to attract better staff, due both to the prospects for an outlet for their ideas and the higher morale resulting from the team approach.

- there are economic and financial benefits arising from the elimination of unnecessary complexity and the better use of resources.

Value Engineering

A useful principle which can be employed in a target costing context is that of value engineering. This takes the approach of value analysis right back to the design stage of the business process. Whereas value analysis tries to reduce the cost whilst maintaining the perceived value of an existing product, value engineering attempts to design the best possible value at the lowest possible cost into a new product. This cost can then be used in a target costing system.

Other cost reduction techniques

Standardisation of materials and components

This relates to a policy of reducing, so far as is possible, the range and variety of materials and components purchased by the manufacturer and of components produced. If the manufacturer is producing a number of models of the product, it is often possible for one component to be used throughout the range. For example, where there is a series of car models it may be possible to use one type of door handle on all models.

The advantages of such a policy are:

(i) the manufacturer can buy, or make, large quantities, gaining the benefit of reduced unit cost

(ii) having proved the efficiency of a material or component, the manufacturer knows that the quality and content will not change

(iii) because of the reduction in variety, inventory control will be easier

(iv) better service can be provided to customers in the provision of spare parts

(v) less time will be needed to train operatives who handle the component.

The possible disadvantages are:

(i)   if there is only one supplier of the material or component, the manufacturer will be at risk if supplies are interrupted

(ii) there may be restrictions on the design of a new model if the manufacturer wishes to continue the policy for economic reasons

(iii) for the same motive, a standard component may be used in one model when it would be better technically if a special component was used.

As an example, many of the major car manufacturers now design vehicles in such a way as to ensure that as many components as possible are common to as wide a range of models as possible.

Standardisation of product

This refers to the production of articles to the same standard, or a range of products each of which is standardised.

The advantages are as follows:

(i)   the manufacturer derives the benefit of long runs of production with reduced unit cost

(ii) tooling is simpler because it is geared to one method of production

(iii) because of the uniformity of the production method, mechanisation can be extensive

(iv) the consequent buying of large amounts of the same materials and parts results in a reduction of unit cost

(v)   production management is simpler, being confined to standard processes

(vi) less training of operatives is required because the processes do not change

(vii) there are fewer demands on the design staff

(viii) inspection costs are low

(ix) customers know they are buying a proven product and that the quality will not change.

A range of products may be basically standardised but with minor differences between models. Again, using the car industry as an example, a particular model of a car may be available in, say, 20 different colours – but apart from this all of the cars are identical.

The policy can produce disadvantages, such as the following:

(i)   The manufacturer may feel safe in doing what he knows best and may become complacent about the success of the product, so that when the product faces new competition or the public becomes disloyal, he is too slow to recognise it.

(ii) If the product has to be altered because of the above circumstances, then equipment, technical knowledge and managerial experience may be too fixed to adapt successfully.

(iii) If production is continued to a level beyond the reduced demand and that demand does not rise, there will be surplus components, materials and finished goods.

Using a cost reduction team

A cost reduction team can be used to identify scope for achieving cost reductions but care must be taken so that costs saved are not outweighed by the costs of the team itself.

A well-defined programme must be instituted so that the cost reduction teams spend their time in fields where there is scope for savings. Furthermore, it is important that a fixed time is allocated to a particular exercise. There may well be a request to continue the exercise in order to complete the study and obtain extra savings, but these may be quite marginal, and the law of diminishing returns will begin to operate. A cost/benefit approach to a cost reduction programme is essential.

Another aspect is the time and trouble taken by line management to accommodate changes brought about by a cost reduction scheme. Departments and whole functions must be given time to adjust and consolidate agreed changes. A permanent state of change may harm morale and upset the proper working of departments. It is important to recognise that cost reduction implies a specific programme aimed at reducing costs at a given time. The concept does not relate to a continuous situation; it should have a definite start and finish and should incorporate well-defined targets. The activity of cost control is a continuous function of management.

7 Chapter summary

```
                        ┌─────────────────┐
                        │   Alternative   │
                        │ costing methods │
                        └─────────────────┘
```

ABC	Target costing	Lifecycle costing	TQM	Cost control and reduction
• Cost pool	• Selling price	• Tracks and	• Get it right,	• Control =
• Cost driver	less profit	accumulates the	first time	setting targets
	margin =	actual costs and	• Continuous	and aiming to
	target profit	evenues from	improvement	meet them
	• Value analysis	inception to	• Customer focus	• Reduction =
	• Value engineering	abandonment		reducing cost

TQM
- Get it right, first time
- Continuous improvement
- Customer focus

Quality costs
- Prevention
- Appraisal
- Internal failure
- External failure

Cost control and reduction
- Control = setting targets and aiming to meet them
- Reduction = reducing cost without reducing value of product

12

Forecasting techniques

Chapter learning objectives

Upon completion of this chapter you will be able to:

- establish a linear function using regression analysis and interpret the results

- explain, calculate and interpret correlation coefficient and coefficient of determination

- use linear regression coefficients to make forecasts of costs and revenues

- explain the advantages and disadvantages of linear regression analysis

- explain the product life cycles importance in forecasting

- explain the principles of time series analysis (cyclical, trend, seasonal variation and random elements)

- calculate moving averages

- calculation of trends, including the use of regression coefficients

- use trend and season variation (additive and multiplicative) to make budget forecasts

- explain the advantages and disadvantages of time series analysis

- explain the purpose of index numbers

- calculate simple index numbers for one or more variables

- adjust historical and forecast data for price and movements

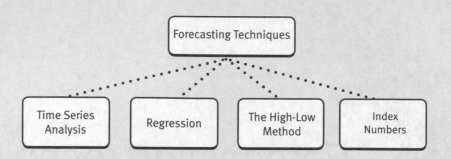

1 Forecasts in budgeting

Budgets are based on forecasts. Forecasts might be prepared for:

* the volume of output and sales

* sales revenue (sales volume and sales prices)

* costs.

The purpose of forecasting in the budgeting process is to establish realistic assumptions for planning. Forecasts might also be prepared on a regular basis for the purpose of feed-forward control reporting.

A forecast might be based on simple assumptions, such as a prediction of a 5% growth in sales volume or sales revenue. Similarly, budgeted expenditure might be forecast using a simple incremental budgeting approach, and adding a percentage amount for inflation on top of the previous year's budget.

On the other hand, forecasts might be prepared using a number of forecasting models, methods or techniques that look to calculate trends and variations over previous years. The reason for using these models and techniques is that they might provide more reliable forecasts.

Possible forecasting techniques:

* the high-low method (seen in a previous chapter)

* linear regression analysis

* time series analysis

* index numbers.

2 Regression analysis

Regression analysis is concerned with establishing the relationship between a number of variables. We are only concerned here with linear relationships between 2 variables.

There are a variety of methods available for identifying the relationship:

(1) Draw a *scatter diagram* and a line of best fit (see Chapter 3)

> The data is plotted on a graph. The y-axis represents the *dependent* variable, i.e. that variable that depends on the other. The *x*-axis shows the *independent* variable, i.e. that variable which is not affected by the other variable.

> From the scatter diagram, the line of best fit can be estimated. The aim is to use our judgement to draw a line through the middle of data with the same slope as the data.

(2) The high-low method (see Chapter 4)

(3) Least Squares Regression Analysis

Least squares regression analysis

Regression analysis finds the line of best fit computationally rather than by estimating the line on a scatter diagram. It seeks to minimise the distance between each point and the regression line.

The equation of a straight line is:

$$y = a + bx$$

where y = dependent variable
  a = intercept (on y-axis)
  b = gradient
  x = independent variable

and $b = \dfrac{n\Sigma xy - \Sigma x \Sigma y}{n\Sigma x^2 - (\Sigma x)^2}$

where n = number of pairs of data

and $a = \bar{y} - b\bar{x}$

Alternative formula for a

$$a = \frac{\sum y}{n} - \frac{b\sum x}{n}$$

Illustration 1 – Regression analysis

A small supermarket chain has 6 shops. Each shop advertises in their local newspapers and the marketing director is interested in the relationship between the amount that they spend on advertising and the sales revenue that they achieve. She has collated the following information for the 6 shops for the previous year:

Shop	Advertising expenditure	Sales revenue
	$000	$000
1	80	730
2	60	610
3	120	880
4	90	750
5	70	650
6	30	430

She has further performed some calculations for a linear regression calculation as follows:

- the sum of the advertising expenditure (x) column is 450

- the sum of the sales revenue (y) column is 4,050

- when the two columns are multiplied together and summed (xy) the total is 326,500

- when the advertising expenditure is squared (x^2) and summed, the total is 38,300, and

- when the sales revenue is squared (y^2) and summed, the total is 2,849,300

Calculate the line of best fit using regression analysis.

Solution

$$b = \frac{n\Sigma xy - \Sigma x \Sigma y}{n\Sigma x^2 - (\Sigma x)^2}$$

$$= \frac{6 \times 326{,}500 - 450 \times 4{,}050}{6 \times 38{,}300 - 450^2}$$

$$= \frac{136{,}500}{27{,}300} = 5$$

$$a = \bar{y} - b\bar{x}$$

$$a = \frac{4{,}050}{6} - 5 \times \frac{450}{6} = 300$$

The regression equation is $\quad y = 300 + 5x$

Interpretation of the line

Mathematical interpretation

If x = 0, then y = 300 and then each time x increases by 1 y increases by 5

Business interpretation

If no money is spent on advertising then sales would still be $300,000. Then for every additional $1 increase in advertising sales revenue would increase by $5.

Linear regression in budgeting

Linear regression analysis can be used to make forecasts or estimates whenever a linear relationship is assumed between two variables, and historical data is available for analysis.

The regression equation can be used for predicting values of y from a given x value.

(1) If the value of x is within the range of our original data, the prediction is known as *Interpolation*.

(2) If the value of x is outside the range of our original data, the prediction is known as *Extrapolation*.

In general, interpolation is much safer than extrapolation.

Test your understanding 1

Marcus Aurelius Ltd has just taken on 2 new stores in the same area. He knows if no money is spent on advertising then sales will be $300,000, but for every $1 spent on advertising sales revenue increases by $5. The predicted advertising expenditure is expected to be $150,000 for one store and $50,000 for the other.

(a) Calculate the predicted sales revenues?

(b) Explain the reliability of the forecasts.

Linear regression can also be used:

- to establish a trend line from a time series. (Time series is explained later in this chapter)

  - The independent variable (x) in a time series is time.

  - The dependent variable (y) is sales, production volume or cost etc.

- as an alternative to using the high-low method of cost behaviour analysis. It should be more accurate than the high-low method, because it is based on more items of historical data, not just a 'high' and a 'low' value.

  - The independent variable (x) in total cost analysis is the volume of activity.

  - The dependent variable (y) is total cost.

  - The value of a is the amount of fixed costs.

  - The value of b is the variable cost per unit of activity.

When a linear relationship is identified and quantified using linear regression analysis, values for a and b are obtained, and these can be used to make a forecast for the budget. For example:

- a sales budget or forecast can be prepared, or

- total costs (or total overhead costs) can be estimated, for the budgeted level of activity.

Test your understanding 2

A company is investigating its current cost structure. An analysis of production levels and costs over the first six months of the year has revealed the following:

Month	Production level (units) (000s)	Production cost ($000)
January	9.0	240
February	10.0	278
March	9.7	256
April	10.5	258
May	11.0	290
June	11.5	300

Further analysis has produced the following data:

$\sum x = 61.7$; $\sum y = 1,622$; $\sum xy = 16,772$; $\sum x^2 = 638.6$

Required:

(a) Use regression analysis to identify:

   (i) Variable cost per unit.

   (ii) Monthly fixed costs

(b) It is expected that in July, production will be 12,000 units. Estimate the cost of July's production and comment on the accuracy of your estimate.

Benefits of simple linear regression

(1) Simple and easy to use.

(2) Looks at the basic relationship between two sets of data.

(3) Can be used to forecast and to produce budgets.

(4) Information required to complete the linear regression calculations should be readily available.

(5) Computer spreadsheet programmes often have a function that will calculate the relationship between two sets of data.

(6) Simplifies the budgeting process.

Limitations of simple linear regression

(1) Assumes a linear relationship between the variables.

(2) Only measures the relationship between two variables. In reality the dependent variable is affected by many independent variables.

(3) Only interpolated forecasts tend to be reliable. The equation should not be used for extrapolation.

(4) Regression assumes that the historical behaviour of the data continues into the foreseeable future.

(5) Interpolated predictions are only reliable if there is a significant correlation between the data.

3 Correlation

Regression analysis attempts to find the straight line relationship between two variables. Correlation is concerned with establishing how strong the relationship is.

Degrees of correlation

Two variables might be:

(a) perfectly correlated

(b) partly correlated

(c) uncorrelated

Positive and negative correlation

Correlation can be positive or negative.

Positive correlation means that high values of one variable are associated with high values of the other and that low values of one are associated with low values of the other.

Negative correlation means that low values of one variable are associated with high values of the other and vice versa.

Perfect correlation

The graph on the left shows perfect positive correlation and the graph on the right show perfect negative correlation

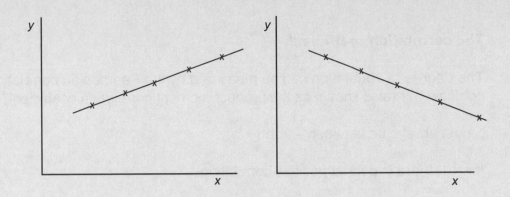

All the pairs of values lie on a straight line. There is an exact linear relationship between the two variables.

Partial correlation

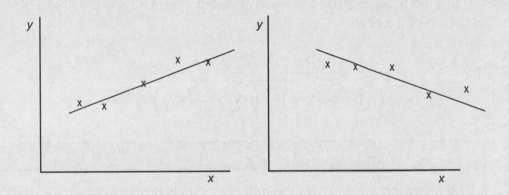

In the first diagram there is not an exact relationship, but low values of x tend to be associated with low values of y, and high values of x tend to be associated with high values of y.

In the second diagram again there is not an exact relationship, but low values of x tend to be associated with high values of y and vice versa.

No correlation

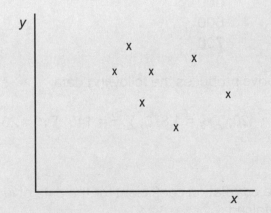

The values of the two variables seem to be completely unconnected.

The correlation coefficient

The degree of correlation can be measured by the Pearsonian correlation coefficient, r (also known as the product moment correlation coefficient).

r must always be between −1 and +1.

If r = 1, there is perfect positive correlation

If r = 0, there is no correlation

If r = −1, there is perfect negative correlation

For other values of r, the meaning is not so clear. It is generally taken that if r > 0.8, then there is strong positive correlation and if r < − 0.8, there is strong negative correlation.

$$r = \frac{n\sum xy - \sum x \sum y}{\sqrt{\left(n\sum x^2 - \left(\sum x\right)^2\right)\left(n\sum y^2 - \left(\sum y\right)^2\right)}}$$

Illustration 2 – Correlation

The following table shows the number of units produced and the total costs incurred.

Units produced	Total costs $
100	40,000
200	45,000
300	50,000
400	65,000
500	70,000
600	70,000
700	80,000

The table above produces the following data:

$\sum x = 28$; $\sum y = 420$; $\sum xy = 1{,}870$; $\sum x^2 = 140$; $\sum y^2 = 26{,}550$; $n = 7$

Required:

Calculate the correlation coefficient for the data given and comment on the result obtained.

Solution

Apply the formula for calculating r

$$r = \frac{(7 \times 1{,}870) - (28 \times 420)}{\sqrt{[(7 \times 140) - (28 \times 28))((7 \times 26{,}550) - (420 \times 420)]}}$$

$$= \frac{(13{,}090 - 11{,}760)}{\sqrt{[(980 - 784)(185{,}850 - 176{,}400)]}}$$

$$= \frac{1{,}330}{\sqrt{(196 \times 9{,}450)}}$$

$$= +0.98$$

A correlation coefficient of + 0.98 indicates a high degree of positive correlation between the variables. In general, the closer that r is to +1 (or − 1) the higher the degree of correlation.

Test your understanding 3

Which of the following is NOT a feasible value for the correlation coefficient?

(a) +1.2

(b) +0.6

(c) 0

(d) −0.9

Test your understanding 4

If $\sum x = 440$, $\sum y = 330$, $\sum x^2 = 17{,}986$, $\sum y^2 = 10{,}366$, $\sum xy = 13{,}467$ and $n = 11$, then the value of r, the coefficient of correlation, to two decimal places, is:

A   0.98

B   0.63

C   0.96

D   0.59

Test your understanding 5

A small supermarket chain has 6 shops. Each shop advertises in their local newspapers and the marketing director is interested in the relationship between the amount that they spend on advertising and the sales revenue that they achieve. She has collated the following information for the 6 shops for the previous year:

Shop	Advertising expenditure $000	Sales revenue $000
1	80	730
2	60	610
3	120	880
4	90	750
5	70	650
6	30	430

She has further performed some calculations for a linear regression calculation as follows:

• the sum of the advertising expenditure (x) column is 450

• the sum of the sales revenue (y) column is 4,050

• when the two columns are multiplied together and summed (xy) the total is 326,500

• when the advertising expenditure is squared (x^2) and summed, the total is 38,300, and

• when the sales revenue is squared (y^2) and summed, the total is 2,849,300

Calculate the correlation coefficient.

The coefficient of determination, r^2

The coefficient of determination, r^2 measures the proportion of changes in y that can be explained by changes in x.

Test your understanding 6

Calculate the coefficient of determination for the small supermarket chain in the previous TYU and comment.

4 Time series analysis

A time series is a series of figures recorded over **time**, e.g. unemployment over the last 5 **years**, output over the last 12 **months**, etc.

Time series analysis is a technique used to:

- identify whether there is any **underlying historical trend**
- use this analysis of the historical trend to forecast the trend into the future
- identify whether there are any **seasonal variations** around the trend
- apply estimated seasonal variations to a trend line forecast in order to prepare a forecast season by season.

A time series has 4 components.

The trend

Most time series follow some sort of long term movement. In time series analysis the trend is measured by:

(1) *Inspection*. A graph of the data is produced and the trend line is drawn by eye with the aim of plotting the line so that it lies in the middle of the data points.

(2) *Least squares regression analysis*. x represents time (each month would be given a number e.g. January =1, February =2 etc) and y is the data.

(3) *Moving averages*. This method attempts to remove seasonal or cyclical variations by a process of averaging.

Seasonal variations

Once the trend has been found, the seasonal variation can be determined. Seasonal variations are **short-term fluctuations** in value due to different circumstances which occur at different times of the year, on different days of the week, different times of day, etc e.g.:

- Sales of groceries are highest on Saturdays

- Traffic is greatest in the morning and evening rush hours.

If there is a straight-line trend in the time series, seasonal variations must cancel each other out. The total of the seasonal variations over each cycle should be zero. Seasonal variations can be measured:

- in units or in monetary values

- as a percentage value or index value in relation to the underlying trend.

Seasonal variations are used to forecast future figures by amending the trend. There are two main models:

(1) *The additive model.* Here the seasonal variation is expressed as an absolute amount to be added on to the trend to find the actual result, e.g. ice-cream sales in summer are expected to be $200,000 above the trend.

> Prediction = Trend + Seasonal variation

(2) *The multiplicative model.* Here the seasonal variation is expressed as a ratio/proportion/percentage to be multiplied by the trend to arrive at the actual figure, e.g. ice-cream sales are expected to be 50% more than the trend.

> Prediction = Trend × Seasonal variation

Cyclical variations

Cyclical variations are **medium-term to long term** influences usually associated with the economy. These cycles are rarely of consistent length. A further problem is that we would need 6 or 7 full cycles of data to be sure that the cycle was there. Cyclical variations are often associated with the economy.

Residual or random variations

Residual or random variations are caused by irregular items, which cannot be predicted.

Forecasting with time series

We are only really interested in the first two components of time series (trend and seasonal variations) when we are looking to forecast for a budget as the cyclical variations are too long term and residual variations are too unpredictable.

A trend over time, established from historical data, and adjusted for seasonal variations, can then be used to make predictions for the future.

e.g

Illustration 3 – Trend and seasonal variation

A business might have a flat trend in sales, of $1 million each six months, but with sales $150,000 below trend in the first six months of the year and $150,000 above trend in the second six months. In this example, the sales would be $850,000 in the first six months of the year and $1,150,000 in the second six months.

5 Moving averages

Calculating a moving average

A moving average is a series of averages calculated from time series historical data.

When moving averages are used to estimate a trend line, an important issue is the choice of the number of time periods to use to calculate the moving average. How many time periods should a moving average be based on?

There is no definite or correct answer to this question. However, where there is a regular cycle of time periods, it would make sense to calculate the moving averages over a full cycle.

- When you are calculating a moving average of daily figures, it is probably appropriate to calculate a seven-day moving average.

- When you are calculating a moving average of quarterly figures, it is probably appropriate to calculate a four-quarter moving average.

- When you are calculating a moving average of monthly figures, it might be appropriate to calculate a 12-month moving average, although a shorter-period moving average might be preferred.

For example

- The first moving average value in the series is the average of the values for time period 1 to time period n. (So, if n = 3, the first moving average in the series would be the average of the historical values for time period 1 to time period 3.)

- The second moving average value in the series is the average of the values for time period 2 to time period (n + 1). (So, if n = 3, the second moving average in the series would be the average of the historical values for time period 2 to time period 4.)

- The third moving average value in the series is the average of the values for time period 3 to time period (n + 2). (So, if n = 3, the third moving average in the series would be the average of the historical values for time period 3 to time period 5.)

The moving average value is associated with the mid-point of the time periods used to calculate the average.

Illustration 4 – Moving averages

A business is forecasting the value of their sales for the first quarter of the coming year. Current year values to date are as follows:

Month	Sales Value $000
June	851
July	771
August	916
September	935
October	855
November	1,000
December	1,019

Using moving averages calculate the forecast sales values for January to March.

Solution

Step 1 – decide on an appropriate 'cycle' to use. This data appears to run in a 3 month cycle - the sales value increases for 3 months then drops down, then increases for 3 months then drops down

Step 2 – calculate the 3 month moving average total

Month	Sales Value $000	Moving average total
June	851	
July	771	2,538
August	916	2,622
September	935	2,706
October	855	2,790
November	1,000	2,874
December	1,019	

Step 3 – calculate the trend by dividing the 3 month moving average total by 3 to get the average for the 3 months.

Month	Sales Value $000	Moving average total	Trend
June	851		
July	771	2,538	846
August	916	2,622	874
September	935	2,706	902
October	855	2,790	930
November	1,000	2,874	958
December	1,019		

Step 4 – compare the trend to the actual sales value to calculate the seasonal variation. Remember that the variation is 'from the trend' so in the case of July the sales value of $771,000 is less than the trend of $846,000 hence the negative variation.

Month	Sales Value $000	Trend	Seasonal variation
June	851		
July	771	846	–75
August	916	874	42
September	935	902	33
October	855	930	–75
November	1,000	958	42
December	1,019		

Step 5 – extrapolate the trend. In this example the trend is increasing by $28,000 each month.

Month	Trend
June	851
July	771
August	916
September	902
October	930
November	958
December	986
January	1,014
February	1,042
March	1,070

Step 6 – apply the season variation to the trend to calculate the forecast sales value. In this example the seasonal variation has a cyclical pattern so we repeat the variation until we have forecast the figures required.

Month	Trend	Seasonal Variation	Forecast Sales Value $000
September	902	33	
October	930	−75	
November	958	42	
December	986	33	
January	**1,014**	**−75**	**939**
February	**1,042**	**42**	**1,084**
March	**1,070**	**33**	**1,103**

KAPLAN PUBLISHING

A more detailed approach

A small business operating holiday homes in Scotland wishes to forecast next year's sales for the budget, using moving averages to establish a straight-line trend and seasonal variations. Next year is 20X7. The accountant has assumed that sales are seasonal, with a summer season and a winter season each year.

Seasonal sales for the past seven years have been as follows:

Sales

	Summer $000	Winter $000
20X4	124	70
20X5	230	180
20X6	310	270
20X7	440	360
20X8	520	470
20X9	650	

Required:

(a) Calculate a trend line based on a two-season moving average.

(b) Calculate the average increase in sales each season.

(c) Calculate seasonal variations in sales.

(d) Use this data to prepare a sales forecast for each season in 20Y0.

(a)

Season and year	Actual sales	Two-season moving total	Seasonal moving average	Centre the moving average (Trend)	Seasonal variation
	(A)			(B)	= (A) – (B)
	$000	$000	$000	$000	$000
Summer 20X4	124				
		194	97		
Winter 20X4	70			123.5	– 53.5
		300	150		
Summer 20X5	230			177.5	+ 52.5
		410	205		
Winter 20X5	180			225.0	– 45.0
		490	245		
Summer 20X6	310			267.5	+ 42.5
		580	290		
Winter 20X6	270			322.5	– 52.5
		710	355		
Summer 20X7	440			377.5	+ 62.5
		800	400		
Winter 20X7	360			420.0	– 60.0
		880	440		
Summer 20X8	520			467.5	+ 52.5
		990	495		
Winter 20X8	470			527.5	– 57.5
		1,120	560		
Summer 20X9	650				

The trend line is shown by the moving averages.

(b) The average increase in sales each season in the trend line is:

($527,500 – $123,500) / 8 seasons = $50,500 each season

(c) Seasonal variations need to add up to zero in the additive model. The seasonal variations calculated so far are:

Year	Summer $000	Winter $000
20X4		− 53.5
20X5	+ 52.5	− 45.0
20X6	+ 42.5	− 52.5
20X7	+ 62.5	− 60.0
20X8	+ 52.5	− 57.5
Total variations	+ 210.0	− 268.5

	Summer	Winter	Total
Number of measurements	4	5	
Average seasonal variation	+ 52.5	− 53.7	− 1.2
Reduce to 0 (share equally)	+ 0.6	+ 0.6	+ 1.2
Adjusted seasonal variation	+ 53.1	− 53.1	0.0

The seasonal variations could be rounded to + $53,000 in summer and − $53,000 in winter.

(d) Using the information above we extrapolate the trend line and then apply the seasonal variation. The average increase in sales is $50,500 each season.

Winter X8 = 527,500 + 50,500 = Summer X9 + 50,500 = Winter X9 + 50,500 = Summer Y0 + 50,500 = Winter Y0

The trend is then adjusted by the season variation

Summer Y0 = 527,500 + (50,500 × 3) + 53,000 = $732,000

Winter Y0 = 527,500 + (50,500 × 4) − 53,000 = $676,500

Test your understanding 7

W plc is preparing its budgets for next year.

The following regression equation has been found to be a reliable estimate of W plc's deseasonalised sales in units:

$y = 10x + 420$

Where y is the total sales units and x refers to the accountancy period. Quarterly seasonal variations have been found to be:

Q1	Q2	Q3	Q4
+10%	+25%	−5%	−30%

In accounting period 33 (which is quarter 4) identify the seasonally adjusted sales units:

A 525

B 589

C 750

D 975

Test your understanding 8

A company will forecast its quarterly sales units for a new product by using a formula to predict the base sales units and then adjusting the figure by a seasonal index.

The formula is BU = 4,000 + 80Q

Where BU = Base sales units and Q is the quarterly period number.

The seasonal index values are:

Quarter 1	105%
Quarter 2	80%
Quarter 3	95%
Quarter 4	120%

Identify the forecast increase in sales units from Quarter 3 to Quarter 4:

A 25%

B 80 units

C 100 units

D 1,156 units

(2 marks)

Advantages and disadvantages of time series analysis

The advantages of forecasting using time series analysis are that:

- forecasts are based on clearly-understood assumptions

- trend lines can be reviewed after each successive time period, when the most recent historical data is added to the analysis; consequently, the reliability of the forecasts can be assessed

- forecasting accuracy can possibly be improved with experience.

The disadvantages of forecasting with time series analysis are that:

- there is an assumption that what has happened in the past is a reliable guide to the future

- there is an assumption that a straight-line trend exists

- there is an assumption that seasonal variations are constant, either in actual values using the additive model (such as dollars of sales) or as a proportion of the trend line value using the multiplicative model.

None of these assumptions might be valid.

However, the reliability of a forecasting method can be established over time. If forecasts turn out to be inaccurate, management might decide that they are not worth producing, and that different methods of forecasting should be tried. On the other hand, if forecasts prove to be reasonably accurate, management are likely to continue with the same forecasting method.

6 The product life cycle and forecasting

The product life cycle (seen in Chapter 11) can also be used during the forecasting procedure.

If an organisation knows where a product is in its life cycle, they can use this knowledge to plan the marketing of that product more effectively and, more importantly, the organisation may be able to derive an approximate forecast of its sales from a knowledge of the current position of the product in its life cycle:

- At the development stage sales are nil.

- At the introduction stage the product is launched on to the market and the sales volume is likely to be at a low level.

- During the growth stage it is hoped that sales volume will increase rapidly.

- At the maturity stage sales are still high but the organisation should not be forecasting any significant growth.

- During the decline stage sales will slow so the forecast figure should be conservative.

The product life cycle model is seen to have a number of uses in management and management accounting. However there are some limitations:

- it is over simplistic to assume that all products comply with the product life cycle curve

- it is difficult for management to establish a precise position of a product in the life cycle curve.

7 Index numbers

Introduction

In a business context there will be many situations where a series of numbers will be produced giving information regarding a number of accounting periods or years. For example, the total revenue produced by a hotel is seen to be increasing year by year which might be interpreted as meaning that the company is generating growth – more rooms, more hotels, more guests.

But there could be another explanation which may be less appealing to management – it may be that the increase in revenue results from an increase in prices charged (room rates) which have been adjusted over time to reflect inflation in the economy. The increase in revenue may not necessarily indicate any increase in volume of activity generated by the company – the company may simply be charging higher prices.

More useful information could be derived in this sort of situation by the use of an index number.

What is an index number?

An index number is a technique for comparing, over time, changes in some feature of a group of items (e.g. price, quantity consumed, etc) by expressing the property each year as a percentage of some earlier year.

The year that is used as the initial year for comparison is known as the **base year**. The base year for an index should be chosen with some care. As far as possible it should be a **'typical year'** therefore being **as free as possible from abnormal occurrences**. The base year should also be fairly recent and revised on a regular basis.

Illustration 5 – Example of an index calculation

The table below shows the sales performance of the Station Hotel. Revenue from rooms let 20X0–20X4 (all figures in $000s)

	20X0	20X1	20X2	20X3	20X4
Station Hotel	1,150	1,250	1,200	1,250	1,300

If 20X0 is the year used for comparison of subsequent selling prices then this is the base year and the index for the 20X0 price is 100.

Year	Selling price $	Index
20X0	20	100
20X1	23	
20X2	26	
20X3	25	
20X4	28	

The index for each subsequent year must then be calculated by comparing that year's price to the price in 20X0.

The calculation of the index for each year is as follows:

Current year figure/base year figure × 100

20X1 23/20 × 100 = 115
20X2 26/20 × 100 = 130
20X3 25/20 × 100 = 125
20X4 28/20 × 100 = 140

The completed table will appear as follows:

Year	Selling Price $	Index
20X0	20	100
20X1	23	115
20X2	26	130
20X3	25	125
20X4	28	140

This now shows that:

- in 20X1 the increase in room rate over the 20X0 price was 15%
- the 20X2 price shows an increase of 30% over the 20X0 price
- the 20X3 price an increase of 25% over 20X0
- the 20X4 price an increase of 40% over 20X0

This simple calculation immediately provides more information for management. Revenue figures can now be adjusted to reflect these changes in the selling price of products.

The revenue figures may be restated at a common price level to reflect the volume changes underlying sales i.e. strip out the extra revenue that is due to an increase the selling price.

The general adjustment carried out to restate costs or revenues at a common price level is to multiply by:

Index number for base year/index number for current year

Where the base year is the year chosen as the common price level.

If revenue were restated at 20X4 prices, the revised revenue figures for Station Hotel would be:

Year	Revenue ($000)	Index adjustment	Adjusted revenue
20X0	1,150	140/100	1,610
20X1	1,250	140/115	1,522
20X2	1,200	140/130	1,292
20X3	1,250	140/125	1,400
20X4	1,300	140/140	1,300

This shows that volume fell considerably between 20X0 and 20X2 but improved in 20X3 and then fell again in 20X4.

This adjustment is often carried out using the Retail Price Index or a specific industry price index as a measure of price inflation. Organisations can restate their sales or costs at a price level which reflects general price inflation to assess their real performance.

KAPLAN PUBLISHING

8 Types of index numbers

Index numbers are used in a variety of situations and to measure changes in all sorts of items. As the uses of index numbers are so diverse a number of different types of indices have been developed.

We shall deal below with the following:

- simple indices
- chain based indices
- multi-item (or weighted) indices.

9 Simple indices

A simple index is one that measures the changes in either price or quantity of a single item.

As was seen in our example earlier relating to hotel rooms a simple index measures the percentage change for a single item in comparison to the base year.

There are therefore two types of simple indices:

- a price index
- a quantity index.

These simple indices are also known as relatives so we may refer to a price or quantity relative. If the index is a price index then this will show the percentage increase in price of the item since the base year. If the index is a quantity index then this will show the increase in quantity or volume sold since the base year.

We can use a formula to calculate a simple index using 0 as the indicator for the base year and 1 as the indicator for the current year.

The formulae for calculating simple indices are:

Simple price index $= \dfrac{p_1}{p_0} \times 100$

Simple quantity index $= \dfrac{q_1}{q_0} \times 100$

Where:

p_0 is the price at time 0
p_1 is the price at time 1
q_0 is the quantity at time 0
q_1 is the quantity at time 1

Illustration 6 – Quantity index

6,500 items were sold in 20X4 compared with 6,000 in 20X3. Calculate the simple quantity index for 20X4 using 20X3 as base year.

$$\text{Simple quantity index} = \frac{q_1}{q_0} \times 100$$

$$= \frac{6,500}{6,000} \times 100$$

$$= 108.3$$

This means that the quantity sold has increased by 8.3% of its 20X3 figure.

10 Chain base index numbers

A chain base index number expresses each year's value as a percentage of the value for the **previous** year.

If a series of index numbers are required for different years, showing the rate of change of the variable from one year to the next, the chain base method is used.

This simply means that each index number is calculated using the previous year as base. If the rate of change is **increasing**, then the index numbers will be rising; if it is **constant**, the numbers will remain the same and if it is **decreasing** the numbers will be falling.

A shop keeper received the following amounts from the sale of radios:

	$
20X1	1,000
20X2	1,100
20X3	1,210
20X4	1,331
20X5	1,464

Is it correct to say that the annual rate of increase in revenue from sales of radios is getting larger?

Year	Sales ($)	Chain base index
20X1	1,000	
20X2	1,100	$\dfrac{1,100}{1,000} \times 100 = 110$
20X3	1,210	$\dfrac{1,210}{1,100} \times 100 = 110$
20X4	1,331	$\dfrac{1,331}{1,210} \times 100 = 110$
20X5	1,464	$\dfrac{1,464}{1,331} \times 100 = 110$

Although the sales revenue from radios has increased each year, the chain base index numbers have remained static at 110. Therefore, the annual rate of increase of sales revenue from radios is remaining constant rather than increasing.

The chain base is also a suitable index to calculate if the weights ascribed to the various items in the index are changing rapidly. Over a period of years, this index would have modified itself to take account of these changes whereas in a fixed-base method after a number of years the whole index would have to be revised to allow for the changed weighting.

$$\text{Chain base index} = \frac{\text{This year's value}}{\text{Last year's value}} \times 100$$

11 Multi-item (weighted) indices

A weighted index measures the change in overall price or overall quantity of a number of different items compared to the base year. So, for example, an organisation might produce three different products and an index is to be constructed to measure the selling price changes of all three products. In order to do this the percentage change in each of the three selling price must first be calculated individually and the results must then be weighted to reflect the relative importance of each of the three products.

For a price index:

Step 1 Calculate the price relative (simple price index) for each of the items.

Step 2 These price relatives must then be weighted in some suitable manner in order to produce an overall price index.

Similarly if a quantity index is to be calculated:

Step 1 Calculate the quantity relative (simple quantity index) for each of the items.

Step 2 These quantity relatives must then be weighted in some suitable manner in order to produce an overall quantity index.

Illustration 8 – A weighted index

Suppose that an organisation produces three products. Information about the selling prices of these three products for the last two years are as follows:

	Selling price 20X2 $	Selling price 20X3 $
Product A	2	3
Product B	9	10
Product C	25	30

In order to produce a weighted index of the overall price increase over the period, weightings are to be assigned to each of the three products based on sales quantities as follows:

	Quantity
Product A	4,000
Product B	3,000
Product C	1,000

Calculate a weighted price index for 20X3 for these three products (with 20X2 as the base year) using the sales quantities given as weights.

	Price index	Quantity weighting	Total Price index × Quantity
A	3/2 × 100 = 150	4,000	600,000
B	10/9 × 100 = 110	3,000	333,000
C	30/25 × 100 = 120	1,000	120,000
		───	───
		8,000	1,053,000

$$\text{Weighted price index} = \frac{1{,}053{,}000}{8{,}000} = 131.6$$

This shows an increase in prices on average of 31.6% over the year.

Test your understanding 9

A production process uses 10 batches of product A and 30 of product B each year. The costs are as follows:

Item	20X2	20X3
Product A	$6.50	$6.90
Product B	$2.20	$2.50

With 20X2 as the base year construct a weighted price index using:

(a) production quantity as the weighting

(b) production cost as the weighting

The best known example of this type of index is in the way inflation is measured in the UK (and many other countries). The UK measure of inflation is known as the Consumer Price Index which is an index built up from a sample of a number of items making up the regular expenditure of families and individuals – various types of food, clothing, travel, etc. As it includes a number of different items it falls into the multi-item or weighted index category.

12 Laspeyre and Paasche indices

So far in the examples the number of batches used of each product have remained the same in each year. These quantities were used to weights the index calculation and, as the quantities were constant year on year, there was no complication caused.

We are now going to look at the calculation of weighted indices where the figures used to weight change over the time period in question.

There are two approaches, named after the individuals who developed them.

Laspeyre index numbers

Laspeyre index numbers use the **base** year quantity or **base** year price to weight the index.

$$\text{Price index} = \frac{\sum(\text{Current year price} \times \text{Base year quantity})}{\sum(\text{Base year price} \times \text{Base year quantity})} \times 100$$

OR **Price index** = $\dfrac{\sum P_1 Q_0}{\sum P_0 Q_0} \times 100$

Quantity index = $\dfrac{\sum(\text{Current year quantity} \times \text{Base year price})}{\sum(\text{Base year quantity} \times \text{Base year price})} \times 100$

OR **Quantity index** = $\dfrac{\sum Q_1 P_0}{\sum Q_0 P_0}$

Illustration 9 – Laspeyre indices

Using the following information calculate the Laspeyre price index and the Laspeyre quantity index.

Product	20X2		20X3	
	Quantity	Unit price $	Quantity	Unit price $
A	10	6.50	5	6.90
B	30	2.20	40	2.50

The base year is 20X2.

Solution

Laspeyre Price index = $\dfrac{\sum P_1 Q_0}{\sum P_0 Q_0} \times 100$

Product	20X2 Price (P_0)	20X3 Price (P_1)	20X2 Quantity (Q_0)	$P_1 Q_0$	$P_0 Q_0$
A	6.50	6.90	10	69	65
B	2.20	2.50	30	75	66
				—	—
			$\sum$	144	131

$$\text{Laspeyre price index} = \frac{144}{131} \times 100 = 110$$

$$\textbf{Laspeyre Quantity index} = \frac{\Sigma Q_1 P_0}{\Sigma Q_0 P_0} \times 100$$

Product	20X2 Quantity (Q_0)	20X3 Quantity (Q_1)	20X2 Price (P_0)	$Q_1 P_0$	$Q_0 P_0$
A	10	5	6.50	32.5	65
B	30	40	2.20	88	66
			Σ	120.5	131

$$\text{Laspeyre quantity index} = \frac{120.5}{131} \times 100 = 92$$

Advantages of Laspeyre indices

- cheaper, as the obtaining of new quantities each year (which may be a costly exercise) is avoided.

- easier to calculate where a series of years are being compared, since the denominator remains the same for all years.

Disadvantages of Laspeyre indices

- an out-of-date consumption pattern may be used, so that trends become unrealistic.

- as prices rise, quantities purchased tend to fall if there are alternative goods available. This decrease is not reflected in the Laspeyre index which tends therefore to overestimate the effect of rising prices.

Paasche index numbers

Paasche index numbers use the **current** year quantity or **current** year price to weight the index.

$$\text{Price index} = \frac{\sum(\text{Current year price} \times \text{Current year quantity})}{\sum(\text{Base year price} \times \text{Current year quantity})} \times 100$$

$$\text{Or Price index} = \frac{\sum P_1 Q_1}{\sum P_0 Q_1} \times 100$$

$$\text{Quantity index} = \frac{\sum(\text{Current year quantity} \times \text{Current year price})}{\sum(\text{Base year quantity} \times \text{Current year price})} \times 100$$

$$\text{Or Quantity index} = \frac{\sum Q_1 P_1}{\sum Q_0 P_1} \times 100$$

Illustration 10 – Paasche indices

Using the following information calculate the Paasche price index and the Paasche quantity index.

Product	20X2		20X3	
	Quantity	Unit price $	Quantity	Unit price $
A	10	6.50	5	6.90
B	30	2.20	40	2.50

The base year is 20X2.

Solution

$$\text{Paasche Price index} = \frac{\Sigma P_1 Q_1}{\Sigma P_0 Q_1} \times 100$$

Product	20X2 Price (P_0)	20X3 Price (P_1)	20X3 Quantity (Q_1)	$P_1 Q_1$	$P_0 Q_1$
A	6.50	6.90	5	34.5	32.5
B	2.20	2.50	40	100	88
				134.5	120.5

$$\text{Paasche price index} = \frac{134.5}{120.5} \times 100 = 112$$

$$\text{Paasche Quantity index} = \frac{\Sigma Q_1 P_1}{\Sigma Q_0 P_1} \times 100$$

Product	20X2 Quantity (Q_0)	20X3 Quantity (Q_1)	20X3 Price (P_1)	$Q_1 P_1$	$Q_0 P_1$
A	10	5	6.90	34.5	69
B	30	40	2.50	100	75
				134.5	144

$$\text{Paasche quantity index} = \frac{134.5}{144} \times 100 = 93$$

Advantage of Paasche indices

- since current year weights are used, this results in an index based on the current pattern of consumption so that a less frequent revision of base year is needed.

Disadvantages of Paasche indices

- where a series of years is involved, the amount of calculation is greater as both the numerator and the denominator need to be recalculated each year.

- can only be constructed if up-to-date quantity information is available.

- rising prices have the opposite effect on the weights, so a Paasche price index tends to underestimate the effect of inflation.

Advantages of index numbers

- They aid the management understanding of information presented to them.

- Indices present changes in data or information over time in percentage terms.

- They make comparison between items of data easier and more meaningful – it is relatively easy to make comparisons and draw conclusions from figures when you are starting from a base of 100.

- The ability to calculate separate price and quantity indices allows management to identify the relative importance of changes in each of two variables.

Disadvantages of index numbers

- There may be no single correct way of calculating an index, especially the more sophisticated index numbers. The user of the information should bear in mind the basis on which the index is calculated.

- The overall result obtained from multi-item index numbers are averages

- They should only be applied to the items which are included in the index calculation.

- They are relative values, not absolute figures and may not give the whole picture.

Index numbers and forecasting

The accuracy of forecasting is affected by the need to adjust historical data and future forecasts to allow for price or cost inflation.

- When historical data is used to calculate a trend line or line of best fit, it should ideally be adjusted to the same index level for prices or costs. If the actual cost or revenue data is used, without adjustments for inflation, the resulting line of best fit will include the inflationary differences.

- When a forecast is made from a line of best fit, an adjustment to the forecast should be made for anticipated inflation in the forecast period.

Test your understanding 10

Production overhead costs at company BW are assumed to vary with the number of machine hours worked. A line of best fit will be calculated from the following historical data, with costs adjusted to allow for cost inflation over time.

Year	Total production overheads $	Number of machine hours	Cost index
20X8	143,040	3,000	192
20X9	156,000	3,200	200
20Y0	152,320	2,700	224
20Y1	172,000	3,000	235

Required:

(a) Reconcile the cost data to a common price level, to remove differences caused by inflation.

(b) If the line of best fit, based on current (20Y1) prices, is calculated as:

$$y = 33,000 + 47x$$

where y = total overhead costs in $ and x = machine hours:

calculate the expected total overhead costs in 20Y2 if expected production activity is 3,100 machine hours and the expected cost index is 250.

Test your understanding 11 – DOMESTIC ELECTRICAL

A domestic electrical appliance was introduced on to the market in 2003. At the point of sale customers are offered the chance to purchase an insurance policy to cover repairs and parts for the first five years of operation. These policies cannot be purchased later on, only when the appliance is first bought. The table below shows the total industry sales of this appliance for the years 2003 to 2009 together with the number of insurance policies sold and a general price index for electrical goods.

Year	Sales of Appliances $000	Policy sales (number)	Price index for Electrical Goods (2001 = 100)
2003	3,600	400	120
2004	6,250	300	125
2005	9,170	600	131
2006	14,000	1,200	140
2007	21,600	1,700	144
2008	27,000	2,200	150
2009	41,600	2,000	160

Required:

(a) Deflate the appliance sales figures to 2001 prices.

(2 marks)

(b) Calculate the coefficient of determination between the deflated appliance sales figures and the insurance policy sales using the following information:

- Total value of deflated appliance sales (x) = $84,000,000
- Total number of policy sales (y) = 8,400
- $\sum xy$ = 136,000,000
- $\sum x^2$ = 1,408,000,000
- $\sum y^2$ = 13,780,000

(2 marks)

(c) The following statement relates to the coefficient of determination calculated in b.

The coefficient of determination means that **(Gap 1)** of the changes in **(Gap 2)** can be explained by changes in the level of the **(Gap 3)**. The other **(Gap 4)** of changes are caused by other factors.

Select the correct phrase to complete the sentences:

– 16.3%

– 87.3%

– deflated appliance sales

– policy sales

(2 marks)

(d) Using the data provided in b calculate the least squares regression equation to predict insurance policy sales from deflated appliance sales.

(2 marks)

(e) The total sales of the electrical appliance in 2010 are estimated at $51million at 2010 prices and the price index for electrical goods in the year 2010 based on 2001 is predicted to be 170.

Use the least squares regression equation to obtain a forecast of insurance policy sales for 2010.

(2 marks)

(Total: 10 marks)

13 Chapter summary

```
                          ┌─────────────────────────┐
                          │  Forecasting Techniques │
                          └─────────────────────────┘
```

Time Series Analysis	Regression	The High-Low Method	Index Numbers
• Trend • Seasonal variations • Moving averages	• $y = a + bx$ • Correlation coefficient • Coefficient of determination	• Trend • Seasonal variations • Moving averages	• Current year base year

Test your understanding answers

Test your understanding 1

(a) The equation of a straight line is $y = a + bx$. The information Marcus has shows that the sales revenue is dependent on the level of advertising. The sales revenue is y and the money spent on advertising is x.

			$
Sales	$= 300{,}000 + 5 \times 150{,}000$	=	1,050,000
Sales	$= 300{,}000 + 5 \times 50{,}000$	=	550,000

(b) The second prediction is the more reliable as it involves interpolation. The first prediction goes beyond the original data upon which the regression line was based and thus assumes that the relationship will continue on in the same way, which may not be true.

Test your understanding 2

(a)

(i) Variable cost (b) $= \dfrac{6 \times 16{,}772 - 61.7 \times 1{,}622}{6 \times 638.6 - 61.7^2}$

$= \dfrac{554.6}{24.71} = \$22.44$

(ii) Fixed cost (a) $= \dfrac{1{,}622}{6} - 22.44 \times \dfrac{61.7}{6}$

$= 270.33 \quad - 230.76$

$= \$39.57$

(b) The estimated cost of 12,000 units will be given by the linear cost equation:

y = $39.57 + $22.44x

y = 39.57 + (22.44 × 12) = 308.85 = $308,850

It should be noted that since this is outside the range of values for which costs are known it might be inaccurate. For example there may be stepped fixed cost such as an additional supervisor that is required at 11,800 units.

Test your understanding 3

A

Test your understanding 4

$$r = \frac{11 \times 13,467 - 440 \times 330}{\sqrt{[(11 \times 17,986 - 440^2)(11 \times 10,366 - 330^2)]}} = 0.63$$

Test your understanding 5

$$r = \frac{n\Sigma xy - \Sigma x\Sigma y}{\sqrt{(n\Sigma x^2 - (\Sigma x)^2)(n\Sigma y^2 - (\Sigma y)^2)}}$$

$$r = \frac{6 \times 326,500 - 450 \times 4,050}{\sqrt{(6 \times 38,300 - 450^2)(6 \times 2,849,300 - 4,050^2)}}$$

$$r = \frac{136,500}{\sqrt{27,300 \times 693,300}}$$

$$r = 0.992$$

Test your understanding 6

The coefficient of determination

$$r^2 = 0.992^2 = 0.984$$

This means that 98.4% of the changes in sales can be explained by changes in advertising. The other 1.6% of changes are caused by other factors.

Test your understanding 7

Answer A

$y = 10x + 420$

We are told that x refers to the accountancy period, which is 33, therefore:

$y = 420 + 33 \times 10 = 750$

This is the trend, however and we need to consider the seasonal variation too. Accounting period 33 is quarter 4. Quarter 4 is a bad quarter and the seasonal variation is -30%, therefore the expected results for period 33 are 30% less than the trend.

Expected sales = 750 × 70% = 525 units

Test your understanding 8

Answer D

Sales in quarter 3 (Q = 3)		
Base = 4000 + (80 × 3)	=	4,240
Seasonal adjustment		95%
Actual sales	=	4,028
Sales in quarter 4 (Q = 4)		
Base = 4000 + (80 × 4)	=	4,320
Seasonal adjustment		120%
Actual sales	=	5,184
Overall increase in sales	=	5,184 − 4,028 = 1,156 units

Test your understanding 9

(a) Quantity weighting

Calculate the simple price index

Product A = $6.90/$6.50 × 100 = 106.2
Product B = $2.50/$2.20 × 100 = 113.6

Determine the weightings to be used - total production batches

Product A	10
Product B	30
	—
	40

Apply weightings to price indices

	Price index	Quantity weighting	Total Price index × Quantity
A	106.2	10	1,062
B	113.6	30	3,408
		—	——
		40	4,470

$$\text{Weighted price index} = \frac{4,470}{40} = 111.8$$

(b) Cost weighting

Use simple price index calculated in a

Determine the weighting to be used - total production cost

	Price in 20X2	Number of units	Total value Price × number of units
A	$6.50	10	65
B	$2.20	30	66
			—
			131

Apply weightings to price indices

	Price index	Quantity weighting	Total Price index × Quantity
A	106.2	65	6,903
B	113.6	66	7,498
		131	14,401

$$\text{Weighted price index} = \frac{14{,}401}{131} = 109.9$$

Test your understanding 10

(a) As the line of best fit is based on 20Y1 prices, use this as the common price level. Costs should therefore be adjusted by a factor:

$$\frac{\text{Index level to which costs will be adjusted}}{\text{Actual index level of costs}}$$

Year	Actual overheads $	Cost index	Adjustment factor	Costs at 20Y1 price level $
20X8	143,040	192	x 235/192	175,075
20X9	156,000	200	x 235/200	183,300
20Y0	152,320	224	x 235/224	159,800
20Y1	172,000	235	x 235/235	172,000

(b) If the forecast number of machine hours is 3,100 and the cost index is 250:

Forecast overhead costs = [$33,000 + ($47 × 3,100 hours)] × (250/235)

= $178,700 × (250/235)

= $190,106

Test your understanding 11 – DOMESTIC ELECTRICAL

(a)

Year	Sales of Appliances $000		Deflated Sales $000
2003	3,600	x 100/120	3,000
2004	6,250	x 100/125	5,000
2005	9,170	x 100/131	7,000
2006	14,000	x 100/140	10,000
2007	21,600	x 100/144	15,000
2008	27,000	x 100/150	18,000
2009	41,600	x 100/160	26,000

(b)

$$r = \frac{n\Sigma xy - \Sigma x \Sigma y}{\sqrt{(n\Sigma x^2 - (\Sigma x)^2)(n\Sigma y^2 - (\Sigma y)^2)}}$$

$$r = \frac{7 \times 136 - 84 \times 8.4}{\sqrt{(7 \times 1,408 - 84^2)(7 \times 13.78 - 8.4^2)}}$$

$$r = \frac{246.4}{\sqrt{2,800 \times 25.9}}$$

$$r = 0.915$$

$$r^2 = 0.915^2 = 0.837$$

(c) The coefficient of determination means that **83.7%** of the changes in **policy sales** can be explained by changes in the level of the **deflated appliance sales**. The other **16.3%** of changes are caused by other factors.

(d)   b $= \dfrac{n\Sigma xy - \Sigma x\Sigma y}{n\Sigma x^2 - (\Sigma x)^2}$

$= \dfrac{7 \times 136 - 84 \times 8.4}{7 \times 1{,}408 - 84^2}$

$= \dfrac{246.4}{2{,}800} \quad = \quad 0.088$

a $= \quad \overline{y} - b\overline{x}$

a $= \quad \dfrac{8.4}{7} \quad - \quad 0.088 \times \quad \dfrac{84}{7} \quad = \quad 0.144$

The Regression equation is $y = 0.144 + 0.088x$

Where   x   is deflated appliance sales ($m)

And   y   is policy sales (000s)

(e)   Deflated appliance sales = $51million × 100/170 = $30million

Policy sales   =   0.144 + 0.088 × 30

                                            =   2.784 (000s)

                                            =   2,784 policies

13

Budgeting

Chapter learning objectives

Upon completion of this chapter you will be able to:

- explain why organisations use budgeting

- describe the planning and control cycle in an organisation

- explain the administrative procedures used in the budgeting process

- describe the stages in the budgeting process

- explain the importance of motivation in performance management

- identify factors in a budgetary planning and control system that influence motivation

- explain the impacts of targets upon motivation

- discuss managerial incentive schemes

- discuss the advantages and disadvantages of a participative approach to budgeting

- explain top down, bottom up approaches to budgeting

- explain the importance of principal budget factor in constructing the budget

- prepare sales budgets

- prepare functional budgets (production, raw materials usage and purchases, labour, variable and fixed overheads)

- prepare cash budgets

- prepare master budgets (income statement and statement of financial position)

- explain and illustrate 'what if' analysis and scenario planning

- explain the importance of flexible budgets in control

- explain the disadvantages of fixed budgets in control

- identify situations where fixed or flexible budgetary control would be appropriate

- flex a budget to a given level of volume

- calculate simple variances between flexed budget, fixed budget and actual sale, costs and profits

- define the concept of responsibility accounting and its significance in control

- explain the concept of controllable and uncontrollable costs

- prepare control reports

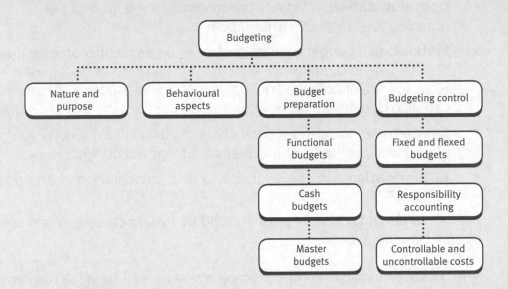

1 The purposes of budgeting

Budget theory

A budget is a **quantitative** expression of a plan of action prepared in advance of the period to which it relates.

Budgets set out the costs and revenues that are expected to be incurred or earned in future periods.

Most organisations prepare budgets for the business as a whole. The following budgets may also be prepared by organisations:

*   Departmental budgets.

*   Functional budgets (for sales, production, expenditure and so on).

*   Income statements and Statements of financial position (in order to determine the expected future profits).

*   Cash budgets (in order to determine future cash flows).

Purposes of budgeting

The main aims of budgeting are as follows:

*   **Planning for the future** – in line with the objectives of the organisation.

*   **Controlling costs** – by comparing the plan of the budget with the actual results and investigating significant differences between the two.

*   **Co-ordination** of the different activities of the business by ensuring that managers are working towards the same common goal (as stated in the budget).

- **Communication** – budgets communicate the targets of the organisation to individual managers.

- **Motivation** – budgets can motivate managers by encouraging them to beat targets or budgets set at the beginning of the budget period. Bonuses are often based on 'beating budgets'. Budgets, if badly set, can also demotivate employees.

- **Evaluation** – the performance of managers is often judged by looking at how well the manager has performed 'against budget'.

- **Authorisation** – budgets act as a form of authorisation of expenditure.

In a management accounting context, the budgeting process is part of the overall planning process.

The overall planning and control process is summarised in the diagram that follows:

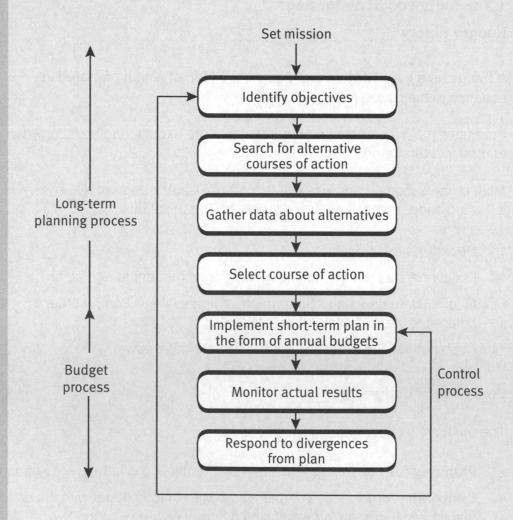

Stages of the planning and control cycle

The eight stages are explained below:

(1) **Set mission**

This involves establishing the broad overall aims and goals of the organisation – these may be both economic and social.

(2) **Identify objectives**

This requires the company to specify objectives towards which it is working. These objectives may be in terms of:

- economic targets
- type of business
- goods/services to be sold
- markets to be served
- market share
- profit objectives
- required growth rates of sales, profits, assets.

(3) **Search for possible courses of action**

A series of specific strategies should be developed dealing particularly with:

- developing new markets for existing products
- developing new products for existing markets
- developing new products for new markets.

(4) **Gathering data about alternatives and measuring pay-offs**

This is an information-gathering stage.

(5) **Select course of action**

Having made decisions, long-term plans based on those decisions are created.

(6) Implementation of short-term plans

This stage signals the move from long-term planning to short-term plans in the form of annual budgeting. The budget provides the link between the strategic plans and their implementation in management decisions. The budget should be seen as an integral part of the long-term planning process.

(7) Monitor actual outcomes

This is the particular role of the cost accountant, keeping detailed financial and other records of actual performance compared with budget targets (variance accounting).

(8) Respond to divergences from plan

This is the control process in budgeting, responding to divergences from plan either through budget modifications or through identifying new courses of action.

2 The stages in budget preparation

How are budgets prepared?

Before any budgets can be prepared, the long-term objectives of an organisation must be defined so that the budgets prepared are working towards the goals of the business.

Once this has been done, the budget committee can be formed, the budget manual can be produced and the limiting factor can be identified.

- **Budget committee is formed** – a typical budget committee is made up of the chief executive, budget officer (management accountant) and departmental or functional heads (sales manager, purchasing manager, production manager and so on). The budget committee is responsible for communicating policy guidelines to the people who prepare the budgets and for setting and approving budgets.

- **Budget manual is produced** – an organisation's budget manual sets out instructions relating to the preparation and use of budgets. It also gives details of the responsibilities of those involved in the budgeting process, including an organisation chart and a list of budget holders.

- **Limiting factor is identified** – in budgeting, the limiting factor is known as the principal budget factor. Generally there will be one factor that will limit the activity of an organisation in a given period. It is usually sales that limit an organisation's performance, but it could be anything else, for example, the availability of special labour skills.

If sales is the principal budget factor, then the sales budget must be produced first. If there is something else limiting the business, i.e. a resource such as material or labour hours, then this would become the principal budget factor that other budgets are based on.

- **Final steps in the budget process** – once the budget relating to the limiting factor has been produced then the managers responsible for the other budgets can produce them. The entire budget preparation process may take several weeks or months to complete. The final stages are as follows.

  (1) Initial budgets are prepared. Budget managers may sometimes try to build in an element of budget slack – this is a deliberate over-estimation of costs or under-estimation of revenues which can make it easier for managers to achieve their targets.

  (2) Initial budgets are reviewed and integrated into the complete budget system.

  (3) After any necessary adjustments are made to initial budgets, they are accepted and the master budget is prepared (budgeted income statement, statement of financial position and cash flow). This master budget is then shown to top management for final approval.

  (4) Budgets are reviewed regularly. Comparisons between budgets and actual results are carried out and any differences arising are known as variances.

3 Behavioural aspects of budgeting

If budgets are to be effective, attention must be paid to the behavioural aspects i.e. the effect of the system on people in the organisation and vice versa. Poor managerial performance and poor financial results are often due to the method of implementation and operation of a control system, rather than to the system itself.

Senior management need to be fully committed to the budgeting system and it is equally important that lower levels of management and operational staff in the organisation should be similarly committed and motivated.

Budgets are one important way of influencing the behaviour of managers within an organisation. There are very few, if any, decisions and actions that a manager can take which do not have some financial effect and which will not subsequently be reflected in a comparison between budgeted and actual results. This all-embracing nature of budgets is probably the most important advantage that a budgetary system has over most other systems in a typical organisation. However, if managers and employees have no confidence in the budgetary processes in operation, it is unlikely that they will operate as an effective control. One reason why objectives may not be met is if those operating the budget are not committed to it.

4 Motivation

Motivation is the drive or urge to achieve an end result. An individual is motivated if they are moving forward to achieving goals or objectives.

Motivation may affect many aspects of the life of an individual. You have to be motivated to pass your ACCA examinations and to gain a recognised accounting qualification. At work you are motivated to achieve promotion and to gain a position of greater authority and responsibility within the organisation.

In a business context, if employees and managers are not motivated, they will lack the drive or urge to improve their performance and to help the organisation to achieve its goals and move forward. Motivation is very important in a business.

Motivation and budgeting

There is evidence which suggests that management accounting planning and control systems can have a significant effect on manager and employee motivation.

These include:

*   the level at which budgets and performance targets are set

*   manager and employee reward systems

*   the extent to which employees participate in the budget setting process.

The setting of budgets and targets

The aim of setting budgets is to provide a challenge for employees and managers that is achievable with an appropriate level of effort.

*   If a budget target is set that is too easy, then actual performance will appear to be a little better than the budget but it will not have challenged the employees. Human behaviour will tend to lead to individuals putting in the minimum possible effort to achieve a set target.

*   If the budget is too difficult, managers become discouraged at what they regard as an unattainable standard. This may de-motivate and as a result, actual performance falls short of what might reasonably have been expected.

The budget should therefore fall between these two extremes and incorporates just the right degree of difficulty which will lead to the optimal level of performance. At this level the budget should be challenging enough to motivate a manager to optimise his performance without being too ambitious.

The right level of difficulty is that which is acceptable to that individual manager. This level of acceptability will differ from manager to manager, as each individual behaves and reacts in a different way in similar circumstances.

5 Incentive schemes

Budgets by themselves have a limited motivational effect. It is the reward structure that is linked to achieving the budget requirements, or lack of reward for non-achievement, which provides the real underlying motivational potential of budgets.

Managers may receive financial rewards (for example, bonuses) and non-financial rewards (for example, promotion or greater responsibility) based on their ability to meet budget targets. The reward will need to be seen as worthwhile if it is to motivate a manager to achieve the budget.

It is usual to assess the performance of a manager by a comparison of budgeted and actual results for his area of responsibility in the organisation. The choice of which particular measures to use is important to ensure that the individual manager sees the attainment of his targets as worthwhile for himself and at the same time in the best interests of the organisation as a whole.

The characteristics of a good employee reward system as follows:

- **Fairness** – the system should reward effort which helps the organisation achieve its objectives.

- **Motivational** – it should motivate the managers and employees to behave congruently i.e. in a way which assists the organisation to achieve its objectives.

- **Understandability** – the system should be such that it is clear to managers what they need to do to achieve the rewards. Unduly complex reward systems, perhaps based on complex bonus formulae are unlikely to be effective in generating improved performance.

- **Consistently applied** – the system should operate in the same way for all employees or, if not possible, for all employees at a given level in the organisation.

- **Objective** – the system should be based on measurable criteria with a minimum of subjectivity. It should also be such that it is not open to manipulation by managers in their own interests.

- **Universal** – all employees and managers at all levels in the organisation should be subject to an appraisal and reward system.

6 Participative budgeting

Top down approach to budgeting

The top down approach is where budgets are set by higher levels of management and then communicated to the lower levels of management to whose areas of responsibility they relate. This is also known as an imposed budget.

In this approach lower level managers are not allowed to participate in the budget setting process.

The main problem with this approach is that those responsible for operating the budget will see it as something in which they have had no say. They lack ownership of the budget and as such they will be reluctant to take responsibility for it. It is unlikely to motivate the employees to achieve the budgetary targets set for them.

However, it can be argued that this top down approach may be the only approach to budgeting which is feasible if:

- lower level employees have no interest in participating in the process

- they are not technically capable of participating in budget setting

- only top level management have access to information which is necessary for budgeting purposes – perhaps information which is commercially sensitive.

The bottom up approach to budgeting

The bottom up approach to budgeting is where lower level managers are involved in setting budget targets. This is known as a participative budget.

The more that individual managers are involved in setting budget targets, the more likely it is that they will accept those targets and strive actively towards the attainment of them. Employees are more likely to internalise the budget – accept it as part of themselves.

In this way actual performances should be improved by the motivational impact of budgets.

The main problem is:

- If budgets are used both in a motivational role and for the evaluation of managerial performance, then the problem of budgetary bias may arise.

Budgetary bias is where a manager deliberately sets a lower revenue target or a higher cost target.

The effects of this sort of bias can be minimised by careful control at the budget setting stage and by monitoring the budget from one year to the next.

An extension of the bottom up approach is the concept of budget challenging – employees are given the chance to question a budget presented to them (in a positive way) before it is finalised.

7 Budget Preparation

The preparation of budgets is illustrated as follows.

Illustration 1 – The stages in budget preparation

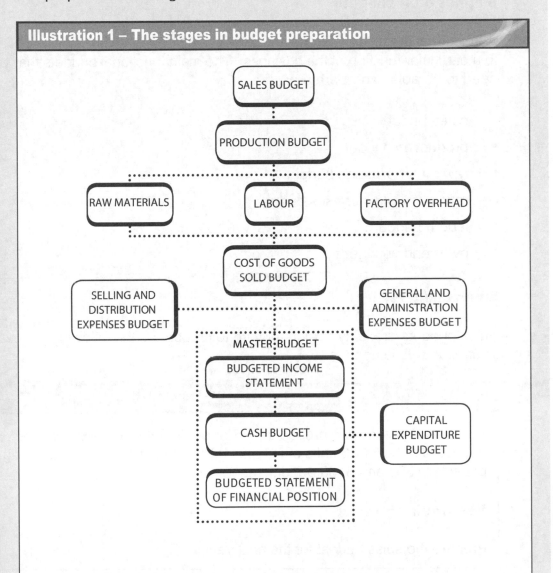

- The diagram shown above is based on sales being the principal budget factor. This is why the sales budget is shown in Step 1.

- Remember that if labour were the principal budget factor, then the labour budget would be produced first and this would determine the production budget.

- Once the production budget has been determined then the remaining functional budgets can be prepared.

Continuous budgets

- **Continuous budget** – this type of budget is prepared a year (or budget period) ahead and is updated regularly by adding a further accounting period (month, quarter) when the first accounting period has expired. If the budget period is a year, then it will always reflect the budget for a year in advance. Continuous budgets are also known as rolling budgets.

8 Functional budgets

A functional budget is a budget of income and/or expenditure which applies to a particular function of the business. The main functional budgets that you need to be able to prepare are:

- sales budget
- production budget
- raw material usage budget
- raw material purchases budget
- labour budget
- overheads budget

Sales budgets

Sales budgets are fairly straightforward to prepare as the following illustration will demonstrate.

Illustration 2 – Sales budgets

A company makes two products – PS and TG. Sales for next year are budgeted to be 5,000 units of PS and 1,000 units of TG. Planned selling prices are $95 and $130 per unit respectively.

Required:

Prepare the sales budget for the next year.

Solution

	Total	PS	TG
Sales units	6,000	5,000	1,000
Sales value	$605,000	$475,000	$130,000

Workings

Sales – PS = 5,000 × $95 = $475,000
Sales – TG = 1,000 × $130 = $130,000

Test your understanding 1

A company makes two products – A and B. The products are sold in the ratio 1:1. Planned selling prices are $100 and $200 per unit respectively. The company needs to earn $900,000 revenue in the coming year.

Required:

Prepare the sales budget for the coming year.

Production budgets

Budgeted production levels can be calculated as follows:

Forecast sales
Closing inventory of finished goods
(Opening inventory of finished goods)

Budgeted production

Illustration 3 – Production budgets

A company makes two products, PS and TG. Forecast sales for the coming year are 5,000 and 1,000 units respectively.

The company has the following opening and required closing inventory levels.

	PS units	TG units
Opening inventory	100	50
Required closing inventory	1,100	50

Required:

Prepare the production budget for the coming year.

Solution		
Production budget	*PS units*	*TG units*
Sales budget	5,000	1,000
+ Closing inventory	1,100	50
– Opening inventory	(100)	(50)
Budgeted production in units	6,000	1,000

Material budgets

There are two types of material budget that you need to be able to calculate, the usage budget and the purchases budget.

- The **material usage budget** is simply the budgeted production for each product multiplied by the quantity (e.g. kg) required to produce one unit of the product.

- The **material purchases budget** is made up of the following elements.

Material usage budget
Closing inventory
(Opening inventory)

Material purchases budget

Illustration 4 – Material budgets

A company produces Products PS and TG and has budgeted to produce 6,000 units of Product PS and 1,000 units of Product TG in the coming year.

The data about the materials required to produce Products PS and TG is given as follows.

Finished products:	*PS* per unit	*TG* per unit
Kg of raw material X	12	12
Kg of raw material Y	6	8

KAPLAN PUBLISHING

Direct materials:

	Raw material	
	X	Y
	kg	kg
Desired closing inventory	6,000	1,000
Opening inventory	5,000	5,000

Standard rates and prices:

Raw material X	$0.72 per kg
Raw material Y	$1.56 per kg

Required:

Prepare the following:

(a) The material usage budget.

(b) The material purchase budget.

Solution

Material budgets

	Material X	Material Y
	kg	kg
For production of PS (W1)	72,000	36,000
For production of TG (W2)	12,000	8,000
Material usage budget	84,000	44,000
+ Closing inventory	6,000	1,000
– Opening inventory	5,000	5,000
Material purchases budget (units)	85,000	40,000
	$	$
Material purchases budget ($)		
X $0.72 per kg ×	85,000	61,200
Y $1.56 per kg ×	40,000	62,400

Workings

(W1) Budgeted production of Product PS = 6,000 units

Therefore: 6,000 × 12 kg per unit = 72,000 kg of Material X required.

Therefore: 6,000 × 6 kg per unit = 36,000 kg of Material Y required.

(W2) Budgeted production of Product TG = 1,000 units

Therefore: 1,000 × 12 kg per unit = 12,000 kg of Material X required.

Therefore: 1,000 × 8 kg per unit = 8,000 kg of Material Y required.

Labour budgets

Labour budgets are simply the number of hours multiplied by the labour rate per hour as the following illustration shows.

Illustration 5 – Labour budgets

A company produces Products PS and TG and has budgeted to produce 6,000 units of Product PS and 1,000 units of Product TG in the coming year.

The data about the labour hours required to produce Products PS and TG is given as follows.

Finished products:

	PS per unit	TG per unit
Direct labour hours	8	12

Standard rate for direct labour = $5.20 per hour

Required:

Prepare the labour budget for the coming year.

Solution

	Hours	$
For Product PS 6,000 × 8 hrs	48,000	
For Product TG 1,000 × 12 hrs	12,000	
	60,000 @ $5.20	312,000

Test your understanding 2

A contract cleaning firm estimates that it will take 2,520 actual cleaning hours to clean an office block. Unavoidable interruptions and lost time are estimated to take 10% of the workers' time. If the wage rate is $8.50 per hour, the budgeted labour cost will be:

A $19,278

B $21,420

C $23,562

D $23,800

Overhead budgets

The following illustration demonstrates the calculation of overhead budgets.

Illustration 6 – Overhead budgets

A company produces Products PS and TG and has budgeted to produce 6,000 units of Product PS and 1,000 units of Product TG in the coming year.

The following data about the machine hours required to produce Products PS and TG and the standard production overheads per machine hour is relevant to the coming year.

	PS per unit	TG per unit
Machine hours	8	12

Production overheads per machine hour

Variable $1.54 per machine hour

Fixed $0.54 per machine hour

Required:

Calculate the overhead budget for the coming year.

Solution

Overhead budget	$
Variable costs 60,000 hours × $1.54	92,400
Fixed costs 60,000 hours × $0.54	32,400
	———
	124,800
	———

Workings

Machine hours – Product PS = 6,000 units × 8 hours = 48,000 machine hours

Machine hours – Product TG = 1,000 units × 12 hours = 12,000 machine hours

Total machine hours = 48,000 + 12,000 = 60,000

Test your understanding 3

Newton Ltd manufactures two products. The expected sales for each product are shown below.

	Product 1	Product 2
Sales in units	3,000	4,500

Opening inventory is expected to be:

Product 1   500 units

Product 2   700 units

Management have stated their desire to reduce inventory levels, and closing inventory is budgeted as:

Product 1	200 units
Product 2	300 units

Two types of material are used in varying amounts in the manufacture of the two products. Material requirements are shown below:

	Product 1	Product 2
Material M1	2 kg	3 kg
Material M2	3 kg	3 kg

The opening inventory of material is expected to be:

Material M1	4,300 kg
Material M2	3,700 kg

Management are keen to reduce inventory levels for materials, and closing inventory levels are to be much lower. Expected levels are shown below:

Material M1 2,200 kg
Material M2 1,300 kg

Material prices are expected to be 10% higher than this year and current prices are $1.10/kg for material M1 and $3.00/kg for material M2.

Two types of labour are used in producing the two products. Standard times per unit and expected wage rates for the forthcoming year are shown below:

	Product 1	Product 2
Hours per unit		
Skilled labour	3	1
Semi-skilled labour	4	4

Skilled labour is to be paid at the rate of $9/hour and semi-skilled labour at the rate of $6/hour.

Production overheads per labour hour are as follows:

Variable $3.50 per labour hour
Fixed $5.50 per labour hour

Calculate the following:

(a) The number of units of product 1 to be produced

(b) The number of units of product 2 to be produced

(c) The quantity of material M1 to be used

(d) The quantity of material M2 to be used

(e) The quantity of material M1 to be purchased and the value of the purchases

(f) The quantity of material M2 to be purchased and the value of the purchases

(g) The number of hours of skilled labour and the cost of this labour

(h) The number of hours of semi-skilled labour and the cost of this labour

(i) The total overhead budget

9 Cash budgets and cash flow forecasts

A **cash forecast** is an estimate of cash receipts and payments for a future period under existing conditions.

A **cash budget** is a commitment to a plan for cash receipts and payments for a future period after taking any action necessary to bring the forecast into line with the overall business plan.

Cash budgets are used to:

• assess and integrate operating budgets

• plan for cash shortages and surpluses

• compare with actual spending.

Cash forecasts can be prepared based on:

• Receipts and payments forecast. This is a forecast of cash receipts and payments based on predictions of sales and cost of sales and the timings of the cash flows relating to these items.

- Statement of financial position forecast. This is a forecast derived from predictions of future statements of financial position. Predictions are made of all items except cash, which is then derived as a balancing figure.

In the exam it is most likely to be part of a receipts and payments forecast i.e. calculating the receipts from receivables or the payments to payables.

Preparing a cash flow forecast

Every type of cash inflow and receipt, along with their timings, must be forecast. Note that cash receipts and payments differ from sales and cost of sales in the income statement because:

- not all cash receipts or payments affect the income statement, e.g. the issue of new shares or the purchase of a non-current asset

- some income statement items are derived from accounting conventions and are not cash flows, e.g. depreciation or the profit/loss on the sale of a non-current asset

- the timing of cash receipts and payments does not coincide with the income statement accounting period, e.g. a sale is recognised in the income statement when the invoice is raised, yet the cash payment from the receivable may not be received until the following period or later.

The following approach should be adopted for examination questions.

Step 1 – Prepare a proforma

Month:	1 $	2 $	3 $	4 $
Receipts (few lines)				
Sub total				
Payments (Many lines)				
Sub total				
Net cash flow				
Balance brought down				
Balance carried down				

Step 2 – Fill in the simple figures

Some payments need only a small amount of work to identify the correct figure and timing and can be entered straight into the proforma. These would usually include:

- wages and salaries
- fixed overhead expenses
- dividend payments
- purchase of non-current assets.

Step 3 – Work out the more complex figures

The information on sales and purchases can be more time consuming to deal with, e.g.:

- timings for both sales and purchases must be found from credit periods
- variable overheads may require information about production levels
- purchase figures may require calculations based on production schedules and inventory balances.

Receipts from receivables

If a business offers credit sales these will be recorded in the income statement at the point when the sale is made. This does not reflect the actual cash received by the business.

To calculate the cash receipts from the credit sales there are two things to consider:

- the value of the receipts – how much cash will be received from the credit sales
- the timing of the receipts – when will the cash be received from the credit sales

Illustration 7 – Forecast cash receipts

The forecast sales for an organisation are as follows:

	January	February	March	April
	$	$	$	$
Sales	6,000	8,000	4,000	5,000

All sales are on credit and receivables tend to pay in the following pattern:

	%
In month of sale	10
In month after sale	40
Two months after sale	45

The organisation expects the rate of irrecoverable debts to be 5%.

Calculate the forecast cash receipts from receivables in April.

Solution

Cash from:		$
April sales:	10% × $5,000	500
March sales:	40% × $4,000	1,600
February sales:	45% × $8,000	3,600
		————
		5,700

Payments to payables

If a business makes credit purchases these will be recorded in the income statement at the point when the purchase is made. This does not reflect the actual cash paid by the business.

To calculate the cash payments for the credit purchases there are two things to consider:

- the value of the payment – how much cash will be paid to the payable
- the timing of the payment – when will the cash be paid to the payable

It may be necessary to calculate the amount due to be paid based on quantities purchased.

Illustration 8 – Forecast cash payments

A manufacturing business makes and sells widgets. Each widget requires two units of raw materials, which cost $3 each. Production and sales quantities of widgets each month are as follows:

Month	Sales and production units
December (actual)	50,000
January (budget)	55,000
February (budget)	60,000
March (budget)	65,000

In the past, the business has maintained its inventories of raw materials at 100,000 units. However, it plans to increase raw material inventories to 110,000 units at the end of January and 120,000 units at the end of February. The business takes one month's credit from its suppliers.

Calculate the forecast payments to suppliers each month, for raw material purchases.

Solution

When inventories of raw materials are increased, the quantities purchased will exceed the quantities consumed in the period. Figures for December are shown because December purchases will be paid for in January, which is in the budget period.

Quantity of raw material purchased in units:

	December	January	February	March
Production	50,000	55,000	60,000	65,000
Usage (× 2)	100,000	110,000	120,000	130,000
+ closing inventory	100,000	110,000	120,000	120,000
– opening inventories	100,000	100,000	110,000	120,000
Purchases (units)	100,000	120,000	130,000	130,000
At $3 per unit	300,000	360,000	390,000	390,000

Having established the purchases each month, we can go on to budget the amount of cash payments to suppliers each month. Here, the business will take one month's credit.

	January $	February $	March $
Payment to suppliers	300,000	360,000	390,000

At the end of March, there will be payables of $390,000 for raw materials purchased, which will be paid in April.

Test your understanding 4

The following budgeted income statement has been prepared for Quest Company for the four months January to April Year 5:

	January $000	February $000	March $000	April $000
Sales	60.0	50.0	70.0	60.0
Cost of production	50.0	55.0	32.5	50.0
(Increase)/decrease in inventory	(5.0)	(17.5)	20.0	(5.0)
Cost of sales	45.0	37.5	52.5	45.0
Gross profit	15.0	12.5	17.5	15.0
Administration and selling overhead	(8.0)	(7.5)	(8.5)	(8.0)
Net profit before interest	7.0	5.0	9.0	7.0

- 40% of the production cost relates to direct materials. Materials are bought in the month prior to the month in which they are used. Purchases are paid for one month after purchase.

- 30% of the production cost relates to direct labour which is paid for when it is used.

- The remainder of the production cost is production overhead.

- $5,000 per month is a fixed cost which includes $3,000 depreciation. Fixed production overhead costs are paid for when incurred.

- The remaining overhead is variable. The variable production overhead is paid 40% in the month of usage and the balance one month later. Unpaid variable production overhead at the beginning of January is $9,000.

- The administration and selling costs are paid quarterly in advance on 1 January, 1 April, 1 July and 1 October. The amount payable is $15,000 per quarter.

- All sales are on credit. 20% of receivables are expected to be paid in the month of sale and 80% in the following month. Unpaid trade receivables at the beginning of January were $44,000.

- The company intends to purchase capital equipment costing $30,000 in February which will be payable in March.

- The bank balance on 1 January Year 5 is expected to be $5,000 overdrawn.

The opening Statement of financial position is expected to be as follows:

	$	$
Non current assets		950,000
Inventory	66,000	
Trade receivables	260,000	
Cash	25,000	
	351,000	
Trade payables	86,000	
Other short-term liabilities	24,000	
	110,000	
Net current assets		241,000
Net assets		1,191,000

Non-current assets in the statement of financial position are expected to increase by $40,000, but no change is expected in trade receivables, trade payables and other short-term liabilities.

There are no plans at this stage to raise extra capital by issuing new shares or obtaining new loans. The company currently has an overdraft facility of $300,000 with its bank.

Required:

Complete the following:

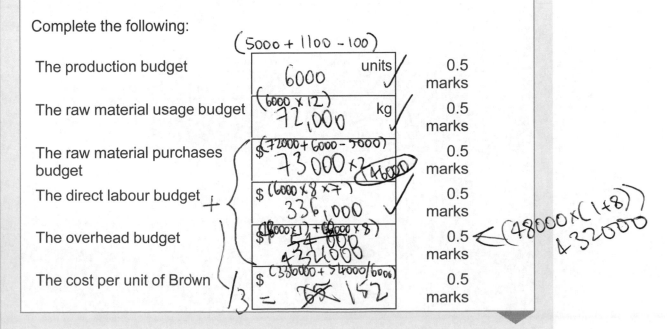

The production budget	(5000 + 1100 - 100) 6000 units ✓	0.5 marks
The raw material usage budget	(6000 x 12) 72,000 kg ✓	0.5 marks
The raw material purchases budget	$(72000 + 6000 - 5000) 73000 x 2 46000	0.5 marks
The direct labour budget	$ (6000 x 8 x 7) 336,000 ✓	0.5 marks
The overhead budget	$ (8000 x 1) + (6000 x 8) 54000 432000	0.5 marks ← (48000 x (1+8)) 432000
The cost per unit of Brown	$ (336000 + 54000/6000) = $$ 152 /3	0.5 marks

Budgeted Income Statement

	$	$	
Sales Revenue		[ ]	0.5 marks
Cost of sales			
Opening inventory	[ ]		0.5 marks
Production cost	[ ]		0.5 marks
Closing inventory	[ ]		0.5 marks
		[ ]	0.5 marks
Gross profit		[ ]	0.5 marks
Administration and marketing		(225,000)	
Profit		[ ]	0.5 marks

chapter 3

Budgeted Statement of Financial Position

	$	$	
Non current assets		☐	0.5 marks
Inventory	☐		1 mark
Trade receivables	260,000		
Cash	☐		1 mark
	─────		
Trade payables	86,000		
Other short term liabilities	24,000		
	─────		
	110,000		
Net current assets		☐	
		─────	
Net assets		☐	1 mark

(Total 10 Marks)

11 'What if' analysis

'What-if' analysis is a form of sensitivity analysis, which allows the effects of changes in one or more data value to be quickly recalculated.

Most budgets are produced under conditions of uncertainty as we are unable to perfectly predict the future. The majority of the costs and revenues (or input values) put in the budget are estimates. These costs and revenues are used to calculate a profit figure for the business (output value). This profit figure may be mathematically accurate, but the level of accuracy may be misleading.

Most budgets are quite complex, involving a large number of inputs. What-if analysis is a technique whereby each of the inputs can be changed both individually and in combination to see the effects on the final results.

An example of basic what-if analysis would be flexing a fixed budget to see how changes in activity levels affect the costs and revenues and therefore the profit of the business. This is discussed in the Budgetary control section of this chapter.

What-if analysis can be very detailed and the 'what-if' function on a spreadsheet package can be a very useful tool to have available.

12 Scenario planning

Scenario planning or scenario thinking is a strategic planning tool used to make flexible long-term plans. It is a strategic planning method that some organisations use to make flexible long-term plans.

Scenario planning has proved a very useful tool in forecasting, strategic planning and business modelling.

The scenario planning process

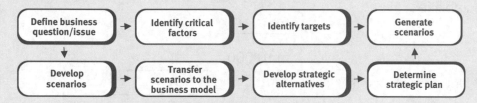

The steps for scenario planning

- **Define the business question**

   The process begins by identifying the fundamental business question or issue that the client wishes to answer or address.

- **Identify the critical factors**

   The next stage of the process asks the question: What do we need to know about the future in order to answer the fundamental business question?

- **Identify the inputs**

   In order to understand how the critical factors will change in the future, all the current and future variables that may impact the critical factors should be identified. This stage is often best performed using a brainstorming or discussion session.

- **Generate scenarios**

  Many different scenarios can now be developed. However, the objective is to narrow down the large number of potential scenarios to 3 or 4 of the most interesting, relevant and challenging ones.

- **Develop the scenarios**

  This involves adding more detail to the broad scenarios which have already been identified.

- **Transfer the scenarios to the business model**

  The scenarios can now be re-created within a market forecast and business model.

- **Develop strategic alternatives and the strategic plan**

  Once the scenario planning process has been completed there is a full, analytical description of a number of potential future environments in which the business may have to operate. Within these virtual worlds and the business planning model the company can begin to explore the potential alternatives and finally to make their strategic choices.

13 Budgetary control

Budgetary control cycle

Control can be defined as the process whereby management take decisions in order to attempt to ensure that an organisation achieves its objectives.

An organisation should establish a mission (the overall reasons for its existence) and set objectives (specific targets to be met in a defined period) for the business. A plan should then be formulated which will, if followed, result in these objectives being achieved. A budget is then prepared, expressing the plan in money terms.

Given our definition of control above, this budget can then be used to establish whether the organisation is on target to achieve its objective. If it is not, the budget may also be able to tell us where things have gone wrong as a basis for taking control action to set the organisation back on track.

The budgetary control cycle can be illustrated as follows.

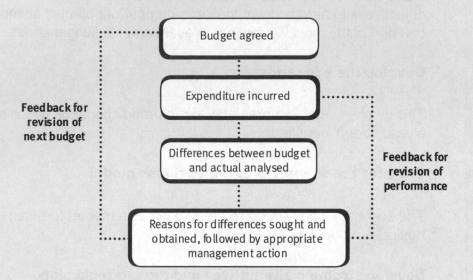

Feedback and feedforward controls

Feedback is the comparison of budget and actual performance with a view to revising plans, budgets or operations. The control action takes place after the event.

Budgetary control systems are typically feedback systems – an expenditure budget is set, a comparison is made with actual expenditure at the end of the budget period. If this shows that actual expenditure exceeds budget then it is not possible to take control action to prevent this overspending as it has already been incurred. The information can be used to avoid the situation happening again in the future.

Feedback controls are of limited use because they operate too late in the control system. It is important, therefore, that an organisation also has in place 'feedforward control'.

Planning is a form of feedforward control.

An example of a feedforward control is cash budgeting which will warn management if a major cash surplus or deficit is expected to arise at some date in the future so that management can take action now.

The essential feature of any budgetary control system is the process of comparing budgeted (expected results) with actual results. The difference between these figures is usually referred to as a variance.

Variances may be either adverse or favourable.

- Adverse variances (Adv) or (A) decrease profits.
- Favourable variances (Fav) or (F) increase profits.

14 Fixed and flexible budgets

A fixed budget is one produced for a single level of activity.

A flexible budget is one which, by recognising cost behaviour patterns, is designed to change as volume of activity changes.

The simplest form of budget report compares the original budget against actual results.

An example of a budget report is shown below:

	Budget	Actual	
	1,000	1,200	
	1,300	1,250	Variance
	$	$	$
Sales revenue	10,000	11,500	1,500 F
Labour costs	2,600	2,125	475 F
Material costs	1,300	1,040	260 F
Overheads	1,950	2,200	250 A
Profit	4,150	6,135	1,985 F

- The fixed budget shown above is not particularly useful because we are not really comparing like with like. For example, the budgeted sales were 1,000 units but the actual sales volume was 1,200 units.

- The overall sales variance is favourable, but from the report shown we don't know how much of this variance is due to the fact that actual sales were 200 units higher than budgeted sales (or whether there was an increase in the sales price).

- Similarly, actual production volume was 50 units less than the budgeted production volume, so we are not really making a very useful comparison. It is more useful to compare actual results with a budget that reflects the actual activity level. Such a budget is known as a flexed budget.

If this control process is to be valid and effective, it is important that the variances are calculated in a meaningful way. One of the major concerns here is to ensure that the budgeted and actual figures reflect the same activity level. As activity levels (output, for example) change, total variable costs will change, but fixed costs stay the same. In order to compare like with like we need to prepare a flexed (or flexible) budget which reflects the actual level of output achieved.

It would be unreasonable to criticise a manager for incurring higher costs if these were a result of a higher than planned volume of activity. Conversely, if the level of activity is low, costs can be expected to fall and the original budget must be amended to reflect this. A variance report based on a flexible budget therefore compares actual costs with the costs budgeted for the level of activity actually achieved. It does not explain any change in budgeted volume, which should be reported on separately.

The key points to note are:

- A fixed budget is set at the beginning of the period, based on estimated production. This is the original budget. At the same time a flexible budget may be produced at a range of activity levels.

- Actual results are compared with the relevant section of the flexible budget, that which corresponds to the actual level of activity. This is usually referred to as the flexed budget.

Illustration 9 – Preparing a flexible budget

Wye Ltd manufactures one product and when operating at 100% capacity can produce 5,000 units per period, but for the last few periods has been operating below capacity.

Below is the flexible budget prepared at the start of last period, for three levels of activity at below capacity:

Level of activity (units)	3,500	4,000	4,500
	$	$	$
Direct materials	7,000	8,000	9,000
Direct labour	28,000	32,000	36,000
Production overheads	34,000	36,000	38,000
Administration, selling and distribution overheads	15,000	15,000	15,000
Total cost	84,000	91,000	98,000

In the event, the last period turned out to be even worse than expected, with production of only 2,500 units. The following costs were incurred:

	$
Direct materials	4,500
Direct labour	22,000
Production overheads	28,000
Administration, selling and distribution overheads	16,500
Total cost	71,000

Required:

Use the information given above to prepare the following.

(a) A flexed budget for 2,500 units.

(b) A budgetary control statement.

Solution

(a) **Flexed budget for 2,500 units**

	$
Direct materials (W1) (2,500 × $2)	5,000
Direct labour (W2) (2,500 × $8)	20,000
Production overheads (W3)	30,000
Administration, selling and distribution overheads (W4)	15,000
Total cost	70,000

Fixed (handwritten annotation)

Handwritten margin notes:
(7000/3500)×2500
(28000/3500)×2500
(38000-34000)/(4500-3500)
= 4
38000
VC 18000 (4×4500)
FC 20000 (38-20)
VC 10,000 (4×2500)
FC 20,000
30,000

Workings

(1) Material is a variable cost – $2 per unit

$$\text{Variable material cost} = \frac{\$7,000}{3,500} = \$2 \text{ per unit}$$

(2) Labour is a variable cost – $8 per unit.

$$\text{Variable labour cost} = \frac{\$28,000}{3,500} = \$8 \text{ per unit}$$

(3) Production overheads are semi-variable. Using the high/low method, the variable cost is $4 per unit, the fixed cost is $20,000. The cost for 2,500 units therefore = $20,000 + (2,500 × $4) = $30,000.

$$\text{Variable cost per unit} = \frac{\$(38,000 - 34,000)}{4,500 - 3,500} = \$4 \text{ per unit}$$

Total fixed cost by substituting at high activity level:

Total cost = $38,000

Total variable cost = 4,500 × $4 = $18,000

Fixed cost = $38,000 – $18,000 = $20,000

(4) Other overheads are fixed.

(b) **Budgetary control statement**

	Flexed budget 2,500 units	Actual 2,500 units	Variance
	$	$	$
Direct materials	5,000	4,500	500 (F)
Direct labour	20,000	22,000	2,000 (A)
Production overheads	30,000	28,000	2,000 (F)
Administration, selling and distribution overheads	15,000	16,500	1,500 (A)
Total cost	70,000	71,000	1,000 (A)

Test your understanding 6

Bug Ltd manufactures one uniform product. Activity levels in the assembly department are an average level of activity of 20,000 units production per four-week period. The actual results for four weeks in October are:

	Budget 20,000 units	Actual 17,600 units
	$	$
Direct labour	20,000	19,540
Direct expenses	800	1,000
Direct material	4,200	3,660
Depreciation	10,000	10,000
Semi-variable overheads	5,000	4,760
	40,000	38,960

Assume that at a level of production of 15,000 units, semi-variable overheads are forecast to be $4,500.

Produce a budgetary control statement showing the actual costs, flexed costs and variances produced.

15 Responsibility accounting

Budgetary control and responsibility accounting are seen to be inseparable.

It is important to ensure that each manager has a well-defined area of responsibility and the authority to make decisions within that area, and that no parts of the organisation remain as 'grey' areas where it is uncertain who is responsible for them. If this is put into effect properly, each area of the organisation's activities is the responsibility of a manager. This structure should then be reflected in the organisation chart.

An area of responsibility may be structured as:

- a cost centre – where the manager is responsible for cost control only

- a revenue centre – where the manager is responsible for generation of revenues only

- a profit centre – the manager has control over sales revenues as well as costs

- an investment centre – the manager is empowered to take decisions about capital investment for his department.

Each centre has its own budget, and the manager receives control information relevant to that budget centre. Costs (and possibly revenue, assets and liabilities) must be traced to the person primarily responsible for taking the related decisions, and identified with the appropriate department.

Identifying costs with responsible managers

It is important to appreciate that in many cases it may not be obvious which centre or manager is responsible for given activities, even if a clearly defined organisation chart is in place and appropriate responsibility accounting units have been set up.

Illustration 10 – Responsibility accounting

The marketing department insists on a special rush order being produced which necessitates additional hours being worked in a number of production departments.

Who should be held responsible for the costs incurred in producing the order?

Possible approaches might include the following:

- Charge the costs to the marketing department as they initiated the transaction and caused the additional costs to be incurred.

- However, this might involve a complex cost accumulation exercise in several production departments as they attempt to identify the costs, including overheads which relate to that order – is this worthwhile?

- The charging of the costs to the marketing department might encourage managers of production departments to over-allocate costs to the order as a means of improving the performance of their department by moving costs across to the marketing department.

Allocation of non-manufacturing costs

Non-manufacturing costs present their own specific problems of budgetary control. Such costs are unlikely to vary with the level of production activity, but they may represent a significant proportion of total costs. Therefore, specific budgetary control techniques must be developed to deal with such costs.

These costs would include such areas as research and development, administration and finance, marketing and distribution.

Since the costs are not related to production activity, some alternative activity measure must be identified. Possible examples would be marketing costs per sales order and purchasing costs per delivery.

The problem of dual responsibility

A common problem is that the responsibility for a particular cost or item is shared between two (or more) managers. For example:

- the responsibility for payroll costs may be shared between the personnel and production departments;

- material costs between purchasing and production departments.

The reporting system should be designed so that the responsibility for performance achievements (i.e. better or worse than budget) is identified as that of a single manager.

The following guidelines may be applied:

(a) If a manager controls quantity and price – that manager is responsible for all expenditure variances.

(b) If manager controls quantity but not price – that manager is responsible only for variances due to usage.

(c) If manager controls price but not quantity – that manager is responsible only for variances due to input prices.

(d) If manager controls neither quantity nor price – all variances are uncontrollable from the point of view of that manager. We should now be asking the question who in the organisation chart is responsible for control of the expenditure – some one must be!

16 Controllable and uncontrollable costs

Controllable costs and revenues are those costs and revenues which result from decisions within the authority of a particular manager or unit within the organisation. These should be used to assess the performance of managers.

Over a long time-span most costs are controllable by someone in the organisation. For example – rent may be fixed for a number of years but there may eventually come an opportunity to move to other premises as such:

- rent is controllable in the long term by a manager fairly high in the organisation structure if the opportunity arises to move premises or negotiate with the land lord.

- but in the short term rent is uncontrollable even by senior managers.

There is no clear-cut distinction between controllable and non-controllable costs for a given manager. There may be joint control with another manager. The aim under a responsibility accounting system will be to assign and report on the cost to the person having primary responsibility.

Illustration 11 – controllable and uncontrollable costs

An example of the two different approaches to controllable and uncontrollable costs is provided by raw materials. The production manager will have control over usage, but not over price, when buying is done by a separate department. For this reason the price and usage variances are separated and, under the first approach, the production manager would be told only about the usage variance, a separate report being made to the purchasing manager about the price variance. The alternative argument is that if the production manager is also told about the price variance, he may attempt to persuade the purchasing manager to try alternative sources of supply.

17 Chapter summary

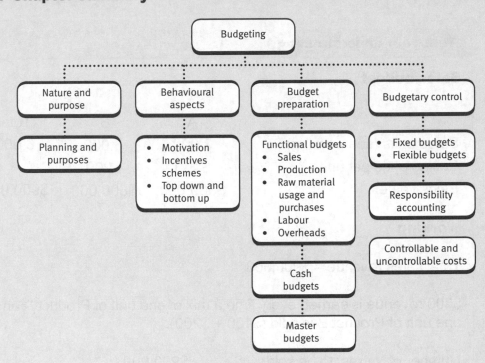

Test your understanding answers

Test your understanding 1

Sales budget

	A	B	Total
Sales units (see working)	3,000	3,000	6,000
Selling price per unit	$100	$200	
Sales value	$300,000	$600,000	$900,000

Working

Total sales revenue = $900,000

$300 revenue is earned every time a mix of one unit of Product A and one unit of Product B is sold ($100 + $200).

Number of 'mixes' to be sold to earn $900,000 = $\dfrac{\$900,000}{\$300}$ = 3,000 'mixes'

3,000 'mixes' = 3,000 units of Product A and 3,000 units of Product B.

Test your understanding 2

The correct answer is D.

The budgeted labour cost is $23,800

Actual expected total time = $\dfrac{2,520}{0.9}$ = 2,800 hours

Budgeted labour cost = 2,800 × $8.50 = $23,800.

Test your understanding 3

Answer a and b

	Product 1	Product 2
Sales forecast	3,000	4,500
+ Closing inventory	200	300
– Opening inventory	500	700
	————	————
Production budget	**2,700**	**4,100**

Answers c, d, e and f

	Material M1	Material M2
Product 1 usage	5,400	8,100
Product 2 usage	12,300	12,300
	————	————
Materials usage budget	**17,700**	**20,400**

	Material M1	Material M2
Material usage	17,700	20,400
+ Closing inventory	2,200	1,300
– Opening inventory	4,300	3,700
	————	————
Material purchases budget(units)	**15,600**	**18,000**
Material price per kg	$1.21	$3.30
Material purchases budget (value)	**$18,876**	**$59,400**

Workings

Material prices are as follows:

M1 : $1.10 × 1.1 = $1.21

M2 : $3.00 × 1.1 = $3.30

Material usages are as follows:

Product 1 – Material M1 usage = 2 × 2,700 = 5,400

Product 2 – Material M1 usage = 3 × 4,100 = 12,300

Product 1 – Material M2 usage = 3 × 2,700 = 8,100

Product 2 – Material M2 usage = 3 × 4,100 = 12,300

Answers g and h

	Skilled	Semi-skilled
Product 1 hours	8,100	10,800
Product 2 hours	4,100	16,400
Labour budget (hours)	**12,200**	**27,200**
Labour rate per hour	$9	$6
Labour budget ($)	**109,800**	**163,200**

Product 1 – skilled hours = 3 × 2,700 = 8,100

Product 2 – skilled hours = 1 × 4,100 = 4,100

Product 1 – semi-skilled hours = 4 × 2,700 = 10,800

Product 2 – semi-skilled hours = 4 × 4,100 = 16,400

Answer i

Number of hours of skilled labour = 12,200 (see above)

Number of hours of semi-skilled labour = 27,200 (see above)

Total hours worked = 12,200 + 27,200 = 39,400

		$
Variable costs	39,400 hours × $3.50	137,900
Fixed costs	39,400 hours × $5.50	216,700
		354,600

Test your understanding 4

	January $	February $	March $
Receipts			
Sales	56,000	58,000	54,000
Payments			
Capital expenditure	–	–	30,000
Direct materials	20,000	22,000	13,000
Direct labour	15,000	16,500	9,750
Fixed production overheads	2,000	2,000	2,000
Variable production overheads	13,000	10,600	8,800
Admin/selling overhead	15,000	–	–
Total outflow	65,000	51,100	63,550
Net cash flow for month	(9,000)	6,900	(9,550)
Opening balance	(5,000)	(14,000)	(7,100)
Closing balance	(14,000)	(7,100)	(16,650)

We can take each item of cash flow in turn, and use workings tables to calculate what the monthly cash flows are.

Cash from sales

	Total sales $	Cash receipts January $	Cash receipts February $	Cash Receipts March $
Opening receivables		44,000	–	–
January	60,000	12,000	48,000	–
February	50,000	–	10,000	40,000
March	70,000	–	–	14,000
		56,000	58,000	54,000

Payments for materials purchases

	December $	January $	February $	March $	April $
Total cost of production	–	50,000	55,000	32,500	50,000
Material cost of production (40%)	–	20,000	22,000	13,000	20,000
Purchases paid in the month prior to usage	20,000	22,000	13,000	20,000	unknown
Payments are made in the month following purchase.	–	20,000	22,000	13,000	20,000

Payments for overheads

	January $	February $	March $
Total cost of production	50,000	55,000	32,500
Overhead cost of production (30%)	15,000	16,500	9,750
Fixed costs	(5,000)	(5,000)	(5,000)
Variable overhead costs	10,000	11,500	4,750

Of the monthly fixed overhead costs of $5,000, $3,000 is depreciation which is not a cash expenditure.

Monthly fixed cost cash expenditure is therefore $2,000.

The opening balance of unpaid variable production overhead cost at the beginning of January is $9,000. This cost should be paid for in January. Variable overheads are paid 40% in the month of expenditure and 60% the following month.

Variable overheads	Cost $	January $	February $	March $
Opening payables for variable overheads		9,000		
January	10,000	4,000	6,000	–
February	11,500	–	4,600	6,900
March	4,750	–	–	1,900
Total payments		13,000	10,600	8,800

The other items of cash flow are straightforward, although it is important to notice that the payments for administration and selling overheads are paid quarterly, and the cash payment ($15,000) is not the same as the total overhead cost for the quarter. Presumably there are depreciation charges within the total costs given.

Test your understanding 5

The production budget (1)	6,000 units
The raw material usage budget (2)	72,000 kg
The raw material purchases budget (3)	$146,000
The direct labour budget (4)	$336,000
The overhead budget (5)	$432,000
The cost per unit of Brown (6)	$152

Budgeted Income Statement

	$	$
Sales Revenue 5,000 × $230		1,150,000
Cost of sales		
Opening inventory 100 × $152	15,200	
Production cost 6,000 × $152	912,000	
Closing inventory 1,100 × $152	(167,200)	
		(760,000)
Gross profit		390,000
Administration and marketing		(225,000)
Profit		165,000

Budgeted Statement of Financial Position

	$	$
Non current assets $950,000 + $40,000		990,000
Inventory (7)	179,200	
Trade receivables	260,000	
Cash (8)	36,800	
	476,000	
Trade payables	86,000	
Other short term liabilities	24,000	
	110,000	
Net current assets		366,000
Net assets $1,191,000 + $165,000		1,356,000

Workings

Production budget		**Raw material budget**	
Sales	5,000	Production	6,000
Opening inventory	(100)	kg per unit	× 12
Closing inventory	1,100		
		(2) *Usage (kg)*	72,000
(1) *Production units*	6,000	Opening inventory	(5,000)
		Closing inventory	6,000
Labour budget		Purchases (kg)	73,000
Production	6,000	Cost per kg	× 2
Hours per unit	× 8		
		(3) *Purchases ($)*	146,000
Labour hours	48,000		
Rate per hour	× 7	**Overhead budget**	
		Labour hours	48,000
(4) *Labour cost ($)*	336,000	Cost per hour ($1 + $8)	× 9

Cost of one unit of Brown				
Direct material (12kg × $2)	$24	(5) *Overhead cost ($)*		432,000
Direct labour (8hr × $7)	$56	**Inventory**		
Overheads (8hr × ($1 + $8))	$72	Raw materials (6,000 × $2)		$12,000
	———	Finished goods (1,100 × $152)		$167,200
(6) *Cost per unit*	$152			———
		(7) *Inventory valuation*		$179,200

Cash	
Opening balance	$25,000
Profit for the period	$165,000
Cash spent on NCA	($40,000)
Change in inventory	($113,200)
	———
(8) *Closing cash balance*	$36,800

Test your understanding 6

(1) **Identify the cost behaviours and calculate the cost per unit based on budget**

	Behaviour	Cost per unit
Direct labour	variable	20,000 / 20,000 = $1
Direct expenses	variable	800 / 20,000 = $0.04
Direct material	variable	4,200 / 20,000 = $0.21
Depreciation	fixed	n/a
Semi-variable overheads	semi variable	see working

Working for Semi-variable overhead (high low method)

Variable cost = change in cost / change in activity

= ($5,000 − $4,500) / (20,000 − 15,000)
= $0.10

Fixed cost = total cost − total variable cost

= $5,000 − ($0.10 × 20,000)

= $3,000

(2) **Produce the budget control statement**

	Actual 17,600 units	Flexed 17,600 units	Variance
	$	$	
Direct labour	19,540	17,600	1,940 A
Direct expenses	1,000	704	296 A
Direct material	3,660	3,696	36 F
Depreciation	10,000	10,000	–
Semi-variable overheads (W)	4,760	4,760	–
	38,960	36,760	2,200 A

Working for Semi-variable overheads

Variable element 17,600 × $0.10 = $1,760
Fixed element $3,000
Total cost = $1,760 + $3,000 = $4,760

Capital budgeting

Chapter learning objectives

Upon completion of this chapter you will be able to:

- discuss the importance of capital investment planning and control

- define and distinguish between capital and revenue expenditure

- outline the issues to consider and the steps involved in the preparation of a capital expenditure budget

- explain and illustrate the difference between simple and compound interest, and between nominal and effective interest rates

- explain and illustrate compounding and discounting

- explain the distinction between cash flow and profit and the relevance of cash flow to capital investment appraisal

- identify and evaluate relevant cash flows for individual investment decisions

- explain and illustrate the net present value (NPV) and internal rate of return (IRR) methods of discounted cash flow

- calculate present value using annuity and perpetuity formulae

- calculate NPV, IRR and payback (discounted and non-discounted)

- interpret the results of NPV, IRR and payback calculations of investment viability

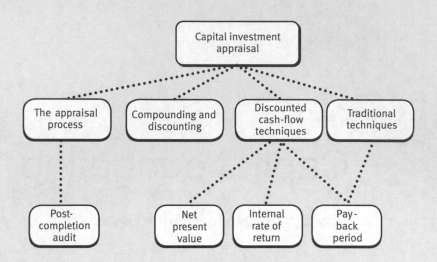

1 Capital investment

When a business spends money on new non-current assets it is known as capital investment or capital expenditure. Spending is normally irregular and for large amounts. It is expected to generate long-term benefits.

Capital investment decisions normally represent the most important decisions that an organisation makes, since they commit a substantial proportion of a firm's resources to actions that are likely to be irreversible.

Many different investment projects exist including:

- replacement of assets
- cost-reduction schemes
- new product/service developments
- product/service expansions
- statutory, environmental and welfare proposals

2 Capital and revenue expenditure

The distinction between capital expenditure and revenue expenditure is important.

Capital expenditure

Capital expenditure is expenditure incurred in:

(a) the acquisition of non-current assets required for use in the business and not for resale

(b) the alteration or significant improvement of non-current assets for the purpose of increasing their revenue-earning capacity.

KAPLAN PUBLISHING

Capital expenditure is initially shown in the **statement of financial position** as non-current assets. It is then **charged to the income statement** over a number of periods, via the **depreciation** charge.

Revenue expenditure

Revenue expenditure is expenditure incurred in:

(a) the purchase of assets acquired for conversion into cash (e.g. goods for resale)

(b) the manufacturing, selling and distribution of goods and the day-to-day administration of the business

(c) the maintenance of the revenue-earning capacity of the non current assets (i.e. repairs, etc).

Revenue expenditure is generally charged to the **income statement** for the period in which the expenditure was incurred.

In practice, there can be some difficulty in clearly distinguishing between alteration/improvement of non-current assets (capital) and their maintenance (revenue). For example, is the installation of a modern heating system to replace an old inefficient system an improvement or maintenance? However, you should not need to make such decisions in your exam.

3 Capital budgeting and investment appraisal

A capital budget:

- is a programme of capital expenditure covering several years

- includes authorised future projects and projects currently under consideration

One stage in the capital budgeting process is **investment appraisal**. This appraisal has the following features:

- estimates of future costs and benefits over the project's life

- assessment of the level of expected returns earned

The capital budgeting process consists of a number of stages:

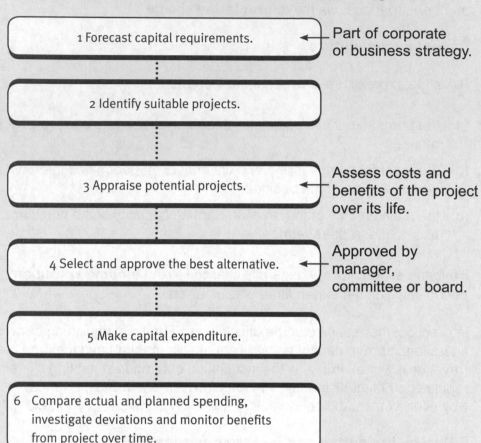

Capital budgeting process

When a proposed capital project is evaluated, the costs and benefits of the project should be evaluated over its foreseeable life. This is usually the expected useful life of the non-current asset to be purchased, which will be several years. This means that estimates of future costs and benefits call for long term forecasting.

A 'typical' capital project involves an immediate purchase of a non-current asset. The asset is then used for a number of years, during which it is used to increase sales revenue or to achieve savings in operating costs. There will also be running costs for the asset. At the end of the asset's commercially useful life, it might have a 'residual value'. For example, it might be sold for scrap or in a second hand market. (Items such as motor vehicles and printing machines often have a significant residual value.)

A problem with long term forecasting of revenues, savings and costs is that forecasts can be inaccurate. However, although it is extremely difficult to produce reliable forecasts, every effort should be made to make them as reliable as possible.

- A business should try to avoid spending money on non-current assets on the basis of wildly optimistic and unrealistic forecasts.

- The assumptions on which the forecasts are based should be stated clearly. If the assumptions are clear, the forecasts can be assessed for reasonableness by the individuals who are asked to authorise the spending.

The capital expenditure committee

The committee is usually responsible for overseeing the capital investment process. The functions of such a committee are to:

- co-ordinate capital expenditure policy

- appraise and authorise capital expenditure on specific projects

- review actual expenditure on capital projects against the budget.

In many organisations, multidisciplinary teams, or working parties, are set up to investigate individual proposals and report back to top management on their findings.

Such a team might comprise:

- project engineer

- production engineer

- management accountant

- relevant specialist, e.g. personnel officer, for a project involving sports facilities or canteens, safety officers, etc.

- economist.

Post-completion audit

The post-completion appraisal of projects provides a mechanism whereby experience gained from current and past projects can be fed into the organisation's decision-making process to aid decisions on future projects. In other words, it aids organisational learning. A post-completion appraisal reviews all aspects of an ongoing project in order to assess whether it has fulfilled its initial expectations. It is a forward-looking rather than a backward-looking technique. The task is often carried out by the Capital Expenditure Committee, or an appointed sub-committee. The committee would meet either annually, bi-annually, or if necessary, quarterly.

Benefits of post-completion audit

(1) If managers know in advance that projects are going to be subject to a post-completion appraisal they ensure that assumptions and plans for the project are more accurate and realistic.

(2) If an appraisal is carried out before the project life ends, and it is found that the benefits have been less than expected because of management inefficiency, then steps can be taken to improve efficiency.

(3) It might identify weaknesses in the forecasting techniques and the estimating techniques used to evaluate the project. The discipline and quality of forecasting for future investments can be improved.

(4) Managers may be motivated to achieve the forecast results if they are aware of a pending post-completion appraisal.

(5) The appraisal reveals the reliability and quality of contractors and suppliers involved in the project.

(6) The appraisal may highlight the reasons for success or failure in previous projects – thereby providing a learning experience for managers to aid better decision making in the future.

Problems with post-completion audits

(1) It may not be possible to identify separately the costs and benefits of any particular project.

(2) It can be a time-consuming and costly exercise.

(3) Applied punitively, post-completion appraisal may lead managers to becoming over-cautious and risk averse.

(4) The strategic effects of a capital investment project may take years to materialise and it may never be possible to identify and quantify them correctly.

(5) There are many uncontrollable factors in long-term investments. A post-completion appraisal will not help managers change these factors in the future.

4 Cash flows used for investment appraisal

In capital investment appraisal it is more appropriate to evaluate future **cash flows rather than accounting profits.** Cash and profit are very different. Profit is calculated on the Income statement and cash is a current asset on the Statement of financial position. The differences arise because:

- Revenue is recognised in the income statement when it is earned but not when the cash is received

- Costs are recognised in the income statement when it is incurred but not when the cash is paid.

- Non-cash expenses – the income statement of a business is charged with a number of non-cash expenses such as depreciation and provisions for doubtful debts. Although these are correctly charged as expenses in the income statement, they are not cash flows and will not reduce the cash balance of the business.

- Purchase of non-current assets – these are often large cash outflows of a business but the only amount that is charged to the income statement is the annual depreciation charge not the entire cost of the non-current asset.

- Sale of non-current assets – when a non-current asset is sold this will result in an inflow of cash to the business but the figure to appear in the income statement is not the sales proceeds but any profit or loss on the sale.

- Financing transactions – some transactions, such as issuing additional share capital and taking out or repaying a loan, will result in large cash flows in or out of the business with no effect on the profit figure at all.

When appraising a possible capital investment it is necessary to use the actual cash flows in and out of the business rather than profits as profits are subjective and cannot be spent.

Cash flows that are appraised should be relevant to or change as a direct result of making a decision to invest. **Relevant cash flows** are:

- future costs and revenues – it is not possible to change what has happened so any relevant costs or revenues are future ones

- cash flows – actual cash coming in or leaving the business not including any non-cash items such as depreciation and notional costs

- incremental costs and revenues - the increase in costs or revenues that occurs as a direct result of a decision to invest.

 Relevant cost terms

Relevant cost terminology

- **Differential costs** are the differences in total costs or revenues between two alternatives.

- **Opportunity cost** is an important concept in decision making. It represents the best alternative that is foregone in taking the decision. The opportunity cost emphasises that decision making is concerned with alternatives and that the cost of taking one decision is the profit or contribution foregone by not taking the next best alternative.

- **Avoidable costs** are the specific costs associated with an activity that would be avoided if that activity did not exist.

Non-relevant cost terminology

- **Sunk costs** are past or historical costs which are not directly relevant in decision making, for example, development costs or market research costs.

- **Committed costs** are future costs that cannot be avoided, whatever decision is taken.

- **Non-cash flow costs** are costs which do not involve the flow of cash, for example, depreciation and notional costs. A notional cost is a cost that will not result in an outflow of cash either now or in the future, for example, sometimes the head office of an organisation may charge a 'notional' rent to its branches. This cost will appear in the accounts of the organisation but will not result in a 'real' cash expenditure.

- **General fixed overheads** are usually not relevant to a decision. However, some fixed overheads may be relevant to a decision, for example, stepped fixed costs may be relevant if fixed costs increase as a direct result of a decision being taken.

- **Carry amount of non-current assets** are not relevant costs because like depreciation, they are determined by accounting conventions rather than by future cash flows.

Illustration 1 – Relevant costs

A company is evaluating a proposed expenditure on an item of equipment that would cost $160,000.

A technical feasibility study has been carried out by consultants, at a cost of $15,000, into benefits from investing in the equipment.

It has been estimated that the equipment would have a life of four years, and annual profits would be $8,000, after deducting annual depreciation of $40,000 and an annual charge of $25,000 for a share of the existing fixed cost of the company.

What are the relevant cash flows for this investment?

Solution

The $160,000 to be spent on the new item of equipment is relevant as it is a future cash flow incurred as a direct result of making the decision.

The $15,000 already spent on the feasibility study is a sunk cost – it has already been spent – therefore it is not relevant.

Depreciation and apportioned fixed overheads are not relevant. Depreciation is not a cash flow and apportioned fixed overheads represent costs that will be incurred anyway.

It is possible to estimate annual cash flows by adjusting profits for non-cash items.

	$
Estimated profit	8,000
Add back depreciation	40,000
Add back apportioned fixed costs	25,000
Annual cash flows	73,000

The $73,000 annual cash flows will also be relevant for the life of the investment.

Test your understanding 1

A manufacturing company is considering the production of a new type of widget. Each widget will take two hours to make.

Fixed overheads are apportioned on the basis of $1 per labour hour.

If the new widgets are produced, the company will have to employ an additional supervisor at a salary of $15,000 per annum. The company will produce 10,000 widgets per annum.

What are the relevant cash flows?

5 The time value of money

One characteristic of all capital expenditure projects is that the cash flows arise over the long term (a period usually greater than 12 months). Under this situation it becomes necessary to carefully consider the time value of money.

Money received today is worth more than the same sum received in the future, i.e. it has a **time value.**

There are three main reasons for the time value of money:

- Potential for earning interest
- Impact of inflation
- Risk

Discounted cash flow (DCF) techniques take account of the time value of money when appraising investments.

The time value of money

Potential for earning interest

If a capital investment is to be justified, it needs to earn at least a minimum amount of profit, so that the return compensates the investor for both the amount invested and also for the length of time before the profits are made. For example, if a company could invest $80,000 now to earn revenue of $82,000 in one week's time, a profit of $2,000 in seven days would be a very good return. However, if it takes four years to earn the money, the return would be very low.

Therefore money has a time value. It can be invested to earn interest or profits, so it is better to have $1 now than in one year's time. This is because $1 now can be invested for the next year to earn a return, whereas $1 in one year's time cannot. Another way of looking at the time value of money is to say that $1 in six years' time is worth less than $1 now.

There are different forms of interest which are discussed in the next section:

- Simple
- Compound
- Nominal
- Effective

Impact of inflation

In most countries, in most years prices rise as a result of inflation. Therefore funds received today will buy more than the same amount a year later, as prices will have risen in the meantime. The funds are subject to a loss of purchasing power over time.

Risk

The earlier cash flows are due to be received, the more certain they are – there is less chance that events will prevent payment. Earlier cash flows are therefore considered to be more valuable.

6 Interest

Simple interest

Simple interest is calculated based on the original sum invested. Any interest earned in earlier periods is not included. Simple interest is often used for a single investment period that is less than a year.

To calculate the future value of an amount invested under these terms you could use the following formula:

$$V = X + (X \times r \times n)$$

Where V = Future value

           X = Initial investment (present value)

           r = Interest rate (expressed as a decimal)

           n = Number of time periods

Illustration 2 – Simple interest

$100 is invested in an account for six months. The interest rate is 10% per annum. Calculate the value of the account after six months.

Solution

$V = X + (X \times r \times n)$

$V = 100 + (100 \times 0.1 \times (6/12)) = \$105$

Compound interest

Compounding calculates the future (or terminal) value of a given sum invested today for a number of years.

To compound a sum, the figure is increased by the amount of interest it would earn over the period. Interest is earned on interest gained in earlier periods.

Illustration 3 – Compounding

$100 is invested in an account for five years. The interest rate is 10% per annum. Calculate the value of the account after five years.

Solution

To compound a sum of money, the value is increased by the amount of interest it will earn over the period it is invested.

Therefore the $100 invested for 5 years will earn:

In year 1 $100 + ($100 × 10%) = $110

In year 2 $110 + ($110 × 10%) = $121

In year 3 $121 + ($121 × 10%) = $133.10

In year 4 $133.10 + (133.10 × 10%) = $146.41

In year 5 $146.41 + (146.41 × 10%) = $161.05

This can also be calculated using a formula:

FORMULA FOR COMPOUNDING

$$V = X(1 + r)^n$$

Where
V = Future value
X = Initial investment (present value)
r = Interest rate (expressed as a decimal)
n = Number of time periods

Illustration 4 – Compounding

$100 is invested in an account for five years. The interest rate is 10% per annum. Calculate the value of the account after five years using the formula.

Solution

$V = X(1+r)^n$

$V = 100 (1.10)^5 = \$161.05$

Test your understanding 2

$450 is invested in an account earning 6.25% interest p.a. Calculate the fund value after 12 years.

Test your understanding 3

$5000 is required in 10 years. $x is invested in an account earning 5% interest p.a. Calculate the value of $x.

Nominal interest rate

The nominal interest rate is the stated interest rate for a time period – for example a month or a year.

Effective interest rate

The effective interest rate is the interest rate that includes the effects of compounding a nominal interest rate.

FORMULA FOR EFFECTIVE INTEREST RATE

$r = (1 + i/n)^n - 1$

Where
r = Effective interest rate
i = Nominal interest rate
n = Number of time periods

Illustration 5 – Nominal and effective interest rates

The nominal interest rate is 10% per year compounded on a monthly basis. A company is going to invest for 12 months what is the effective interest rate?

Solution

$r = (1 + i/n)^n - 1$

$r = (1 + 0.1/12)^{12} - 1$

$r = 0.1047$

The effective interest rate of receiving 10% interest per annum compounded on a monthly basis for 12 months is the same as receiving 10.47% interest per annum with no compounding.

Test your understanding 4

A company has $1,000,000 to invest for 12 months.

The choices available are:

- a deposit account offering nominal interest at 10% per year, with interest calculated quarterly
- a deposit account offering nominal interest at 10.25% per year, with interest calculated annually

Which deposit account gives the higher effective interest rate?

7 Discounting

Discounting performs the opposite function to compounding. Compounding finds the future value of a sum invested now, whereas discounting considers a sum receivable in the future and establishes its equivalent value today. This value in today's terms is known as the **Present Value (PV).**

In potential investment projects, cash flows will arise at many different points in time. Calculating the present value of future flows is a key technique in investment appraisal decisions.

Assumptions used in discounting

Unless told otherwise you should assume:

- **All cash flows occur at the start or end of a year.**

  Although in practice many cash flows accrue throughout the year, for discounting purposes they are all treated as occurring at the start or end of a year. Note also that if today (T_0) is 01/01/20X0, the dates 31/12/20X1 and 01/01/20X2, although technically separate days, can be treated for discounting as occurring at the same point in time, i.e. at T_1.

- **Initial investments occur at once (T_0), other cash flows start in one year's time (T_1).**

  In project appraisal, the investment needs to be made before the cash flows can accrue. Therefore, unless the examiner specifies otherwise, it is assumed that investments occur in advance. The first cash flows associated with running the project are therefore assumed to occur one year after the project begins, i.e. at T_1.

FORMULAE FOR DISCOUNTING

Present value = Future value x discount factor **LEARN**

Where: Discount factor $= \dfrac{1}{(1+r)^n}$ or $(1+r)^{-n}$ **GIVEN**

where: r is the interest rate expressed as decimal

n is the number of time periods

$(1 + r)^{-n}$ can be looked up in discounting tables. It is known as the discount factor.

Test your understanding 5

Calculate how much should be invested now in order to have $250 in eight years' time? The account pays 12% interest per annum.

Test your understanding 6

Calculate the present value of $25,000 receivable in six years' time, if the interest rate is 10% p.a.

The cost of capital

In the above discussions we referred to the rate of interest. There are a number of alternative terms used to refer to the rate a firm should use to take account of the time value of money:

- cost of capital
- discount rate
- required return.

Whatever term is used, the rate of interest used for discounting reflects the cost of the finance that will be tied up in the investment.

8 Capital investment appraisal

Appraisal methods

There are three widely used appraisal methods:

(1) The payback period (using both discounted and non-discounted cash flows)

(2) Net present value (NPV).

(3) Internal rate of return (IRR).

All three methods consider the time value of money, assuming the discounted payback method is used. They are known as discounted cash flow (DCF) techniques.

9 The payback period

The payback period is the time a project will take to pay back the money spent on it. It is based on expected cash flows and provides a measure of liquidity.

This is the time which elapses until the invested capital is recovered. It considers cash flows only. Unlike DCF techniques, it is assumed that the **cash flows** occur evenly during the year.

Decision criteria

- Compare the payback period to the company's maximum return time allowed and if the payback is quicker the project should be accepted.
- Faced with mutually-exclusive projects choose the project with the quickest payback.

Calculation – Constant annual flows

$$\text{Payback period} = \frac{\text{Initial investment}}{\text{Annual cash inflow}}$$

A payback period may not be for an exact number of years. To calculate the payback in years and months you should multiply the decimal fraction of a year by 12 to get the number of months.

Test your understanding 7

An expenditure of $2 million is expected to generate net cash inflows of $500,000 each year for the next seven years.

Calculate the payback period for the project?

Test your understanding 8

A project will involve spending $1.8 million now. Annual cash flows from the project would be $350,000.

Calculate the payback period for the project.

Calculations – Uneven annual flows

If cash inflows are uneven (a more likely state of affairs), the payback has to be calculated by working out the cumulative cash flow over the life of a project

Illustration 6 – Mickey Ltd

Mickey Ltd is considering two mutually-exclusive projects with the following details:

Project A

Initial investment	$450,000				
Scrap value in year 5	$20,000				
Year:	1	2	3	4	5
Annual cash flows ($000)	200	150	100	100	100

Project B

| Initial investment | $100,000 |
| Scrap value in year 5 | $10,000 |

Year:	1	2	3	4	5
Annual cash flows ($000)	50	40	30	20	20

Assume that the initial investment is at the start of the project and the annual cash flows accrue evenly over the year.

Required:

Calculate which project the company should select if the objective is to minimise the payback period?

Solution

Project A	Cashflow	Cumulative cash flow
	$000	$000
Year 0	(450)	(450)
Year 1	200	(250)
Year 2	150	(100)
Year 3	100	0
Payback period = 3 years		

Project B		
Year 0	(100)	(100)
Year 1	50	(50)
Year 2	40	(10)
Year 3	30	20
Payback period = 2 years 4 months		

Note:

Project B – requires $10,000 during year 3 to payback. Over the 3rd year $30,000 cash is being received. Assuming that cash accrues evenly over the year it will take 1/3 of a year to recoup the remaining cash to payback. 1/3 × 12 months = 4 months

Discounted payback

One of the major criticisms of using the payback period is that it does not take into account the time value of money. The discounted payback technique attempts to overcome this criticism by measuring the time required for the **present values** of the cash inflows from a project to equal the present values of the cash outflows.

The technique is identical – but the present value of the cash flow is calculated before calculating the cumulative cash flow.

Illustration 7 – Mickey Ltd cont.

Mickey Ltd is considering two mutually-exclusive projects with the following details:

Project A

| Initial investment | $450,000 |
| Scrap value in year 5 | $20,000 |

Year:	1	2	3	4	5
Annual cash flows ($000)	200	150	100	100	100

Project B

| Initial investment | $100,000 |
| Scrap value in year 5 | $10,000 |

Year:	1	2	3	4	5
Annual cash flows ($000)	50	40	30	20	20

Assume that the initial investment is at the start of the project and the annual cash flows accrue evenly over the year.

Required:

Calculate the discounted payback period for both projects if the relevant cost of capital is 10%.

Solution

Year	Discount factor 10%	Project A Cash flow $000	Project A Present value $000	Project A Cumulative cash flow $000	Project B Cash flow $000	Project B Present value $000	Project B Cumulative cash flow $000
0	1.000	(450)	(450)	(450)	(100)	(100)	(100)
1	0.909	200	181.8	(268.2)	50	45.45	(54.55)
2	0.826	150	123.9	(144.3)	40	33.04	(21.51)
3	0.751	100	75.1	(69.2)	30	22.53	1.02
4	0.683	100	68.3	(0.9)			
5	0.621	120	74.52	73.62			

Project A now pays back in just over 4 years and Project B in just under 3 years. Project B is still preferable to Project A but the payback period has increased as time value of money is applied to the cash flows

Advantages	Disadvantages
• Simple to understand	• Is not a measure of absolute profitability
• A project with a long payback period tends to be riskier than one with a short payback period. Payback is a simple measure of risk	• Ignores the time value of money. **Note:** A discounted payback period may be calculated to overcome this problem
• Uses cash flows, not subjective accounting profits	• Does not take into account cash flows beyond the payback period
• Emphasises the cash flows in the earlier years	
• Firms selecting projects on the basis of payback periods may avoid liquidity problems	

Advantages and disadvantages of Payback

Payback has a number of advantages

- As a concept payback is easily understood and is easily calculated.

- Rapidly changing technology. If new plant is likely to be scrapped in a short period because of obsolescence, a quick payback is essential.

- Improving investment conditions. When investment conditions are expected to improve in the near future, attention is directed to those projects that will release funds soonest, to take advantage of the improving climate.

- Payback favours projects with a quick return. It is often argued that these are to be preferred for three reasons.

  - Rapid project payback leads to rapid company growth – but in fact such a policy will lead to many profitable investment opportunities being overlooked because their payback period does not happen to be particularly swift.

  - Rapid payback minimises risk (the logic being that the shorter the payback period, the less there is that can go wrong). Not all risks are related to time, but payback is able to provide a useful means of assessing time risk (and only time risk). It is likely that earlier cash flows can be estimated with greater certainty.

  - Rapid payback maximises liquidity – but liquidity problems are best dealt with separately, through cash forecasting.

- Payback uses cash flows, rather than profits, and so is less likely to produce an unduly optimistic figure distorted by assorted accounting conventions which might permit certain costs to be carried forward and not affect profit initially.

The disadvantages of payback are:

- Project returns may be ignored. In particular, cash flows arising after the payback period are totally ignored.

- Timing of cash flows are ignored. Cash flows are effectively categorised as pre-payback or post-payback, but no more accurate measure is made.

- The time value of money is ignored (unless discounted payback is used)

- There is no objective measure as to what length of time should be set as the minimum or maximum payback period. Investment decisions are therefore subjective.

> - Payback takes no account of the effects on business profits and periodic performance of the project, as evidenced in the financial statements. This is critical if the business is to be reasonably viewed by users of the accounts.

10 Net present value (NPV)

The net benefit or loss of benefit in present value terms from an investment opportunity.

The NPV represents the surplus funds earned on a project. This means that it tells us the impact on shareholder wealth.

Decision criteria

- Any project with a positive NPV is viable.

- Projects with a negative NPV are not viable.

- Faced with mutually-exclusive projects, choose the project with the highest NPV.

What does the NPV actually mean?

Suppose, in an investment problem, we calculate the NPV of certain cash flows at 12% to be – $97, and at 10% to be zero, and yet at 8% the NPV of the same cash flows is + $108. Another way of expressing this is as follows.

- If the funds were borrowed at 12% the investor would be $97 out of pocket – i.e. the investment earns a yield below the cost of capital.

- If funds were borrowed at 10% the investor would break even – i.e. the investment yields a return equal to the cost of capital.

- If funds were borrowed at 8% the investor would be $108 in pocket – i.e. the investment earns a return in excess of the cost of capital.

In other words, a positive NPV is an indication of the surplus funds available to the investor now as a result of accepting the project.

Illustration 8 – Mickey Ltd cont

Mickey Ltd is considering two mutually-exclusive projects with the following details:

Project A

Initial investment	$450,000
Scrap value in year 5	$20,000

Year:	1	2	3	4	5
Annual cash flows ($000)	200	150	100	100	100

Project B

Initial investment	$100,000
Scrap value in year 5	$10,000

Year:	1	2	3	4	5
Annual cash flows ($000)	50	40	30	20	20

Assume that the initial investment is at the start of the project and the annual cash flows accrue evenly over the year.

Required:

Calculate the Net Present Value to the nearest $000 for Projects A and B if the relevant cost of capital is 10%.

		Project A		Project B	
Year	Discount factor 10%	Net cash flow $000	PV $000	Net cash flow $000	PV $000
0					
1					
2					
3					
4					
5					

Calculate which project has the highest NPV.

Year	Discount factor	Project A		Project B	
		Cash flow $000	Present value $000	Cash flow $000	Present value $000
0		(450)	(450)	(100)	(100)
1	0.909	200	182	50	45
2	0.826	150	124	40	33
3	0.751	100	75	30	23
4	0.683	100	68	20	14
5	0.621	120	75	30	19
		NPV =	74	NPV =	34

Test your understanding 9

An organisation is considering a capital investment in new equipment. The estimated cash flows are as follows.

Year	Cash flow $
0	(240,000)
1	80,000
2	120,000
3	70,000
4	40,000
5	20,000

The company's cost of capital is 9%.

Calculate the NPV of the project to assess whether it should be undertaken.

Advantages	Disadvantages
• Does consider the time value of money	• Fairly complex
• It is a measure of absolute profitability	• Not well understood by non-financial managers
• Considers cash flows	• It may be difficult to determine the cost of capital
• It considers the whole life of the project	
• A company selecting projects on the basis of NPV maximisation should maximise shareholders wealth	

Advantages and disadvantages of NPV

When appraising projects or investments, NPV is considered to be superior (in theory) to most other methods. This is because it:

- considers the time value of money – discounting cash flows to PV takes account of the impact of interest, inflation and risk over time.

- is an absolute measure of return – the NPV of an investment represents the actual surplus raised by the project. This allows a business to plan more effectively.

- is based on cash flows not profits – the subjectivity of profits makes them less reliable than cash flows and therefore less appropriate for decision making.

- considers the whole life of the project – NPV takes account of all relevant flows associated with the project. Discounting the flows takes account of the fact that later flows are less reliable

- should lead to maximisation of shareholder wealth. If the cost of capital reflects the investors' (i.e. shareholders') required return, then the NPV reflects the theoretical increase in their wealth. For a company, this is considered to be the primary objective of the business.

However, there are some potential drawbacks:

- It is difficult to explain to managers. To understand the meaning of the NPV calculated requires an understanding of discounting. The method is not as intuitive as techniques such as payback.

- It requires knowledge of the cost of capital. The calculation of the cost of capital is, in practice, more complex than identifying interest rates. It involves gathering data and making a number of calculations based on that data and some estimates. The process may be deemed too protracted for the appraisal to be carried out.

- It is relatively complex. For the reasons explained above, NPV may be rejected in favour of simpler techniques.

11 Internal rate of return (IRR)

This is the rate of return, or discount rate, at which the project has a NPV of zero.

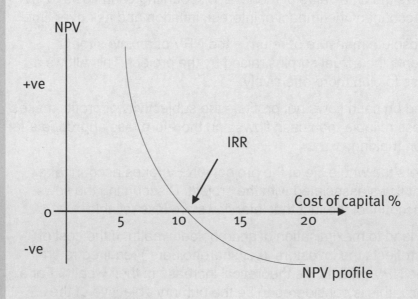

Graph showing the NPV of one project appraised at different discount rates

Decision criteria

- If the IRR is greater than the cost of capital the project should be accepted.

- Faced with mutually-exclusive projects choose the project with the higher IRR.

Further explanation of IRR

Using the NPV method, PVs are calculated by discounting cash flows at a given cost of capital, and the difference between the PV of costs and the PV of benefits is the NPV. In contrast, the IRR method of DCF analysis is to calculate the exact DCF rate of return that the project is expected to achieve.

If an investment has a positive NPV, it means it is earning more than the cost of capital. If the NPV is negative, it is earning less than the cost of capital. This means that if the NPV is zero, it will be earning exactly the cost of capital.

Conversely, the percentage return on the investment must be the rate of discount or cost of capital at which the NPV equals zero. This rate of return is called the IRR, or the DCF yield and if it is higher than the target rate of return then the project is financially worth undertaking.

Calculating the IRR (using linear interpolation)

The steps in linear interpolation are:

(1) Calculate two NPVs for the project at two different costs of capital

(2) Use the following formula to find the IRR:

FORMULA FOR IRR

$$IRR = L + \frac{N_L}{N_L - N_H} \times (H - L)$$

where:

L = Lower rate of interest

H = Higher rate of interest

N_L = NPV at lower rate of interest

N_H = NPV at higher rate of interest.

Illustration 9 – Mickey Ltd cont.

(a) Calculate the internal rate of return of Project A.

Year	Discount factors at ?%	Project A Net cash flow $000	PV $000
0		(450)	
1		200	
2		150	
3		100	
4		100	
5		120	

The NPV of Project A at a discount rate of 10% is $73,620

(b) Calculate the internal rate of return of Project B.

You are given the following:

At 10% the NPV was $33,310
At 20% the NPV is $8,510
At 30% the NPV is – $9,150

Solution

(a)

Year	Discount factors at 20%	Project A Net cash flow $000	PV $000
0	1.000	(450)	(450)
1	0.833	200	167
2	0.694	150	104
3	0.579	100	58
4	0.482	100	48
5	0.402	120	48
		NPV @ 20% =	(25)

KAPLAN PUBLISHING

$$IRR = L + \frac{N_L}{N_L - N_H} \times (H - L)$$

$$IRR = 10 + \frac{74}{74 - (25)} \times (20 - 10)$$

$$IRR = 10 + \frac{74}{99} \times (10)$$

$$IRR = 10 + (0.747 \times 10)$$

IRR = 17.5%

(b) **Project B**

At 10% the NPV was $33,310
At 20% the NPV is $8,510
At 30% the NPV is – $9,150

$$IRR = 20 + \frac{8,510}{8,510 - (-9,150)} \times (30 - 20)$$

$$IRR = 20 + \frac{8,510}{17,660} \times 10$$

$$IRR = 20 + (0.482 \times 10)$$

IRR = 24.8%

Test your understanding 10

A potential project's predicted cash flows gives a NPV of $50,000 at a discount rate of 10% and –$10,000 at a rate of 15%.

Calculate the IRR.

Test your understanding 11

Identify the correct explanation of the internal rate of return - it is the interest rate that equates the present value of expected future net cash flows to:

A   the initial cost of the investment outlay

B   the depreciation value of the investment

C   the terminal (compounded) value of future cash receipts

D   the firm's cost of capital

(2 marks)

For examination purposes, the choice of rates to estimate the IRR is less important than your ability to perform the calculation to estimate it.

Advantages	Disadvantages
• Does consider the time value of money	• It is not a measure of absolute profitability
• It is a percentage so should be easily understood by non-financial managers	• Interpolation only provides an estimate of the true IRR
• Considers cash flows	• Fairly complicated to calculate – although spreadsheets now have built-in programs
• It considers the whole life of the project	• The IRR of projects may conflict with the NPV. If this occurs the NPV must take precedence
• It can be calculated without reference to the cost of capital	
• A company selecting projects where the IRR exceeds the cost of capital should increase shareholders' wealth	

Advantages and disadvantages of IRR

Using IRR an as appraisal technique has many advantages:

- IRR considers the time value of money. The current value earned from an investment project is therefore more accurately measured.

- IRR is a percentage and therefore easily understood. Although managers may not completely understand the detail of the IRR, the concept of a return earned is familiar and the IRR can be simply compared with the required return of the organisation.

- IRR uses cash flows not profits. These are less subjective as discussed above.

- IRR considers the whole life of the project rather than ignoring later flows.

- a firm selecting projects where the IRR exceeds the cost of capital should increase shareholders' wealth. This holds true provided the project cash flows follow the standard pattern of an outflow followed by a series of inflows, as in the investment examples above.

However there are a number of difficulties with the IRR approach:

- It is not a measure of absolute profitability. A project of $1,000 invested now and paying back $1,100 in a year's time has an IRR of 10%. If a company's required return is 6%, then the project is viable according to the IRR rule but most businesses would consider the absolute return too small to be worth the investment.

- Interpolation only provides an estimate (and an accurate estimate requires the use of a spreadsheet programme).

- The cost of capital calculation itself is also only an estimate and if the margin between required return and the IRR is small, this lack of accuracy could actually mean the wrong decision is taken. For example if the cost of capital is found to be 8% (but is actually 8.7%) and the project IRR is calculated as 9.2% (but is actually 8.5%) the project would be wrongly accepted.

- Non-conventional cash flows may give rise to no IRR or multiple IRRs. For example a project with an outflow at T0 and T2 but income at T1 could, depending on the size of the cash flows, have a number of different profiles on a graph (see below). Even where the project does have one IRR, it can be seen from the graph that the decision rule would lead to the wrong result as the project does not earn a positive NPV at any cost of capital.

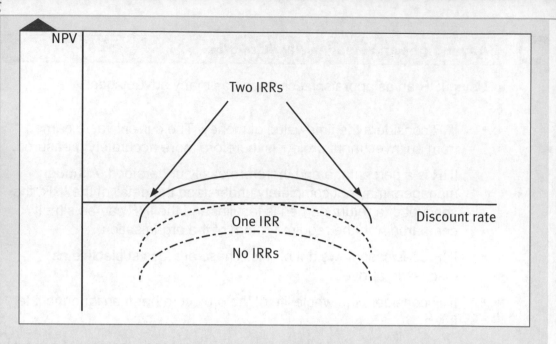

NPV v IRR

Both NPV and IRR are investment appraisal techniques which discount cash flows. However only NPV can be used to distinguish between two mutually-exclusive projects, as the diagram demonstrates.

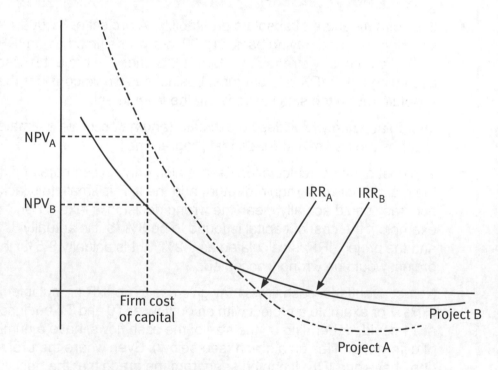

The profile of project A is such that it has a lower IRR and applying the IRR rule would prefer project B. However in absolute terms, A has the higher NPV at the company's cost of capital and should therefore be preferred.

NPV is therefore the better technique for choosing between projects.

The advantage of NPV is that it tells us the absolute increase in shareholder wealth as a result of accepting the project, at the current cost of capital. The IRR simply tells us how far the cost of capital could increase before the project would not be worth accepting.

12 NPV and IRR with equal cash flows

Discounting annuities

An annuity is a constant annual cash flow for a number of years.

Calculating the NPV of a project with even cash flows

When a project has equal annual cash flows the annuity factor may be used to calculate the NPV.

The **annuity factor** (AF) is the name given to the sum of the individual DF.

The PV of an annuity can therefore be quickly found using the formula:

PV = Annual cash flow × AF

Like with calculating a discount factor, the AF can be found using an annuity formula or annuity tables.

The formula is:

$$AF = \frac{1 - (1+r)^{-n}}{r}$$

For example, for a six-year annuity at 10%:

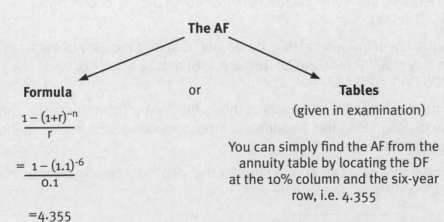

The AF

Formula

$$\frac{1 - (1+r)^{-n}}{r}$$

$$= \frac{1 - (1.1)^{-6}}{0.1}$$

$$= 4.355$$

or

Tables
(given in examination)

You can simply find the AF from the annuity table by locating the DF at the 10% column and the six-year row, i.e. 4.355

Calculating the IRR of a project with even cash flows

There is a simpler technique available, using annuity tables, if the project cash flows are annuities.

(1) Find the cumulative DF, Initial investment ÷ Annual inflow

(2) Find the life of the project, n.

(3) Look along the n year row of the cumulative DF until the closest value is found.

(4) The column in which this figure is found is the IRR.

Illustration 10 – Calculating IRR using annuities

Find the IRR of a project with an initial investment of $1.5 million and three years of inflows of $700,000 starting in one year.

Solution

NPV calculation:

Time		Cash flow $000	DF (c) %	PV $000
0	Investment	(1,500)	1	(1,500)
1–3	Inflow	700	(b)	(a)
NPV				Nil

- The aim is to find the discount rate (c) that produces an NPV of nil.

- Therefore the PV of inflows (a) must equal the PV of outflows, $1,500,000.

- If the PV of inflows (a) is to be $1,500,000 and the size of each inflow is $700,000, the DF required (b) must be 1,500,000 ÷ 700,000 = 2.143.

- The discount rate (c) for which this is the 3-year factor can be found by looking along the 3-year row of the cumulative DFS shown in the annuity table.

- The figure of 2.140 appears under the 19% column suggesting an IRR of 19% is the closest.

Test your understanding 12

(a) Pluto Ltd has been offered a project costing $50,000. The returns are expected to be $10,000 each year for seven years. Cost of capital is 10%. Calculate whether the project be accepted.

(b) Calculate the IRR of the project?

Discounting perpetuities

A perpetuity is an annual cash flow that occurs forever.

It is often described by examiners as a cash flow continuing 'for the foreseeable future'.

Calculating the NPV of a project with a perpetuity

The PV of a perpetuity is found using the formula:

$$PV = \frac{cashflow}{r}$$

or

$$PV = cashflow \times \frac{1}{r}$$

$\frac{1}{r}$ is known as the perpetuity factor.

Calculating the IRR of a project with a perpetuity

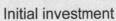

$$IRR \text{ of a perpetuity} = \frac{Annual\ inflow}{Initial\ investment} \times 100$$

Annuities/perpetuities in advance

The use of annuity factors and perpetuity factors both assume that the first cash flow will be occurring in one year's time. If this is not the case, you will need to adjust your calculation.

Advanced annuities and perpetuities

Some regular cash flows may start now (at T_0) rather than in one years time (T_1).

Calculate the PV by ignoring the payment at T_0 when considering the number of cash flows and then adding one to the annuity or perpetuity factor.

Illustration – Advanced annuities and perpetuities

A 5-year $600 annuity is starting today. Interest rates are 10%. Find the PV of the annuity.

Solution

This is essentially a standard 4-year annuity with an additional payment at T_0. The PV could be calculated as follows:

	T_0	T_1	T_2	T_3	T_4
CF	600	600	600	600	600
PV	600	+	600 × 4-year 10% AF

PV = 600 + 600 × 3.17 = 600 + 1902 = $2,502

The same answer can be found more quickly by adding 1 to the AF:

PV = 600 × (1 + 3.17) = 600 × 4.17 = $2,502.

Illustration – Advanced perpetuities

A perpetuity of $2,000 is due to commence immediately. The interest rate is 9%. What is the PV?

Solution

This is essentially a standard perpetuity with an additional payment at T_0. The PV could be calculated as follows:

T_0		T_1	T_2	T_3		T_4 ....
2,000		2,000 $\to \infty$				

PV $(2000) + (2000 \times 9\%$ perpetuity formula$)$

Again, the same answer can be found more quickly by adding 1 to the perpetuity factor.

$$2000 \times \left(1 + \frac{1}{0.09}\right) = 2000 \times 12.11 = \$24{,}222$$

Annuities/perpetuities in arrears

Delayed annuities and perpetuities

Some regular cash flows may start later than T_1.

These are dealt with by:

(1) applying the appropriate factor to the cash flow as normal

(2) discounting your answer back to T_0.

Illustration – Delayed annuities and perpetuities

What is the PV of $200 incurred each year for four years, starting in three year's time, if the discount rate is 5%?

Solution

Method: A four-year annuity starting at T_3
                                (1-4)

T_0	T_1	T_2	T_3	T_4	T_5	T_6
			200	200	200	200
PV	2.					
		1.				

Step 1   Discount the annuity as usual

$$200 \times 4\text{yr } 5\% \text{ AF} = 200 \times 3.546 = 709.2$$

Note that this gives the value of the annuity at T_2

Step 2   Discount the answer back to T_0

$$709.2 \times 2\text{yr } 5\% \text{ DF} = 709.2 \times 0.907 = \$643$$

Annuity or perpetuity factors will discount the cash flows back to give the value one year before the first cash flow arose. For standard annuities and perpetuities this gives the present (T_0) value since the first cash flow started at T_1.

However for delayed cash flows, applying the factor will find the value of the cash flows one year before they began, which in this example is T_2. To find the PV, an additional calculation is required – the value must be discounted back to T_0.

Care must be taken to discount back the appropriate number of years. The figure here was discounted back two years because the first step gave the value at T_2. It can help to draw a timeline as above and mark on the effect of the first step (as shown with a 1. here) to help you remember.

Test your understanding 13

An investment of $50,000 is expected to yield $5,670 per annum in perpetuity. Calculate the net present value of the investment opportunity if the cost of capital is 9%.

Test your understanding 14

$100,000 is deposited in a bank account paying 8% interest each year. Calculate the maximum sum that can be withdrawn from the account at the end of each year in perpetuity.

Test your understanding 15

In order to earn a perpetuity of $2,000 per annum calculate how much would need to be invested today. The account will pay 10% interest.

Test your understanding 16

What is the IRR of an investment that costs $20,000 and generates $1,600 for an indefinitely long period.

Test your understanding 17

A company is considering a project with a three-year life producing the following costs and revenues:

	$
Cost of machine	100,000
Depreciation of machine (for three years)	20,000 p.a.
Residual value of machine	40,000
Annual cost of direct labour	20,000
Annual charge for foreman (10% apportionment)	5,000
Annual cost of components required	18,000
Annual net revenues from machine	80,000
Cost of capital	20%

Identify which of the following is closest to the net present value of the machine:

A ($13,000)

B ($11,380)

C $11,610

D $22,370

(2 marks)

Test your understanding 18

A project has a normal pattern of cash flows (i.e. an initial outflow followed by several years of inflows).

Identify what would be the effects of an increase in the company's cost of capital on the internal rate of return (IRR) of the project and its discounted payback period (DPP)?

	IRR	DPP
A	Decrease	Decrease
B	Decrease	Increase
C	No change	Increase
D	No change	Decrease

(2 marks)

Test your understanding 19

Blue Inc produces paint and is considering investing in a new mixing machine. The expected costs and benefits of the new mixing machine are as follows:

- The machine will cost $30,000 to purchase

- Depreciation will be charged at 20% on a straight line basis

- Sales are predicted to increase by 10% on the current predicted sales for the next 5 years. The current predictions are as follows: Year 1 $20,000; Year 2 $22,000; Year 3 $23,000; Year 4 $25,000; Year 5 $28,000

- Staff training costs are currently $1,200 per annum, this will increase to $1,400 in the first year but will then drop to $1,000 in subsequent years

- Operating costs will be reduced from current levels of $15,000 per annum to $10,000 per annum.

The following information is relevant to this decision:

- The payback period will be 4 years and 1 month. The company's policy is for projects to pay back within 5 years.

- The net present value is $5,774 negative.

- The internal rate of return is 7%. The company's cost of capital is 16%.

Required

Calculate and state the relevant value of the cash flow for each of the following. A zero should be used to indicate no relevant value. Use brackets to indicate an outflow of cash.

	Year 0	Year 1	Year 2	Year 3	Year 4	Year 5	
Purchase cost							0.5 marks
Depreciation							0.5 marks
Sales revenue							2 marks
Training costs							2 marks
Operating cost							1 mark

Complete the phrases below, deleting words/phases where appropriate (marked with *)

The payback period of 4 years and 1 month is *within/outside** the company's policy of 5 years, and on this criterion the investment *should go/should not go** ahead.

1 mark

The NPV is *positive/negative** and on this criterion the investment *should go /should not go** ahead.

1 mark

The IRR, at 7%, is *above/below** the company's 16% cost of capital and on this criterion the investment *should go/should not go** ahead.

1 mark

Overall the investment *should/should not** proceed because the *Payback/NPV/IRR** is the dominant criterion.

1 mark

Total 10 marks

13 Chapter summary

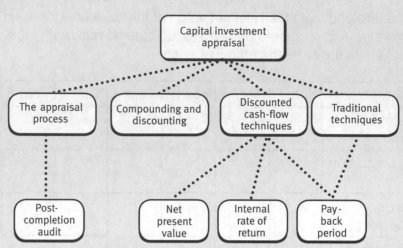

Test your understanding answers

Test your understanding 1

Of the costs mentioned, only the $15,000 salary is relevant as it is incurred as a direct result of making the decision to manufacture the new widgets. The fixed overheads are not incremental to the decision and should be ignored.

Other costs that would be relevant include any direct material, direct labour and direct expenses incurred as a result of the production of the new widgets. Also any variable production overheads.

Test your understanding 2

$V = 450(1.0625)^{12} = \$931.45$

Test your understanding 3

$$x = \frac{5,000}{1.05^{10}} = \$3,070$$

Test your understanding 4

It might seem that the better investment is the deposit account offering 10.25% per year, but this is not the case.

When interest is quoted at 10% per year, payable quarterly, this means the effective annual interest rate is:

$r = (1+0.1/4)^{4} - 1$

$r = 10.38\%$ per year

This is a higher rate.

Test your understanding 5

$x = 250 \times 0.404 = \$101$

Test your understanding 6

PV = 25,000 × 0.564 = $14,100

Test your understanding 7

$$\text{Payback Period} \quad = \quad \frac{\$2m}{\$\,500,000}$$

Payback Period = 4 years

Test your understanding 8

$$\text{Payback} = \quad \frac{\$1,800,000}{£350,000} \quad = 5.1429 \text{ years}$$

0.1429 of a year × 12 months = 1.7 months (rounded = 2 months)

The answer can therefore be stated as either:

• 5.1 years

• 5 years 2 months

assuming cash flows occur evenly throughout the year.

Test your understanding 9

Year	Cash flow	DF at 9%	PV
	$		$
0	(240,000)	1.000	(240,000)
1	80,000	0.917	73,360
2	120,000	0.842	101,040
3	70,000	0.772	54,040
4	40,000	0.708	28,320
5	20,000	0.650	13,000
NPV			+ 29,760

The PV of cash inflows exceeds the PV of cash outflows by $29,760, which means that the project will earn a DCF return in excess of 9%, i.e. it will earn a surplus of $29,760 after paying the cost of financing. It should therefore be undertaken.

Test your understanding 10

$$IRR = 10\% + \frac{50,000}{50,000-(-10,000)} \times (15\%-10\%) = 14.17\%$$

Test your understanding 11

At the IRR, PV of future net cash flows = initial capital outlay.

Answer A

Test your understanding 12

(a)

Year	Cash flow $	Discount factor	Present value $
0	(50,000)		(50,000)
1–7	10,000	4.868	48,680
			(1,320)

(b) $10,000 × annuity factor = $50,000

Annuity factor = 5

Using the tables and a life of seven years, the closest annuity factor to 5 is 5.033. This means the IRR is approximately 9%

Test your understanding 13

NPV = ($50,000) + $5,670 ÷ 0.09 = $13,000

Test your understanding 14

Maximum withdrawal = $100,000 × 0.08 = $8,000 per annum in perpetuity.

Test your understanding 15

Initial investment required = $2,000 ÷ 0.10 = $20,000.

Test your understanding 16

$$\text{IRR} = \frac{\text{Annual inflow}}{\text{Initial investment}} \times 100 = \frac{\$1,600}{\$20,000} \times 100 = 8\%$$

Test your understanding 17

Revenue – components – labour = $80,000 – $18,000 – $20,000 = $42,000

Year	Cash flow $000		Discount factor	Present value $000
0	Initial cost	(100)		(100)
1 – 3	Annual cash	42	2.106	88.452
3	Residual	40	0.579	23.16
				11.612

Net present value = $11,612

Answer C

Test your understanding 18

The IRR will be unaffected by the cost of capital. As the discount rate increases future cash flow reduce in present value terms, therefore the discounted payback period will increase.

Answer C

Test your understanding 19

	Year 0	Year 1	Year 2	Year 3	Year 4	Year 5	
Purchase cost	(30,000)	0	0	0	0	0	0.5 marks
Depreciation	0	0	0	0	0	0	0.5 marks
Sales revenue	0	2,000	2,200	2,300	2,500	2,800	2 marks
Training costs	0	(200)	200	200	200	200	2 marks
Operating cost	0	5,000	5,000	5,000	5,000	5,000	1 mark

Notes

The business is already operating therefore the capital appraisal process will look at the **incremental** costs/revenues that the new machine will produce.

- **Depreciation** is not an actual cash flow so it is not included in the capital appraisal calculation.

- **Sales revenue** should only include the increase (or extra revenue) of 10% on current predictions.

- **Training costs** should only include the extra cost (year 1) or the saving (years 2 to 5) when compared to current predicted costs.

- **Operating costs** are actually classed as an inflow as there is a saving in cost when compared to the current predicted cost.

Completed sentences

The payback period of 4 years and 1 month is **within** the company's policy of 5 years, and on this criterion the investment **should go** ahead.

The NPV is **negative** and on this criterion the investment **should not go** ahead.

The IRR, at 7%, is **below** the company's 16% cost of capital and on this criterion the investment **should not go** ahead.

Overall the investment **should not** proceed because the **NPV** is the dominant criterion.

Standard costing

Chapter learning objectives

Upon completion of this chapter you will be able to:

- explain the purpose and principles of standard costing

- explain and illustrate the difference between standard, marginal and absorption costing

- establish the standard cost per unit under marginal costing and absorption costing

- calculate sales price and volume variances

- calculate materials total, price and usage variances

- calculate labour total, price and efficiency variances

- calculate the variable overhead total, expenditure and efficiency variances

- calculate fixed overhead total, expenditure and, where appropriate, volume, capacity and efficiency variances

- interpret the variances

- explain factors to consider before investigating variances (including the relative significance), explain possible causes of the variances and recommend control action (potential action to eliminate variances)

- explain the interrelationships between the variances

- calculate actual figures or standard figures where the variances are given

- reconcile budgeted profit with actual profit under standard absorption costing

- reconcile budgeted profit or contribution with actual profit or contribution under standard marginal costing.

- prepare control reports suitable for presentation to management.

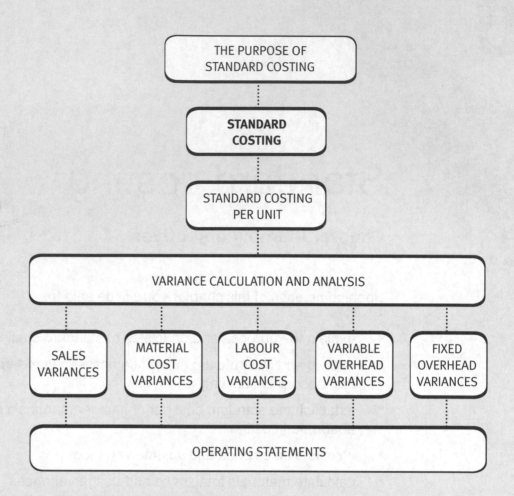

1 The purposes of standard costing

Introduction to standard costing

A **standard cost** is the planned unit cost of a product or service. It is an indication of what a unit of product or service **should** cost.

Standard costs represent 'target' costs and they are therefore useful for planning, control and motivation.

Types of cost standards

There are four main types of cost standards.

- Basic standards.
- Ideal standards.
- Attainable standards.
- Current standards.

Basic standards – these are **long-term standards** which remain unchanged over a period of years. Their sole use is to show trends over time for items such as material prices, labour rates, and labour efficiency. They are also used to show the effect of using different methods over time. Basic standards are the least used and the **least useful** type of standard.

Ideal standards – these standards are based upon **perfect operating conditions**. Perfect operating conditions include: no wastage; no scrap; no breakdowns; no stoppages; no idle time. In their search for perfect quality, Japanese companies use ideal standards for pinpointing areas where close examination may result in large cost savings. Ideal standards may have an **adverse motivational impact** because they are unlikely to be achieved.

Attainable standards – these standards are the **most frequently encountered** type of standard. They are based up**on efficient (but not perfect) operating conditions**. These standards include allowances for the following: normal or expected material losses; fatigue; machine breakdowns. Attainable standards must be based on a high performance level so that with a certain amount of hard work they are achievable (unlike ideal standards).

Current standards – these standards are based on current **levels of efficiency** in terms of allowances for breakdowns, wastage, losses and so on. The main disadvantage of using current standards is that they **do not provide any incentive to improve** on the current level of performance.

2 Standard costs per unit

In order to prepare budgets we need to know what an individual unit of a product or service is expected to cost.

- A standard cost may be based on either a marginal cost basis, including only variable costs, or under absorption costing.

- Standard costs also provide an easier method of accounting since it enables simplified records to be kept.

- Once estimated, standard costs are usually collected on a standard cost card.

Illustration 1 – Standard costs per unit

K Ltd manufactures Product 20K. Information relating to this product is given below.

Budgeted output for the year: 900 units

Standard details for one unit:

Direct materials: 40 square metres at $5.30 per square metre

Direct wages: Bonding department 24 hours at $5.00 per hour

Finishing department 15 hours at $4.80 per hour

Budgeted costs and hours per annum are as follows:

	$	*Hours*
Variable overhead		
Bonding department	45,000	30,000
Finishing department	25,000	25,000
Fixed overhead apportioned to this product:		
Production	$36,000	
Selling, distribution and administration	$27,000	

[handwritten margin note: PRIME]

[handwritten margin note: MARGINAL ABSORPTION]

Note: Variable overheads are recovered (absorbed) using hours, fixed overheads are recovered on a unit basis.

Required:

Prepare a standard cost card in order to establish the standard cost of one unit of Product 20K and enter the following subtotals on the card:

(1) prime cost

(2) marginal cost

(3) total absorption cost

(4) total standard cost.

Solution

Standard cost card – Product 20K	$
Direct materials (40 × $5.30)	212
Direct labour:	
Bonding (24 hours at $5.00)	120
Finishing (15 hours at $4.80)	72
	———
(1) **Prime cost**	404
Variable overhead:	
Bonding ($45,000/30,000 × 24 hours)	36
Finishing ($25,000/25,000 × 15 hours)	15
	———
(2) **Marginal cost**	455
Production overheads ($36,000/900)	40
	———

(3) **Total absorption cost**	495
Non-production overheads ($27,000/900)	30
	——
(4) **Total standard cost**	525
	——

Test your understanding 1

The following statement shows budgeted and actual costs for the month of October for Department X.

Month ended 31 October	Original budget	Actual result
	$	$
Sales	600,000	550,000
	———	———
Direct materials	150,000	130,000
Direct labour	200,000	189,000
Production overhead		
Variable with direct labour	50,000	46,000
Fixed	25,000	29,000
	———	———
Total costs	425,000	394,000
Profit	175,000	156,000
	———	———
Direct labour hours	50,000	47,500
Sales and production units	5,000	4,500

Note: There is no opening and closing inventory.

(a) Calculate the standard cost per unit under absorption costing.

(b) Calculate standard cost per unit under marginal costing.

3 Variance analysis

Basic variance analysis has been seen in the Budgeting chapter when comparing the flexed budget with the actual results.

The following variance analysis produces more detailed results as to the causes of the differences between what the costs and revenues should have been and what they actually were.

As well as being the basis for preparing budgets, standard costs are also used for calculating and analysing variances.

The variances that will be looked at are:

- Sales variances
- Raw material variances
- Labour variances
- Variable overhead variances
- Fixed overhead variances

4 Sales variances

Introduction

There are two causes of sales variances

- a difference in selling price
- a difference in sales volume

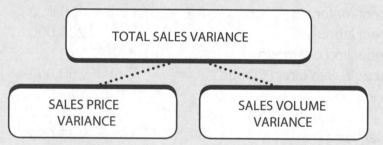

Sales volume variance

The sales volume variance calculates the effect on profit of the actual sales volume being different from that budgeted. The effect on profit will differ depending upon whether a marginal or absorption costing system is being used.

- Under absorption costing any difference in units is valued at the standard profit per unit.
- Under marginal costing any difference in units is valued at the standard contribution per unit.

Sales volume variance

(Actual Quantity Sold – Budget Quantity sold) × **Standard Margin**

The **Standard Margin** equals the Standard contribution per unit (marginal costing), or the standard profit per unit (absorption costing).

If the actual quantity sold is greater that the budget this will produce a favourable variance as it increases profit.

Sales price variance

The sales price variance shows the effect on profit of selling at a different price from that expected.

Sales price variance

(Actual Price – Budget Price) × Actual Quantity sold

If the actual price is greater that the budget this will produce a favourable variance as it increases profit.

Illustration 2 – Sales variances

The following data relates to 20X8.

Actual sales:	1,000 units @ $650 each
Budgeted output and sales for the year:	900 units
Standard selling price:	$700 per unit
Budgeted contribution per unit:	$245
Budgeted profit per unit:	$205

Required:

Calculate the sales volume variance (under absorption and marginal costing) and the sales price variance.

Solution

Sales volume variance – absorption costing

(1,000 units – 900 units) × $205 = $20,500 Fav

Sales volume variance – marginal costing

(1,000 units – 900 units) × $245 = $24,500 Fav

Sales price variance

($650 – $700) × 1,000 = $50,000 Adv

Test your understanding 2

Radek Ltd has budgeted sales of 400 units at $2.50 each. The variable costs are expected to be $1.80 per unit, and there are no fixed costs.

The actual sales were 500 units at $2 each and costs were as expected.

Calculate the sales price and sales volume variances (using marginal costing).

Test your understanding 3

W Ltd budgeted sales of 6,500 units but actually sold only 6,000 units. Its standard cost card is as follows:

	$
Direct materials	25
Direct wages	8
Variable overhead	4
Fixed overhead	18
	___
Total standard cost	55
Standard gross profit	5
	___
Standard selling price	60
	___

The actual selling price for the period was $61.

Calculate the sales price and sales volume variances for the period (using absorption costing).

Possible causes of sales variances

Causes of sales variances include the following:

- unplanned price increases (sales price variance)

- unplanned price reduction, for example, when trying to attract additional business (sales price variance)

- unexpected fall in demand due to recession (sales volume variance)

- additional demand attracted by reduced price (sales volume variance)

- failure to satisfy demand due to production difficulties (sales volume variance).

5 Materials cost variances

Introduction

There are two causes of material cost variances

- a difference in purchase price
- a difference in quantity used

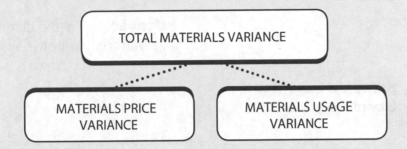

Materials total variance

The materials total variance is the difference between:

(a) the actual cost of direct material and

(b) the standard material cost of the actual production (flexed budget).

- It can be analysed into two sub-variances: a materials price variance and a materials usage variance.
    - A materials price variance analyses whether the company paid more or less than expected for materials.
    - The purpose of the materials usage variance is to quantify the effect on profit of using a different quantity of raw material from that expected for the actual production achieved.

Material variances

Material Price Variance = (Actual quantity bought × Actual Price) – (Actual quantity bought × Standard Price)

Material Usage Variance = (Actual quantity used × Standard Price) – (Standard quantity used for actual production × Standard Price)

OR

(1) **Actual quantity × Actual price**

| | **Price variance** | (the difference between row 1 and row 2) |

(2) **Actual quantity × Standard price**

| | **Usage variance** | (the difference between row 2 and row 3) |

(3) **Standard quantity* × Standard price**

| | **Total variance** | (the total of the price and the usage variances) |

* the standard quantity is the amount of material that should have been used to produce the actual output

Illustration 3 – Material cost variances

The following information relates to the production of Product X.

Extract from the standard cost card of Product X

Direct materials (40 square metres × $5.30 per square metre) $212

Actual results for direct materials in the period: 1,000 units were produced and 39,000 square metres of material costing $210,600 in total were used.

Required:

Calculate the materials total, price and usage variances for Product X in the period.

Solution

Actual quantity × Actual price		$210,600
	Price variance	**$3,900 (A)**
Actual quantity × Standard price 39,000 × $5.30		$206,700
	Usage variance	**$5,300 (F)**
Standard quantity x Standard price 1,000 × 40 × $5.30		$212,000
	Total variance	**$1,400 (F)**

Test your understanding 4

James Marshall Ltd makes a single product with the following budgeted material costs per unit:

2 kg of material A at $10/kg

Actual details:

Output 1,000 units

Material purchased and used 2,200 kg

Material cost $20,900

Calculate materials price and usage variances.

Possible causes of materials variances

Materials price variances may be caused by:

- supplies from different sources
- unexpected general price increases
- changes in quantity discounts
- substitution of one grade of material for another
- materials price standards are usually set at a mid-year price so one would expect a favourable price variance early in a period and an adverse variance later on in a budget period.

Materials usage variances may be caused by:

- a higher or lower incidence of scrap

- an alteration to product design

- substitution of one grade of material for another. A lower grade of material may be more difficult to work with, so there may be a higher wastage rate and, in turn, an adverse usage variance may arise.

6 Labour cost variances

Introduction

There are two causes of labour cost variances

- a difference in rate paid

- a difference in hours worked

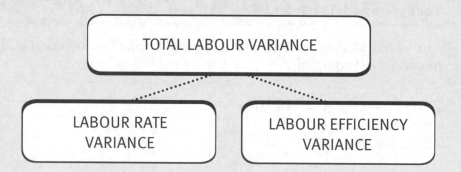

Labour total variance

The labour total variance is the difference between:

(a) the actual cost of direct labour and

(b) the standard direct labour cost of the actual production (flexed budget).

- A labour rate variance analyses whether the company paid more or less than expected for labour.

- A labour efficiency variance analyses whether the company used more or less labour than expected.

(1) Actual hours × Actual rate

	Rate variance	(the difference between row 1 and row 2)

(2) Actual hours × Standard rate

	Efficiency variance	(the difference between row 2 and row 3)

(3) Standard hours* × Standard rate

	Total variance	(the total of the rate and the efficiency variances)

* the standard hours are the number of hours that should have been worked to produce the actual output

Illustration 4 – Labour cost variances

The following information relates to the production of Product X.

Extract from the standard cost card of Product X

	$
Direct labour:	
Bonding (24 hrs @ $5 per hour)	120

Actual results for wages:

Production   1,000 units produced

Bonding   23,900 hours costing $131,450 in total

Required:

Calculate the labour total, rate and efficiency variances in the Bonding department for Product X in the period.

Solution

Labour variances in Bonding department

Actual hours × actual rate		$131,450
	Rate variance	$11,950 (A)
Actual hours × standard rate		
23,900 × $5.00		$119,500
	Efficiency variance	$500 (F)
Standard hours x standard rate		
1,000 × 24 hours × $5.00		$120,000

The labour total variance in the Bonding department is the sum of the rate and efficiency variances, i.e.

$11,950 (A) + $500 (F) = $11,450 (A)

Test your understanding 5

Roseberry Ltd makes a single product and has the following budgeted information:

Budgeted production	1,000 units
Budgeted labour hours	3,000 hours
Budgeted labour cost	$15,000

Actual results:

Output	1,100 units
Hours paid for	3,400 hours
Labour cost	$17,680

Possible causes of labour variances

Labour price variances may be caused by:

- an unexpected national wage award
- overtime or bonus payments which are different from planned/budgeted
- substitution of one grade of labour for another higher or lower grade.

Labour efficiency variances may be caused by:

- changes in working conditions or working methods, for example, better supervision
- consequences of the learning effect
- introduction of incentive schemes or staff training
- substitution of one grade of labour for another higher or lower grade.

7 Variable overhead variances

Introduction

Variable overhead variances are very similar to those for materials and labour because, like these direct costs, the variable overhead cost also changes when activity levels change.

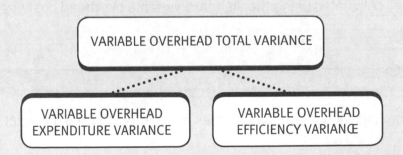

Variable overhead total variance

It is normally assumed that variable overheads vary with direct labour hours of input and the variable overhead total variance will therefore be due to one of the following:

- the variable overhead cost per hour was different to that expected (an expenditure variance)
- working more or fewer hours than expected for the actual production (an efficiency variance)

(1) **Actual hours × Actual rate**

| | **Expenditure variance** | (the difference between row 1 and row 2) |

(2) **Actual hours × Standard rate**

| | **Efficiency variance** | (the difference between row 2 and row 3) |

(3) **Standard hours* × Standard rate**

| | **Total variance** | (the total of the rate and the efficiency variances) |

* the standard hours are the number of hours that should have been worked to produce the actual output

Variable overhead variances

- if variable overhead cost changes, not as a result of a change in direct labour hours, but as a result of a change in the production volume it is not possible to calculate the sub-variances: expenditure and efficiency

- in such situations, only the variable overhead total variance can be calculated using the standard variable overhead cost per unit.

Illustration 5 – Variable overhead variances

The following information relates to the production of Product X.

Extract from the standard cost card of Product X

	$
Direct labour:	
Bonding (24 hrs @ $5 per hour)	120
Variable overhead:	
Bonding (24 hrs @ $1.50 per hour)	36

Actual results for production and labour hours worked:

Production	1,000 units produced
Bonding	23,900 hours

Actual results for variable overheads:

Bonding Total cost $38,240

Required:

Calculate the variable overhead total, expenditure and efficiency variances in the Bonding department for Product X for the period

Solution

Variable overhead variances in Bonding department

Actual hours × Actual rate		$38,240
	Expenditure variance	**$2,390 (A)**
Actual hours × Standard rate		
23,900 hours × $1.50		$35,850
	Efficiency variance	**$150 (F)**
Standard hours × Standard rate		
1000 × 24 hours × $1.50		$36,000
	Total variance	**$2,240 (A)**

Test your understanding 6

The budgeted output for Carr Ltd for May was 1,000 units of product A. Each unit requires two direct labour hours. Variable overheads are budgeted at $3/labour hour.

Actual results:

Output	900 units
Labour hours worked	1,980 hours
Variable overheads	$5,544

Calculate variable overhead total, expenditure and efficiency variances.

Possible causes of variable overhead variances

Variable overhead expenditure variances may be caused by:

- incorrect budgets being set at the beginning of a period.

- overheads consisting of a number of items, such as: indirect materials, indirect labour, maintenance costs, power, etc. Consequently, any meaningful interpretation of the expenditure variance must focus on individual cost items.

Variable overhead efficiency variances may be caused by:

- changes in working methods and condition, for example, better supervision

- consequences of the learning effect

- introduction of incentive schemes or staff training

- substitution of one grade of labour for another higher or lower grade.

Note that the possible causes of variable overhead efficiency variances are the same as those for the labour efficiency variance.

8 Fixed overhead variances

Introduction

Fixed overhead variances show the effect on profit of differences between actual and expected fixed overheads.

- By definition, actual and expected fixed overheads do not change when there is a change in the level of activity, consequently many of the variances calculated are based upon budgets.

- However, the effect on profit depends upon whether a marginal or absorption costing system is being used.

Fixed overhead variances in a marginal costing system

Marginal costing does not relate fixed overheads to cost units. There is no under- or over-absorption and the fixed overhead incurred is the amount shown in the income statement (as a period cost).

- Since fixed overhead costs are fixed, they are not expected to change when there is a change in the level of activity.

- There is only one Fixed overhead variances in a marginal costing system

Fixed overhead expenditure variance (marginal costing principles)

	$
Actual Expenditure	x
Less: Budget Expenditure	(x)
	___
Fixed overhead expenditure variance	x
	___

Fixed overhead variances in an absorption costing system

- In absorption costing, fixed overheads are related to cost units by using absorption rates. This means that the calculation for fixed overhead variances in an absorption costing system can relate to both a change in expenditure and a change in production levels or volume.

The fixed overhead variances in an absorption costing system are as follows:

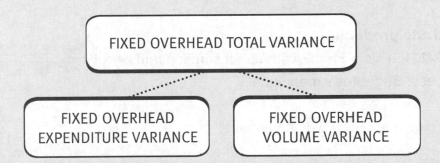

Fixed overhead total variance

In an absorption costing system, the fixed overhead total variance measures the effect on profit of there being a difference between the actual cost incurred and the amount absorbed by the use of the absorption rate based on budgeted costs and activity. This means that the fixed overhead total variance is equivalent to the under- or over-absorption of overhead in a period.

Under absorption costing, this variance can be further subdivided into an expenditure and volume variance.

Fixed overhead expenditure variance

The fixed overhead expenditure variance shows the effect on profit of the actual fixed overhead expenditure differing from the budgeted value. It is calculated in exactly the same way for both marginal and absorption costing.

	$
Actual Expenditure	X
Less: Budget Expenditure	(X)
	―
Fixed overhead expenditure variance	X
	―

Fixed overhead volume variance

The fixed overhead volume variance is the difference between the budgeted overhead expenditure and the amount of overhead that was absorbed by actual production.

The calculation for this differs depending on whether the OAR at the start of the period was based on **units** produced or **hours** worked to produce the units.

Units produced

	$
Actual units × Fixed overhead absorption rate per unit	X
Less: Budgeted expenditure	(X)
	―
Fixed overhead volume variance	X

OR:

Hours worked

	$
Standard hours for actual production × FOAR per standard hour	X
Less: Budgeted expenditure	(X)
	―
Fixed overhead volume variance	X

Illustration 6 – Fixed overhead variances

The following information is available for a company for Period 4.

Budget

Output	$22,960
Unit	6,560

Actual

Fixed production overheads	$24,200
Unit	6,460

Required:

Calculate the following:

(a) fixed overhead absorption rate per unit *3.5*

(b) fixed overhead expenditure variance for marginal costing *N/A B 50) 24200 - 22960 =*

(c) fixed overhead expenditure variance for absorption costing *(350)* *1 240 A.*

"

(d) fixed overhead volume variance for marginal costing *N/A*

(e) fixed overhead volume variance for absorption costing

(f) fixed overhead total variance for marginal costing

(g) fixed overhead total variance for absorption costing.

Solution

(a) FOAR = $22,960/6,560 = $3.50 per unit

(b) Fixed overhead expenditure variance for marginal costing.

Actual expenditure	$24,200
Less Budgeted expenditure	$22,960
Fixed overhead expenditure variance	$1,240 (A)

(c) The fixed overhead expenditure variance for absorption costing is calculated in exactly the same way as that for marginal costing.

(d) There is no fixed overhead volume variance for marginal costing. This is because under marginal costing, fixed overheads are not expected to change when there is a change in volume of activity.

(e) Fixed overhead volume variance for absorption costing

Actual units × FOAR per unit*	$22,610
Less Budgeted expenditure	$22,960
Fixed overhead volume variance	$350 (A)

* (6,460 × $3.50 = $22,610)

The variance is adverse because fewer units were produced than expected.

(f) The fixed overhead total variance for marginal costing is the same as the expenditure variance for marginal costing, i.e. $1,240 (A).

(g) The fixed overhead total variance for absorption costing is the total of the expenditure and volume variances for absorption costing, i.e. $1,240 (A) + $350 (A) = $1,590 (A).

Fixed overhead capacity and efficiency variances

In absorption costing systems, if the fixed overhead is absorbed based on **hours**, then the fixed overhead volume variance can be subdivided into capacity and efficiency variances.

- The capacity variance measures whether the workforce worked more or fewer hours than **budgeted** for the period:

	$
Actual hours × FOAR per hour	X
Less Budgeted expenditure	(X)
Fixed overhead capacity variance	X

The efficiency variance measures whether the workforce took more or less time than **standard** in producing their output for the period:

	$
Standard hours for actual production × FOAR per hour	X
Less Actual hours × FOAR per hour	(X)
Fixed overhead efficiency variance	X

Together, these two sub-variances explain why the level of activity was different from that budgeted, i.e. they combine to give the fixed overhead volume variance.

Illustration 7 – Fixed overhead variances

The following information is available for a company for Period 4.

Fixed production overheads	$22,960
Units	6,560

The standard time to produce each unit is 2 hours

Actual

Fixed production overheads	$24,200
Units	6,460
Labour hours	12,600 hrs

Required:

Calculate the following:

(a) fixed overhead absorption rate per hour *3.5*

(b) fixed overhead capacity variance *–350*

(c) fixed overhead efficiency variance *–350*

(d) fixed overhead volume variance.

Solution

(a) FOAR = $22,960/(6,560 units × 2 hours) $1.75 per hour

(b)	Actual hours × FOAR	
	12,600 × $1.75	$22,050
	Less Budgeted expenditure	($22,960)
		———
	Capacity variance	$910 (A)

(c)	Standard hours × FOAR	
	6,460 × 2 × $1.75	$22,610
	Less Actual hours x FOAR	
	12,600 × $1.75	($22,050)
		———
	Efficiency variance	$560 (F)

(d) The fixed overhead volume variance is the sum of the capacity and efficiency variances, i.e.

$910 (A) + $560 (F) = 350 (A).

This can be proved as follows:

Standard hours × FOAR per hour (6,460 × 2 hours × $1.75)	$22,610
Less: Budgeted expenditure	($22,960)
Total variance	$350(A)

Test your understanding 7

Last month, 40,000 production hours were budgeted in CTD, and the budgeted fixed production overhead cost was $ 250,000. Actual results show that 38,000 hours were worked and paid, and the standard hours for actual production were 35,000. CTD operates a standard absorption costing system.

What was the fixed production overhead capacity variance for last month?

A $12,500 Adverse

B $12,500 Favourable ✓

C $31,250 Adverse

D $31,250 Favourable

The fixed overhead **total** variance in an absorption costing system is the same as any **under/over-absorption** of overhead.

Illustration 8 – Under/over absorption

Gatting Ltd produces a single product. Fixed overheads are budgeted at $12,000 and budgeted output is 1,000 units.

Actual results:

Output	1,100 units
Overheads incurred	$13,000

Calculate the following:

(a) fixed overhead expenditure variance   1000 (A)

(b) fixed overhead volume variance

(c) fixed overhead total variance.

(d) under/over-absorption   200

Cup
Eff Var   1200 A
Cup Var

Solution

(a) Fixed overhead expenditure variance

Actual expenditure	$13,000
Less Budgeted expenditure	$12,000
Expenditure variance	$1,000 (A)

(b) Fixed overhead volume variance

Actual units × FOAR (1,100 × $12)	$13,200
Less Budgeted expenditure	$12,000
Expenditure variance	$1,200 (F)

(c) Fixed overhead total variance

Fixed overhead expenditure variance	$1,000 (A)
Fixed overhead volume variance	$1,200 (F)
Total variance	$200 (F)

(d) FOAR per unit = $12,000/1,000 = $12 per unit

Overhead absorbed = 1,100 × $12	$13,200
Overheads incurred	$13,000
Over-absorption	$200

Possible causes of fixed overhead variances

Fixed overhead expenditure variances may be caused by:

- changes in prices relating to fixed overhead expenditure, for example, increase in factory rent

- seasonal differences, e.g. heat and light costs in winter. When the annual budget is divided into four equal quarters, no allowances are given for seasonal factors and the fact that heat and light costs in winter are generally much higher than in the summer months. (Of course, over the year, the seasonal effect is cancelled out.)

Fixed overhead volume variances may be caused by:

- changes in the production volume due to changes in demand or alterations to stockholding policies

- changes in the productivity of labour or machinery

- lost production through strikes.

9 Possible interrelationships between variances

The cause of a particular variance may affect another variance in a corresponding or opposite way. This is known as interrelationships between variances. Here are some examples:

- if supplies of a specified material are not available, this may lead to a favourable price variance (use of cheaper material), an adverse usage variance (more wastage caused by cheaper material), an adverse fixed overhead volume variance (production delayed while material was unavailable) and an adverse sales volume variance (inability to meet demand due to production difficulties)

- a new improved machine becomes available which causes an adverse fixed overhead expenditure variance (because this machine is more expensive and depreciation is higher) offset by favourable wages efficiency and fixed overhead volume variances (higher productivity)

- workers trying to improve productivity (favourable labour efficiency variance) might become careless and waste more material (adverse materials usage variance)

- in each of these cases, if one variance has given rise to the other, there is an argument in favour of combining the two variances and ascribing them to the common cause. In view of these possible interrelationships, care has to be taken when implementing a bonus scheme. If the chief buyer is rewarded for producing a favourable price variance, this may cause trouble later as shoddy materials give rise to adverse usage variances.

10 Operating statements

Variances are often summarised in an operating statement. The statement allows for budgeted values to be reconciled with actual values.

If the statement starts with budgeted profit (absorption costing) or budgeted contribution (marginal costing) then:

- Add the favourable variances as these increase profit
- Subtract the adverse variance as these decrease profit

The main differences between absorption and marginal costing operating statements are as follows:

- The marginal costing operating statement has a sales volume variance that is calculated using the standard contribution per unit rather than a standard profit per unit as in absorption costing.
- There is no fixed overhead volume variance in the marginal costing operating statement.

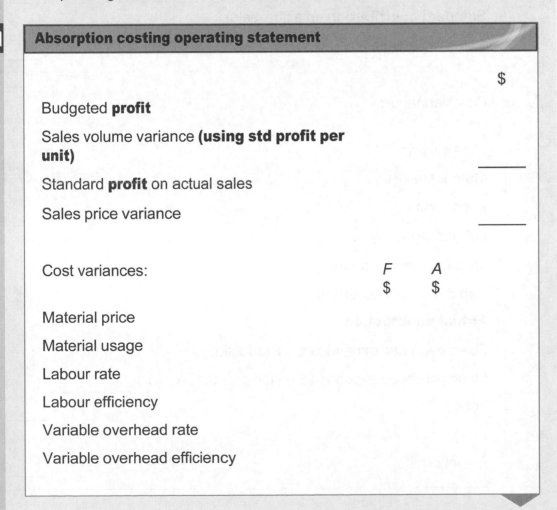

Absorption costing operating statement

		$
Budgeted **profit**		
Sales volume variance **(using std profit per unit)**		____
Standard **profit** on actual sales		
Sales price variance		____
Cost variances:	F $	A $
Material price		
Material usage		
Labour rate		
Labour efficiency		
Variable overhead rate		
Variable overhead efficiency		

Fixed overhead volume – **Production**

Fixed overhead expenditure – Production

Fixed overhead expenditure – Non-production

Total

Actual profit

(Note the bold highlight the differences from the marginal costing version.)

Marginal costing operating statement

$

Budgeted **contribution**

Sales volume variance **(using std contribution per unit)**

Standard **contribution** on actual sales

Sales price variance

	F	A
Cost variances:	$	$
Material price		
Material usage		
Labour rate		
Labour efficiency		
Variable overhead rate		
Variable overhead efficiency		

Actual contribution

Fixed overhead expenditure – Production

Fixed overhead expenditure – Non-production

Total

Actual profit

Illustration 9 – Reconciliation of budget to actual

Below is a statement of variances for A Ltd:

Sales price variance	$2,100 (F)
Sales volume variance	$1,800 (F)
Materials price variance	$6,000 (A)
Materials usage Variance	$2,000 (A)
Labour rate variance	$1,000 (A)
Labour efficiency Variance	$1,500 (F)
Fixed overhead expenditure variance	$2,800 (A)
Fixed overhead volume variance	$2,100 (A)

The budgeted profit for the period was $300,000

Requirement

Calculate the actual profit.

Solution

Budgeted profit	**$300,000**
Sales price variance	+$2,100 (F)
Sales volume variance	+$1,800 (F)
Materials price variance	–$6,000 (A)
Materials usage Variance	–$2,000 (A)
Labour rate variance	–$1,000 (A)
Labour efficiency Variance	+$1,500 (F)
Fixed overhead expenditure variance	–$2,800 (A)
Fixed overhead volume variance	–$2,100 (A)
Actual profit	**$291,500**

Test your understanding 8

Chapel Ltd manufactures a chemical protective called Rustnot. The following standard costs apply for the production of 100 cylinders:

		$
Materials	500 kg @ $0.80 per kg	400
Labour	20 hours @ $1.50 per hour	30
Fixed overheads	20 hours @ $1.00 per hour	20
		450

Chapel Ltd uses absorption costing.

The monthly production/sales budget is 10,000 cylinders sold at $6 per cylinder.

For the month of November the following actual production and sales information is available:

Produced/sold		10,600 cylinders
Sales value		$63,000
Material purchased and used	53,200 kg	$42,500
Labour	2,040 hours	$3,100
Fixed overheads		$2,200

(a) Calculate the following variances were calculated for November:

Sales volume variance		1 mark
Sales price variance		1 mark
Materials price variance		0.5 marks
Materials usage variance		0.5 marks
Labour rate variance		0.5 marks
Labour efficiency variance		0.5 marks
Fixed overhead expenditure variance		1 mark
Fixed overhead volume variance		1 mark

6 marks

(b) Prepare the operating statement for November using the variances you have calculated.

	$
Budgeted profit	
Sales volume variance	
Sales price variance	
	————

Cost variances:	F	A
	$	$
Material price		
Material usage		
Labour rate		
Labour efficiency		
FIxed overhead expenditure		
Fixed overhead volume	————	———— ————
Total		
Actual profit		

4 marks

11 Working backwards

One way that the examiner can easily test your understanding of variances is to ask you to calculate the following instead of straightforward variance calculations:

- actual figures from variances and standards
- standards from variances and actual figures.

Illustration 10 – Working backwards (materials)

ABC Ltd uses standard costing. It purchases a small component for which the following data are available:

Actual purchase quantity	6,800 units
Standard allowance for actual production	5,440 units
Standard price	$0.85/unit
Material price variance (Adverse)	($544)

Required:

Calculate the actual price per unit of material.

Solution

		$
Actual quantity × Actual price = 6,800 × AP =		?
Actual quantity × Standard price = 6,800 × $0.85 =		5,780
		___
Material price variance (given) =		544 (A)

Because the material price variance is adverse, this means that the actual cost of the materials was $544 more than standard, i.e.

Actual quantity (6,800) × Actual price = $(5,780 + 544) = $6,324

$$\text{Actual price per unit} = \frac{\$6,324}{\text{Actual quantity}} = \frac{\$6,324}{\$6,800} = \$0.93$$

Illustration 11 – Working backwards (fixed overheads)

A business has budgeted to produce and sell 10,000 units of its single product. The standard cost per unit is as follows:

Direct materials	$15
Direct labour	$12
Variable overhead	$10
Fixed production overhead	$8

During the period the following variances occurred:

fixed overhead expenditure variance	$4,000 adverse
fixed overhead volume variance	$12,000 favourable

Calculate the following.

(a) Actual fixed overheads in the period.

(b) Actual production volume in the period.

Solution

(a) The actual fixed overheads are calculated as follows.

Actual fixed overheads	?
Budgeted fixed overheads ($8 × 10,000)	$80,000
Fixed overhead expenditure variance	$4,000 (A)

Because the fixed overhead expenditure variance is adverse, this means that the actual fixed overheads were $4,000 more than budgeted.

Actual fixed overheads	= Budgeted fixed overheads	+ Fixed overhead expenditure variance
	= $80,000 + $4,000	= $84,000

(b) The actual production volume is calculated as follows.

$$\text{The fixed overhead volume variance (in units)} = \frac{\text{Fixed overhead volume variance in \$}}{\text{Standard fixed overhead rate per unit}}$$

$$= \frac{\$12,000}{\$8} = 1,500 \text{ units (F)}$$

Because the variance is favourable, this means that 1,500 more units were produced than budgeted, i.e. 10,000 + 1,500 = 11,500 units.

This can also be proved as follows

Actual units × standard fixed overhead rate per unit ? × $8	?
Budgeted expenditure	$80,000
Fixed overhead volume variance	$12,000 (F)

Actual units × standard fixed overhead rate per unit = $80,000 + $12,000 = $92,000

$$\text{Actual units} = \frac{\$92,000}{\$8} = 11,500 \text{ units}$$

Test your understanding 9

In a period, 11,280 kilograms of material were used at a total standard cost of $46,248. The material usage variance was $492 adverse.

Required:

Calculate the standard allowed weight of material for the period.

Test your understanding 10

In a period 6,500 units were made and there was an adverse labour efficiency variance of $26,000. Workers were paid $8 per hour, total wages were $182,000 and there was a nil rate variance.

Calculate how many standard labour hours there were per unit.

Test your understanding 11

A company uses standard marginal costing. Last month the standard contribution on actual sales was $44,000 and the following variances arose:

Total Variable costs variance	$6,500 Adverse
Sales Price variance	$2,000 Favourable
Sales Volume Contribution variance	$4,500 Adverse

What was the actual contribution for last month?

A $33,000

B $35,000

C $37,500

D $39,500

Test your understanding 12

Brake Ltd manufactures and distributes brake discs to the automotive sector. The company operates an integrated standard cost system in which:

- Purchases of materials are recorded at standard cost

- Direct material costs and direct labour costs are variable

- Production overheads are fixed and absorbed using direct labour hours.

Actual and budgeted data for May are shown below:

- Budgeted direct materials per unit – 2kg at $5 per kg

- Direct labour – 0.5hours per unit

- Budgeted production for the month was 10,000 units

- 22,500 Kgs of material were purchased

- The total standard cost of the materials was $115,000

- 6,000 direct labour hours were worked at a cost of $6 per hour.

- Budgeted Fixed production overheads in the period were $240,000

- Actual fixed production overheads in the period were $260,000

Variances calculated for May are as follows:

- Material price variance $11,250A

- Labour efficiency variance $1,750A

Required

(1) Calculate the actual number of brake discs manufactured

(2) Calculate the actual price paid per kg of material

(3) Calculate the material usage variance

(4) Calculate the standard rate per labour hour

(5) Calculate the labour rate variance

(6) Calculate the fixed overhead expenditure variance

(7) Calculate the overhead absorption rate

(8) Calculate the fixed overhead capacity variance

(9) Calculate the fixed overhead efficiency variance

(10) Calculate the fixed overhead volume variance

10 Marks

12 Reporting of variances

In reporting variances, the concept of responsibility accounting should be followed so a variance report to an individual manager should only include figures relating to his own area of responsibility i.e. within his area of control. If more figures are given, then they are usually reported in the form of 'for information only' as a help to a manager in seeing the total picture or context in which his figures arise.

Several questions may be asked before deciding whether or not to investigate a variance. These include:

- Is the variance controllable?

- Is the expected benefit from control action likely to exceed the expected cost?

- Is there a reasonable probability of successfully being able to correct a variance?

- Is the variance material (significant)?

- Is the variance steadily getting worse?

Cost versus benefit

For some variances, especially small variances, the cost of investigating its causes might be more than the likely benefit from any control measures. In such circumstances, investigation of the variance is not worthwhile.

However, not all significant controllable variances will necessarily lead to control action. Managers should also consider:

- what it would cost to implement control action

- what would be the benefits from taking control action.

Control action is only worthwhile if the expected benefits from the control measures exceed the cost of implementing them.

The benefits from control action are not the same as the amount of the variance.

Illustration 12

A variance report indicates that there have been adverse material variances of $5,000 last month. Investigation has shown that the problem is due to a high wastage rate in a particular process. The wastage rate could be reduced, but only if the work force spends more time on the process, and this would add $6,000 a month to labour costs.

The control action is not worthwhile unless monthly savings exceed $6,000. Management should investigate if it is possible to source better quality material to reduce wastage or is an improvement to the process can be made.

Probability of successful correction

Measures to correct a variance might not be successful. The probability of control action having the desired effect should therefore be taken into consideration as well.

e.g

Illustration 13

Investigation of the adverse material variances of $5,000 last month suggests that the variance will continue at this level in the future unless control measures are taken.

Control action would cost an extra $3,500 a month in labour costs. However, there is only a 50% probability that the corrective action would succeed in reducing the variance.

Here, the extra costs will be $3,500 each month, and the expected benefits either $0 or $5,000 (weighted average value = 0.50 × $0 + 0.50 × $5,000 = $2,500.) It is questionable whether the control measures will be worthwhile.

Significance of variances

Variance reports might apply the principle of management by exception. Variances are differences between actual and standard/budget. Some differences are inevitable, but it is only large or potentially significant variances that matter for control purposes. With exception reporting, only large and potentially significant items are reported to management and drawn to their attention. Exception reporting means that managers do not have to read through large amounts of insignificant cost data to find the information that really matters.

The amount of detail included in reports will vary according to the needs of management. As a guide, they should be in sufficient detail to motivate the individual manager to take the most appropriate action in all the circumstances. If a report lacks the required amount of detail, then an individual manager should request this from the management accountant.

13 Control reports

General criteria may be laid down for such reports:

(a) Reports should be **relevant** to the information needs of their recipients. This means that the report should contain all relevant information to the decisions to be made, and responsibilities exercised by the manager who receives the report. Generally, other information should be excluded although there is an argument for including background information on divisional/company performance.

(b) Reporting should be linked to **responsibility**.

(c) Reports should be **timely**. One of the most frequent reporting problems is that reports are received after the decision for which they are required. In such cases managers must often rely on informal information sources outside the budget system. This may be less efficient and also reduces the credibility of the budgetary control system in the eyes of that manager.

(d) Reports should be **reliable**. The reports should be regarded as containing reliable information (though not necessarily exact to the penny). There may be a conflict between reliability and timeliness, and often an assessment must be made of what is an acceptable error rate and/or degree of approximation.

(e) Reports should be designed to **communicate effectively,** often with managers who are not professional accountants. Reports should avoid jargon, be concise, but contain sufficient detail (often in supporting schedules). Maximum use should be made of graphical presentation.

(f) Reports should be **cost-effective**. A report is only worthwhile if the benefits from its existence exceed the cost of producing it.

14 Chapter summary

> **The purposes of standard costing**
>
> - Provide 'targets'
> - Useful for planning, control and decision making
> - Essential for calculating and analysing variances
> - Variances provide 'feedback' to management
> - Easier method of accounting
> - Standards may be on marginal or absorption costing basis

STANDARD COSTING

> **Standard costs per unit**
>
> - Collected on standard cost card
> - Allow variances to be calculated
> - In marginal costing includes variable costs only
> - In absorption costing includes a fixed cost per unit also

> **Variance calculation and analysis**
> You need to know how to calculate and interpret the following variances

| SALES VARIANCES | MATERIAL COST VARIANCES | LABOUR COST VARIANCES | VARIABLE OVERHEAD VARIANCES | FIXED OVERHEAD VARIANCES |

> **Operating statements**
>
> - Variances summarised in operating statement
> - Reconcile budgeted profit (or contribution) with actual profit
> - Marginal costing operating statements do not have fixed overhead volume variances (and therefore capacity and efficiency variances)
> - Marginal costing operating statements calculate a sales volume variance using standard contributions per unit
> - Absorption costing operating statements calculate a sales volume variance using standard profit per unit

Test your understanding answers

Test your understanding 1

(a) **Standard cost per unit under absorption costing**

	$
Direct materials	150,000
Direct labour	200,000
Production overhead	
Variable	50,000
Fixed	25,000
Total production cost	425,000

Budgeted production units = 5,000

Standard cost per unit – absorption costing = $425,000/5,000 units = $85

(b) **Standard cost per unit under marginal costing**

	$
Direct materials	150,000
Direct labour	200,000
Variable overhead costs	50,000
Total variable cost	400,000

Budgeted production units = 5,000

Standard cost per unit – marginal costing = $400,000/5,000 units = $80

Test your understanding 2

Sales price variance	= ($2.00 – $2.50) × 500	= $250 (A)
Sales volume variance	= (500 – 400) × $0.70*	= $70 (F)
Total sales variance		$180 (A)

*Standard contribution per unit = $(2.50 – 1.80) = $0.70

Test your understanding 3

Price variance = ($61 − $60) × 6,000 = $6,000 (F)
Volume variance = (6,000 − 6,500) × $5* = $2,500 (A)

$3,500 (F)

* Standard gross profit per unit

Test your understanding 4

	$	
Actual quantity × Actual price	20,900	
Price variance		$1,100 (F)
Actual quantity × Standard price 2,200 × $10	$22,000	
Usage variance		$2,000 (A)
Standard quantity × Standard price 1,000 × 2 × $10	$20,000	
Total variance		$900 (A)

Test your understanding 5

Labour variances	$	$
Actual hours × Actual rate	17,680	
Price variance		680 (A)
Actual hours × Standard rate 3,400 hours × ($15,000/3,000)	17,000	
Efficiency variance		500 (A)
Standard hours × Standard rate 1,100 × (3,000/1,000) × $5	16,500	
Total variance		1,180 (A)

Test your understanding 6

Actual hours × Actual rate	$5,544

Expenditure variance	**$396 (F)**

Actual hours × Standard rate
1,980 hours × $3 $5,940

Efficiency variance	**$540(A)**

Standard hours × Standard rate
900 × 2 hours × $3 $5,400

Total variance	**$144 (A)**

Test your understanding 7

Answer A

	$
Actual hours × FOAR per hour	
38,000 × $250,000/40,000 hours	$237,500
Budgeted expenditure	$250,000
Capacity variance	$12,500 (A)

Test your understanding 8

(a) Variances

Sales price

$$[(63,000/10,600) - \$6] \times 10,600 = \textbf{\$600 (A)}$$

Sales volume

$$(10,600 - 10,000) \times [\$6 - (450/100)] = \textbf{\$900 (F)}$$

Materials price and usage

Actual quantity × Actual price		$42,500
	Price variance	$60 (F)
Actual quantity × Standard price **53,200 × $0.80**		$42,560
	Usage variance	$160 (A)
Standard quantity × Standard price **10,600 × (500/100) × $0.80**		$42,400

Labour rate and efficiency

Actual hours × Actual rate		$3,100
	Rate variance	$40 (A)
Actual hours × Standard rate **2,040 × $1.50**		$3,060
	Efficiency variance	$120 (F)
Standard hours × Standard rate **10,600 × (20/100) × $1.50**		$3,180

Fixed overhead expenditure

The standard fixed overhead cost is $20 per 100 cylinders. Monthly production is budgeted at 10,000 cylinders. Therefore the budgeted fixed overhead cost is:

10,000 × $20/100 = $2,000.

The actual cost was $2,200.

The extra cost of **$200** is an **adverse** fixed overhead expenditure variance.

Fixed overhead volume

	$
Actual units × FOAR per unit	
10,600 × 20/100	2,120
Budgeted units × FOAR per unit	
10,000 × 20/100	2,000
	———
Volume variance	**120 (F)**

(b) **Chapel Ltd – Operating statement for November**

Budgeted profit (W1)	15,000
Sales volume variance	900F
Sales price variance	600A
	———
	15,300F

Cost variances:

	F	A	
Materials price	60		
Materials usage		160	
Labour rate		40	
Labour efficiency	120		
Fixed overhead expenditure		200	
Fixed overhead volume	120		
	———	———	———
Total	300	400	100A
Actual profit (W2)			15,200

Workings

(W1) Budgeted profit

	$
10,000 cylinders @ $6.00	60,000
Total cost	(45,000)
Profit	15,000

(W2) Actual profit

	$	$
Sales		63,000
Less: Materials	42,500	
Labour	3,100	
Fixed overheads	2,200	
		47,800
		15,200

Test your understanding 9

Standard price = $\dfrac{\$46,248}{11,280}$ = $4.10 per kg

Material usage variance in kg = $\dfrac{\text{Usage variance in \$}}{\text{Standard price per kg}}$ = $\dfrac{\$492 \text{ (A)}}{\$4.10}$ = 120 kg

If the usage variance is adverse, then this means that the actual quantity was greater than the standard quantity, i.e.

Standard allowed = Actual quantity – material usage variance in kg
                  = 11,280 – 120 = 11,160 kg

This can be proved as follows:

	$
Actual quantity × Standard price = (11,280 × $4.10) =	46,248
Standard quantity × Standard price = (11,160 × $4.10) =	45,756
Material usage variance =	492 (A)

Test your understanding 10

	$	$
Actual hours × Actual rate	182,000	
Rate variance		Nil
Actual hours × Standard rate		
= ? × $8 = 4	182,000	
Efficiency variance		26,000 (A)
Standard hours × Standard rate		
= 6,500 × Standard hours × $8 =	156,000	

$$\text{Standard labour hours per unit} = \frac{\$156,000}{6,500 \times 8} = 3$$

Test your understanding 11

D $39,500

Standard Contribution on actual sales	$44,000
Add: Favourable Sales Price variance	$2,000
Less: Adverse total variable costs variance	($6,500)
Actual Contribution	$39,500

Test your understanding 12

Material variances

(1) The actual number of brake discs manufactured was **11,500 units**

(2) The material usage variance was **$2,500F**

(3) The actual price paid per kg of material was **$5.50**

Actual quantity × **Actual price**
22,500kg × **$5.50** $123,750

                                        Price $11,250A

Actual quantity × Standard price
22,500kg × $5 $112,500

                                        Usage $2,500F

Standard quantity × Standard price
2kg × **11,500 units** × $5 $115,000

Labour variances

(4) The standard rate per labour hour was **$7**

(5) The labour rate variance was **$6,000F**

Actual hours × Actual rate
6,000 hours × $6 $36,000

                                        Rate $6,000F

Actual quantity × **Standard price**
6,000 hours × **$7** $42,000

                                        Efficiency $1,750A

Standard quantity × **Standard price**
0.5 hours × 11,500 units × **$7** $40,250

Fixed overhead variances

(6) The fixed overhead expenditure variance was **$20,000A**

Actual fixed overhead – Budgeted fixed overhead

$260,000 – $240,000 = **$20,000A**

(7) The overhead absorption rate was **$48 per labour hour**

$$\frac{\text{Overhead cost}}{\text{Overhead activity}} = \frac{\$240,000}{10,000 \text{ units} \times 0.5 \text{ hours}} = \textbf{\$48 per labour hour}$$

(8) The fixed overhead capacity variance was **$48,000F**

Actual hours × OAR = 6,000 hours × $48	$288,000
Budgeted hours × OAR = 0.5 hours × 10,000 units × $48	$240,000
Capacity variance	**$48,000F**

(9) The fixed overhead efficiency variance was **$12,000A**

Standard hours × OAR = 0.5 hours × 11,500 units × $48	$276,000
Actual hours × OAR = 6,000 hours × $48	$288,000
Efficiency variance	**$12,000A**

(10) The fixed overhead volume variance was **$36,000F**

Capacity variance + Efficiency variance = 48,000F + 12,000A = **$36,000F**

Performance measurement techniques

Chapter learning objectives

Upon completion of this chapter you will be able to:

- discuss the purpose of mission statements and their role in performance measurement

- discuss the purpose of strategic and operational and tactical objectives and their role in performance measurement

- discuss the impact of economic and market conditions on performance measurement

- discuss the impact of government regulation on performance management

- discuss the relationship between short-term and long-term performance

- discuss and establish critical success factors and key performance indicators and their link to objectives and mission statements

- establish critical success factors and key performance indicators in a specific situation

- discuss and calculate measures of financial performance (profitability, liquidity, activity and gearing) and non-financial measures

- discuss the importance of non-financial performance measure

- Perspectives of the balanced scorecard
    - discuss the advantages and limitations of the balanced scorecard
    - describe performance indicators for financial success, customer satisfaction, process efficiency and growth

- discuss the role of benchmarking in performance measurement

- Economy, efficiency and effectiveness
  - discuss the meaning of each of the efficiency, capacity and activity ratios
  - calculate the efficiency, capacity and activity ratios in a specific situation

- Resource utilisation
  - describe measures of performance utilisation in service and manufacturing environments
  - establish measures of resource utilisation in a specific situation

- discuss the measurement of quality of service

- distinguish performance measurement issues in service and manufacturing industries in relation to quality

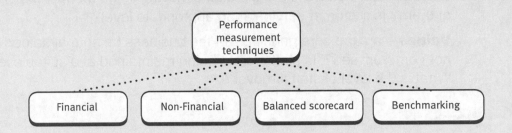

1 Introduction

Performance measurement is the monitoring of budgets or targets against actual results to establish how well the business and it's employees are functioning as a whole and as individuals.

Performance measurements can relate to short-term objectives (e.g. cost control) or longer-term measures (e.g. customer satisfaction).

Objectives and goals of a business will vary depending on the type of business that is being operated. For example:

*   A company's overall goal will be to maximise their shareholders wealth so they will want to monitor profitability (based on increasing sales and reducing costs) and growth or market share compared to competitors.

*   A non-profit organisation, for example a government department, will want to provide the best service possible for the lowest cost so that the residents being cared for achieve value for money from the taxes they pay.

What these businesses have in common is that they will have long term (strategic) goals or objectives. These long term goals will be broken down into tactical and operational targets which will need to be monitored. To be able to do this they will identify critical success factors and key performance indicators to monitor to ensure targets are met.

The mission statement

A mission statement, as discussed in chapter 1, should describe the overall long term purpose of the organisation.

The different elements of the mission statement can be used as a guide for producing performance measures for the business.

*   **Purpose** – is the business meeting it's main aims? Maximisation of shareholder wealth? Maintaining customer satisfaction? Producing innovative products/services?

*   **Strategy** – is the business providing the products and services it planned to? Is the product or service being provided in the manner it intended?

- **Policies and culture** – are the staff behaving in the manner expected of them? Is customer service at an appropriate level?

- **Values** – are the core principles of the business being maintained and not compromised? Is staff morale being maintained at a suitable level? What is the level of staff turnover?

Planning

As seen in chapter 1 there are three different planning levels:

- **Strategic** or corporate planning – planning for the longer term and for the whole business

- **Tactical** – breaking the strategic plan into manageable chunks for each business unit or department

- **Operational** – turning the strategic and tactical plans into the day to day running of the business.

The planning level will influence the performance measures that are used to monitor achievement of the overall goals of the business.

- **Strategic** – measurement of the overall profitability of the business and/or the return made on investing surplus cash

- **Tactical** – comparison of the actual costs and revenues with the budgeted costs and revenues for each business unit or department

- **Operational** – measurement of day to day targets such as meeting production requirements, meeting sales targets and reducing wastage.

As you can see there are short term objectives (operational) and long term (tactical and strategic) goals and objectives.

The short term objectives will enable the businesses to monitor progression towards the ultimate long term goal and to enable performance of employees to be measured along the way. Suitable performance measures therefore need to be set to monitor the achievement of each objective.

2 Critical success factors

Critical success factors (CSFs) are the essential areas of the business that must be performed well if the mission, objectives and goals of the business are to be achieved.

CSFs act as a common point of reference to measure the success of your business. CSFs help everyone in the team to know exactly what they need to do to ensure the success of the business. This helps employees perform their own work in the right context and so pull together towards the same overall aims to achieve goal congruence.

CSFs are related to the mission and goals of the business:

- The mission focuses on the overall long term aims and what is ultimately to be achieved

- Objectives break down the mission into quantifiable goals

- CSFs are the essential areas that must be perfected to achieve the objectives and therefore the mission of the business.

Measurement of CSFs is possible by the creation of Key performance indicators (KPIs). KPIs can be based on financial and non-financial information.

Examples of CSFs and KPIs

The table below shows a number of non-financial performance indicators grouped against CSFs. The organisation will formulate its own, specific KPIs which best suit its business.

CSFs	KPIs
Competitiveness	• sales growth by product or service
	• measures of customer base
	• relative market share and position
Resource utilisation	• efficiency measurements of resources planned against consume
	• measurements of resources available against those used
	• productivity measurements
Quality of service	• quality measures in every unit
	• evaluate suppliers on the basis of quality
	• number of customer complaints received
	• number of new accounts lost or gained
Customer satisfaction	• speed of response to customer needs
	• informal listening by calling a certain number of customers each week
	• number of customer visits to the factory or workplace
	• number of factory and non-factory manager visits to customers

Quality of working life	• days absence
	• labour turnover
	• overtime
	• measures of job satisfaction
Innovation	• proportion of new products and services to old one
	• new product or service sales levels
Responsiveness (lead time)	• order entry delays and errors
	• wrong blueprints or specifications
	• long set-up times and large lots
	• high defect count
	• machines that break down
Quality of output	• returns from customers
	• reject rates
	• reworking costs
	• warranty costs
Flexibility (ability to react to changing demand and a changing environment)	• product/service introduction flexibility
	• product/service mix flexibility
	• volume flexibility
	• delivery flexibility
	• time to respond to customer demands

External factors affecting performance measurement

External factors may be an important influence on an organisation's ability to achieve objectives. In particular market conditions and government policy will be outside of the control of the organisation's management and will need to be carefully monitored to ensure forecasts remain accurate.

Economic and market conditions

Any performance measure that is used by a business will need to be flexible to allow to peaks and troughs in economic and market conditions that are beyond the control of the business or the specific employee or manager.

The actions of competitors must also be considered. For example, company demand may decrease if a competitor reduces its prices or launches a successful advertising campaign.

Government regulation

The government can have a direct affect on the workings of a business by introducing regulations or by having departments that monitor business activity such as

- The Competition Act which prohibits anti-competitive agreements and any abuse of a dominant market position.

- The Office of Fair Trading who investigates any businesses suspecting of breaching the Competition Act.

Other regulations that the government can enforce include:

- **Setting maximum or minimum selling prices** – prescription charges in the UK.

- **Taxation** – tax on alcohol and petrol with the intention of reducing consumption

- **Subsides** – subsides given to firms providing training for employees

- **Fines and quotas** – quotas or maximums are set to limit production and if exceeded fines are imposed. For example fishing quotas are set to prevent over fishing of the seas and if a trawler brings in too much then a fine is incurred.

If a business is affected by government regulation then the performance measures should take account of this externally imposed limitation i.e. a sales team target should not exceed a quota or exceed/undercut a price set by the government.

3 Financial performance measures

Financial performance measures are used to monitor the inflows (revenue) and outflows (costs) and the overall management of money in the business. These measures focus on information available from the Income Statement and Statement of financial position of a business.

Financial measures can be used to record the performance of cost centres, profit centres and investment centres within a responsibility accounting system but they can also be used to assess the overall performance of the organisation as a whole. For example, if cost reduction or cost control is identified as a critical success factor, cost based performance measures might be an appropriate performance indicator to be used.

Cost based performance measures can be calculated as a simple cost per unit of output. The organisation will have to determine its policy for establishing cost per unit for performance measurement purposes. The chosen method should then be applied consistently.

4 Measuring profitability

The primary objective of a company is to maximise profitability. Profitability ratios can be used to monitor the achievement of this objective.

Return on capital employed (ROCE)

This is a key measure of profitability. It is the profit from operations as a percentage of the capital employed. The ROCE shows the profit that is generated from each $1 of assets employed.

$$ROCE = \frac{\text{Profit from operations}}{\text{Capital employed}} \times 100$$

Where capital employed = total assets less current liabilities **or** total equity plus long term debt.

A high ROCE is desirable. An increase in ROCE could be achieved by:

- Increasing profit, e.g. through an increase in sales price or through better control of costs.

- Reducing capital employed, e.g. through the repayment of long term debt.

The ROCE can be understood further by calculating the profit from operations margin and the asset turnover:

ROCE = profit from operations margin × asset turnover

Gross profit margin

This is the gross profit as a percentage of revenue.

$$\text{Gross profit margin \%} = \frac{\text{Gross profit}}{\text{Revenue}} \times 100$$

A high gross profit margin is desirable. It indicates that either sales prices/volumes are high or that **production** costs are being kept well under control.

Profit for the period margin

This is the profit (revenue less all expenses) as a percentage of revenue.

$$\text{Profit from operations margin \%} = \frac{\text{Profit from operations}}{\text{Revenue}} \times 100$$

A high profit margin is desirable. It indicates that either sales prices/volumes are high or that **all** costs are being kept well under control.

Asset turnover

This is the revenue divided by the capital employed. The asset turnover shows the revenue that is generated from each $1 of assets employed.

$$\text{Asset turnover} = \frac{\text{Revenue}}{\text{Capital employed}}$$

A high asset turnover is desirable. An increase in the asset turnover could be achieved by:

- Increasing revenue, e.g. through the launch of new products or a successful advertising campaign.

- Reducing capital employed, e.g. through the repayment of long term debt.

Test your understanding 1

The following figures are extracted from the accounts of Super Soups, a company selling gourmet homemade soups.

	20X9	20X8
	$	$
Total production costs	6,538,000	5,082,000
Gross profit	3,006,000	2,582,000
Profit from operations	590,000	574,000
Total capital employed	6,011,000	5,722,000

Required:

Using appropriate ratios, comment on the profitability of Super Soups.

Test your understanding 2

Companies X and Y are both involved in retailing.

Relevant information for the year ended 30 September 20X5 was as follows:

	X	Y
	$000	$000
Sales revenue	50,000	200,000
Profit before tax	10,000	10,000
Capital employed	50,000	50,000

Required:

Prepare the following ratios for both companies and comment on the results:

(a) ROCE

(b) profit margin

(c) asset turnover.

5 Measuring liquidity

A company can be profitable but at the same time encounter cash flow problems. Liquidity and working capital ratios give some indication of the company's liquidity.

Current ratio

This is the current assets divided by the current liabilities.

$$\text{Current ratio} = \frac{\text{Current assets}}{\text{Current liabilities}}$$

The ratio measures the company's ability to meet its short term liabilities as they fall due.

A ratio in excess of 1 is desirable but the expected ratio varies between the type of industry.

A decrease in the ratio year on year or a figure that is below the industry average could indicate that the company has liquidity problems. The company should take steps to improve liquidity, e.g. by paying payables as they fall due or by better management of receivables in order to reduce the level of bad debts.

Quick ratio (acid test)

This is a similar to the current ratio but inventory is removed from the current assets due to its poor liquidity in the short term.

$$\text{Quick ratio} = \frac{\text{Current assets} - \text{inventory}}{\text{Current liabilities}}$$

The comments are the same as for the current ratio.

Inventory holding period

$$\text{Inventory holding period (in days)} = \frac{\text{Inventory}}{\text{Cost of sales}} \times 365$$

This indicates the average number of days that inventory items are held for.

An increase in the inventory holding period could indicate that the company is having problems selling its products and could also indicate that there is an increased level of obsolete inventory. The company should take steps to increase inventory turnover, e.g. by removing any slow moving or unpopular items of inventory and by getting rid of any obsolete inventory.

A decrease in the inventory holding period could be desirable as the company's ability to turn over inventory has improved and the company does not have excess cash tied up in inventory. However, any reductions should be reviewed further as the company may be struggling to manage its liquidity and may not have the cash available to hold the optimum level of inventory.

Receivables collection period

$$\text{Receivables collection period (in days)} = \frac{\text{Receivables}}{\text{Revenue}} \times 365$$

This is the average period it takes for a company's receivables to pay what they owe.

An increase in the receivables collection period could indicate that the company is struggling to manage its debts. Possible steps to reduce the ratio include:

- Credit checks on customers to ensure that they will pay on time

- Improved credit control, e.g. invoicing on time, chasing up bad debts.

A decrease in the receivables collection period may indicate that the company's has improved its management of receivables. However, a receivables collection period well below the industry average may make the company uncompetitive and profitability could be impacted as a result.

Payables period

$$\text{Payables period (in days)} = \frac{\text{Payables}}{\text{Purchases}} \times 365$$

This is the average period it takes for a company to pay for its purchases.

An increase in the company's payables period could indicate that the company is struggling to pay its debts as they fall due. However, it could simply indicate that the company is taking better advantage of any credit period offered to them.

A decrease in the company's payables period could indicate that the company's ability to pay for its purchases on time is improving. However, the company should not pay for its purchases too early since supplier credit is a useful source of finance.

Test your understanding 3

Calculate the liquidity ratios for P for the year ended 31 December 20X9.

	$m
Sales revenue	1,867.5
Gross profit	489.3
Inventory	147.9
Trade receivables	393.4
Trade payables	275.1
Cash	53.8
Short-term investments	6.2
Other current liabilities	284.3

6 Measuring risk

In addition to managing profitability and liquidity it is also important for a company to manage its risk. The following ratios may be calculated to see how risky a company is:

Financial gearing

This is the long term debt as a percentage of equity.

$$\text{Gearing \%} = \frac{\text{Debt}}{\text{Equity}} \times 100$$

or

$$\text{Gearing \%} = \frac{\text{Debt}}{\text{Debt + equity}} \times 100$$

A high level of gearing indicates that the company relies heavily on debt to finance its long term needs. This increases the level of risk for the business since interest and capital repayments must be made on debt, whereas there is no obligation to make payments to equity.

The ratio could be improved by reducing the level of long term debt and raising long term finance using equity.

Interest cover

This is the operating profit (profit before finance charges and tax) divided by the finance cost.

$$\text{Interest cover} = \frac{\text{Profit before interest}}{\text{Finance cost}}$$

A decrease in the interest cover indicates that the company is facing an increased risk of not being able to meet its finance payments as they fall due.

The ratio could be improved by taking steps to increase the profit, e.g. through better management of costs, or by reducing finance costs through reducing the level of debt.

Dividend cover

This is the profit for the year divided by the dividend.

$$\text{Dividend cover} = \frac{\text{Profit for the year}}{\text{Dividend}}$$

A decrease in the dividend cover indicates that the company is facing an increased risk of not being able to make its dividend payments to shareholders.

7 Problems with using only financial performance indicators

All of the ratios reviewed so far have concentrated on the financial performance of the business. Many of these ratios, e.g. ROCE, gross profit margin, may be used to assess the **performance of a division** and of the **manager** in charge of that division.

Achievement of these target ratios (financial performance indicators) may be linked to a reward system in order to motivate managers to improve financial performance.

However, there are a number of problems associated with the use of financial performance indicators to monitor performance:

Short-termism vs long term performance

Linking rewards to financial performance may tempt managers to make decisions that will improve short-term financial performance but may have a negative impact on long-term profitability. E.g. they may decide to cut investment or to purchase cheaper but poorer quality materials.

As mentioned at the start of this chapter any targets that are set at the different planning levels should all aim towards achieving the overall aim or mission of the business. There should be goal congruence to reduce the risk of a short termist view being taken by the managers.

Manipulation of results

In order to achieve the target financial performance and hence their reward, managers may be tempted to manipulate results. For example:

- **Accelerating revenue** – revenue included in one year may be wrongly included in the previous year in order to improve the financial performance for the earlier year.

- **Delaying costs** – costs incurred in one year may be wrongly recorded in the next year's accounts in order to improve performance and meet targets for the earlier year.

- **Understating a provision or accrual** – this would improve the financial performance and may result in the targets being achieved.

- Manipulation of **accounting policies** – for example, closing inventory values may be overstated resulting in an increase in profits for the year.

Do not convey the full picture

The use of only financial performance indicators has limited benefit to the company as it does not convey the full picture regarding the factors that will drive long-term profitability, e.g. customer satisfaction, quality.

Therefore, when monitoring performance, a broader range of measures should be used.

8 Non-financial performance indicators (NFPIs)

Although profit cannot be ignored as it is the main objective of commercial organisations, critical success factors (CSFs) and key performance indicators (KPIs) should not focus on profit alone. The view is that a range of performance indicators should be used and these should be a mix of financial and non-financial measures.

Examples of Non-Financial Performance Indicators (NFPI) include:

- measurements of customer satisfation e.g. returning customers, reduction in complaints

- resource utilisation e.g. are the machines being operated for all the available hours and producing output as efficiently as possible?

- measurement of quality e.g. reduction in conformance and non-conformance costs

The large variety in types of businesses means that there are many NFPIs. Each business will have its own set of NFPIs that provide relevant measures of the success of the business. However, NFPIs can be grouped together into 2 broad groups:

- Productivity
- Quality

9 Productivity

A productivity measure is a measure of the efficiency of an operation, it is also referred to as **resource utilisation**. It relates the goods or services produced to the resources used (and therefore ultimately the cost incurred) to produce output. The most productive or efficient operation is one that produces the maximum output for any given set of resource inputs or alternatively uses the minimum inputs for any given quantity or quality of output.

It is important to be able to distinguish between production and productivity.

*   Production is the quantity of goods or services that are produced.

*   Productivity is a measure of how efficiently those goods or services have been produced.

Types of productivity measures

Productivity measures are usually given in terms of labour efficiency. However productivity measures are not restricted to labour and can also be expressed in terms of other resource inputs of the organisation such as the machine hours used for production.

Productivity is often analysed using three control ratios:

Production-volume ratio

The production/volume ratio assesses the overall production relative to the plan or budget. A ratio in excess of 100% indicates that overall production is above planned levels and below 100% indicates a shortfall compared to plans.

The production/volume ratio is calculated as:

$$\frac{\text{Actual output measured in standard hours}}{\text{Budgeted production hours}} \times 100$$

Capacity ratio

The capacity ratio provides information in terms of the hours of working time that have been possible in a period.

The capacity ratio is calculated as follows:

$$\frac{\text{Actual production hours worked}}{\text{Budgeted production hours}} \times 100$$

Efficiency ratio

The efficiency ratio is a useful indicator of productivity based on output compared with inputs.

The efficiency ratio is calculated as follows:

$$\frac{\text{Actual output measured in standard hours}}{\text{Actual production hours worked}} \times 100$$

Illustration 1 – Productivity measures

Suppose that the budgeted output for a period is 2,000 units and the budgeted time for the production of these units is 200 hours.

The actual output in the period is 2,300 units and the actual time worked by the labour force is 180 hours.

Required

Calculate how productive the work force has been.

Solution

Production/volume ratio

$$\frac{\text{Actual output measured in standard hours}}{\text{Budgeted production hours}} \times 100$$

$$\text{Standard hours per unit} = \frac{200 \text{ hours}}{2{,}000 \text{ units}} = 0.1 \text{ hours per unit of output}$$

Actual output measured in standard hours $= 2{,}300 \text{ units} \times 0.1 \text{ hours} = 230 \text{ standard hours}$

$$\text{Production/volume ratio} = \frac{230}{200} \times 100 = \textbf{115\%}$$

This shows that production is 15% up on planned production levels.

Capacity ratio

$$\frac{\text{Actual production hours worked}}{\text{Budgeted production hours}} \times 100$$

$$\text{Capacity ratio} = \frac{180}{200} \times 100 = \textbf{90\%}$$

Therefore this organisation had only 90% of the production hours anticipated available for production.

Efficiency ratio

$$\frac{\text{Actual output measured in standard hours}}{\text{Actual production hours worked}} \times 100$$

$$\text{Efficiency ratio} = \frac{230}{180} \times 100 = \textbf{127.78\%}$$

The workers were expected to produce 10 units per hour, the standard hour.

Therefore, in the 180 hours worked it would be expected that 1,800 units would be produced. In fact 2,300 units were produced. This is 27.78% more than anticipated.

NB: production/volume ratio = capacity ratio × efficiency ratio

Examples of productivity measures

Productivity measures are not restricted to use in manufacturing industries but can be adapted for use in both the service and public sectors

Public sector

A nurse in a fracture clinic should be able to complete the plastering of an average broken bone in 45 minutes.

The data on one nurse showed the following:

Hours worked in one week	55 hours
Actual number of casts completed	70

Each nurse is expected to work a 10 hour shift 5 days a week.

Calculate the production/volume ratio, capacity ratio and efficiency ratio for this nurse.

$$\text{Production/volume ratio} = \frac{70 \times 45/60}{50} \times 100 = \textbf{105\%}$$

$$\text{Capacity ratio} = \frac{55}{50} \times 100 = \textbf{110\%}$$

$$\text{Efficiency ratio} = \frac{52.5}{55} \times 100 = \textbf{95.45\%}$$

Service Sector

It should be possible to deliver a fast food meal in 1 minute 30 seconds. The information for one fast food restaurant is as follows:

Opening hours	8.30am to 7pm
Actual meals in one day	380 meals
Budgeted meals in one day	420 meals

Calculate the production/volume ratio, capacity ratio and efficiency ratio for this day.

$$\text{Production/volume ratio} = \frac{380 \times 1.5/60}{10.5} \times 100 = \textbf{90.5\%}$$

$$\text{Capacity ratio} = \frac{10.5}{10.5} \times 100 = \textbf{100\%}$$

$$\text{Efficiency ratio} = \frac{9.5}{10.5} \times 100 = \textbf{90.5\%}$$

The budgeted output for a period is 1,500 units and the standard time allowed per unit is 30 minutes. The actual output in the period was 1,400 units and these were produced in 720 hours. Calculate the production/volume ratio, capacity ratio and efficiency ratio. Explain the meaning of your answer.

10 Quality

Quality is an issue whether manufacturing products or providing a service. Poor quality products or services will lead to a loss of business and damage to the businesses reputation. Targets of an appropriate level need to be set. Examples of NFPIs that could be used to monitor quality both from an internal and external (customer) perspective include:

- Wastage levels
- Internal re-working of finished products
- Customer complaints
- Speed of delivery
- Accuracy of delivery
- Number of returns
- Repeat sales
- New customers
- Growth in sales
- Labour turnover
- Staff absences
- Evaluation of development plans
- Job satisfaction
- Overtime working
- Product improvements
- Sales from new products
- Cost of research and development
- Cleanliness
- Tidiness
- Meeting staff needs
- Meeting government targets on emissions

11 Problems with non-financial performance indicators

The use of NFPI measures such as those mentioned is now common place, but it is not without problems:

- Setting up and operating a system involving a wide range of performance indicators can be time-consuming and costly

- It can be a complex system that managers may find difficult to understand

- There is no clear set of NFPIs that the organisation must use - it will have to select those that seem to be most appropriate

- The scope for comparison with other organisations is limited as few businesses may use precisely the same NFPIs as the organisation under review.

12 The balanced scorecard

To get an effective system of performance appraisal a business should use a combination of financial and non-financial measures.

One of the major developments in performance measurement techniques in recent years that has been widely adopted is the balanced scorecard.

The concept was developed by Kaplan and Norton, 1993 at Harvard. It is a device for planning that enables managers to set a range of targets linked with appropriate objectives and performance measures.

The four perspectives

The framework looks at the strategy and performance of an organisation from four points of view, known in the model as four perspectives:

- financial
- customer
- internal
- learning and growth.

The approach is shown in the following diagram:

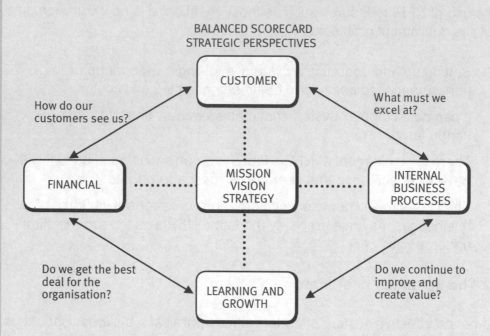

Financial perspective

This focuses on satisfying shareholder value.

Appropriate performance measures would include:

- return on capital employed
- return on shareholders' funds.

Customer perspective

This is an attempt to measure customers' view of the organisation by measuring customer satisfaction. Examples of relevant performance measures would include:

- customer satisfaction with timeliness
- customer loyalty.

Internal perspective

This aims to measure the organisation's output in terms of technical excellence and consumer needs. Indicators here would include:

- unit costs
- quality measurement.

Learning and growth perspective

This focuses on the need for continual improvement of existing products and techniques and developing new ones to meet customers' changing needs.

- A measure would include % of revenue attributable to new products.

Illustration 2 – The balanced scorecard

The following is Horn Ltd's income statement for year ended 20X3, together with additional analysis of revenue and costs.

From this summary we can develop a series of performance indicators relevant to the four perspectives used by the balanced scorecard.

Horn Ltd

Income statement for the year ended X3

	$m
Revenue	1.35
Cost of sales	0.83
Gross profit	0.52
Admin and distribution costs	0.15
Profit from operations	0.37
Taxation	0.04
Profit after taxation	0.33
Dividends	0.13
Profit for the period	0.20
Total assets less current liabilities	2.40

An analysis of revenue and costs show:

Revenue	$m
Existing products	1.03
New products	0.32
Sales to existing customers	0.82
Sales to new customers	0.53

Included in the cost structure is:	$m
Research and development	0.08
Training	0.14
Customer support costs	0.04
Quality assurance	0.03

Solution

Balanced scorecard

Potential Horn Ltd performance indicators

- Financial perspective

  Return on capital employed = 0.37/2.40 × 100 = 15.42%
  Profit from operations margin = 0.37/1.35 × 100 = 27.41%

- Customer perspective

  Customer support as % of revenue = 0.04/1.35 × 100 = 2.96%
  % of business from existing customers = 0.82/1.35 × 100 = 60.74%

- Learning and growth perspective

  Training costs as % of total costs = 0.14/(0.15 + 0.83) × 100 = 14.29%
  % of revenue from new products = 0.32/1.35 × 100 = 23.70%

- Internal perspective

  Quality assurance % of revenue = 0.03/1.35 × 100 = 2.22%
  Admin and distribution costs % of revenue = 0.15/1.35 × 100 = 11.11%

This list is not exhaustive - there will other indicators that Horn Ltd could calculate for each of the four perspectives.

To be useful these performance indicators would need to be compared with benchmarked or target levels for the current period and undergo analysis with previous years.

Advantages and disadvantages of the balanced scorecard

The model can be seen as an extension of the use of a range of performance indicators, including non-financial measures and a move away from the traditional over-reliance on profit based and other financial measures.

Advantages

- uses four perspectives

- less able to distort the performance measure

- harder to hide bad performance

- long term rather than short term

- focuses on KPIs

- KPIs can be changed as the business changes

Disadvantages

- large numbers of calculations required

- subjective

- comparison with other businesses is not easy

- arbitrary nature of arriving at the overall index of performance

Advantages and disadvantages of the Balanced Scorecard

The advantages of the approach include the following:

- It looks at performance from the point of view of the four perspectives outlined above, not just from the narrow view of the shareholders as traditional analysis would.

- Managers are unlikely to be able to distort the performance measure.

- Bad performance is more difficult to hide.

- It should lead to the long-term success of the business rather than focusing on short-term improvements.

- It focuses on key performance indicators. The process of identifying these indicators can make senior managers question strategy and focus on the core elements of the business.

- As the core elements of the business change, the performance indicators can be changed accordingly. It is therefore a flexible measure.

The disadvantages of the model include the following:

- It can involve a large number of calculations which may make performance measurement time-consuming and costly to operate.

- The selection of performance indicators under each of the four perspectives is subjective.

- This in turn will make comparisons with the performance of other organisations difficult to achieve satisfactorily.

- The weighting used to arrive at an overall index of performance are arbitrary and may need to be arrived at by trial and error.

Test your understanding 5

Faster Pasta is an Italian fast food restaurant that specialises in high quality, moderately priced authentic Italian pasta dishes and pizzas. The restaurant has recently decided to implement a balanced scorecard approach and has established the following relevant goals for each perspective:

Perspective	Goal
Customer perspective	- To increase the number of new and returning customers
	- To reduce the % of customer complaints
Internal	- To reduce the time taken between taking a customer's order and delivering the meal to the customer.
	- To reduce staff turnover
Innovation and learning	- To increase the proportion of revenue from new dishes
	- To increase the % of staff time spent on training
Financial	- To increase spend per customer
	- To increase gross profit margin

The following information is also available for the year just ended and for the previous year.

	20X8	20X9
Total customers	11,600	12,000
– of which are new customers	4,400	4,750
– of which are existing customers	7,200	7,250
Customer complaints	464	840
Time between taking order and customer receiving meal	4 mins	13 mins
% staff turnover	12 %	40 %
% time staff spend training	5 %	2%
Revenue	$110,000	$132,000
– revenue from new dishes	$22,000	$39,600
– revenue from existing dishes	$88,000	$92,400
Gross profit	$22,000	$30,360

Required:

Using appropriate measures, calculate and comment on whether or not Faster Pasta has achieved its goals.

13 Benchmarking

The term 'benchmarking' has become fashionable in management culture and is now widely used in board-rooms throughout the UK. Johnson and Scholes, in their book *Exploring Corporate Strategy*, give the following meaning to the term.

Benchmarking is the management process which involves comparison of competences with best practice including comparison beyond the organisation's own industry.

Through benchmarking, organisations can learn about their own business practices and the best practice of others.

It therefore requires organisations to:

- identify what they do and why they do it

- have knowledge of what the industry does and in particular what competitors do

- be fully committed to achieving best practice.

Any activity can be benchmarked and an organisation should focus on those:

- that are central to business strategy
- where significant improvement is required without increasing resources
- where staff are committed and eager for improvement.

Types and levels of benchmarking

There are several types and levels of benchmarking, which are mainly defined by whom an organisation chooses to measure itself against.

These include:

Internal benchmarks

Comparisons between different departments or functions within an organisation.

Competitive benchmarks

Comparisons with competitors in the business sector – through inter-firm comparison schemes.

Functional benchmarks

Comparisons with organisations with similar core activities that are not a competitor.

Strategic benchmarks

Comparisons of market share and profit margins.

The benchmarking process

The following steps are required in a systematic benchmarking exercise:

- planning
- analysis
- action
- review.

Planning includes selecting the activity to be benchmarked, involving fully the staff engaged with that activity and identifying the key stages of the activity relating to inputs, outputs and outcomes. It is important to establish the benchmark to a level of 'best practice'.

Analysis includes identifying the extent to which the organisation is under performing and to stimulate ideas as to how this can be met.

This may include whether new processes or methods are required. Implementation concerns the use of an action plan to achieve the improvement or the maintenance of the pre-determined standards. Management should ensure that resources are made available to meet the objectives set.

Action involves putting an appropriate plan into force in order to improve performance in the benchmarked areas.

Review includes monitoring progress against the plan and reviewing the appropriateness of the performance measure.

In practice, businesses establishing benchmarks will use a variety of information sources for their programmes. The most relevant and useful information would be that from a benchmarking partner. Such partnerships can be organised through trade associations and inter-firm comparison links.

All organisations can benefit with comparisons with others. Ideally, it should be judged against best practice wherever that may be found.

Benchmarking analysis can provide such comparisons of the resources, competences in separate activities and overall competence of the organisation.

14 Chapter summary

```
                    ┌─────────────────┐
                    │   Performance   │
                    │   measurement   │
                    │   techniques    │
                    └─────────────────┘
```

Financial	Non-Financial	Balanced scorecard	Benchmarking
• Profitability	• Productivity	• Financial	• Internal
• Liquidity	• Quality	• Customer	• Competitive
• Risk		• Process efficiency	• Functional
		• Learning and growth	• Strategic

Test your understanding answers

Test your understanding 1

Profitability ratios

	20X9	20X8
Gross profit margin = gross profit/revenue (%)	31.50%	33.69%
Profit margin = profit from operations/revenue (%)	6.18%	7.49%
ROCE = profit from operations/CE (%)	9.82%	10.03%
Asset turnover = revenue/CE	1.59	1.34
Note: Revenue= total production cost + gross profit	9,544,000	7,664,000

Comment

Overall, profitability has deteriorated slightly year on year.

Gross profit margin – Despite an increase in revenue of 24.6%, the gross profit margin has fallen by over 2% to 31.5%. Although revenue has shown a significant increase, the production costs have increased at a faster rate of 28.7% year on year. The falling gross profit margin may indicate that the company is unable to achieve the same level of sales prices as it was in 20X8 or is not as efficient at controlling its production costs.

Profit from operations margin – Again, despite an increase in revenue of 24.6%, the profit margin has fallen from 7.49% to 6.18%. The falling profit margin may indicate that the company is unable to achieve the same level of sales prices as it was in 20X8 or is not as efficient at controlling all of its costs.

Asset turnover – this has actually shown a small improvement year on year from 1.34 in 20X8 to 1.59 in 20X9. This shows that the company is getting better at generating revenue from the capital employed within the business.

ROCE – Despite the improvement in asset turnover, the ROCE has actually fallen slightly from 10.03% in 20X8 to 9.83% in 20X9. This means that the company is not as good at generating profit from its capital employed. The decrease in the ROCE is due to the fall in the profit margin.

It would be useful to obtain a further breakdown of revenue and costs, in order to fully understand the reasons for the changes and to prevent any further decline in the ratios discussed. It would also be useful to obtain the average ratios for the industry in order to gauge Super Soups performance against that of its competitors.

Test your understanding 2

	X		Y	
ROCE	$\dfrac{10,000}{50,000} \times 100\%$		$\dfrac{10,000}{50,000} \times 100\%$	
	= 20%		= 20%	
Profit margin	$\dfrac{10,000}{50,000} \times 100\%$		$\dfrac{10,000}{200,000} \times 100\%$	
	= 20%		= 5%	
Asset turnover	$\dfrac{50,000}{50,000}$		$\dfrac{200,000}{50,000}$	
	= 1		= 4	

The ROCE for both companies is the same. X has a higher profit margin, whilst Y shows a more efficient use of assets. This indicates that there may be a trade-off between profit margin and asset turnover.

Test your understanding 3

Current ratio	(147.9 + 393.4 + 53.8 + 6.2)/(275.1 + 284.3) = 601.3/559.4	= 1.07
Quick ratio	(601.3 – 147.9)/559.4	= 0.81
Receivables collection period	393.4/1,867.5 × 365	= 77 days
Inventory holding period	147.9/(1,867.5 – 489.3) × 365	= 39 days
Payables payment period	275.1/(1,867.5 – 489.3) × 365	= 73 days

Test your understanding 4

Output per standard hour is 2 units as each unit has a standard time allowance of 30 minutes.

Budgeted labour hours are 1,500/2 = 750

The actual output measured in standard hours is 1,400/2 = 700 standard hours

The production/volume ratio = 700/750 × 100% = 93.3%

The capacity ratio = 720/750 × 100% = 96%

The efficiency ratio = 700/720 × 100% = 97.2%

Production is 6.7% less than planned. This is due to a shortfall in capacity available of 4% and lower productivity of 2.8%.

Test your understanding 5

Customer perspective

Goal: To increase the number of new and returning customers

Measure: The number of new customers has increased year on year from 4,400 to 4,750. This is an 8.0% increase. The number of returning customers has also increased slightly from 7,200 to 7,250, i.e. a 1.0% increase.

Comment: The company has achieved its goal of increasing the number of new and existing customers. It is worth noting that the proportion of customers who are returning customers has fallen slightly from 62.1% to 60.4% of the total customers. This could indicate a small drop in the level of customer satisfaction.

Goal: To decrease the % customer complaints

Measure: The percentage of customer complaints has increased from 4% (464 ÷ 11,600) to 7% (840 ÷ 12,000).

Comment: Faster Pasta should investigate the reasons for the increase in customer complaints and take the required action immediately in order to ensure that it can meet this goal in the future.

Internal perspective

Goal: To reduce the time taken between taking the customer's order and delivering the meal to the customer

Measure: The time taken has more than tripled from an average of 4 minutes in 20X8 to an average of 13 minutes in 20X9.

Comment: Customers may place a high value on the fast delivery of their food. The increase in time may be linked to the increased number of customer complaints. If this continues customer satisfaction, and therefore profitability, will suffer in the long-term. The restaurant should take steps now in order to ensure that this goal is achieved going forward.

Goal: To reduce staff turnover

Measure: This has risen significantly from 12% to 40% and hence the business has not achieved its goal.

Comment: The reasons for the high staff turnover should be investigated immediately. This may be contributing to longer waiting times and the increase in customer complaints. This will impact long-term profitability.

Innovation and learning perspective

Goal: To increase the proportion of revenue from new dishes

Measure: This has increased year on year from 20% ($22,000 ÷ $110,000) in 20X8 to 30% ($39,600 ÷ $132,000) in 20X9. Therefore, the restaurant has achieved its goal.

Comment: This is a favourable increase and may have a positive impact on long-term profitability if the new products meet the needs of the customers.

Goal: To increase the % of staff time spent on training.

Measure: This has fallen significantly from 5% to only 2% and hence the company is not achieving its goal.

Comment: Staff may be unsatisfied if they feel that their training needs are not being met. This may contribute to a high staff turnover. In addition, staff may not have the skills to do the job well and this would impact the level of customer satisfaction.

Financial perspective

Goal: to increase spend per customer

Measure: Spend per customer has increased from $9.48 ($110,000 ÷ 11,600) to $11.00 ($132,000 ÷ 12,000), i.e. a 16.0% increase.

Comment: This is a favourable increase. However, the issues discussed above must be addressed in order to ensure that this trend continues.

Goal: To increase gross profit margin.

Measure: The gross profit margin has increased year on year from 20% ($22,000 ÷ $110,000) to 23% ($30,360 ÷ $132,000).

Comment: This is a favourable increase. However, the issues discussed above must be addressed in order to ensure that this trend continues.

Performance measurement in specific situations

Chapter learning objectives

Upon completion of this chapter you will be able to:

- discuss measures that may be used to assess managerial performance and the practical problems involved

- Profitability
  - calculate return on investment and residual income
  - explain the advantages and limitations of return on investment and residual income

- describe performance measures which would be suitable in contract and process costing environments

- describe performance measures appropriate for service industries

- discuss the measurement of performance in service industry situations

- discuss the measurement of performance in non-profit seeking and public sector organisations

- Economy, efficiency and effectiveness
  - explain the concepts of economy, efficiency and effectiveness
  - describe performance indicators for economy, efficiency and effectiveness
  - establish performance indicators for economy, efficiency and effectiveness in a specific situation

1 Introduction

There are many different types of business which can broadly be placed into one the following groups:

- Manufacturing industry
- Service provider
- Non-profit organisation (charities)
- Public sector organisation (government departments)

Each of these business sectors will have different objectives, for example:

- Manufacturing – reduce the cost of the product
- Service provider – improve the quality of the service
- Non-profit organisation – to meet the demands of the 'customer'
- Public sector organisation – to stay within a tight budget.

Each business will need to monitor the performance of their objectives to ensure they are able to succeed in their chosen field but each will face their own difficulties in deciding on appropriate measures to use. For example, as seen in a previous chapter, measurement of a service providers output can be difficult due to:

- Intangible nature of the service
- The variability of the service
- Simultaneous production and consumption of the service
- Perishability of the service

Non-profit and public organisations will have difficulties deciding on performance measures as the usually financial performance measures, such as profit as a percentage of revenue, will not be applicable.

2 Divisional performance measurement

Measuring managerial performance

There are practical problems involved in isolating managerial performance from the performance of the division being managed. The personal performance of the manager is not the same as the overall performance of the division due to external factors which are outside of the control of the organisation. For example:

- a manager may be in control of a division which faces fierce competition and difficult operating conditions and therefore will not be able to grow the business easily

- another manager may be given a division which faces less competition and an easier business environment.

Measures which reflect the performance of the division as a whole, therefore, may not reflect the performance of the manager.

There are two main ways of measuring managerial performance.

(1) **Set specific managerial objectives**

Individual managers can be set specific objectives against which their performance can be measured at regular intervals. These objectives will be linked to the overall objectives of the organisation as a whole.

For example, the organisation may have an objective to increase overall sales by 5% per annum. The specific objective for a manager operating in a very competitive environment may be to maintain sales at the current level rather than try to increase them. This objective should be agreed with the individual manager as being set at a level which is tough but achievable in order to provide motivation. The payment of bonuses or other performance-related pay may also be linked to the achievement of the agreed objectives.

(2) **Use measures based on controllable costs and revenue i.e. controllable profit**

Budget targets can distinguish between controllable and uncontrollable costs and revenue. The divisional performance can be measured against the total budget using traceable costs and revenues whereas managerial performance can be measured based ont what the controllable element is.

Responsibility centres

Performance measures will also differ according to the type of centre a manager is responsible for:

Responsibility centre	Example	Examples of measures used to assess performance
Cost centre	Production line in a manufacturing business Costs only	• total cost and cost per unit • cost variances • non-financial performance indicators (NFPIs) related to quality, productivity and efficiency.
Revenue centre	Sales team for a car show room. Revenues only	• total sales and market share • sales variances • NFPIs related to customer satisfaction.
Profit centre	Retail division of a carpet manufacturer. Costs and revenues	All the above plus: • profit percentages • working capital ratios
Investment centre	The European business unit in an international organisation Costs, revenues and authority to invest in new assets and dispose of old ones	All of the above plus: • Return on Investment (ROI) • Residual Income (RI)

Return on investment (ROI)

This is a similar measure to ROCE but is used to appraise the investment decisions of an individual division.

$$\text{ROI \%} = \frac{\text{Controllable profit}}{\text{Controllable capital employed}} \times 100$$

- Controllable profit is usually taken after depreciation but before tax. However, in the exam you may not be given this profit figure and so you should use the profit figure that is closest to this. Assume the profit is controllable, unless told otherwise.

- Capital employed is total assets less current liabilities <u>or</u> total equity plus long term debt. Use net assets if capital employed is not given in the question.

- Non-current assets might be valued at cost, net replacement cost or carrying amount. The value of assets employed could be either an average value for the period as a whole or a value as at the end of the period. An average value for the period is preferable. However, in the exam you should use whatever figure is given to you.

Illustration 1 – ROI

The following data has been collected in respect of investment centre A:

Controllable profit $50,000

Controllable assets $250,000

Required

Calculate the ROI for investment centre A

Solution

$$\text{ROI} = \frac{50,000}{250,000} \times 100 = 20\%$$

This means that the centre has made a rate of return of 20% on the assets under its control.

Test your understanding 1

The following data relate to the operational performance of the four divisions of Questor plc.

Division	A	B	C	D
	$000	$000	$000	$000
Profit	250	400	320	80
Net assets	1,300	2,500	1,600	320

Using return on investment to evaluate performance, which division has been most successful?

A Division A

B Division B

C Division C

D Division D

Residual Income (RI)

Residual income is the net operating income that an investment centre or division earns above the minimum required return on its operating assets.

RI = Controllable profit – Notional interest on capital

- Controllable profit is calculated in the same way as for ROI.

- Notional interest on capital = the capital employed in the division multiplied by a notional cost of capital or interest rate.
  - Capital employed is calculated in the same way as for ROI.
  - The selected cost of capital could be the company's average cost of funds (cost of capital). However, other interest rates might be selected, such as the current cost of borrowing, or a target ROI. (You should use whatever rate is given in the exam).

Illustration 2 – RI calculation

An investment centre's statement of financial position shows assets under its control amounting to $300,000. The profit of the centre, in its own income statement amounts to $50,000. The notional cost of capital of 10%.

Required

Calculate the RI for this centre.

Solution

The residual income calculation of the investment centre would show:

Controllable profit	$50,000
Less notional cost of capital $300,000 × 10%	($30,000)
	————
Residual income	$20,000

Test your understanding 2

An investment centre has net assets of $800,000, and made profits before interest and tax of $160,000. The notional cost of capital is 12%.

Required:

Calculate and comment on the RI for the period.

Illustration 3 – ROI versus RI

A division currently has:

Controllable profit of $20m

Controllable assets of $100m

Cost of capital 10%.

An investment opportunity has arisen that would increase the controllable profit by $10m and increase the controllable assets by $50m.

Should the manager of the division take advantage of the opportunity?

Solution

The investment does not change the ROI of the division:

Current ROI = $20m/$100m × 100 = 20%

With investment ROI = $30m/$150m × 100 = 20%

The investment improves the RI of the division:

Current RI = $20m - (10% × $100m) = $10m

With investment RI = $30m – (10% × $150m) = $15m

Based on RI the investment should be accepted as it produces a higher absolute level of income.

This suggests that the use of ROI as a performance measure may lead to sub-optimal decisions which do not maximise profit (and therefore wealth) generated by the organisation.

Test your understanding 3

A division has a residual income of $280,000 and a controllable profit before interest of $740,000.

If it uses a notional rate of 10% for interest on its invested capital, what is its return on investment to the nearest whole percentage?

A   4%

B   10%

C   16%

D   27%

Evaluation of ROI as a performance measure

ROI is a popular measure for **divisional performance** but has some serious failings which must be considered when interpreting results.

Advantages	Disadvantages
• familiar and simple calculation	• based on accounting information
• uses readily available information	• open to manipulation
• widely used measure	• may be distorted by inflation
• gives result in percentage terms so can be used to compare business units of different sizes.	• may discourage investment in new assets
	• use of a percentage comparison can be misleading
	• may lead to non-goal congruence

Advantage and disadvantages of ROI

Advantages

- It is a familiar and simple calculation – everyone with a basic knowledge of accounting will be familiar with the return on capital concept.

- It uses readily available information taken from the investment centres normal accounting system. It is therefore a low cost measure – no additional information is usually required in order to be able to carry out the calculations.

- It is a widely used measure, so comparisons with other organisations should be readily available.

- As ROI gives a result in percentage terms, it can be used to compare units which differ in size – their performance is reduced to a common base as a result of the percentage calculation.

Disadvantages

- The measure is based on accounting information (profit figures and asset figures). Different accounting policies, such as the depreciation policy, may impact on the figure calculated.

- It may be open to manipulation. Managers may be tempted to massage the figures to present a better picture of their performance, especially if bonuses are at stake.

- The measure may be distorted by inflation as historical cost accounts do not reflect the current value of the assets used in the revision.

- ROI may discourage investment and re-equipment in more technologically up to date assets. Old assets, almost fully depreciated will give a low asset base in the ROI calculation, which will result in an increased figure for ROI and give the impression of an improved level of performance.

- ROI gives a percentage value – useful for making comparisons as we have mentioned above. However, the use of comparatives can also be misleading.

- Importantly, ROI may lead managers to take decisions which are to their advantage but which do not benefit the organisation as a whole. In technical terms, ROI may lead to dysfunctional decision making.

Evaluation of RI as a performance measure

Compared to using ROI as a measure of performance, RI has several advantages and disadvantages:

Advantages	Disadvantages
• encourages new investment	• not comparable with different size business units
• interest charge	• based on accounting measures
• absolute measure	• determination of the appropriate cost of capital

Advantages and disadvantages of RI

Advantages

- It encourages investment centre managers to make new investments if they add to RI. A new investment might add to RI but reduce ROI. In such a situation, measuring performance by RI would not result in dysfunctional behaviour, i.e. the best decision will be made for the business as a whole.

- Making a specific charge for interest helps to make investment centre managers more aware of the cost of the assets under their control.

- RI gives an absolute measure, not a percentage measure – it therefore avoids some of the problem of ROI

Disadvantages

- It does not facilitate comparisons between divisions since the RI is driven by the size of divisions and of their investments.

- It is based on accounting measures of profit and capital employed which may be subject to manipulation, e.g. in order to obtain a bonus payment.

- There is a major problem inherent in the RI calculation – that is, the determination of an appropriate notional cost of capital

3 Manufacturing industries

Introduction

Manufacturing industries are able to use the performance indicators mentioned in the previous chapter along with some of the calculations in earlier chapters to assess the performance of managers and divisions. For example:

- Financial indicators for overall profitability and liquidity of the business

- Non-financial indicators for productivity and quality

- Variance analysis for sales, materials, labour and overheads

- Labour turnover

We need to consider what would be appropriate measures of performance for the different costing techniques that occur in manufacturing situations.

Contract costing

Contract costing is used when a job or project is large and will take a significant length of time (usually more than one accounting period) to complete.

In view of the large scale of many contracting operations, cost control is vital and frequent comparisons of budgeted and actual data are needed to monitor:

- cost over-runs
- time over-runs.

In addition a note should to be made of the:

- ratio of cost incurred to value of work certified
- amount of remedial work subsequently required.

Effectively, the level of profit being earned on the contract can be checked as each architect or quantity surveyor's certificate is received.

In addition checks should be made on:

- levels of idle time
- amounts of wasted material
- inventory levels
- utilisation of plant.

Illustration 4 – Contract costing

To be able to evaluate the progress of a contract against budget it is necessary to calculate the attributable profit at certain stages of the contract.

There is a four step procedure for calculating attributable profit on long-term contracts.

Step 1: Determine the total sales value for the contract

Step 2: Compute the total expected costs to complete the contract

Step 3: Calculate the overall expected profit on the contract. If there is a loss anticipated then the whole loss is recognised immediately.

Step 4: Calculate the cumulative attributable profit based on either

$$\frac{\text{Value of work certified to date}}{\text{Contract price}} \times \text{Overall expected profit}$$

OR

$$\frac{\text{Costs incurred to date}}{\text{Total expected costs to completion}} \times \text{Overall expected profit}$$

These figures can be calculated based on budget and can then be used as guidance through a long-term contract.

Test your understanding 4

JK Housing is currently undertaking a contract to build a block of flats. The contract value is $62m. The following information is available:

Value of work certified	$38m
Costs incurred to date	$28m
Future cost to complete	$28m

Calculate the profit to be recognised using:

(1) work certified

(2) costs incurred to date

Job costing

Job costing is used to cost individual, unique jobs. Job costing is contract costing on a smaller scale both in value and time therefore many of the performance measures will be identical:

- cost control
- time management.

The type of firm that is using job costing will influence the type of measure used. Examples could include:

- Practising accountants – ratio of chargeable time for a job to total time required to complete the job

- Garages – average age of inventories of spares

- Printers – cost per printed page

- Tree surgeons – tipping time to chipping time

Process costing

Process costing is used when manufacturing consists of a sequence of continuous operations or processes. This system, used by (for example) chemical companies, food manufacturers, makers of nuts and bolts and brewers would require several key performance measures:

- levels of abnormal loss

- levels of rejected production

- production time.

In addition, inventory levels and cost targets would be monitored as well as any bottlenecks identified and cured.

Batch costing

Being a 'half-way house' between job and process costing, performance measures used in those two systems may be equally appropriate for batch costing. Again, individual businesses could be considered together with areas to monitor and therefore areas for which performance measures are required.

- Clothing manufacturers – quantity of material loss

- Furniture manufacturers – levels of inventories held

- Bakers – baking time to oven heating time

- Electrical goods makers – number of quality control failures

4 The service sector

Many of the basic principles will apply in service industries – CSFs, KPIs etc, but their application will require special attention if they are to be useful in assessing performance.

The service sector of the economy

In many western economies one of the major changes that has taken place in recent years has been a change in the structure of those economies – the manufacturing sector has declined in size and significance and the service sector has grown in importance. The service sector consists of banks, airlines, transport companies, accountancy and consultancy firms and service shops.

We shall consider two main aspects of performance in relation to service organisations:

- financial performance
- service quality. Quality is seen to be a particularly important non-financial performance indicator in the service sector.

Financial performance

Conventional financial analysis distinguishes four types of ratio: profitability, liquidity, gearing and activity ratios. Analysis of a company's performance using accounting ratios involves comparisons with past trends and/or competitors' ratios. Typical ratios that could be used by a service organisation include:

- revenue per 'service
- revenue per 'principal' or partner in, say, a management consultancy
- staff costs as a % of revenue
- space costs as a % of revenue
- training costs as a % of revenue
- profit %
- current ratio
- quick asset ratio
- market share
- market share increase year by year.

Financial ratio analysis is of limited use due to the 'human' nature of a service provider - the quality of the service also needs to be considered.

Illustration 5 – Service sector examples

Barclays Bank plc (a major UK based banking group)

Barclays Bank has split its business between corporate and retail customers. The bank has over 350 products and services, most of which are variants on borrowing or lending, whose profitability is tied to borrowing and lending rates as affected by transactions with the Bank of England and government economic policy. Individual retail customers can make use of a mix of these services – albeit in most cases a limited sample of the total range – via several possible 'service delivery processes': by post, telephone, automatic teller machines (ATMs), cashiers or the branch manager. Whilst the gross margins of individual services are known, no attempt is made to trace costs, even labour costs, to them.

Commonwealth Hotels

Each hotel has a general manager and a number of responsibility centres: rooms, food, bar, reception (including telephones) and marketing. Individual customers can use any mix of these services. Here gross margins (after deducting all direct costs) are known, but indirect costs are not allocated to the responsibility centres. The management team is rewarded by a bonus system related to the hotel's total profit.

Service quality

BAA plc

BAA (British Airports Authority) is a large company which operates many of the UK's major airports. The company uses regular customer surveys for measuring customer perceptions of a wide variety of service quality attributes, including, for example, the cleanliness of its facilities, the helpfulness of its staff and the ease of finding one's way around the airport.

The quality measure and the mechanisms used to gather information will depend on the 'quality issue'.

Quality	Measures	Mechanisms
Access	Walking distance/ease of finding way around	Surveys operational data
Aesthetics	Staff appearance/airport appearance, quality of catering	Surveys inspection
Availability	Equipment availability	Internal fault monitors
Cleanliness	Environment and equipment	Surveys/inspection
Comfort	How crowded it is	Surveys/inspection
Communication	Information clarity/clarity of labelling and pricing	Surveys/inspection
Competence	Staff efficiency	Management inspection
Courtesy	Courtesy of staff	Surveys/inspection
Friendliness	Staff attitude	Surveys/inspection
Reliability	Equipment faults	Surveys/inspection
Responsiveness	Staff responsiveness	Surveys/inspection
Security	Efficiency of security checks/number of urgent safety reports	Surveys/internal data

Internal quality measurement

Inspection and monitoring of the inputs to the service process is important for all organisations. The quality of the solicitors in a practice or the number and grades of staff available in a consultancy organisation are crucial to the provision of service quality. BAA monitors the availability and condition of equipment and facilities.

Many service companies use internal mechanisms to measure service quality during the process of service delivery. BAA has advanced systems to monitor equipment faults and the terminal managers are expected to report any problems they see.

The quality of the service may be measured after the event, that is by measuring the results by outputs of the service.

5 Non-profit seeking and public sector organisations

There are said to be two main problems involved in assessing performance of these organisations:

- the problem of identifying and measuring objectives

- the problem of identifying and measuring outputs.

Objectives

One of the issues in performance evaluation, in any sector, is defining organisational objectives. Once that is done, performance indicators can be devised that indicate the extent to which such objectives have been achieved.

In non profit seeking organisations the objectives may be much more varied, reflecting the variety of organisations included in the sector:

- charities
- professional institutions
- educational establishments
- government bodies

Although the detail will vary depending on the organisation involved, we could suggest that the general objective of non profit seeking organisations is to provide the best possible service within a limited resource budget:

- **Charities** will have a limited amount of funds available – they will seek to use these funds to provide services to as many of their beneficiaries as possible. It will be important not to waste money or any other resources.

- A central **government department** (health or education for example) or a local authority typically has a limited amount of finance available. Its objective will be to provide the best possible service to the community with the financial constraints imposed upon it.

The problems of output measurement

Outputs of organisations in these sectors are often not valued in a money terms. How do we measure the output of a school or hospital?

Output targets can be set in these situations, but they will always be open to debate and argument.

Illustration 6 – Schools

In the UK, Government sets targets for schools in the form of GCSE pass rates – a form of output for the school. League tables are then published which rank schools based on their pupils' examination results but:

- There are many people who argue that the output of a school cannot be measured by examination results. They argue the output is a wider concept than this – and one which is not so easily measured – the concept of value added education. This would look at the improvement in knowledge and ability of pupils over their life at the school. But how do we measure this?

- Comparing schools performance by publishing league tables of examination results is also open to question. It is of course an attempt to carry out comparative analysis of performance – one school against another. But, many people make the point that the tables do not compare like with like. Different schools have children from different social backgrounds for example, which may be reflected in examination results.

Value for Money (VFM)

The value for money (VFM) concept has been developed as a useful means of assessing performance in an organisation which is not seeking profit.

VFM concept revolves around the 3Es, as follows:

- **Economy** (an input measure) – measures the relationship between money spent and the inputs. Are the resources used the cheapest possible for the quality required?

- **Efficiency** (link inputs with outputs) – is the maximum output being achieved from the resources used?

- **Effectiveness** (links outputs with objectives) – to what extent to which the outputs generated achieve the objectives of the organisation.

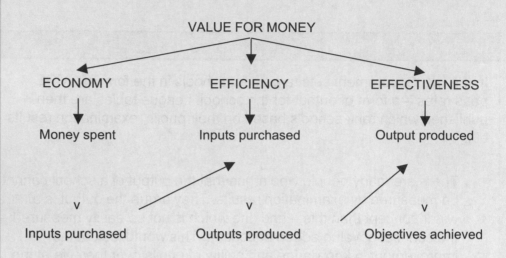

If you follow through the diagram above, you will see that, ultimately, VFM relates money spent to objectives achieved.

You should note that VFM still focuses on financial performance. Non profit seeking organisations will also need to consider non-financial performance, particularly quality.

Value for money

The non-profit sector incorporates a diverse range of operations including national government, local government, charities, executive agencies, trusts and so on. The critical thing about such operations is that they are <u>not</u> motivated by a desire to maximise profit.

Many, if not all, of the benefits arising from expenditure by these bodies are non-quantifiable (certainly not in monetary terms, e.g. social welfare). The same can be true of costs. So any cost/benefit analysis is necessarily quite judgemental, i.e. social benefits versus social costs as well as financial benefits versus financial costs. The danger is that if benefits cannot be quantified, then they might be ignored.

Another problem is that these organisations often do not generate revenue but simply have a fixed budget for spending within which they have to keep (i.e. a capital rationing problem). Value for money ('VFM') is often quoted as an objective here but it does not get round the problem of measuring 'value'.

Illustration 7 – Value for money

Value for money in a university would comprise the three element of:

Economy – this is about balancing the cost with the quality of the resources. Therefore, it will review areas such as the cost of books, computers and teaching compared with the quality of these resources. It recognises that the organisation must consider its expenditure but should not simply aim to minimise costs. e.g. low cost but poor quality teaching or books will hinder student performance and will damage the reputation of the university.

Efficiency – this focuses on the efficient use of any resources acquired. For example:

- How often are the library books that are bought by the university taken out on loan by students?
- What is the utilisation of IT resources?
- What % of their working time do lecturers spend teaching or researching?

Effectiveness – this measures the achievement of the organisation's objectives. For example:

- The % of students achieving a target grade.
- The % of graduates who find full time employment within 6 months of graduating.

The 3E's

Below are the calculations for economy, efficiency and effectiveness:

(1) **Economy**

$$\frac{\text{Standard input}}{\text{Actual input}} \times 100$$

(2) **Efficiency**

$$\frac{\text{Actual output}}{\text{Actual input}} \times 100$$

(3) **Effectiveness**

$$\frac{\text{Actual output}}{\text{Standard output}} \times 100$$

Illustration 8 – Examples of performance measures using the 3Es

Hospitals

(1) **Economy**

Comparing the standard cost of drugs used in treatments with the actual cost of drugs

(2) **Efficiency**

Comparing the number of beds in use in a ward with the number of beds available in the ward

(3) **Effectiveness**

Comparing the current waiting time for patients with the desired waiting time for patients.

A College

(1) **Economy**

Comparing the standard cost of tutors with the actual cost of the tutors.

(2) **Efficiency**

Comparing actual tutor utilisation in hours with planned tutor utilisation in hours.

(3) **Effectiveness**

Comparing actual exam results (% over a certain grade or percentage passes) with desired exam results.

Test your understanding 5

St Alice's Hospice is a charity which collects funds and donations and utilises these in the care of terminally ill patients. The governing body has set the manager three performance objectives for the three months to 30 June 20X7:

* to achieve a level of donations of $150,000 over the 3 month period

* to keep administration costs to no more than 8% of donations per month

* to achieve 80% of respite care requested from the community.

Actual results were as follows:

	April	May	June
Donations($)	35,000	65,000	55,000
Administration costs ($)	2,450	5,850	4,400
Respite care requests (days)	560	570	600
Respite care provided (days)	392	430	510

Calculate appropriate performance measures to evaluate the managers performance.

Test your understanding 6

A government is looking at assessing state schools by reference to a range of both financial and non-financial factors, one of which is average class sizes.

Which of the three E's best describes the above measure?

A   Economy

B   Effectiveness

C   Efficiency

D   Externality

Test your understanding 7

A government is looking at assessing the performance of teachers in a state school by reference to a range of both financial and non-financial factors, one of which is pass rates.

Which of the three E's best describes the above measure?

A   Economy

B   Effectiveness

C   Efficiency

D   Externality

6 Chapter summary

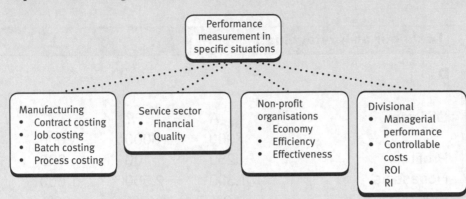

Test your understanding answers

Test your understanding 1

D

Division	A	B	C	D
	$000	$000	$000	$000
Profit	250	400	320	80
Net assets	1,300	2,500	1,600	320
ROI	19%	16%	20%	25%

Test your understanding 2

If performance is measured by RI, the RI for the period is:

	$
Profit before interest and tax	160,000
Notional interest (12% × $800,000)	96,000
RI	64,000

(**Note:** Capital employed is not available in this question and therefore net assets should be used as a substitute value).

Investment centre managers who make investment decisions on the basis of short-term performance will want to undertake any investments that add to RI, i.e. if the RI is positive.

Test your understanding 3

c

RI = Controllable profit – Notional interest on capital

$280,000 = $740,000 – (10% × invested capital)

$740,000 – $280,000 = 10% × invested capital

$460,000 = 10% of the capital invested

Capital invested = $460,000/10 × 100 = $4,600,000

ROI = Controllable profit/controllable capital employed × 100

ROI = $740,000/$4,600,000 × 100

ROI = 16%

Test your understanding 4

Step 1: Determine the total sales value for the contract

$62m (given in the question)

Step 2: Compute the total expected costs to complete the contract

$28m + $28m = $56m

Step 3: Calculate the overall expected profit on the contract. If there is a loss anticipated then the whole loss is recognised immediately.

$62m – $56m = $6m

Step 4: Calculate the cumulative attributable profit based

(1)
$$\frac{\text{Value of work certified to date}}{\text{Contract price}} \times \text{Overall expected profit}$$

$$\frac{\$38m}{\$62m} \times \$6m$$

$$= \$3.68m$$

(2)
$$\frac{\text{Costs incurred to date}}{\text{Total expected costs to completion}} \times \text{Overall expected profit}$$

$$\frac{\$28m}{\$56m} \times \$6m$$

$$= \$3m$$

Test your understanding 5

	April	May	June
Administration costs as a % of donations	7%	9%	8%
Respite care provided	70%	75.4%	85%

Total donations of $155,000 have been received which exceeds the target for the period.

Administration costs have been within the target of 8% in April and June but exceeded the target in May.

There has been a steady improvement in the level of respite care provided and in June the target was exceeded.

Test your understanding 6

C

Class sizes are the result of the number of pupils educated (output), the number of teachers employed (input) and how well the timetable is organised in using those teachers. Therefore this is a measure of efficiency.

Test your understanding 7

B

Pass rates (objective) are the result of how well the teachers educate the pupils (output). Therefore this is a measure of effectiveness.

18

Spreadsheets

Chapter learning objectives

Upon completion of this chapter you will be able to:

* explain the role, features and uses of a spreadsheet package.

* identify applications for computer spreadsheets and their use in cost management

Most of this chapter has been included as expandable text as many students will already have detailed knowledge of such software through practical experience. However, spreadsheets are examinable and should be expected to come up every time in the exam.

1 Uses of spreadsheets

Introduction

A spreadsheet is a computer package that is used to manipulate data. Much of the data of a company is likely to be held on a number of spreadsheets. Spreadsheets can be used for anything with a rows and columns format. One of the most useful functions of a spreadsheet is being able to input formulae to enable calculation to happen automatically when data is input in specific cells.

Entering formulae

- A formula always starts with an equal sign (=) in Excel.

- Formulae consist of numbers, cell co-ordinates (e.g. A2, F7), operators and functions. Operators perform actions on numbers and co-ordinates. Examples of operators are plus, minus, divide and multiply. Functions perform more advanced actions on numbers and co-ordinates.

The arithmetic operations and method of writing the basic formulae are very similar in all packages. The **BODMAS (Brackets off, Division, Multiplication, Addition, Subtraction)** rule must be used to evaluate an arithmetic problem:

- use brackets to clarify the correct order of operations and evaluate expressions within the brackets first

- perform division and multiplication before addition and subtraction

- work from left to right if the expression contains only addition and subtraction.

Steps involved in entering formulae

To enter a formula:

- select the cell where you want to enter the formula

- press the equal sign (=) on the keyboard (or click on the sign in the formula bar, if one is shown)

- key in the formula directly from the keyboard or use the mouse to select the cells you want in the formula. There are no spaces in a formula

- press the <Enter> key

- when you have entered a formula, the resulting value appears in that cell. The formula is only visible in the formula bar

- typical formulae:

  = (A6+C10) – E25   Adds A6 with C10 and subtracts E25

  = (H19*A7)/3   Multiplies H19 with A7 and divides the total by 3

  = SUM(L12:L14)   A quick way of adding L12 + L13 + L14

Statistical functions

The basic commands for statistical functions that operate on lists of values are also very similar throughout the range of spreadsheet packages. Examples of these are:

- SUM – the total of the values in the list

- AVG – the average of the values in the list

- MAX – the highest value in the list

- MIN – the lowest value in the list

Practical application of spreadsheets in the workplace

Spreadsheets are a convenient way of setting up all sorts of charts, records and tables. Uses include:

- 'what if?' analysis

- budgeting and forecasting

- reporting performance

- variance analysis

- inventory valuation.

'What if?' analysis

- The power of spreadsheets is that the data held in any one cell can be made dependent on that held in other cells by the use of formulae.

- This means that changing a value in one cell can set off a chain reaction of changes through other related cells.

- This allows 'what-if?' analysis to be quickly and easily carried out, e.g. 'what if sales are 10% lower than expected?'

Budgeting and forecasting

Preparing budgets and forecasts are classic applications of spreadsheets, as they allow estimates to be changed without having to recalculate everything manually. Here is an extract from a cash flow forecast:

	A	B	C	D	E
1	Revised cashflow forecast for 05/06				
2	£000	Jul-05	Aug-05	Sep-05	Oct-05
3					
4	Sales receipts	1867	1828	1893	1939
5					
6	Payments				
7	Purchases	1691	1644	1701	1798
8	Overheads	57	57	57	57
9	Capex	50	50	50	25
10	Bank loan	12	12	12	12
11	VAT	160			171
12	CT				
13	Bank o/d interest	2	2	2	1
14		1972	1765	1822	2064
15					
16	Net cash in/out flow	-105	63	71	-125
17					
18	Bal b/f *	-134	-239	-176	-105
19	Bal c/f	-239	-176	-105	-230
20					

The key formulae are as follows:

- Total payments: e.g. B14: = SUM(B7:B13)

- Net cashflow: e.g. B16: = B4-B14

- Bal c/f: e.g. B19: = B18+B16

Reporting performance

Performance appraisal usually involves calculating ratios, possibly involving comparatives between companies and from one year to the next.

- A neat way of doing this is to input the raw data, such as financial statements on one sheet and calculate the ratios on another.

- For example, here is an extract from the five years results for a company called Parkland, input on a sheet titled "historic data":

	A	Formula Bar	D	E	
1					
2				Rutwater	
3	£000	2005	2004	2003	2
4					
5	Revenue	319,361	316,197	309,119	30
6	Cost of sales	-81,428	-84,627	-83,039	-8
7	Gross profit	237,933	231,570	226,080	22
8					
9	EBITDA	157,485	154,999	145,910	11

- Here are some ratios that have been set up on a separate sheet (titled "current and historic ratios") in the same workbook:

KAPLAN PUBLISHING

	A	B	C	D	E
1					
2	**Historic ratio analysis**			**Rutwater**	
3			**2005**	**2004**	**2003**
4					
5	RoC		11.7%	12.5%	12.5%
6	Margin		27.8%	27.8%	26.8%
7	Asset turnover		£0.42	£0.45	£0.47
8	Gross margin		74.5%	73.2%	73.1%
9	EBITDA margin		49.2%	48.1%	47.2%
10					

- Taking just one as an example, gross margin – this is calculated as gross profit divided by revenue. The answer has been formatted to show as a percentage to one decimal place and the formula for cell C8 is as follows: ='Historic data'!C7/'Historic data'!C5

- The 'historic data'! part indicates which worksheet the information came from. While this looks complex, setting up the formula was simply a matter of clicking on the correct cells in the first place:

  - On the sheet "current and historic ratios" click on cell C8 and press "="

  - Switch to sheet "historic data" and click on cell C7

  - Type "/"

  - Click on cell C5 while still on sheet "historic data"

  - Press enter and you will automatically return to the "current and historic ratios" sheet.

Variance analysis

Variance analysis involves management comparing actual results with budget and then investigating the differences. A relatively simple statement could be along the lines of the following:

	A	B	C	D	E	F	G
1					Variance Report		
2	Project Name:						
3	Employee Name:						
4							
5	ID#		Task Name		Planned Effort (Baseline)	Actual Effort (or Estimated Completion)	Variance / Slippage	Comments
6							0.0	
7							0.0	
8							0.0	
9							0.0	
10							0.0	
11							0.0	

2 Advantages and disadvantages of spreadsheets

Introduction

Many users use spreadsheets to store data, even though the data could be better managed in a database. This confusion stems from the basic similarity that the key function of both spreadsheets and databases is to store and manipulate data.

- A database is designed to store and manipulate large amounts of data.
- A spreadsheet is designed mainly to run formulas and reports on numbers

Advantages of spreadsheets

Spreadsheets are designed to analyse data and sort list items, not for long-term storage of raw data. A spreadsheet should be used for 'crunching' numbers and storage of single list items. Advantages of spreadsheets include the following:

- Spreadsheet programs are relatively easy to use.
- Spreadsheet functions enable data to processed more quickly.
- They include graphing functions that allow for quick reporting and analysis of data.
- Spreadsheets are often easier to read than hand written tables
- They should reduce calculation errors.

Disadvantages of spreadsheets

- Data must be re-copied over and over again to maintain it in separate data files.
- Spreadsheets are not able to identify data input errors.
- Spreadsheets lack detailed sorting and querying abilities.
- There can be sharing violations among users wishing to view or change data at the same time.
- Spreadsheets are restricted to a finite number of records.
- Spreadsheets are open to cyber attack through viruses, hackers and general system failure.

KAPLAN PUBLISHING

Using a spreadsheet package

For those unfamiliar with spreadsheet packages, this section will provide the basic introduction needed to feel confident to use Microsoft Excel and carry out simple information analysis tasks.

- This package has been chosen because it is the most popular and therefore the most likely to be used in your college or work environment.

- The editions and programs that you are using may not be the same as those used in this section. In that case, the screens you produce will not be identical to those shown here.

- However, all spreadsheet packages will have the basic features described in this section and access to a different package will not cause too many problems.

- If you are at all unsure, you should read the manual that accompanies your chosen spreadsheet.

In order to explain the role, features and uses of a spreadsheet package, the following instructions should be read and attempted in full if you are unfamiliar with the use of spreadsheets. If you are confident with using spreadsheets check through the notes for any areas you may not have covered previously.

What is a spreadsheet?

A spreadsheet could be defined as a table of rows and columns that intersect to form cells.

- Each row is identified by a number.

- Each column is identified by a letter (or letters).

- Each cell has a unique identifier formed by a letter (or letters) and a number.

- Numbers, text or formulae may be entered into these cells.

- A formula normally involves a mathematical calculation on the content of other cells, the result being inserted in the cell containing the formula. These are not visible when you are entering data but reside in the background.

- Some or all of a spreadsheet can be printed out directly or saved on disk for insertion into reports or other documents using a word processing package.

Basic spreadsheet terms

Make sure you learn the following basic spreadsheet terms if you don't know them already.

- **Worksheet:** a worksheet or spreadsheet is the basis of all the work you do. It could be considered to be the electronic equivalent of an accountant's ledger.

- **Workbook:** is a collection of worksheets. The workbook is simply a folder that binds together your worksheets.

- **Columns:** each column is referenced by one or two letters in the column heading. The whole worksheet consists of 256 columns, labelled A through IV.

- **Rows:** each row is referenced by the row number shown in the row heading to the left of a row. There are 65,536 rows in Excel.

- **Cells:** The intersection of a column and a row is known as a 'cell'. To refer to a particular cell, use its column and row location. This is called a 'cell address', for example A1, B22, etc.

- **Sheet tabs:** these are between the worksheet and the status bar and are used to move between worksheets in your workbook.

- **Window:** you can only see part of the worksheet at any time; you could consider the screen to be a window onto the worksheet. You have the facility to move this window, so that you can view any part of the spreadsheet.

- **Cell pointer:** indicates the active cell on by highlighting the border around the cell

A good way of testing your understanding of spreadsheets in an examination is to ask you to select the correct definition of one of the basic spreadsheet terms from a list of possible options.

Running a spreadsheet program

The way to gain access to a spreadsheet package depends upon the type of computer system in use.

*   A **menu** may be available to allow access to the chosen software by entering a single number or letter or by use of a cursor or mouse.

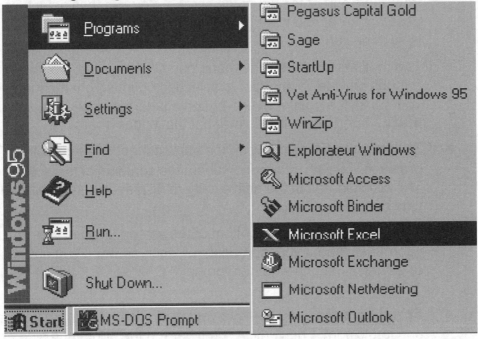

*   If you are working in a **Windows** environment, you will access the spreadsheet package using the mouse.

*   Click on the Start button in the bottom left hand corner of the Window.

*   Keep the mouse button depressed and highlight the 'Programs' and then the package that you want to use. Click on the icon.

*   The opening screen in Microsoft Excel might look like this.

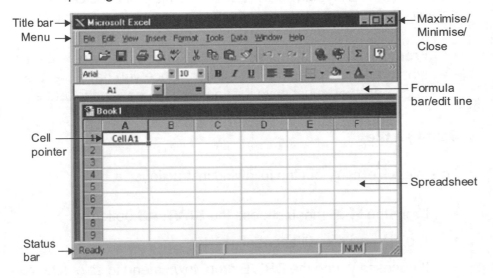

(Yours might look a little different if you have a different version of Excel).

- On the screen you will see the **title bar**, the **menu bar**, **the function tool bar** and in the top right corner the buttons to **minimise**, **maximise**/restore and close the worksheet. As with most Windows programs you can change the size and move the Excel Window.

- If your screen does not have a formula bar, a formatting bar or a toolbar you can show these by accessing **View** and then **Toolbars** from the menu at the top of the screen. You can then select (or deselect) what you want to show on the screen. A tick signifies that it is switched on.

- The toolbars are below the menu bar. Clicking on any of these buttons provides a shortcut to selecting options from the menu bar. If you pause the pointer over a button a label will appear and, in the **status bar**, Excel will tell you what that button does.

- The **formula bar** is between the spreadsheet and the toolbar. This provides you with information about the contents of the active cell. The co-ordinates of the active cell are displayed on the left-hand side of the formula bar.

- The **status bar** is at the bottom of the screen. It gives you information about your spreadsheet, such as when you are opening or saving a file and whether you have CAPS LOCK, NUM LOCK or SCROLL LOCK on.

- **Scroll bars** are used to move your spreadsheet both up and down and left to right. The vertical scroll bar (on the right hand side of the spreadsheet) is used to move up and down. The horizontal scroll bar (below the spreadsheet and above the status bar) is used to move left and right.

Creating a new file

When you first open Excel, a blank spreadsheet appears on the screen and you can start typing straight away. At this point you can work on an established spreadsheet or start on a new one by creating a file.

- From the file menu choose the NEW option, and a new Excel workbook will appear on the screen. Once you have created a document, you must save it if you wish to use it in the future.

Saving a file

To save a file, carry out the following instructions:

- From the **FILE** menu choose the **SAVE AS** option.

- A dialogue box will appear.

- If necessary, use the DRIVE drop down menu to select the relevant drive.

- In the **FILE NAME** text box type in the name you wish to use. All spreadsheet packages automatically add an extension to your filename.

- Click on the **OK** button.

- When you have saved a file once, you do not need to choose the **SAVE AS** option again, but simply choose **SAVE** from the **FILE** menu or click on the icon on the tool bar (picture of a floppy disk).

Closing a file/Quitting

When you have finished working on a spreadsheet and you have saved it, you will need to close it down.

- You can do this by either pressing the button at the top right hand side of the worksheet with a cross on it or by choosing the CLOSE or EXIT option from the FILE menu.

- If you only want to exit Excel briefly and prefer not to close down the whole package you can switch to another application or back to the Windows Program Manager by pressing <Alt><Tab> repeatedly. This allows you to step through all the opened packages in rotation.

- If you have changed the file, Excel will ask if you wish to save the changes you made before closing. Click on the appropriate button.

Moving directly to a cell: the GOTO command

Sometimes you may want to move to a specific address in the spreadsheet that is too far from your present position to warrant using the arrow keys to get there. On the top of the keyboard you can see a row of keys labelled F1 through to F12; these are known as 'function keys'.

- When the function keys are pressed, a special function is invoked. For example, the F5 key is the GOTO key in Excel.

- If you wish to go to cell D19, press F5 and a dialogue box will appear. You are prompted to enter an address or range. Enter D19 and the cell pointer will go directly to cell D19.

The help facility

Excel has a comprehensive help facility, which provides both **general** help and **context sensitive** help.

- To invoke the help command press the 'Help' button on the menu bar, the ? box on the toolbar or the shortcut key F1.

- To obtain information on any particular subject shown, move the mouse pointer over the required topic and click, or you may be prompted to type in a question.

- Context sensitive help is available either when a help button is displayed in a dialogue box or when an error message is flashed onto the screen.

- Asking for help at this stage by either clicking on the help button, ? box or by pressing F1 will result in the help window appearing at the topic relevant to the problem encountered.

Putting data onto a worksheet

Entering data on a worksheet is very easy. You simply type your entry, press return and whatever you typed will be placed in the current cell, i.e. where the cell pointer is.

- As you type, each character will be displayed on the edit line at the top of the screen. The entry is not put onto the worksheet until you press the return key.

- When you have finished entering data you can either press the <Enter> key on the keyboard or click on the Enter Box (a green tick) on the formula bar.

- If you change your mind about entering the data then either press the <Esc> key on the keyboard or click on the Cancel Box (a red cross) on the formula bar.

- If you have made a mistake, you can press the 'backspace key' (the key above the ENTER key) to delete what you have done one character at a time. If you have already pressed the ENTER key, you can delete it by highlighting the cell or cells and pressing the Delete key.

- There are three types of data that can be entered into your worksheet – text, numbers and formulae.

Entering text

Text is entered by simply typing into a cell. Typing any letter at the beginning of a cell entry causes it to be accepted as a 'label', rather than a 'value'.

- If the text you enter is longer than the width of the cell then the text will 'run over' into the next cell. But if the next cell also contains data/information then you will only see part of the text you entered, i.e. the label will be truncated.

- There will be times when you want a spreadsheet to treat a number or a formula as text. To do this you must type an apostrophe in front of the number or formula you are entering, e.g. '01707 320903 or '=A4+D5.

Entering numbers

Numbers can be entered on a spreadsheet by simply typing into a cell.

- If the space in the cell is insufficient, the number will be shown in an exponential form on the spreadsheet, but the number will still be retained in full in the formula bar.

- If you want to see the contents of cells in full, the columns can be widened to accommodate the number (or text).

- It is not necessary to put the commas in manually when entering large numbers (1,000 or more), because it is easy to format the data to display commas and decimal places to make the data easier to understand. For example:

    - if you wish to enter 123,456, enter 123456 into a cell and press Enter

    - move the cursor back onto that cell, click on 'Format' in the menu bar, then 'Cells'

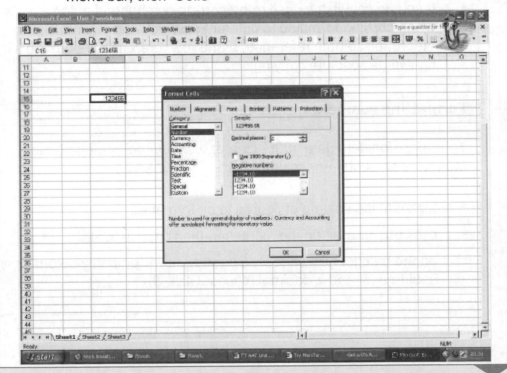

- choose the 'Number' tab and then 'Number' from the category list

- now reduce the decimal places to '0' by clicking on the down arrow and tick the 'Use 1000 separator' box

- press OK. Your number should now be shown as 123,456

- you can also use the 'Currency' option from the category list to put $s in front.

Cut, Copy and Paste

- **Cut** then **paste** is used to **move** cells from one area of the spreadsheet to another.

- **Copy** then **paste** is used to **copy** cells from one area to another.

- Copying and pasting or cutting and pasting operations always have two parts:

  - define the range you want to copy or cut **from**; then

  - define the range that you want to copy or move to.

- You can copy formulae to different cells by the same method. Note that the cell references change automatically when formulae are copied – this is known as relative copying.

- If you do not wish for cell references to be changed automatically when copying formulae to different cells you can insert $ signs before the column reference, or the row reference or both. This is known as absolute copying.

Formatting numbers

To make monetary data 100% clearer it should be formatted into monetary amounts. For columns with a '$' at the top:

- highlight the column of figures to be formatted

- click on 'Format' on the menu bar, then choose 'Cells'

- on the category list choose 'Currency'. It will probably automatically assign a '$' and 2 decimal places. Click OK.

Formatting text

Making a spreadsheet look good is more than just a cosmetic exercise. Proper formatting, underlining and emboldening can make the spreadsheet easier to follow, draw attention to important figures and reduce the chance of errors.

- For example, to change the font to Times New Roman throughout a spreadsheet: click on the first cell with an entry in it and drag the mouse to the last cell with an entry in it. The area covered should be shaded. Go to the Format menu and select Cells. Select the Font tab and then the chosen style.

- For example, to put titles in bold: click and drag the cursor over them, then click on the **B** button (**B**old) on the tool bar. Alternatively, all entries in a row or column can be selected by clicking on the letter at the head of the column or the number at the very left of the row.

- For example, to change the width of a column: place the mouse pointer in the column heading at the intersection and a two headed arrow should appear. Drag this to the right until the column is wide enough. Adjust the width of the other columns to accommodate the entries comfortably.

- For example, to align column headings use the align buttons on the formatting toolbar (to the right of the underline U).

- For example, to underline totals by highlighting the cells containing the totals: click on 'Format' on the menu bar, then click on 'Cells' then 'Border' tab, and a window similar to the following will appear.

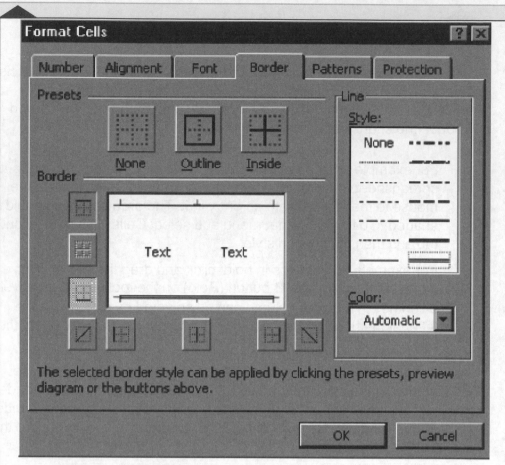

- The box on the left shows the edges of the cell or selection of cells, which will have a border.

- The box on the right shows the types of lines that are available.

- Click on the top line on the left-hand list and then on the single, non-bold line (probably already selected) in the right hand options.

- The top of the 'totals' cells should now have a single underlining.

- Now click on the bottom line and then on the double under-lining style. Click on OK.

Test your understanding 1

Which of the following is not an advantage of spreadsheet software over manual approaches?

A   Security

B   Speed

C   Accuracy

D   Legibility

Test your understanding 2

Angelina wants to calculate the expected value of the following cash flows using a spreadsheet

	A	B	C
1	Cash flow	Probability	CF × probability
2	250	0.3	
3	350	0.2	
4	450	0.4	
5	600	0.1	
6	Total	1	

What should the formulae be in

A   Cell C3

B   Cell C6?

Test your understanding 3

The following spreadsheet has been set up to look at the relationship between 20 sets of data relating to production volume (x) and costs (y).

		A	B	C	D	E
1		x	y	xy	x^2	y^2
25	Totals					

What formula is required to calculate the variable cost per unit?

Test your understanding 4

A company manufactures a single product. In a computer spreadsheet, the cells C1 to C12 contain the budgeted monthly sales units for the twelve months of next year in sequence with January sales in cell C1 and finishing with December sales in cell C12. The company policy is for closing inventory of finished goods each month to be 10% of the budgeted sales units for the following month.

Which of the following formulae will generate the budgeted production (in units) for May next year?

A = [(C5 + (0.1* C6)]

B = [(C5 – (0.1* C6)]

C = [(1.1*C5) – (0.1* C6)]

D = [(0.9*C5) + (0.1* C6)]

Test your understanding answers

Test your understanding 1

A   A computer-based approach exposes the firm to threats from viruses, hackers and general system failure.

Test your understanding 2

A   C3 = A3*B3

B   C6 = SUM(C2:C5)

Test your understanding 3

The variable cost per unit is the gradient ("b") of the linear regression line, given in this case by

$$b = \frac{n\Sigma xy - (\Sigma x)(\Sigma y)}{n\Sigma x2 - (\Sigma x)} = (20*C25 - A25*B25)/(20*D25 - A25^2)$$

Test your understanding 4

Answer D

	April	May	June
Sales	C4	C5	C6
Less opening inventory		−C5 × 0.1	
Closing inventory		C6 × 0.1	
Production		(C5 × 0.9) + (C6 × 0.1)	

Questions

Chapter 1: The nature and purpose of management accounting

(1) **Data is information that has been processed in such a way as to make it meaningful for use by management in making decisions.**

Is this statement TRUE or FALSE?

A   True

B   False

(2) **Which of the following is not a fundamental attribute of good information?**

A   Complete

B   Concise

C   Cost effective

(3) **Good information should be:**

(i)   Relevant

(ii) Timely

(iii) Accurate

(iv) Motivating

A   (i) and (ii)

B   All of them

C   (ii), (iii) and (iv)

D   (i) (ii) and (iii)

(4) **Which of the following steps does not form part of the planning process?**

A   Set objectives for achievement

B   Identify ways in which objectives can be achieved

C   Take corrective action to improve chances of achieving objectives

(5) **Which of the following is the appropriate name for planning which considers how the functional heads within a business unit will coordinate employees on a day-to-day basis?**

A   Strategic planning

B   Tactical planning

C   Operational planning

(6) **The manager of a division is responsible for costs and revenues as well as capital invested?**

Which is the appropriate classification for the division?

A   Revenue centre

B   Investment centre

C   Profit centre

D   Cost centre

(7) **The following assertions relate to management accounting:**

(i)   The purpose of management accounting is to provide accounting information to the managers of the business and other internal users.

(ii) Management accounts are only concerned with the cost of goods, services and operations.

Which of the following statements are true?

A   Assertion (i) and)ii) are both correct

B   Only assertion (i) is correct

C   Only assertion (ii) is correct

Chapter 2: Sources of data

(8) **If you choose the 10th or the 100th unit after the first has been chosen. This type of sampling is known as:**

A   Simple random

B   Stratified

C   Cluster

D   Systematic

(9) **Which of the following is an example of external information?**

A   Payroll system

B   Government statistics

C   Accounting system

D   Strategic planning system

(10) If you select a sample for a national opinion poll prior to a general election. The process would start by dividing the country into areas and a random sample of areas is taken. Next divide the country into town and cities and a sample is taken again. Then perhaps a sample of streets and a random sample of houses are then chosen. This is an example of which type of sampling:

A   Simple

B   Random

C   Multi-stage

D   Cluster

(11) Here are possible reasons why sampling is used over other methods of gathering data?

(i)   The whole population may not be known

(ii) Testing all items in a population may not be possible

(iii) Items may be destroyed in the testing process

Which of the statements are correct?

A   (i), (ii) and (iii)

B   (ii) and (iii)

C   (i) and (ii)

D   (iii) only

(12) When sampling a population if there are several well defined groups which method would be used?

A   Random sampling

B   Systematic sampling

C   Stratified sampling

D   Quota sampling

KAPLAN PUBLISHING

Chapter 3: Presenting information

(13) **What type of graph is this?**

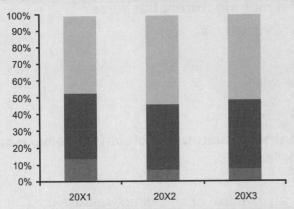

A   line graph

B   compound bar chart

C   percentage compound bar chart

D   percentage component bar chart

(14) **Below is a pie chart showing the colours of shirts ordered by one shop.**

Shirt colours

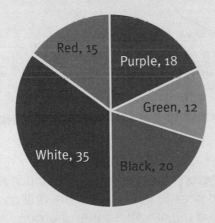

What is the angle of the wedge showing black shirts ordered?

A   44°

B   54°

C   65°

D   72°

Chapter 4: Types of cost and cost behaviour

(15) **Which of the following costs should not be included in the inventory valuation of a manufacturing business?**

A   Depreciation on the plant and machinery

B   Salary of salesman

C   Factory supervisor's salary

D   Electricity for factory

(16) **A shop carries out repairs on customers' electrical items, e.g. televisions, video recorders, etc.**

Which of the following is an example of an indirect variable cost?

A   Business rates for repair shop

B   Salary of repair shop supervisor

C   Repair person paid per hour worked

D   Electricity for recharging repair tools

(17) **The following diagram represents a cost behaviour pattern.**

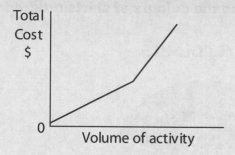

Which of the following statements is consistent with the above diagram?

A   Annual factory costs when the electricity supplier sets a tariff based on a fixed charge plus a constant unit cost for consumption but subject to a maximum annual charge

B   Weekly total labour cost when workers are paid an hourly wage during normal working hours and a higher hourly rate if they are required to work outside those hours

C   Total direct material cost for a period if the supplier charges a lower unit cost on all units once a certain quantity has been purchased in that period

D   Total direct material cost for a period if the supplier has agreed to a maximum charge for that period

(18) **The following diagram represents a cost behaviour pattern.**

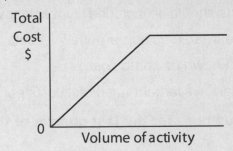

Which of the following statements is consistent with the above diagram?

A   Annual factory costs when the electricity supplier sets a tariff based on a fixed charge plus a constant unit cost for consumption but subject to a maximum annual charge

B   Weekly total labour cost when workers are paid an hourly wage during normal working hours and a higher hourly rate if they are required to work outside those hours

C   Total direct material cost for a period if the supplier charges a lower unit cost on all units once a certain quantity has been purchased in that period

D   Total direct material cost for a period if the supplier has agreed to a maximum charge for that period

(19) **The telephone costs of a business are likely to be classified as a stepped fixed cost.**
Is this statement TRUE or FALSE?

A   True

B   False

(20) **A company has a performance related pay scheme in operation.**

What is the most appropriate cost classification for the salaries of the managers?

A   Fixed cost

B   Stepped fixed cost

C   Semi-variable cost

(21) **Which of the following statements is correct?**

   A   Only direct production costs should be included in inventory valuation

   B   All indirect costs should be treated as non-production costs.

   C   The sum of direct costs is known as prime cost.

   D   Indirect costs per unit are always larger than direct costs per unit

(22) **The costs and output of a business for the last quarter of the year were as follows:**

	Output (units)	Cost ($)
Oct	1,800	8,850
Nov	2,000	8,750
Dec	800	3,950

Using the high low method which of the following represents the estimated cost in January of producing 1,500 units if the monthly fixed costs are expected to increase by $100 at the start of next year?

   A $6,750

   B $6,850

   C $7,380

   D $7,480

(23) **A business has experienced the following labour costs:**

Output (units)	Cost ($)
7,000	86,000
12,000	141,000
9,000	102,000

Fixed costs increase by $15,000 for output in excess of 10,000 units.

Using the high low method what is the estimated cost of producing 14,000 units ?

   A $142,000

   B $157,000

   C $163,000

   D $178,000

Chapter 5: Accounting for inventory

(24) **Which of the following could be used to document the transfer of materials from one production department to another?**

    A   Materials requisition note

    B   Materials returned note

    C   Materials transfer note

(25) **The following represent the materials transactions for a company for a year:**

	$000
Materials purchases	240
Issued to production	215
Materials written off	12
Returned to stores	6
Returned to suppliers	2

The material inventory at 31 December 20X1 was $42,000.

What was the opening balance on the materials inventory account at 1 January 20X1?

    A $1,000

    B $25,000

    C $33,000

    D $59,000

(26) **Continuous stocktaking is the process of checking the balance of every item of inventory on the same date, usually at the end of an accounting period.**

Is this statement TRUE or FALSE?

    A   True

    B   False

This information is relevant for TYUs 27–32.

A business has inventory of material A of 400 units valued at $2.20 per unit at 1 September. During the month of September the movements of material A were as follows:

5 September	Issue	250 units
10 September	Receipt	500 units @ $2.50 per unit
15 September	Issue	340 units
18 September	Receipt	400 units @ $2.70 per unit
27 September	Issue	600 units

(27) **What is the cost of issues using the FIFO method?**

    A $2,913

    B $2,980

    C $2,975

    D $2,990

(28) **What is the value of the closing inventory using the FIFO method?**

    A $242

    B $251

    C $286

    D $297

(29) **What is the value of issues using the LIFO method?**

    A $2,913

    B $2,924

    C $2,980

    D $2,968

(30) **What is the value of closing inventory using the LIFO method?**

    A $242

    B $251

    C $286

    D $297

(31) **What is the cost of issues using the weighted average cost method?**

    A $2,913

    B $2,926

    C $2,980

    D $2,968

(32) **What is the value of closing inventory using the weighted average cost method?**

    A $242

    B $251

    C $284

    D $297

(33) **The objective of holding buffer inventory is to take advantage of quantity discounts.**

Is this statement TRUE or FALSE ?

    A   True

    B   False

(34) **Which of the following is not a stockholding cost:**

    A   The opportunity cost of capital tied up

    B   The cost of insurance

    C   Shipping and handling costs

    D   Inventory obsolescence

(35) **A manufacturer uses 100,000 components costing $1each at a constant rate throughout the year. The cost of making a single order for more components is $10 and the holding costs for each component are 0.5% of the average inventory value.**

What is the EOQ?

    A   1,411

    B   14,142

    C   20,000

(36) **A retailer has a steady demand for rugby balls at 50 a month. Each ball costs $6 from the supplier. The costs involved in placing an order are $10 and the stockholding costs are 20% of the stockholding value per annum.**

How many orders will be placed per annum?

    A   1.73

    B   6

    C   8.48

    D   100

(37) Annual demand for raw material is 1,000,000 units. Each unit costs 15 cents. Procurement costs for each order are $20 and lead time has been estimated as 2 days. There are 250 working days per annum, the carrying cost of inventory is 10 cents per unit and the cost of a stockout is 20 cents per unit. What is the optimal reorder level?

A   125

B   8,000

C   20,000

Chapter 6: Accounting for labour

(38) Which of the following should be classified as direct labour?

A   The site foreman of a building company

B   Workers assembling components on a production line

C   The storeman handling parts requisitions in a factory.

(39) A company employs 100 direct workers in the factory, who are paid a basic rate of $5 per hour for a 35 hour week. In addition to working their normal hours last month, each worker was asked to work an additional 5 hours overtime per week to meet general production requirements. All overtime hours are paid at time and a half. As a result of some faulty material, 150 hours of direct labour time were registered as idle.

What is the indirect labour cost for last month, assuming a 4 week period?

A $750

B $2,000

C $5,750

D $15,750

(40) An employee receives a bonus according to the Rowan scheme. The employee's basic rate of pay is $6 per hour. The allowed time for the job was 1 hour and the employee completed it in 40 minutes.

What is the total payment for the job (to the nearest cent) ?

A $1.33

B $ 4.00

C $ 5.00

D $ 5.33

(41) At 31 March 20X1 an organisation had 5,400 employees. During the previous year 750 had left the organisation, although the management had decided that only 600 needed replacing and had recruited accordingly.

What was the labour turnover rate for the year to 31 March 20X1 (to 2 decimal places)?

A   10.96%

B   11.11%

C   11.27%

D   13.89%

(42) The data below relates to last month's production of product Z:

Standard time allowed per unit = 20 minutes

Budgeted hours available = 210 hours

Actual output = 600 units in 220 hours

Which of the following is the correct labour capacity and efficiency ratio?

	Labour capacity	Labour efficiency
A	95.24%	90.91%
B	95.24%	104.76%
C	104.76%	90.91%
D	104.76%	95.24%

Chapter 7: Accounting for overheads

(43) A company manufactures two products, E and F, in a factory divided into two production cost centres, Primary and Finishing. In order to determine a budgeted fixed overhead cost per unit of product, the following budgeted data are relevant.

	Primary	Finishing
Allocated and apportioned fixed costs	$84,000	$93,000
Direct labour – minutes per unit		
E	36	25 = 61
F	30	40 = 70
	66	65

Total

549,000

420,000

_____

969,000

Budgeted production is 9,000 units of E and 6,000 units of F. Fixed overheads are to be absorbed on a direct labour hour basis.

What is the budgeted fixed overhead cost of a unit of product E?

A $10

B $11

C $12

D $13

(44) **Billecarte Ltd manufactures two products, Zonk and Tink, in a factory divided into two production cost centres, Machining and Assembly. In order to find a fixed overhead cost per unit, the following budgeted data are relevant.**

	Machining	Assembly
Direct and allocated fixed costs	$120,000	$72,000
Labour hours per unit		
Zonk	0.50 hours	0.20 hours
Tink	1.00 hours	0.25 hours

Budgeted production is 4,000 units of each product (8,000 units in all) and fixed overheads are to be absorbed by reference to labour hours.

What should be the budgeted fixed overhead cost of a unit of Zonk?

A $28

B $24

C $20

D $18

(45) **Products alpha and beta are made in a factory that has two production cost centres: assembly and finishing. Budgeted production is 8,000 alpha and 10,000 beta. Fixed overheads are absorbed on a labour hour basis.**

The following budgeted information is available:

	Production	Finishing
Allocated and apportioned fixed costs	$ 55,000	$ 63,000
Direct labour hours per unit		
Product alpha	1.5 hrs	2 hrs
Product beta	1 hr	0.5 hrs

What is the budgeted fixed cost per unit for product beta?

A $3.46

B $4.00

C $9.75

D $10.425

(46) **Here are three statements on the determination of overhead absorption rates:**

(1)   Costs can be allocated where it is possible to identify the department that caused them.

(2)   Costs need to be apportioned where they are shared by more than one department.

(3)   Service centre costs should not be included in unit overhead costs.

Which of these statements are correct?

A   (1) and (2) only

B   (1) and (3) only

C   (2) and (3) only

D   (1), (2) and (3)

(47) **The following statements refer to overhead absorption:**

(1)   Factory rent and rates are typically allocated to departments rather than apportioned.

(2)   A single product firm does not need to apportion overheads to find a cost per unit.

(3)   If departmental overhead recovery rates are similar it makes little difference if overheads are applied on a departmental or business wide basis.

Which of these statements are correct?

A   (1) and (2) only

B   (1) and (3) only

C   (2) and (3) only

D   (1), (2) and (3)

(48) **A manufacturing company has the following budgeted and actual results for the year:**

Budgeted fixed overhead expenditure	$504,000
Budgeted activity	42,000 machine hours
Actual fixed overhead expenditure	$515,000
Actual activity	45,000 machine hours

What is the result of using the pre-determined fixed overhead rate for the year?

A $11,000 under-absorbed

B $25,000 under-absorbed

C $25,000 over-absorbed

D $36,000 over-absorbed

(49) **A manufacturing organisation has two production departments (Machining and finishing) and two service departments (Quality control and Maintenance). After primary apportionment the overheads for the factory are as follows: What is the total overhead to be apportioned to the Finishing department?**

	Total	Machining	Finishing	QC	Maintenance
Overheads	$633,000	$220,000	$160,000	$140,000	$113,000
Work done by QC		45%	35%	–	20%
Work done by Maint'ce		30%	40%	30%	–

A $124,750

B $284,750

C $285,821

D $348,250

Chapter 8: Marginal and absorption costing

(50) **The following statements relate to costing and overheads:**

(i)   Products create a demand for support activities in service cost centres in direct proportion to the volume of each product manufactured   *NOT TRUE*

(ii) Where overheads form a large proportion of total costs, then the arbitrary nature of apportionment is more of an issue

(iii) When closing inventory levels are lower than opening inventory levels, marginal costing gives a lower profit than absorption costing   *NOT TRUE*

(iv) Only fixed and variable production costs should be included in unit costs for inventory valuation purposes under absorption costing

Which TWO of the statements are correct?

A   Statements (i) and (iii)

B   Statements (i) and (iv)

C   Statements (ii) and (iii)

D   Statements (ii) and (iv)

(51) **The number of units of finished goods inventory at the end of a period is greater than at the beginning.**

What would the effect be of using the marginal costing method of inventory valuation?

A   less operating profit than the absorption costing method

B   the same operating profit as the absorption costing method

C   more operating profit than the absorption costing method

D   more or less operating profit than the absorption costing method depending on the ratio of fixed to variable costs

(52) **Accounting standards support the use of the marginal costing approach to inventory valuation when preparing the published accounts of a company, as it achieves a better matching of sales and expenses for the period.**

Is this statement TRUE or FALSE?

A   True

B   False

FALSE AS MC DOES NOT TAKE INTO ACCOUNT FIXED OH SO IT CANT BE A BETTER MATCH OF SALES AND EXPENSES!

(53) **A business has just completed its first year of trading. The following information has been collected from the accounting records.**

	$
Variable cost per unit	
Manufacturing	6.00
Selling and administration	0.20
Fixed costs	
Manufacturing	90,000
Selling and administration	22,500

Production was 75,000 units and sales were 70,000 units. The selling price was $8 per unit throughout the year.

What is the difference in profit using marginal costing for inventory valuation, rather than absorption costing?

A $8,500

B $7,500

C $6,000 ✓

D $2,500

Handwritten annotations:
$Fixed = 90,000 + (6.20 \times 75000) = 555,000 \quad 121,000$
$Marg = 6.2 \times 5000 \quad = 34,000$
$\frac{90,000}{75000} \times 5000 = 6000$

Chapter 9: Job, batch and process costing

(54) **The cost of output goods is found by calculating the net costs of the manufacturing process and dividing by the number of units produced.**

What is this approach known as?

A   Job costing

B   Batch costing

C   Process costing

(55) **Which one of the following industries is most likely to use batch costing as the method for establishing the cost of products?**

A   Car repairs

B   Clothing

C   Oil refining

(56) **The following statements refer to calculating the cost of a unit of output:**

(1) In process and batch costing the cost per unit of output is found by dividing total costs by the number of units produced.

(2) In process and job costing the cost per unit of output is found directly by accumulating costs for each unit.

Which of the following is true?

A   Only statement (1) is correct.

B   Only statement (2) is correct.

C   Both statement (1) and statement (2) are correct.

(57) **The following data relates to a process for the month of May:**

	$
Input materials (500 litres)	3,000
Labour and overhead	2,670

Normal output is expected to be 9 litres for every 10 litres input.

Actual output was 460 litres.

What is the cost per unit of finished output (to 2 decimal places)?

A $11.33

B $11.67

C $12.33

D $12.60

(58) **4,000kg of material are input to a chemical process. Normal losses are expected to be 10% of input and because of their toxic nature will incur a disposal cost of $2 per kg.**

The process cost $11,800 and actual output was 3,550kg

What is the total cost of the abnormal loss (to the nearest $)?

A $53

B $153

C $175

D $275

The following information available for a process for the month of December relates to questions 59 and 60.

WIP @ 1 December	12,000 units (40% converted) Material element $33,600 Conversion costs $22,980
Materials added	48,000 units at a cost of $144,000
Conversion costs	$307,500
WIP @ 31 December	15,000 units (60% converted)

All material is input at the start of the process whereas conversion occurs evenly through the process.

(59) **What is the value of closing WIP at 31 December, using the Weighted average method of valuation?**

A $84,680

B $99,480

C $101,250

D $136,200

(60) **What is the value of finished production in December, using the FIFO method of valuation?**

A $305,250

B $406,830

C $408,600

D $416,250

(61) **Which of the following is not a possible method of apportioning the joint costs of a manufacturing process?**

A   Physical quantity

B   Market value at point of separation

C   Carrying amount

Chapter 10: Service and operation costing

(62) **The principles used to calculate unit costs in manufacturing industries can equally be applied to service industries.**

Is this statement TRUE or FALSE?

A   True

B   False

(63) **Which of the following would not be an appropriate situation for the use of service costing?**

A   Power supply industry

B   Oil refinery

C   Restaurant in a factory

D   Haulage business

(64) **Which of the following statistics is unlikely to be used by the Rooms department of a hotel business?**

A   Room occupancy

B   Cleaning cost per room

C   Meals served per guest

D   Average cost per occupied bed

(65) **Many service applications involve high fixed costs and the higher the number of cost units produced the higher the fixed costs per unit.**

Is this statement TRUE or FALSE?

A   True

B   False

(66) **A transport business has 6 lorries in operation, 5 days a week for 50 weeks of the year.**

Each vehicle is expected to make 4 journeys a day, delivering an average load of 5 tonnes to each customer. The average customer is located 25 kilometres from the transport headquarters. Fuel and other variable running costs per kilometre travelled (laden or unladen) are budgeted to be $0.50. Other fixed running costs amount to $225,000 per annum.

What is the standard running cost per tonne kilometre?

A $0.45

B $0.50

C $0.77

D $1.25

Chapter 11: Alternative costing principles

(67) **Which ONE of the following is an advantage of Activity Based Costing?**

A   It provides more accurate product costs

B   It is simple to apply

C   It is a form of marginal costing and so is relevant to decision making

D   It is particularly useful when fixed overheads are very low

(68) **Quality control costs can be categorised into internal and external failure costs, appraisal costs and prevention costs. In which of these four classifications would the following costs be included?**

–   The costs of a customer service team

–   The cost of equipment maintenance

–   The cost of operating test equipment

	Customer service team	Equipment maintenance	Test Equipment
A	Prevention costs	Appraisal costs ✓	Internal failure costs
B	Prevention costs	Internal failure costs	Appraisal costs
C	External failure costs	Internal failure costs	Prevention costs
D	External failure costs	Prevention costs ✓	Appraisal costs ✓

(69) **In calculating the life cycle costs of a product, which of the following items would be excluded?**

(i)   Planning and concept design costs

(ii)   Preliminary and detailed design costs

(iii) Testing costs

(iv) Production costs

(v)   Distribution and customer service costs

A   (iii)

B   (iv)

C   (v)

D   None of them

(70) **As part of a process to achieve a target cost, GYE Inc are interviewing prospective customers to determine why they would buy the product and how they would use it. What term best describes this process?**

A   Value analysis

B   Operational research

C   TQM

D   Lifecycle costing

Chapter 12: Forecasting techniques

(71) **Regression analysis has been used to find the line of best fit for two variables, x and y and the correlation coefficient has then been calculated to assess the reliability of the line as a forecasting tool.**

What is the value of the correlation coefficient for the line that will provide the most reliable forecast?

A   −0.9

B   0

C   +0.2

(72) **Using the data below, calculate the price index for 2003.**

Year	Selling price $	Index
2000	22	100
2001	23	
2002	26	
2003	25	
2004	28	

A   105

B   118

C   114

D   127

(73) **Using the information below, restate the 2006 revenue to 2008 prices**.

Year	Revenue ($000)	Index
2004	1,150	100
2005	1,250	115
2006	1,200	130
2007	1,250	115
2008	1,300	140

A   1,610

B   1,522

C   1,400

D   1,292

The following data relate to Questions 74 and 75

H is forecasting its sales for next year using a combination of time series and regression analysis models. An analysis of past sales units has produced the following equation for the quarterly sales trend:

$$y = 26x + 8{,}850$$

where the value of x represents the quarterly accounting period and the value of y represents the quarterly sales trend in units. Quarter 1 of next year will have a value for x of 25.

The quarterly seasonal variations have been measured using the multiplicative (proportional) model and are:

Quarter 1 – 15%
Quarter 2 – 5%
Quarter 3 + 5%
Quarter 4 + 15%

Production is planned to occur at a constant rate throughout the year.

The company does not hold inventories at the end of any year.

(74) **The difference between the budgeted sales for quarter 1 and quarter 4 next year are:**

A   78 units

B   2,850 units

C   2,862 units

D   2,940 units

(75) **The number of units to be produced in each quarter of next year will be nearest to:**

A   9,454 units

B   9,493 units

C   9,532 units

D   9,543 units

(76) **Z plc has found that it can estimate future sales using time series analysis and regression techniques.**

The following trend equation has been derived:

$$y = 25,000 + 6,500x$$

where:

y is the total sales units per quarter
x is the time period reference number

Using the above model, what is the forecast for sales units for the third quarter of year 7, assuming that the first quarter of year 1 is time period reference number 1.

A   194,000 units

B   200,500 units

C   207,000 units

D   213,500 units

(77) **Regression analysis has been used to calculate the line of best fit from a series of data. Using this line to predict a value which lies between the two extreme values observed historically is known as extrapolation.**

Is this statement TRUE or FALSE?

A   True

B   False

(78) **Regression analysis has produced the following results from the batch production costs for each of the past 5 months.**

$\Sigma x = 540$, $\Sigma y = 755$, $\Sigma x^2 = 61{,}000$, $\Sigma xy = 83{,}920$

Which of the following is the appropriate value for b in the regression line to 2 decimal places?

A   −1.40

B   0.01

C   0.89

D   1.40

(79) **A company is preparing its budgets for next year. The following regression equation has been found to be a reliable estimate of XYZ's deseasonalised sales in units:**

y = 10x + 150

Where y = total sales units and x refers to the accountancy period.

What is the expected figure for actual sales in accounting period 19?

A   255

B   315

C   340

Chapter 13: Budgeting

(80) **The following statements relate to budgeting:**

(i)   A forecast is an attempt to predict what will happen

(ii) A budget is a plan of what is intended to happen

(iii) All budgets are prepared in financial terms

(iv) The master budget consists of a budgeted income statement and budgeted statement of financial position

(v)   A flexible budget adjusts both fixed and variable costs for the level of activity

Which of the following is true?

A   All statements are correct

B   Statements (i) and (ii) are correct

C   Statements (ii), (iii) and (iv) are correct

D   Statements (i), (iii) and (v) are correct

(81) **Which of the following statements is true?**

A   The principal budget factor is the person who is responsible for controlling and coordinating the budget process

B   A business must always produce its sales budget first, before any other budgets can be decided on

C   The budget committee consists of managers with final responsibility for agreeing the budget

(82) **An organisation is preparing its quarterly budget. It has consistently maintained inventory levels at 10% of the following month's sales. Budgeted sales for January are 2,000 units and sales are expected to increase by 500 units per month for the following three months.**

What is the budgeted production in units for February?

A   2,050

B   2,450

C   2,500

D   2,550

(83) **The management accountant is preparing the master budget for her retail firm. The following information has been supplied.**

Sales	$300,000
Opening inventory	$40,000
Closing inventory	$60,000
Required profit	20%

What amount should be budgeted for purchases?

A $220,000

B $225,000

C $240,000

D $260,000

(84) **An extract from next year's budget for a manufacturing company is shown below.**

	Month 3	Month 4
Sales	100,000units	120,000units
Closing inventory of finished goods	6,000units	8,000units
Closing inventory of raw materials	22,000kg	12,000kg

Each unit requires 2kg material.

What is the budgeted material usage for month 4?

A   230,000 kg

B   234,000 kg

C   240,000 kg

D   244,000 kg

(85) **The following information has been supplied in connection with an organisation's labour and overhead budget:**

	Product alpha Cost per unit	Product beta Cost per unit
	$	$
Unskilled labour (@$5/hr)	15	10
Skilled labour (@ $8/hr)	16	24
	—	—
Total labour cost	31	34
	—	—
Budgeted production	8,000 units	12,000 units

What is the total amount of skilled labour hours required in the period?

A   40,000 hours

B   48,000 hours

C   52,000 hours

D   60,000 hours

(86) **Performance-related pay involves:**

A   rewarding employees with a proportion of total profits

B   rewarding employees with a proportion of total profits in excess of a target minimum level

C   rewarding employees on the basis of the amount of work they have done

D   rewarding employees for achieving agreed personal targets

(87) **In the context of budget preparation the term 'goal congruence' is:**

A   the alignment of budgets with objectives using feed-forward control

B   the setting of a budget which does not include budget bias

C   the alignment of corporate objectives with the personal objectives of a manager

D   the use of aspiration levels to set efficiency targets

(88) **Which of the following statements about imposed budgets are correct?**

(i)   Imposed budgets are likely to set realistic targets because senior management have the best idea of what is achievable in each part of the business.

(ii)   Imposed budgets can be less effective than budgets set on a participative basis, because it is difficult for an individual to be motivated to achieve targets set by someone else.

(iii) Imposed budgets are generally quicker to prepare and finalise than participative budgets.

A   (i) and (ii) only

B   (i) and (iii) only

C   (ii) and (iii) only

D   (iii) only

(89) **A flexible budget is**

A   a budget for semi-variable overhead costs only;

B   a budget which, by recognising different cost behaviour patterns, is designed to change as volume of activity changes;

C   a budget for a twelve month period which includes planned revenues, expenses, assets and liabilities;

D   a budget which is prepared for a rolling period which is reviewed monthly, and updated accordingly.

(90) **A purpose of a flexible budget is:**

A   to cap discretionary expenditure

B   to produce a revised forecast by changing the original budget when actual costs are known

C   to control resource efficiency

D   to communicate target activity levels within an organisation by setting a budget in advance of the period to which it relates.

(91) **A fixed budget is:**

A   a budget for a single level of activity

B   used when the mix of products is fixed in advance of the budget period

C   a budget which ignores inflation

D   an overhead cost budget.

(92) **In a responsibility accounting system for which of the following should the production line manager be held responsible?**

A   Raw material prices and labour wage rates

B   Raw material usage and labour wage rates

C   Raw material prices and labour hours worked

D   Raw material usage and labour hours worked

Chapter 14: Captital Budgeting

(93) **A company is evaluating a new product proposal that will last 6 years.**

The initial outlay is $2 million. The proposed product selling price is $220 per unit and the variable costs are $55 per unit and sales are planned to be 2,750 units each year. The incremental cash fixed costs for the product will be $3,750 per annum.

What is the NPV of this project is the cost of capital is 10%.

A $40,250

B   −$40,250

C $190,600

D   −£190,600

(94) **The details of an investment project are as follows:**

Cost of asset bought at the start of the project $80,000
Annual cash inflow $25,000
Cost of capital 5% each year
Life of the project 8 years

The present value of the cash flows that occur in the second year of the project is:

A $23,800

B $22,675

C $21,000

D $20,575

The following data relates to Questions 95 and 96.

Year	Item	Cash flow
0	Cost of machine	(50,000)
1	Net cash flow from sales	22,000
2	Net cash flow from sales	22,000
3	Net cash flow from sales	20,000

A company uses a cost of capital of 10%. Assume all cash flows accrue evenly through the year.

(95) **What is the payback period of the data above:**

A   1 year 4 months

B   1 year 10 months

C   2 years 4 months

D   2 years 10 months

(96) **What is discounted payback of the data above:**

A   1 year 4 months

B   1 year 10 months

C   2 years 4 months

D   2 years 10 months

(97) **An education authority is considering the implementation of a CCTV (closed circuit television) security system in one of its schools. Details of the proposed project are as follows:**

Life of project 5 years
Initial cost $75,000
Annual savings:
Labour costs $20,000
Other costs $5,000
Cost of capital 15% per annum

What is the internal rate of return for this project?

A   20.1%

B   19.9%

C   19.1%

D   18.9%

(98) **The details of an investment project are:**

Life of the project 10 years
Cost of asset bought at the start of the project $100,000
Annual cash inflow $20,000
Cost of capital 8% each year

What is the payback of the cash flows that occur?

A $34,200

B $100,000

C   5 years

D   6 years and 8 months

(99) **A company has determined that the net present value of an investment project is $12,304 when using a 10% discount rate and $(3,216) when using a discount rate of 15%.**

What is the internal rate of return of the project to the nearest 1%?

A   13%

B   14%

C   16%

D   17%

(100)**An investment project with no residual value has a net present value of $87,980 when it is discounted using a cost of capital of 10%. The annual cash flows are as follows:**

Year	$
0	(200,000)
1	80,000
2	90,000
3	100,000
4	60,000
5	40,000

Calculate the Internal Rate of Return (IRR) of the project.

A   17.3%

B   17.9%

C   18.3%

D   18.9%

The following data relates to Questions 101 to 103.

M plc is evaluating three possible investment projects and uses a 10% discount rate to determine their net present values.

Investment	A	B	C
	$000	$000	$000
Initial investment	400	450	350
Incremental cash flows			
Year 1	100	130	50
Year 2	120	130	110
Year 3	140	130	130
Year 4	120	130	150
Year 5	100	150	100
Net present value	39	55	48

(101)**What is the payback period of investment A?**

A   3 years

B   3 years 4 months

C   4 years

D   4 years 4 months

(102) **What is the discounted payback period of investment B?**

    A   3 years 1 month

    B   3 years 6 months

    C   4 years 5 months

    D   4 years 8 months

(103) **What is the Internal Rate of Return (IRR) of investment C?**

    A   12.3%

    B   13.5%

    C   14.9%

    D   15.4%

Chapter 15: Standard costing

(104) **A company's standard labour rate for its factory workers is set at $5 per hour.**

The standard time allowed for producing one unit is 20 minutes.

During the period 4,800 units were produced and the factory workers were paid $5.25 per hour. The actual hours worked were 1,560.

What was the total labour cost variance?

    A $390 adverse

    B $190 adverse

    C $190 favourable

    D $390 favourable

(105) **Which of the following would explain an adverse materials usage variance?**

    A   The volume of activity was more than originally expected

    B   A higher quality of materials than anticipated was used

    C   There was a major spillage resulting in the loss of raw materials

The following information relates to questions 106 and 107:

The materials budget for producing 5,000 units of product is 25,000 litres at $3.30 per litre. In the first month of production the company purchased 30,000 litres at a cost of $105,000, of which 28,000 litres were used to produce an actual output of 5,900 units.

(106)**What was the material usage variance?**

A $9,900 adverse

B $650 adverse

C $4,950 favourable

D $5,250 favourable

(107)**What was the material price variance?**

A $6,000 adverse

B $12,600 adverse

C $6,000 favourable

D $12,600 favourable

The following information relates to questions 108 and 109:

A company's product results for the month are as follows:

	Actual	Budget
Sales units	9,500	9,000
	$	$
Sales revenue	104,500	108,000
Manufacturing costs at standard	76,000	72,000
Contribution	28,500	36,000

(108)**What was the sales price variance?**

A $3,500 adverse

B $9,000 adverse

C $9,500 adverse ✓

D $9,500 favourable

Act (9500 × 11) = 104500 ← you sold for less than standard

Stan (9500 × 12) = 114 000 ← standard

VAR   9500 (A)

(109)**What was the sales volume contribution variance?**

A $1,500 favourable

B $2,000 favourable

C $6,000 favourable

D $7,500 adverse

9500 - 9000 = 500

Standard contribution per unit

36000 / 9000 = 4

500 × 4 = 2000

(110)**A company's standard variable overhead rate for manufacturing is $7 per hour and the standard time allowed for production is 2.5 hours per unit.**

During the period 3,200 units were produced in 8,320 hours. The variable overhead expenditure variance was $1,664 favourable. What was the actual variable overhead rate per hour?

A $6.53 ✗

B $6.80 ✓

C $6.93

D $7.20

(111)**If a manufacturing organisation is absorbing fixed overheads on a labour hour basis, the fixed overhead volume variance can be split into expenditure and efficiency variances.**

Is this statement TRUE or FALSE?

A True ✓

B False

(112)**A company's budgeted fixed overhead for the last quarter of the financial year was $280,000 for 7,000 units of output. It actually spent $284,400 manufacturing 7,200 units.**

What was the fixed overhead volume variance?

A $ 8,000 adverse ✓

B $ 4,400 adverse

C $ 7,900 favourable

D $ 8,000 favourable

B $\frac{280,000}{7000} = 40$

40 x 7200a = 288,000 ← 8k above budget

or

40 x 200 (volume var) = 8000

This means an over absorption has occured = favourable.

(113) **A company uses standard marginal costing. Last month, when all sales were at the standard selling price, the standard contribution from actual sales was $85,600 and the following variances arose:**

Total variable costs variance	$12,600	Adverse
Total fixed costs variance	$10,500	Favourable
Sales volume contribution variance	$20,500	Favourable

What was the Actual contribution for last month?

A $62,500

B $73,000

C $83,000

D $93,500

Standard Contribution = 85600
Total VC variance (12600)
73,000

Chapter 16: Performance measurement techniques

(114) **A division has a residual income of $240,000 and a net profit before imputed interest of $640,000.**

If it uses a rate of 10% for computing imputed interest on its invested capital, what is its return on investment (ROI) to the nearest whole number?

A 4%

B 10%

C 16%

D 27%

The following information is for questions 115 – 117

The budgeted output for a period is 1,500 units and the standard time allowed per unit is 30 minutes. The actual output in the period was 1,400 units and these were produced in 720 hours.

(115) **Calculate the production/volume ratio**

A 97.2%

B 93.3%

C 96.0%

D 95.8%

(116) **Calculate the capacity ratio**

A 97.2%

B 93.3%

C 96.0%

D 95.8%

(117) **Calculate the efficiency ratio**

    A   97.2%

    B   93.3%

    C   96.0%

    D   95.8%

(118) **HH plc monitors the % of total sales that derives from products developed in the last year. Which part of the balanced scorecard would this metric be classified under?**

    A   Financial perspective

    B   Customer perspective

    C   Internal perspective

    D   Learning perspective

(119) **If the current ratio for a company is equal to its acid test (that is, the quick ratio), then:**

    A   the current ratio must be greater than one

    B   the company does not carry any inventory

    C   trade receivables plus cash is greater than trade payables minus inventory

    D   working capital is positive

Chapter 17: Performance measurement in specific situations

(120) **A government is looking at assessing hospitals by reference to a range of both financial and non-financial factors, one of which is survival rates for heart by-pass operation.**

Which of the three E's best describes the above measure?

    A   Economy

    B   Effectiveness

    C   Efficiency

    D   Externality

(121) **An organisation is divided into a number of divisions, each of which operates as a profit centre. Which of the following would be useful measures to monitor divisional performance?**

(i) Contribution

(ii) Controllable profit

(iii) Return on investment

(iv) Residual income

A (i) only

B (i) and (ii) only

C (iii) and (iv) only

D All of them

Chapter 18: Spreadsheets

(122) **The benefit of using a spreadsheet to prepare a budget is that estimates can be varied without everything having to be recalculated manually.**

Is this statement TRUE or FALSE?

A True

B False

(123) **A spreadsheet is more useful than a database when the primary objective is to store large amounts of raw data that needs to be accessed by multiple users.**

Is this statement TRUE or FALSE?

A True

B False

(124) **Which of the following is not a disadvantage of using spreadsheets?**

A Spreadsheets are restricted to a finite number of records, and can require a large amount of hard-drive space for data storage

B There can be sharing violations among users wishing to view or change data at the same time

C Spreadsheets do not have the ability to generate graphs and charts for the analysis of data

(125) **Which of the following is the least suitable application of a spreadsheet package?**

A   Budgeting and forecasting

B   Maintenance of customer records

C   Inventory valuation

D   Variance analysis

20

Answers

Chapter 1: The nature and purpose of management accounting

(1) **B FALSE**

Data consists of numbers, letters and raw facts that have been recorded but not yet processed into a suitable form. Data that has been processed so as to make it meaningful is known as information.

(2) **B**

(3) **D**

(4) **C**

(5) **C**

(6) **B**

(7) **B**

Chapter 2: Sources of data

(8) **D**

Data collection can be simplified by selecting say every 10th or 100th unit after the first unit has been chosen randomly as discussed below. Such a procedure is called systematic random sampling.

(9) **B**

(10) **C**

This method is often applied if the population is particularly large, for example all TV viewers in the UK.

(11) **A**

(12) **C**

Chapter 3: Presenting information

(13) **D**

(14) **D**

The black shirts are 20% of the order therefore will be 20% of the degrees in a circle.

$360° × 20\% = 72°$

Chapter 4: Types of cost and cost behaviour

(15) **B**

B is a non-production costs and as such should not be used to value inventory.

(16) **D**

    A   Indirect and fixed

    B   Indirect and fixed

    C   Direct and variable

    D   Indirect and variable

(17) **B**

(18) **D**

(19) **B FALSE**

Telephone costs are likely to consist of a fixed element for line rental and a variable element for calls, hence are semi-variable.

(20) **C**

(21) **C**

(22) **B**

Take the highest and lowest output and associated costs.

	Output (units)	Cost ($)
High	2,000	8,750
Low	800	3,950
Change	+1,200	+4,800

Hence VC = $4,800/1,200 = $4 per unit.

FC = 3,950 − (800 × 4) = 750 this year and therefore 850 next.

So cost of 1,500 units = 850 + (1500 × 4) = 6850

(23) **B**

Take the highest and lowest output and associated costs when fixed costs are constant.

	Output (units)	Cost ($)
High	9,000	102,000
Low	7,000	86,000
Change	2,000	16,000

Hence VC = $16,000/2,000 = $8 per unit.

FC = 102,000 – (9,000 × 8) = 30,000 at output under 10,000 units.

So cost of 14,000 units = 30,000 + 15,000 + (14,000 × 8) = 157,000

Chapter 5: Accounting for inventory

(24) **The correct answer is C**

(25) **The correct answer is B**

Material inventory account

	$000		$000
Opening balance (bal fig)	25	Issued to production	215
Creditors for purchases	240	Materials returned to suppliers	2
Materials returned to stores	6	Written off	12
		Closing balance	42
	271		271

(26) **FALSE**

The statement refers to periodic stocktaking.

In continuous stocktaking a business counts and values selected items of inventory on a rotating basis. Specialist teams count and check certain inventory items on each day.

(27) **A**

				$
Issue on 10th Sept	250	$2.20	=	550
Issue on 15th Sept	150	$2.20	=	330
	190	$2.50	=	475
Issue on 27th Sept	310	$2.50	=	775
	290	$2.70	=	783
				2,913

(28) **D**

Closing inventory	110	$2.70	=	$297

(29) **D**

				$
Issue on 10th Sept	250	$2.20	=	550
Issue on 15th Sept	340	$2.50	=	850
Issue on 27th Sept	400	$2.70	=	1,080
	160	$2.50	=	400
	40	$2.20	=	88
				2,968

(30) **A**

Closing inventory	110 × $2.20	=	$242

(31) **B**

			$
Issue on 10th Sept ($880/400 = $2.20)	250	$2.20	550
Issue on 15th Sept ($1,580/650 = $2.43077	340	$2.43077	826
Issue on 27th Sept ($1,834/710 = $2.5831)	600	$2.5831	1,550
			2,926

(32) **C**

Closing inventory	110 × $2.582 = $284

(33) **B FALSE**

The objective of holding buffer inventories is to reduce the risk of a stockout occurring e.g. where supplier lead times are uncertain (the time taken between placing and receiving an order).

The availability of quantity discounts would affect the order quantity not the reorder level.

(34) **C** – which is a cost of ordering and obtaining the inventory.

(35) **C**

EOQ = $\sqrt{(2CoD/Ch)}$
Co = 10, D=100,000, Ch= $0.005
EOQ = $\sqrt{(2 \times 10 \times 100000 / 0.005)}$ = 20,000

(36) **B**

Co=10, D= 50x12 = 600, Ch=0.2 x $6
EOQ = $\sqrt{(2CoD/Ch)}$ = $\sqrt{(2 \times 10 \times 600/1.20)}$
EOQ = 100
Therefore place 6 orders p.a (600/100).

(37) **B**

ROL = demand in the lead time

Demand per day = 1,000,000 / 250 = 4,000 units.

So expected demand in the lead time and hence ROL is 8,000

C is the EOQ and A the number of orders that would be placed p.a.

Chapter 6: Accounting for labour

(38) **B**

(39) **C**

Idle time = 150 hours @ $5 = $750

Overtime (premium only) = 100 × 5 × 4 @ $2.50 = $5000

Total indirect labour element = $5,750

(40) **D**

Basic rate = 40/60 × $6 = $4

Bonus = 40/60 × $6/60 × 20 = $1.33

Total payment = $5.33

Note: Under Halsey scheme, bonus payment would be:

$$\frac{60 - 40}{2} \times \frac{\$6}{60} = \$1.00$$

(41) **A**

No. of leavers requiring replacement = 600
Employees at 1 April 20X0 = 5400 + 750 − 600 = 5550

Average no. of employees = $\dfrac{5550 + 5400}{2}$ = 5475

Labour turnover rate = 600/5475 x 100 = 10.96%

(42) **C**

Expected hours to produce actual output (standard hours):

600 units × 20/60 = 200 hours

Labour efficiency ratio = 200/220 × 100 = 90.91%

Labour capacity ratio = 220/ 210 × 100 = 104.76%

Production volume ratio = 200/210 × 100 = 95.24%

Chapter 7: Accounting for overheads

(43) **B**

		Primary hours		Finishing hours
E 9,000	X36/60	5,400	X25/60	3,750
F 6,000	X30/60	3,000	X40/60	4,000
		8,400		7,750

Rate per hour $\dfrac{\$84,000}{8,400}$ = $10 $\dfrac{\$93,000}{7,750}$ = $12

E $10 X36/60 + $12 X25/60 = $11

(44) **D**

Machining hours = 4,000 × 0.5 hours + 4,000 × 1.0 hours = 6,000 hours

Assembly hours = 4,000 × 0.2 hours + 4,000 × 0.25 hours = 1,800 hours

Machine absorption rate $= \dfrac{\$120,000}{6,000 \text{ hours}} = \$20$ per hour

Assembly absorption rate $= \dfrac{\$72,000}{1,800 \text{ hours}} = \$40$ per hour

Fixed overhead per unit of Zonk = 0.5 hours × $20 + 0.2 hours × $40 = $18

(45) **B**

	Production	Finishing
Allocated and apportioned fixed costs	$ 55,000	$ 63,000
Total Direct labour hours:		
Product alpha	1.5 × 8,000	2 × 8,000
Product beta	**1 × 10,000**	**0.5 × 10,000**
	22,000 hrs	**21,000 hrs**
Fixed overhead per labour hour	$2.50	$3.00

Product beta: (1 hr @ $2.5) + (0.5 hrs @ $3) = $4

(46) **A**

(47) **C**

(48) **C**

Pre-determined overhead rate = $504,000/42,000 = $12 per hour

	$
Overhead absorbed (45,000 hours @ $12) =	540,000
Overhead incurred	515,000
Fixed overhead over-absorbed	25,000

(49) **B**

    (1) $Q = 140,000 + 0.3M$

    (2) $M = 113,000 + 0.2Q$

Substitute (1) in equation (2):

$M = 113,000 + 0.2 (140,000 + 0.3M)$

$M = 113,000 + 28,000 + 0.06M$

$0.94M = 141,000$

$M = 150,000$

Substituting this into equation (1)

$Q = 140,000 + 0.3(150,000) = 185,000$

Total overheads for departments

	Machining	Finishing
Primary apportionment	220,000	160,000
Share of QC (45%/35%)	83,250	64,750
Share of maint'ce (30%/40%)	45,000	60,000
TOTAL	348,250	284,750

Chapter 8: Marginal and absorption costing

(50) **D**

    (i) Incorrect. Smaller volume products often cause a disproportionate amount of cost.

    (ii) Correct

    (iii) Incorrect. Marginal costing gives a higher profit.

    (iv) Correct

(51) **A**

(52) **B FALSE**

The absorption costing approach charges fixed overheads to units produced and as a result achieves a better matching of sales and costs during a period and a more realistic measure of profit.

(53) **C**

Closing inventory = 5,000 units

Under full absorption costing a proportion of the fixed manufacturing overhead will be carried forward in this inventory.

$$\frac{\$90,000}{75,000} \times 5,000 = \$6,000 \quad \checkmark$$

This is the difference in profit.

Chapter 9: Job, batch and process costing

(54) **C**

(55) **B**

(56) **A**

Statement (2) is true for job costing but not process costing.

(57) **D**

Expected output = 90% × 500 = 450 litres

Cost per unit = ($3,000 + $2,670)/450 = $12.60

(58) **D**

	$	Units
Process costs	11,800	4,000
Normal loss @ disposal cost	800	(400)
Total	12,600	3,600

Cost per unit = $12,600/3,600 = $3.50

Abnormal loss = 3,600 − 3,550 = 50kg

Cost of abnormal loss = 50 @ ($3.50 + $2) = $275

(59) **B**

Physical flow:

Opening WIP + Units added   Finished units + start closing WIP

12,000   + 48,000   = 45,000   + 15,000

Equivalent units calculation:

	Completed units	Start closing WIP	Total EU
Physical units	45,000	15,000	
Material	45,000	15,000	60,000
Conversion	45,000	9,000	54,000

Cost per EU:

	Material	Conversion
Costs in op WIP	$33,600	$22,980
Costs of period	$144,000	$307,500
Total costs	$177,600	$330,480
EU	60,000	54,000
Cost per EU	$2.96	$6.12

Value of finished output:

Completed units = 45,000 @ ($2.96 + $6.12) = $408,600

Closing WIP:

Material 15,000 @ $2.96 = $44,400

Conversion costs 9,000 @ $6.12 = $55,080

Total closing WIP = $99,480

(60) **B**

Physical flow:

Opening WIP   + Units added   Finished units   + units start to finish   + start closing WIP

12,000   + 48,000   = 12,000   + 33,000   + 15,000

	Finish opening WIP	Start to finish	Start closing WIP	Total EU
Physical units	12,000	33,000	15,000	
Material	0	33,000	15,000	48,000
Conversion	7,200	33,000	9,000	49,200

	Material	Conversion
Costs of period	$144,000	$307,500
EU	48,000	49,200
Cost per EU	$3	$6.25

Value of finished output = value of units start to finish + completed opening WIP:

Units start to finish = 33,000 @ ($3 + $6.25) = $305,250

Completed Opening WIP:

Costs b/fwd	$56,580
Material added	0
Conversion costs (7,200@$6.25)	$45,000

Total value = $101,580

Hence total value of finished production = $305,250 + $101,580 = $406,830

Note: Closing WIP
Material 15,000@$3 = $45,000
Conversion 9000 @ $6.25 = $56,250
Total value = $101,250

(61) **C**

Chapter 10: Service and operation costing

(62) **A TRUE**

(63) **B** – which would use process costing to establish the cost of a physical product

(64) **C** – which would be of use to the Restaurant/ Kitchen

(65) **B FALSE**

Many service applications do involve high fixed costs but a higher number of cost units will result in a lower fixed cost per unit.

(66) **B**

Total km travelled p.a. = 200km × 5 days x 50 weeks × 6 vehicles = 300,000 km

Total VC = 300,000 km @ $0.50 = $150,000

Total Running costs = $150,000 VC + $225,000 FC = $375,000 p.a.

Total tonne km p.a. = 4 journeys × 25 km × 5 tonnes × 5 days × 50 weeks × 6 vehicles = 750,000 km

Standard cost per tonne km = $375,000 / 750,000 = $0.50

Chapter 11: Alternative costing systems

(67) **A**

ABC is fairly complicated, is a form of absorption (not marginal) costing and is particularly useful when fixed overheads are high and not primarily volume driven.

(68) **D**

A customer service team deals with customer queries and complaints from outside the organisation, typically after goods have been delivered to the customer. The costs of this team arise from quality failures and are preventable. They are external failure costs. Maintenance is intended to prevent machine breakdowns and so to prevent quality failures, and they are therefore prevention costs. Test equipment is used for inspection.

(69) **D**

A product's life cycle costs are very inclusive; none of these would be excluded.

(70) **A**

Value analysis involves identify why and how customers value a product to enable cost savings to be made without compromising the value to the customer.

Chapter 12: Forecasting techniques

(71) **A**

The correlation coefficient measures the strength of the connection between two variables. A correlation coefficient of 0 suggests that the two variables are unrelated and as a result there is no linear relationship between them. The closer the value to +1 or –1 the greater the correlation and the more reliable the line of best fit.

(72) **C**

The calculation of the index for each year is as follows:

20X3 25/22 ×100 = 114

(73) **D**

Year	Revenue ($000)	Index adjustment	Adjusted revenue ($000)
2004	1,150	140/100	1,610
2005	1,250	140/115	1,522
2006	1,200	140/130	1,292

(74) **D**

Quarter	Value of x	Trend units	Forecast sales units
1	25	26×25+8,850=9,500	9,500×85%=8,075
2	26	26×26+8,850=9,526	9,526×95%=9,049.7
3	27	26×27+8,850=9,552	9,552×105%=10,029.6
4	28	26×28+8,850=9,578	9,578×115%=11,014.7

Difference between Q1 and Q4 budgeted sales = 11,014.7 – 8,075.0 =2,939.7 units

(75) **D**

Budgeted production each quarter = 38,169/4 = 9,542.25 units

(76) B

X is the time period reference number and for the first quarter of year 1 is 1. The time period reference number for the third quarter of year 7 is 27.

y = 25,000 + 6,500 × 27 = 200,500 units

(77) B FALSE

Using the line to predict values within the range observed is known as interpolation.

(78) C

$$b = \frac{(5 \times 83,920) - (540 \times 755)}{(5 \times 61,000) - (540^2)} = 0.89$$

(79) C

y= (10 × 19) + 150 = 340

Chapter 13: Budgeting

(80) B

(i) Correct

(ii) Correct

(iii) Incorrect, e.g. budget for number of employees required

(iv) Incorrect. Master budget also includes budgeted cash flow

(v) Incorrect. Adjusts variable costs. Fixed are fixed.

(81) C

(82) D

	Jan	Feb	Mar
Sales	2,000	2,500	3,000
–Opening inventory	(200)	(250)	(300)
+Closing inventory	250	300	350
Production	2,050	2,550	3,050

(83) **D**

Profit = $300,000 × 0.2 = 60,000
Cost of sales = $240,000
Cost of sales = opening inventory + purchases – closing inventory
240,000 = 40,000 + P – 60,000
P = 240,000 – 40,000 + 60,000
P= $260,000

(84) **D**

Month 4 production = 120,000 + 8,000 – 6,000 = 122,000 units

Month 4 usage = 122,000 units @ 2kg = 244,000 kg

(85) **C**

Total hours required = 16,000 + 36,000 = 52,000

	Alpha	Beta
Skilled Hours per unit	2	3
units	8,000	12,000
Total hours	16,000	36,000

(86) **D**

Answers A and B refer to profit-related pay and answer C describes either piece work payment or payment by the hour/day.

(87) **C**

Where there is goal congruence, managers who are working to achieve their own personal goals will automatically also be working to achieve the organisation's goals. Although the use of aspiration levels to set targets (option D) is likely to help in the achievement of goal congruence, it is not of itself a definition of the term.

(88) **C**

Statement (i) is incorrect. Managers at an operational level are more likely to know what is realistically achievable than a senior manager imposing budget targets from above. Statement (ii) is arguably correct: participation in budgeting could improve motivation. Statement (iii) is correct: imposed budgets should be much quicker to prepare, because less discussion time and negotiation time is required than with participative budget-setting.

(89) **B**

Option C is a fixed budget and option D is a rolling budget. Option A is incorrect as a flexible budget includes all costs.

(90) **C**

A flexible budget helps to control resource efficiency by providing a realistic budget cost allowance for the actual level of activity achieved. Control action can therefore be more effective because the effects of any volume change have been removed from the comparison.

(91) **A**

A fixed budget is a budget prepared for a planned single level of activity. It does not ignore inflation (option C is incorrect) and it includes direct costs as well as overhead costs (option D is incorrect). A fixed budget can be prepared for a single product as well as a mix of products (option B is incorrect).

(92) **D**

The production-line manager does not control prices or rates

Chapter 14: Capital Budgeting

(93) **B**

	Cash flow $	Discount rate 10%	Present value $
Year 0 Initial outlay	(2,000,000)	1.000	(2,000,000)
Year 1–6 Annual cash flow	450,000	4.355	1,959,750
Net present value			(40,250)

(94) **B**

Year	Cash flow $	Discount factor 5%	Present value $
0	(80,000)	1.000	(80,000)
1	25,000	0.952	23,800
2	25,000	0.907	22,675

(95) **C**

Year	Cash flow $	Cumulative cash flow $
0	(50,000)	(50,000)
1	22,000	(28,000)
2	22,000	(6,000)
3	20,000	14,000

2 years and 4 months

Months calculated = 6,000/20,000 × 12 = 3.6 months

(96) **D**

Year	Item	Cash flow $	Discount factor 10%	PV	Cumulative cash flow $
0	Cost of machine	(50,000)	1.000	(50,000)	(50,000)
1	Net cash flow from sales	22,000	0.909	19,998	(30,002)
2	Net cash flow from sales	22,000	0.826	18,172	(11,830)
3	Net cash flow from sales	20,000	0.751	15,020	3,190

2 years and 10 months

Months calculated = 11,830/15,020 × 12 = 9.5 months

(97) **B**

Year	Cash flow $	Discount factor 15%	Present value $	Discount factor 20%	Present value $
0	(75,000)	1.000	(75,000)	1.000	(75,000)
1–5	25,000	3.352	83,800	2.991	74,775
NPV			8,800		(225)

IRR = 15 + [8,800/(8,800 − 225) × 5] = 19.9%

(98) **C**

$100,000/$20,000 = 5 Years

(99) **B**

IRR = 10 + [12,304/(12,304 − 3,216) × 5] = 13.96% therefore 14%

(100)**A**

Year	Cash flow $	Discount factor 20%	Present value $
0	(200,000)	1.000	(200,000)
1	80,000	0.833	66,640
2	90,000	0.694	62,460
3	100,000	0.579	57,900
4	60,000	0.482	28,920
5	40,000	0.402	16,080
		NPV	(32,000)

IRR = 10 + [87,980/(87,980 − 32,000) × 10] = 17.3%

(101)**B**

Investment	Cash flow $000	Cumulative cash flow
Initial investment	(400)	(400)
Incremental cash flows		
Year 1	100	(300)
Year 2	120	(180)
Year 3	140	(40)
Year 4	120	80

(102)**C**

Investment	Cash flow $000	Discounted cash flow $000	Cumulative cash flow $000
Initial investment	450	450	(450)
Incremental cash flows			
Year 1	130	118.17	(331.83)
Year 2	130	107.38	(224.45)
Year 3	130	97.63	(126.82)
Year 4	130	88.79	(38.03)
Year 5	150	93.15	55.12

(103)**D**

Investment	Cash flows	Discounted cash flows (20%)
	$000	$000
Initial investment	350	350
Incremental cash flows		
Year 1	50	41.65
Year 2	110	76.34
Year 3	130	75.27
Year 4	150	72.3
Year 5	100	40.2
Net present value	48 (10%)	41.24

IRR = 10 + [48/(48 − 41.24) × 10] = 15.4%

Chapter 15: Standard costing

(104)**B**

Aq × Ap =
1,560 × $5.25 = $8,190

Sq × Sp =
4,800 × 20/60 × $5 = $8,000
                         _____
                         $190A
                         _____

(105)**C**

(106)**C**

Actual materials used × standard rate

28,000 × $3.30   97,350

Standard cost of actual production

5,900 × 5 × $3.30   97,350
                                            _____
                                            4,950 favourable
                                            _____

(handwritten annotations: equivalent figure; Actual Output; Standard litre per unit; Standard cost per unit)

(107)**A**

$105,000 − 30,000 × $3.30 = $6,000 adverse

(108)**C**

Budget selling price = $108,000/9,000 = $12

$104,500 – 9,500 × $12 = $9,500 adverse

(109)**B**

Standard contribution = $36,000/9,000 = $4 per unit

Volume variance = 500 × $4 = $2,000 favourable.

(110)**B**

	$
Actual hours x standard rate 8,320 × $7	58,240
Less favourable expenditure variance	(1,664)
	_____
Actual expenditure	56,576
	_____

Therefore actual rate per hour = $56,576/8,320 = $6.80

(111)**B FALSE**

The fixed overhead volume variance can be subdivided into a capacity and an efficiency variance.

(112)**D**

Standard fixed overhead rate per unit = $280,000 / 7,000 = $40 per unit

Fixed overhead volume variance = 200 units × $40 = $8,000 favourable (over-absorbed)

(113)**B**

Standard contribution on actual Sales	$85,600
Less: Adverse total variable costs variance	($12,600)
Actual Contribution	$73,000

Chapter 16: Performance measurement techniques

(114)**C**

RI = Net profit before interest − (10% × invested capital)
Therefore £240,000 = £640,000 − (10% × invested capital)
So 10% × invested capital = £400,000
Therefore invested capital = £4m
ROI = Net profit before interest/Invested capital
ROI = £640,000/£4,000,000 × 100 = 16%

(115)**B**

Output per standard hour is 2 units as each unit has a standard time allowance of 30 minutes.
Budgeted labour hours are 1,500/2 = 750
The actual output measured in standard hours is 1,400/2 = 700 standard hours

The PV ratio = 700/750 × 100% = 93.3%

(116)**C**

The capacity ratio = 720/750 × 100% = 96%

(117)**A**

The efficiency ratio = 700/720 × 100% = 97.2%

(118)**D**

(119)**B**

The current ratio is all current assets including inventory divided by current liabilities, while the acid test is the current asset figure less inventory divided by current liabilities. These can only be equal if a firm carries no inventory.

KAPLAN PUBLISHING

Chapter 17: Performance measurement in specific situations

(120)B

Reducing mortality rates is likely to be a stated objective of the hospital and as such is a measure of output, or effectiveness

(121)B

The manager of a profit centre can exercise control over revenues and controllable costs, but has no influence concerning the capital invested in the centre.

Contribution (i) would be a useful performance measure because a profit centre manager can exercise control over sales revenue and variable costs. Controllable profit (ii) would also be useful as long as any overhead costs charged in deriving the profit figure are controllable by the profit centre manager. Apportioned central costs would not be deducted when calculating controllable profit. Return on investment (iii), residual income (iv) would not be useful because they require a measure of the capital invested in the division.

Chapter 18: Spreadsheets

(122)A TRUE

(123)B FALSE

A database would be more useful.

Spread sheets are designed to analyse data and sort list items, not for long-term storage of raw data.

(124)C

Spreadsheet packages do include a graphical function.

(125)B

Where a database would be more suitable.

Index

A

Abnormal losses and gains.....223
Absorption.....174
Absorption costing.....163, 197
Activity based costing (ABC).....274
Allocation.....163
Annuities.....423
Apportionment.....163
Appraisal cost......282
Asset turnover.....497
Attainable standards.....441
AVCO.....115
Average cost per unit.....221
Avoidable costs.....400

B

Balanced scorecard.....509
Bar charts..... 46
Bases of apportionment.....163
Basic pay.....136
Basic standards.....441
Batch costing.....214, 538
Behaviour.....66
Benchmarking.....515
Budget committee.....344
Budget manual.....344
Budgetary control.....371
Budgeting.....341, 559
By-product.....248, 249

C

Capital expenditure.....392
Capacity ratio.....504
Cash budgets.....356
Chain based index numbers.....3168
Charts.....45
Closing work in progress (CWIP).....234
Cluster sampling..... 36
Coefficient of determination.....302
Committed costs.....400
Component bar chart.....47
Composite cost unit.....267
Compound bar chart.....50
Compound interest.....401
Compounding.....402
Conformance cost.....283
Continuous budget.....350
Continuous operation costing.....212
Continuous stocktaking.....114
Contract costing.....536
Contribution.....194, 459
Control.....6, 108

Control reports.....476
Controllable costs.....379
Conversion costs.....236
Correlation.....298
Correlation coefficient..... 300
Cost accounting.....16
Cost behaviour..... 66
Cost card.....80
Cost centre.....13, 61, 448, 504
Cost coding.....83
Cost control.....283
Cost driver.....275
Cost equations.....78
Cost objects.....60
Cost of capital.....406
Cost per service unit.....264
Cost pool.....274
Cost reduction.....284
Cost units.....61
Critical success factors.....492
Current ratio.....498
Current standards.....441
Cyclical variations.....304

D

Data..... 2
Decision making.....6
Dependent variable.....51, 78, 301
Differential costs.....399
Differential piecework systems.....144
Direct costs.....65
Discounting.....400, 404
Dividend cover.....502
Divisional performance.....527

E

Economic Batch Quantity (EBQ).....108
Economic Order Quantity (EOQ).....108
Economic environment.....33
Element.....61
Effective interest rate.....403
Efficiency ratio.....505
Equation of a straight line.....78
Equivalent units (EU)..... 234, 235
External failure cost.....283
External information.....22, 29
Extrapolation.....304, 306

Index

F

Financial accounting.....16
Financial performance measures.....495
First In First Out (FIFO).....115, 241
Fixed budget.....373
Fixed costs.....67
Fixed overhead variances.....456
Flexible budget.....373
Forecasting.....290, 557
Function.....62
Functional budgets.....350

G

Gearing ratio.....501
Goods received note (GRN).....93
Graphs.....45
Gross profit margin.....496

H

High low method.....72
Holding costs.....98

I

Ideal standards.....441
Idle time ratio.....152
Index numbers.....314
Incentive schemes.....146, 347
Independent variable.....51, 78, 301
Indirect costs.....65
Information.....2
Interest.....401
Interest cover.....501
Internal failure cost.....282
Internal information.....28
Internal rate of return (IRR).....416
Interpolation.....304
Inventory.....97
Inventory account.....123
Inventory holding period.....499
Inventory valuation.....114
Investment appraisal.....393
Investment centres.....14

J

Job costing.....212, 537
Joint costs.....248
Joint products.....248

L

Labour account.....141
Labour budget.....354
Labour capacity ratio.....152

Labour cost variances.....450
Labour efficiency ratio.....152
Labour production volume ratio.....153
Labour turnover.....149
Laspeyre index.....322
Last In First Out (LIFO).....115
Least squares regression analysis.....293
Life cycle costing.....277
Linear regression.....295
Line graph.....51
Line of best fit.....53, 301
Liquidity measures.....519

M

Management accounting.....16
Managerial performance.....527
Marginal costing.....194
Marginal production cost.....81
Master budgets.....365
Material purchases budget.....352
Material usage budget.....352
Material cost variances.....446
Materials requisition notes.....93
Materials returned notes.....93
Materials transfer notes.....94
Maximum inventory level.....111
Minimum inventory level.....111
Mission statements.....8, 491
Motivation.....347
Moving averages.....305
Multiple line graphs.....51
Multistage Sampling.....35

N

Nature.....65
Net present value (NPV).....412
Nominal interest rate.....403
Non-conformance cost.....283
Non-financial information.....21
Non-financial performance indicators (NFPI).....503
Non-profit seeking organisations.....541
Normal loss.....220

O

Opening work in progress (OWIP).....234, 239
Operating statement.....464
Operational costing.....266
Operational planning.....11
Ordering costs.....99
Over absorption.....180
Overhead account.....183
Overhead absorption rate (OAR).....175

Index

Overhead budget.....355
Overheads.....162
Overtime premiums.....137

P

Paasche index.....325
Participative budgeting.....348
Payables payment period.....450
Payback period.....406
Percentage component bar chart.....48
Periodic stocktaking.....112
Perpetual inventory.....114
Perpetuities.....425
Piecework systems.....144
Pie chart.....55
Planning.....6, 10, 492
Prevention cost.....282
Prime cost.....65, 81
Principal budget factor.....344
Process costing.....217,538
Production budget.....351
Product life cycle.....277, 313
Production-volume ratio.....504
Productivity measures.....504
Profit centre.....14
Profit for the period margin.....497
Public sector.....541
Purchase invoice.....93
Purchase order form.....93
Purchase requisition.....93
Purchasing procedure.....92

Q

Quality.....508
Quantity discounts.....106
Quick ratio.....499
Quota sampling.....36

R

Random sampling.....34
Random variations.....304
Reapportionment.....167
Receivables collection period.....499
Reciprocal reapportionment.....170
Reconciliation statement.....481
Regression analysis.....293
Relevant costs.....20, 397
Remuneration methods.....143
Reorder level.....102
Reorder quantity.....103
Repeated distribution reapportionment.....170
Report writing.....42

Residual income (RI).....530
Residual variations.....304
Responsibility accounting.....13, 377
Responsibility centre.....13, 528
Return on capital employed.....496
Return on investment (ROI).....529
Revenue centre.....13
Revenue expenditure.....393
Risk measures.....522

S

Sales budget.....350
Sales variances.....444
Sampling.....33
Scatter diagram.....53
Scenario planning.....370
Scrap value.....221
Seasonal variations.....304
Semi-variable costs.....69
Service cost centre.....169
Service cost unit.....263
Service costing.....262
Service sector.....539
Simple bar chart.....46
Simple index numbers.....317
Simple interest.....401
SMART.....10
Specific order costing.....212
Spreadsheets.....556
Standard costing.....440
Stepped fixed costs.....68
Stocktaking.....112
Stores ledger cards.....115
Straight piecework systems.....144
Strategic planning.....11
Stratified sampling.....35
Sunk costs.....340
Systematic sampling.....34

T

Tables.....44
Tactical planning.....11
Target costing.....276
Time records.....139
Time series analysis.....303
Time value of money.....399
Total quality management (TQM).....281
Trend.....303

U

Uncontrollable costs.....379
Under-absorption.....180

Index

V

Value analysis…..284

Value engineering…..286

Value for money (VFM 3Es)…..543

Variable costs…..66

Variable overhead cost variances…..453

Variance analysis…..443, 557

Variance reporting…..474

W

Weighted average cost (AVCO)…..115, 239

Weighted index numbers…..320

'What if' analysis…..369, 555

Work in Progress (WIP)…..234